Find the Beat online!
Check us out at
www.shojobeat.com!

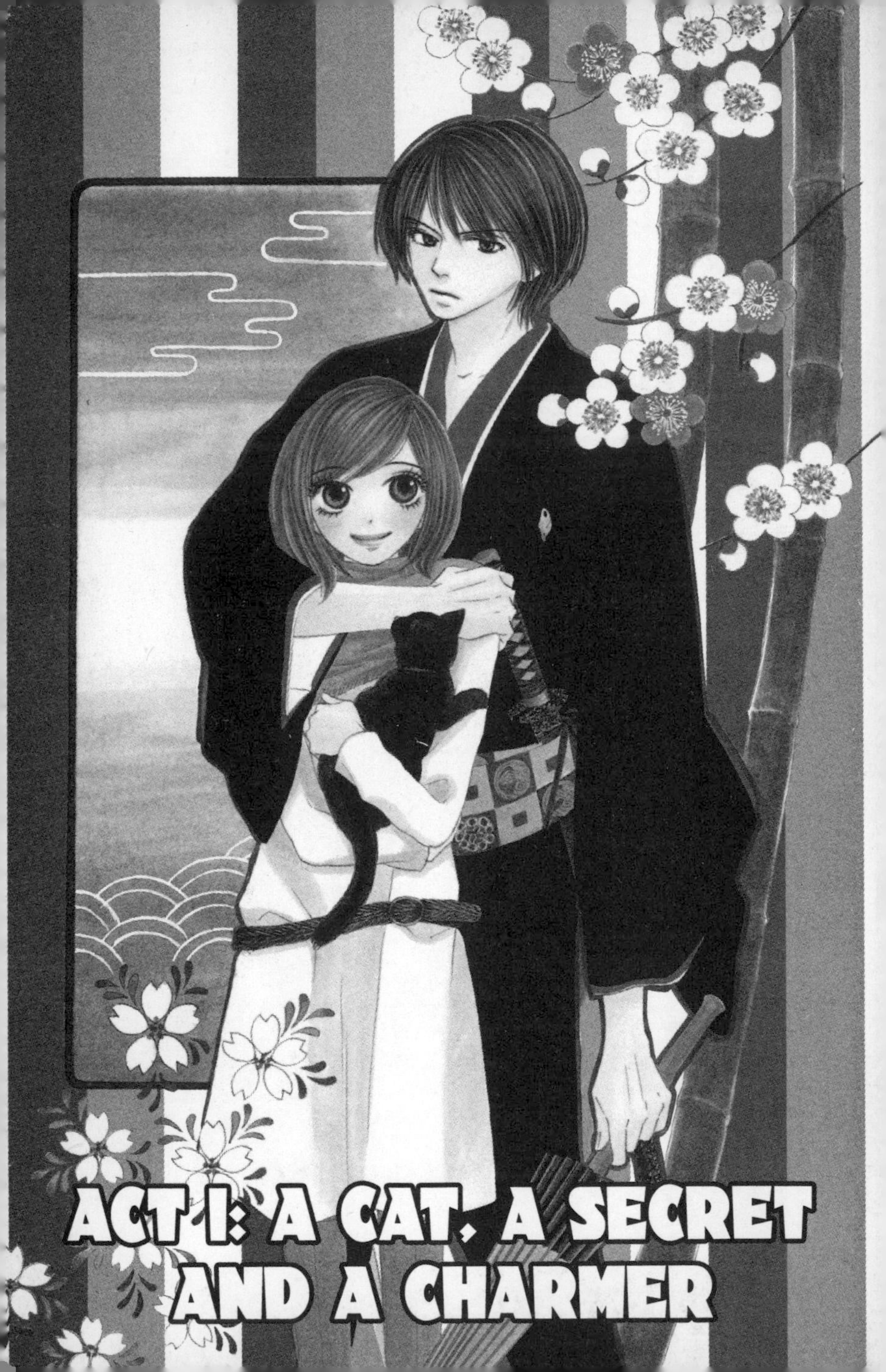
ACT 1: A CAT, A SECRET AND A CHARMER

GREETINGS, I'M
KANOKO SAKURAKOJI.
I WANTED TO PERSONALLY
EXPRESS MY GRATITUDE
TO YOU FOR PICKING UP
BACKSTAGE PRINCE.

Many
thanks.

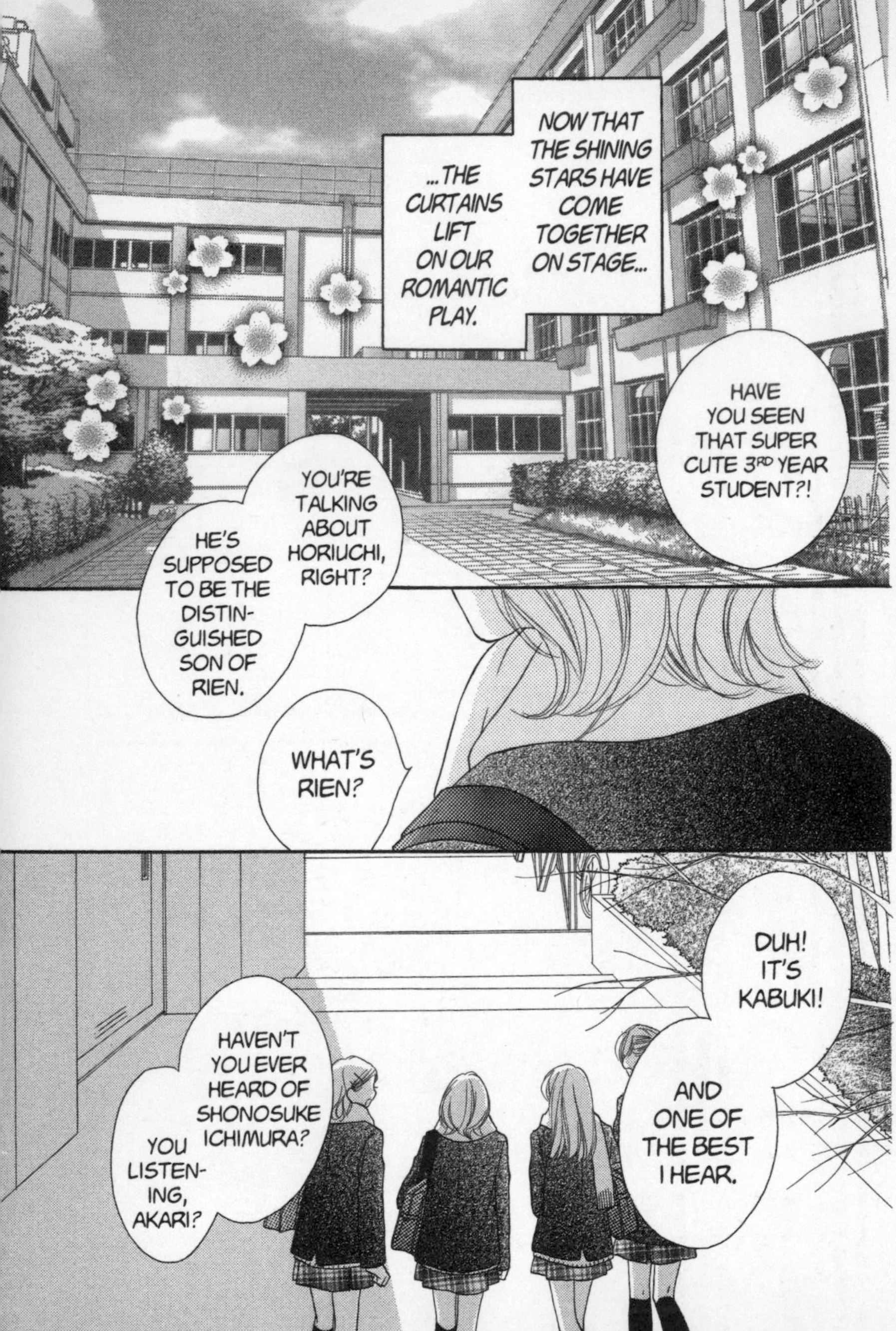
NOW THAT THE SHINING STARS HAVE COME TOGETHER ON STAGE...
...THE CURTAINS LIFT ON OUR ROMANTIC PLAY.
HAVE YOU SEEN THAT SUPER CUTE 3RD YEAR STUDENT?!
YOU'RE TALKING ABOUT HORIUCHI, RIGHT?
HE'S SUPPOSED TO BE THE DISTIN-GUISHED SON OF RIEN.
WHAT'S RIEN?
DUH! IT'S KABUKI!
AND ONE OF THE BEST I HEAR.
HAVEN'T YOU EVER HEARD OF SHONOSUKE ICHIMURA?
YOU LISTEN-ING, AKARI?

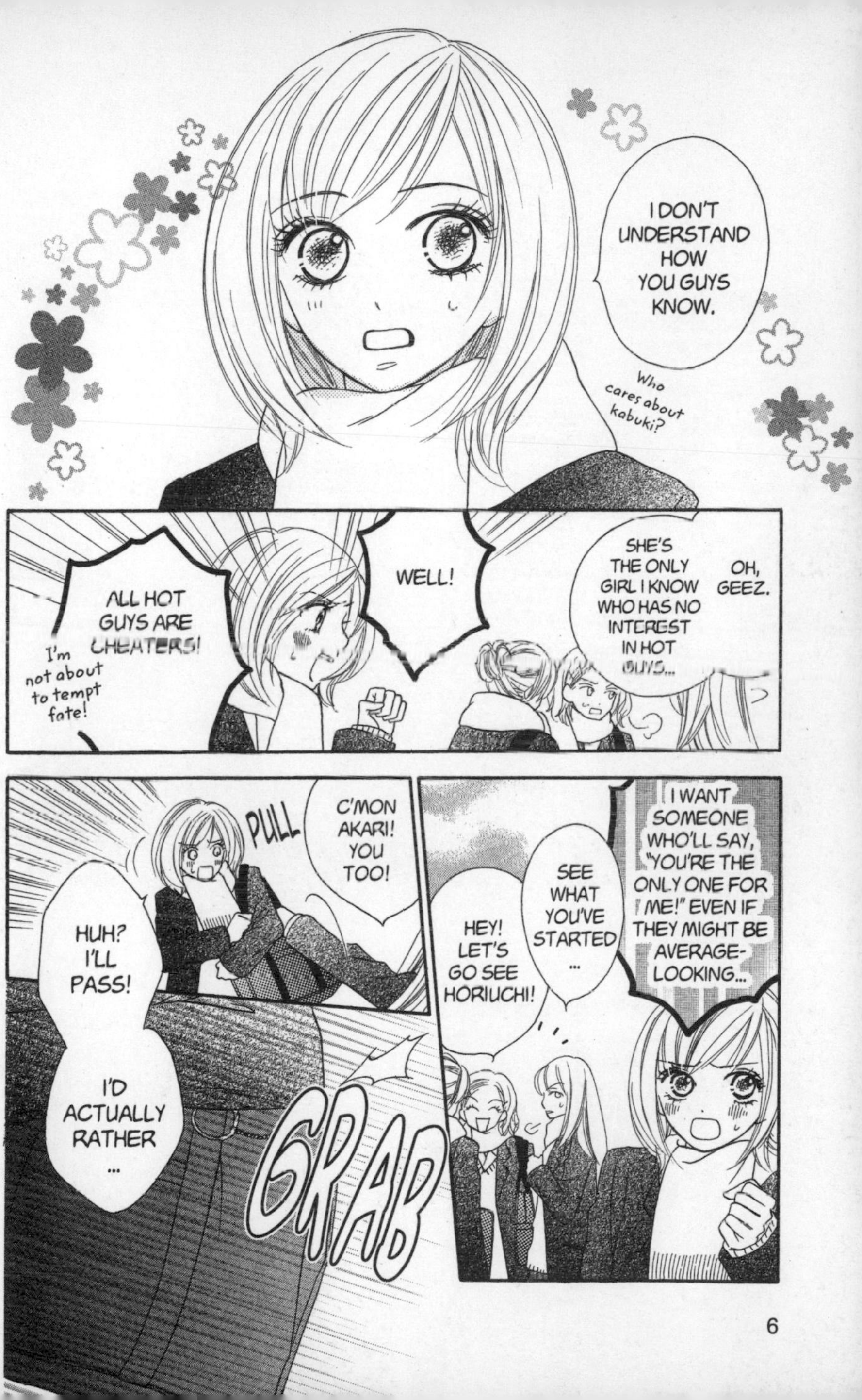
I DON'T UNDERSTAND HOW YOU GUYS KNOW.
Who cares about kabuki?
OH, GEEZ.
SHE'S THE ONLY GIRL I KNOW WHO HAS NO INTEREST IN HOT GUYS...
WELL!
ALL HOT GUYS ARE CHEATERS!
I'm not about to tempt fate!
I WANT SOMEONE WHO'LL SAY, "YOU'RE THE ONLY ONE FOR ME!" EVEN IF THEY MIGHT BE AVERAGE-LOOKING...
SEE WHAT YOU'VE STARTED ...
HEY! LET'S GO SEE HORIUCHI!
C'MON AKARI! YOU TOO!
PULL
HUH? I'LL PASS!
I'D ACTUALLY RATHER ...
GRAB

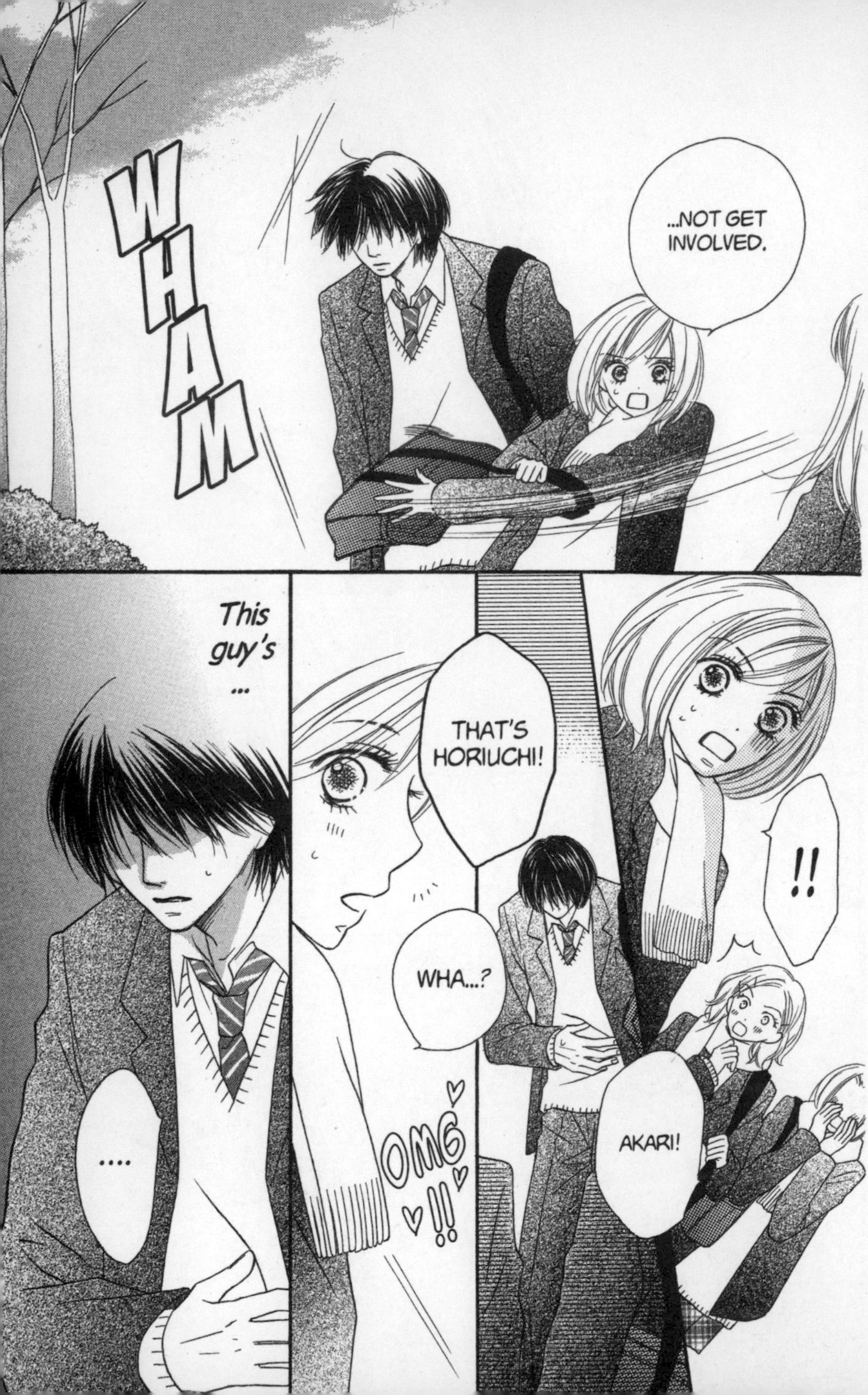
...NOT GET INVOLVED.
WHAM
!!
AKARI!
THAT'S HORIUCHI!
WHA...?
OMG !!
This guy's ...
....

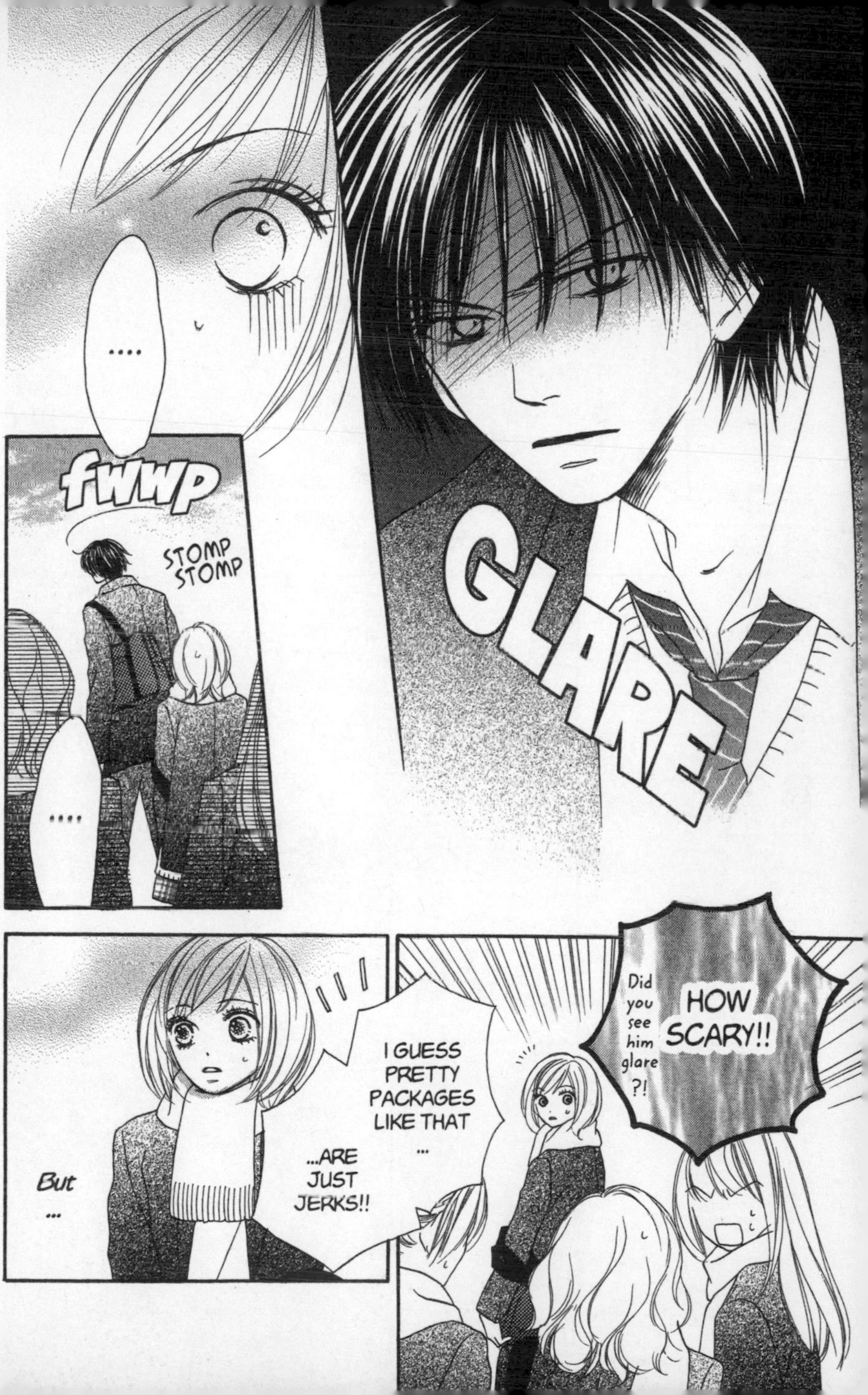
....
GLARE
fwwp
STOMP STOMP
....
Did you see him glare?!
HOW SCARY!!
I GUESS PRETTY PACKAGES LIKE THAT ...
...ARE JUST JERKS!!
But ...

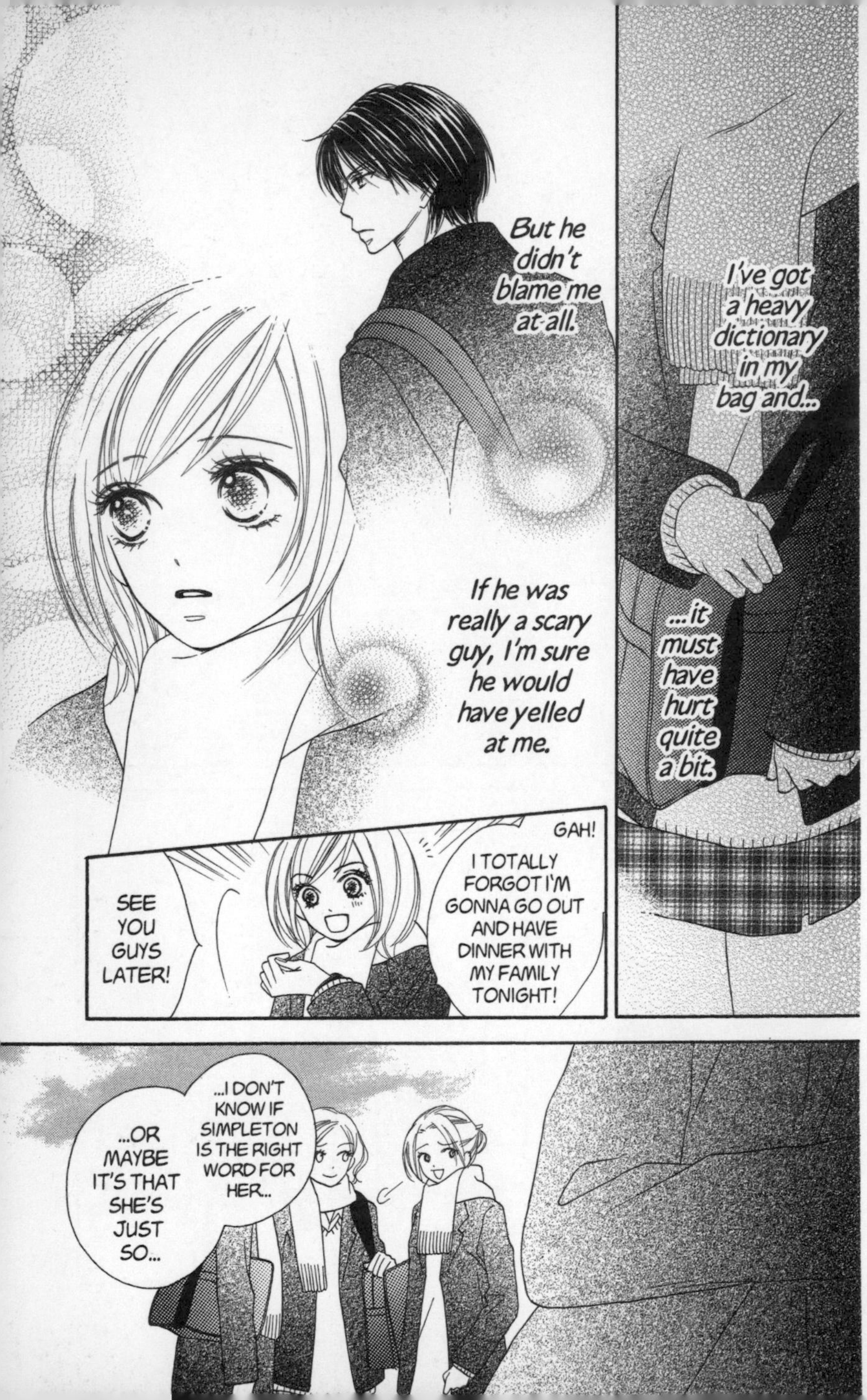
I've got a heavy dictionary in my bag and...
...it must have hurt quite a bit.
But he didn't blame me at all.
If he was really a scary guy, I'm sure he would have yelled at me.
GAH!
I TOTALLY FORGOT I'M GONNA GO OUT AND HAVE DINNER WITH MY FAMILY TONIGHT!
SEE YOU GUYS LATER!
...I DON'T KNOW IF SIMPLETON IS THE RIGHT WORD FOR HER...
...OR MAYBE IT'S THAT SHE'S JUST SO...

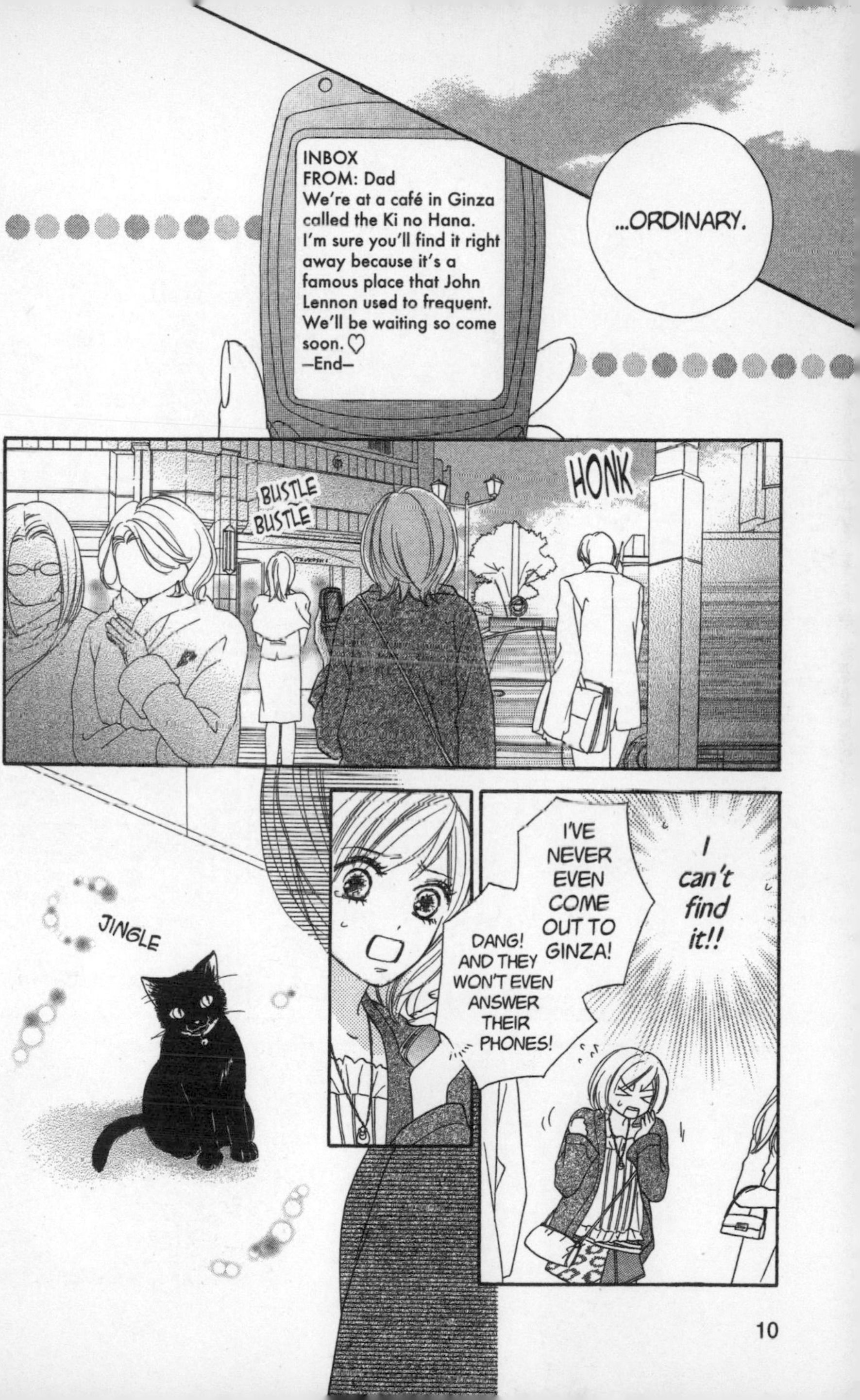
...ORDINARY.
INBOX
FROM: Dad
We're at a café in Ginza called the Ki no Hana. I'm sure you'll find it right away because it's a famous place that John Lennon used to frequent. We'll be waiting so come soon. ♡
—End—
HONK
BUSTLE BUSTLE
I can't find it!!
I'VE NEVER EVEN COME OUT TO GINZA!
DANG! AND THEY WON'T EVEN ANSWER THEIR PHONES!
JINGLE

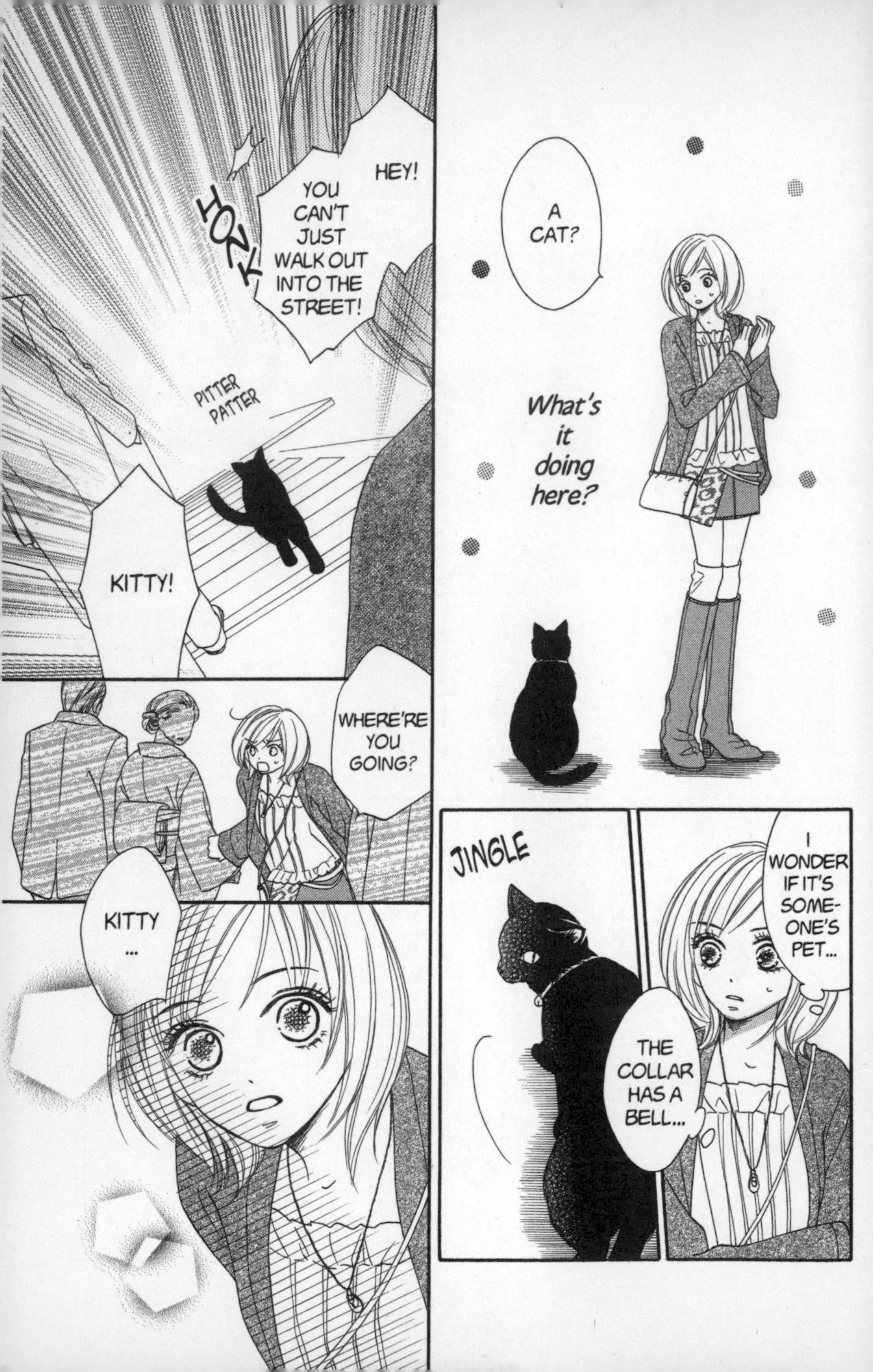
A CAT?
What's it doing here?
I WONDER IF IT'S SOME-ONE'S PET...
JINGLE
THE COLLAR HAS A BELL...
HEY!
YOU CAN'T JUST WALK OUT INTO THE STREET!
HONK
PITTER PATTER
KITTY!
WHERE'RE YOU GOING?
KITTY ...

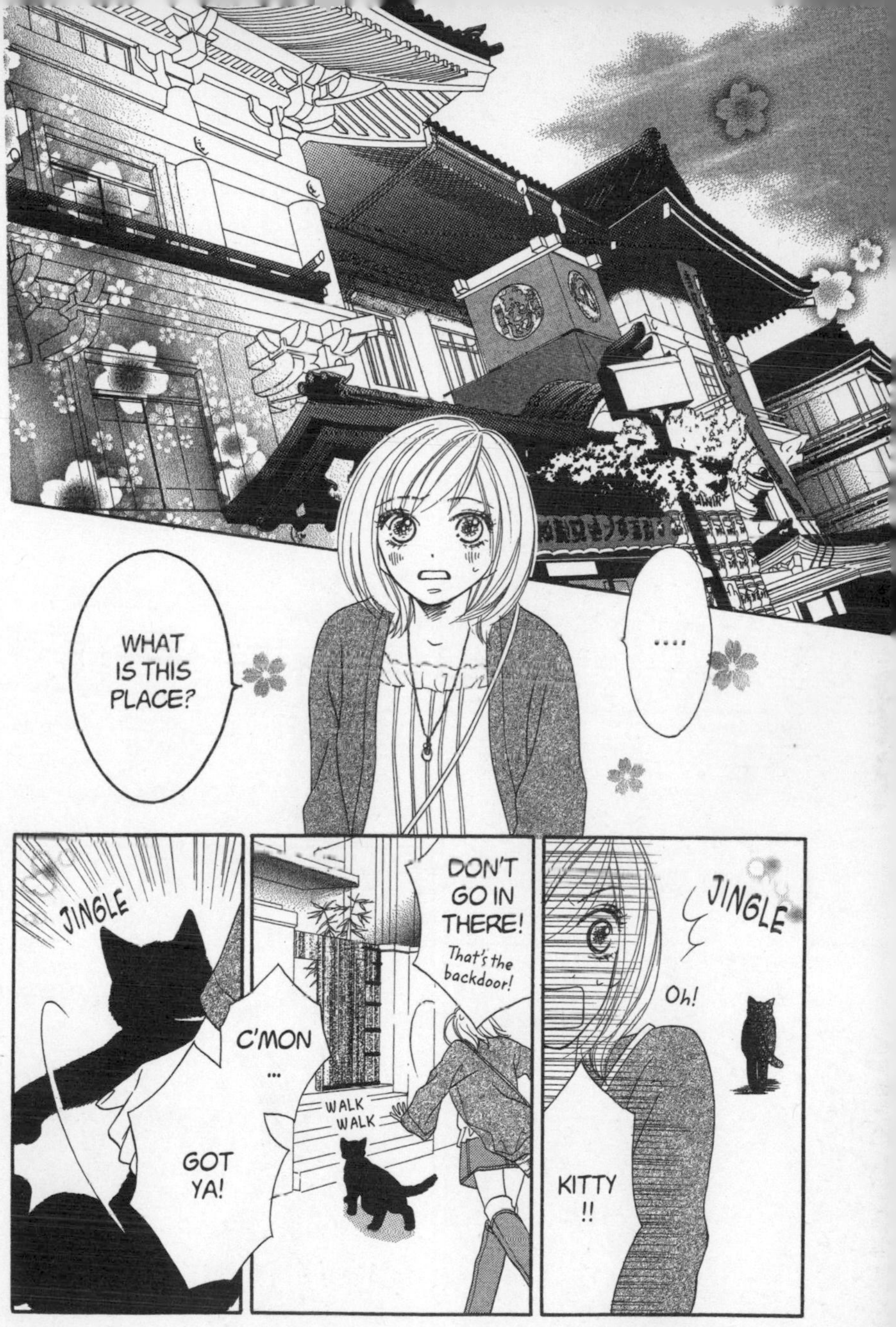
....
WHAT IS THIS PLACE?
JINGLE
Oh!
KITTY !!
DON'T GO IN THERE!
That's the backdoor!
WALK WALK
JINGLE
C'MON ...
GOT YA!

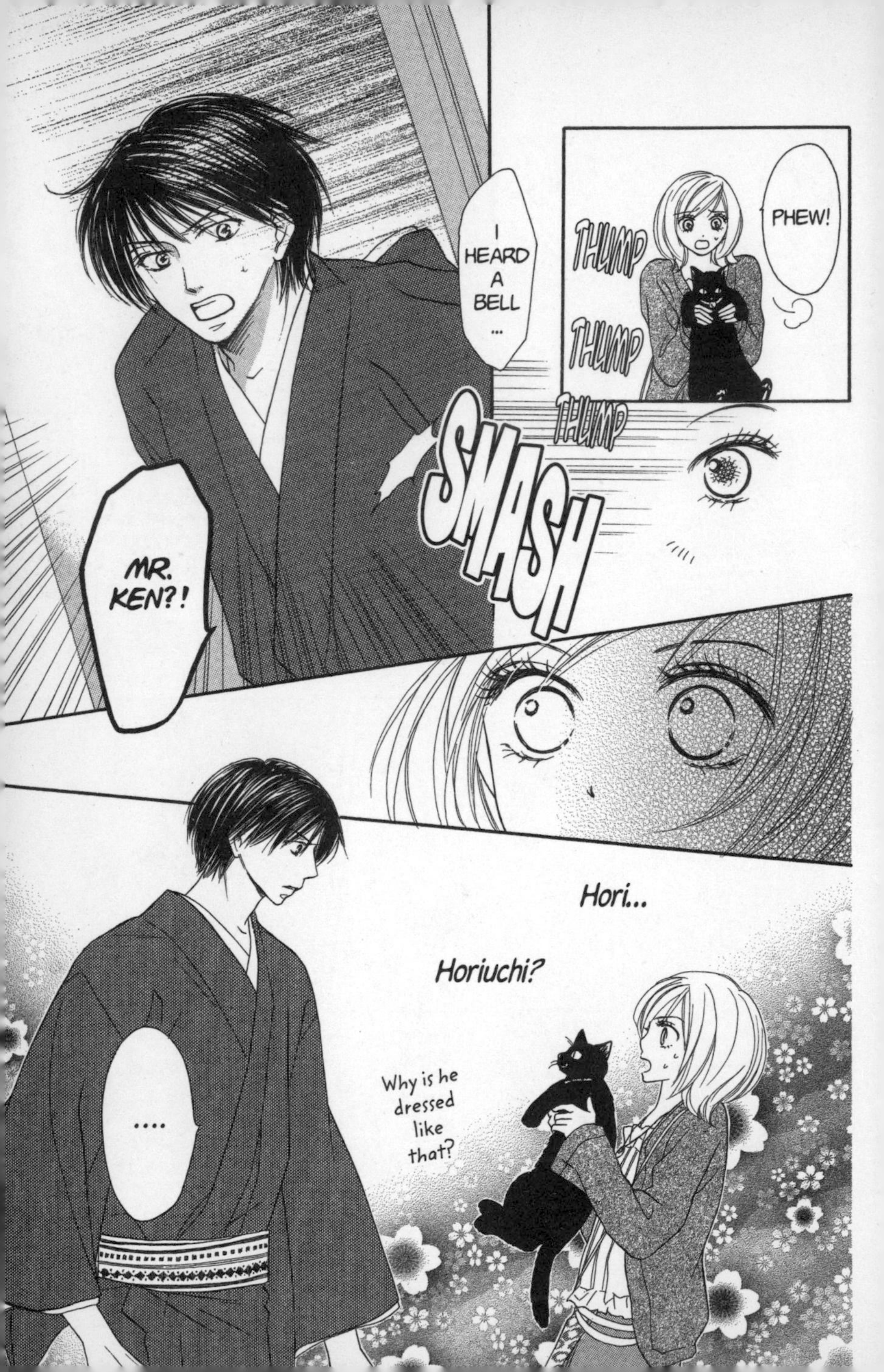
THUMP
THUMP
PHEW!
THUMP
I HEARD A BELL ...
SMASH
MR. KEN?!
Hori...
Horiuchi?
Why is he dressed like that?
....

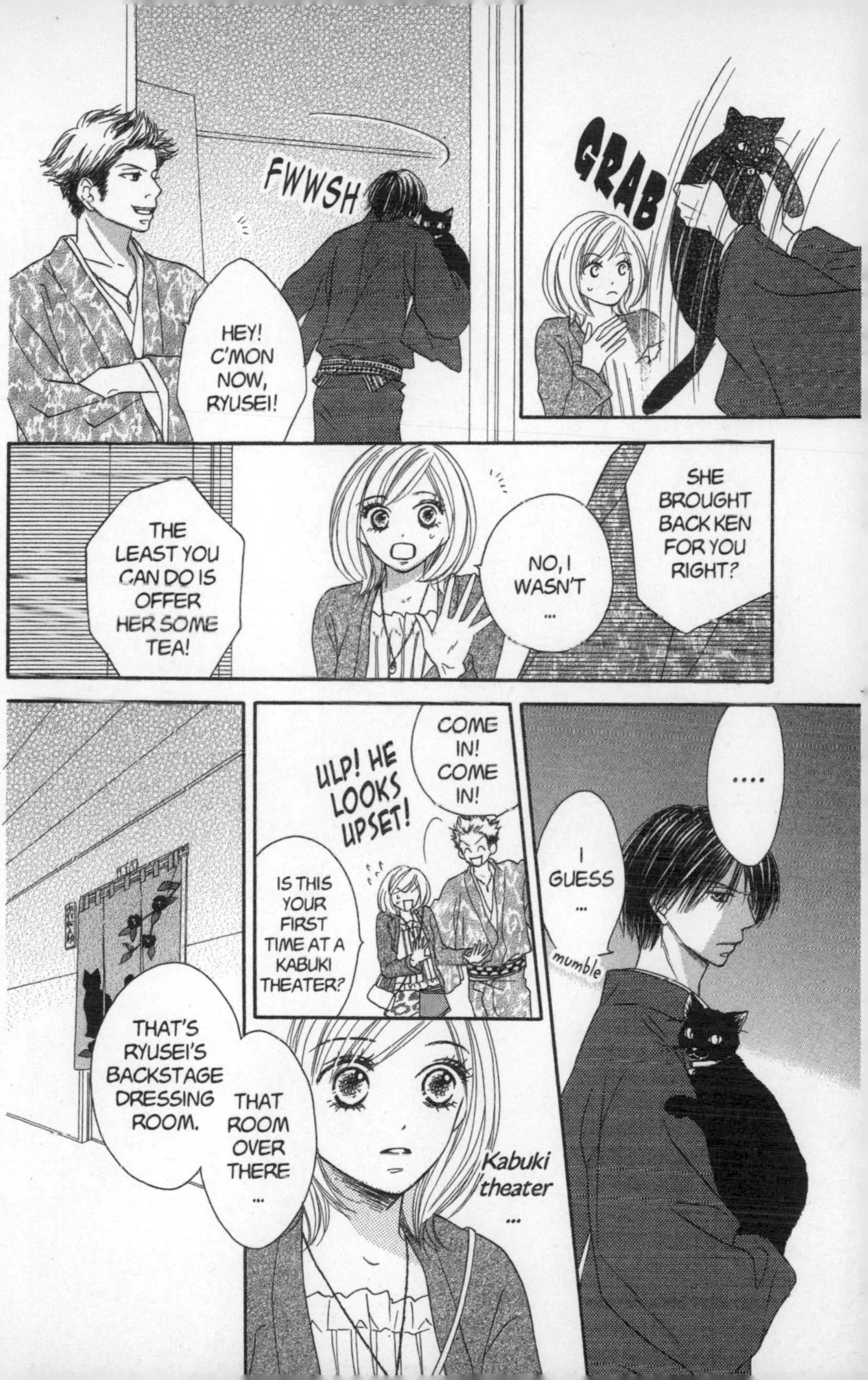
GRAB
FWWSH
HEY! C'MON NOW, RYUSEI!
SHE BROUGHT BACK KEN FOR YOU RIGHT?
NO, I WASN'T ...
THE LEAST YOU CAN DO IS OFFER HER SOME TEA!
....
I GUESS ...
mumble
COME IN! COME IN!
ULP! HE LOOKS UPSET!
IS THIS YOUR FIRST TIME AT A KABUKI THEATER?
THAT ROOM OVER THERE ...
THAT'S RYUSEI'S BACKSTAGE DRESSING ROOM.
Kabuki theater ...

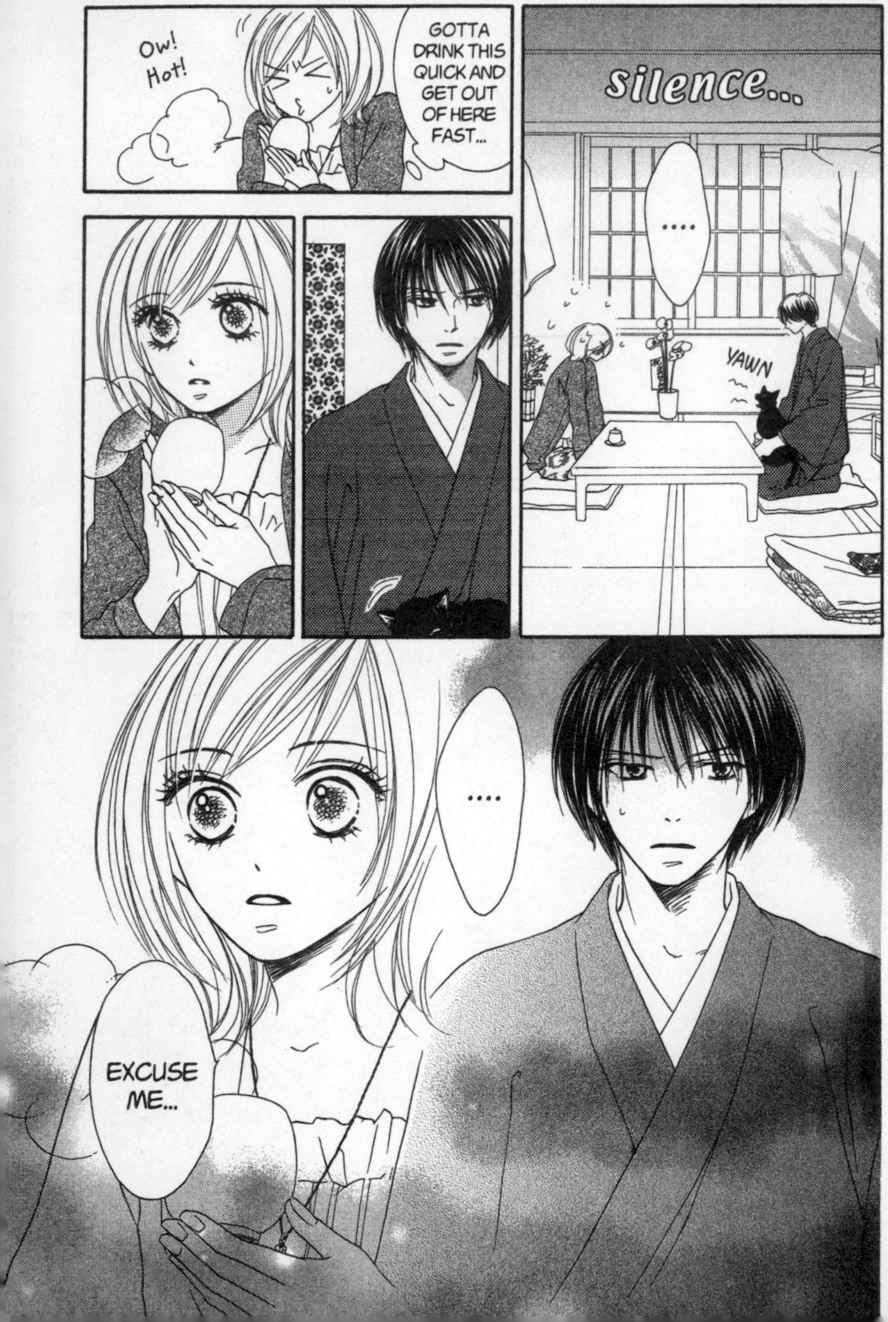
silence...
....
YAWN
GOTTA DRINK THIS QUICK AND GET OUT OF HERE FAST...
Ow! Hot!
....
EXCUSE ME...

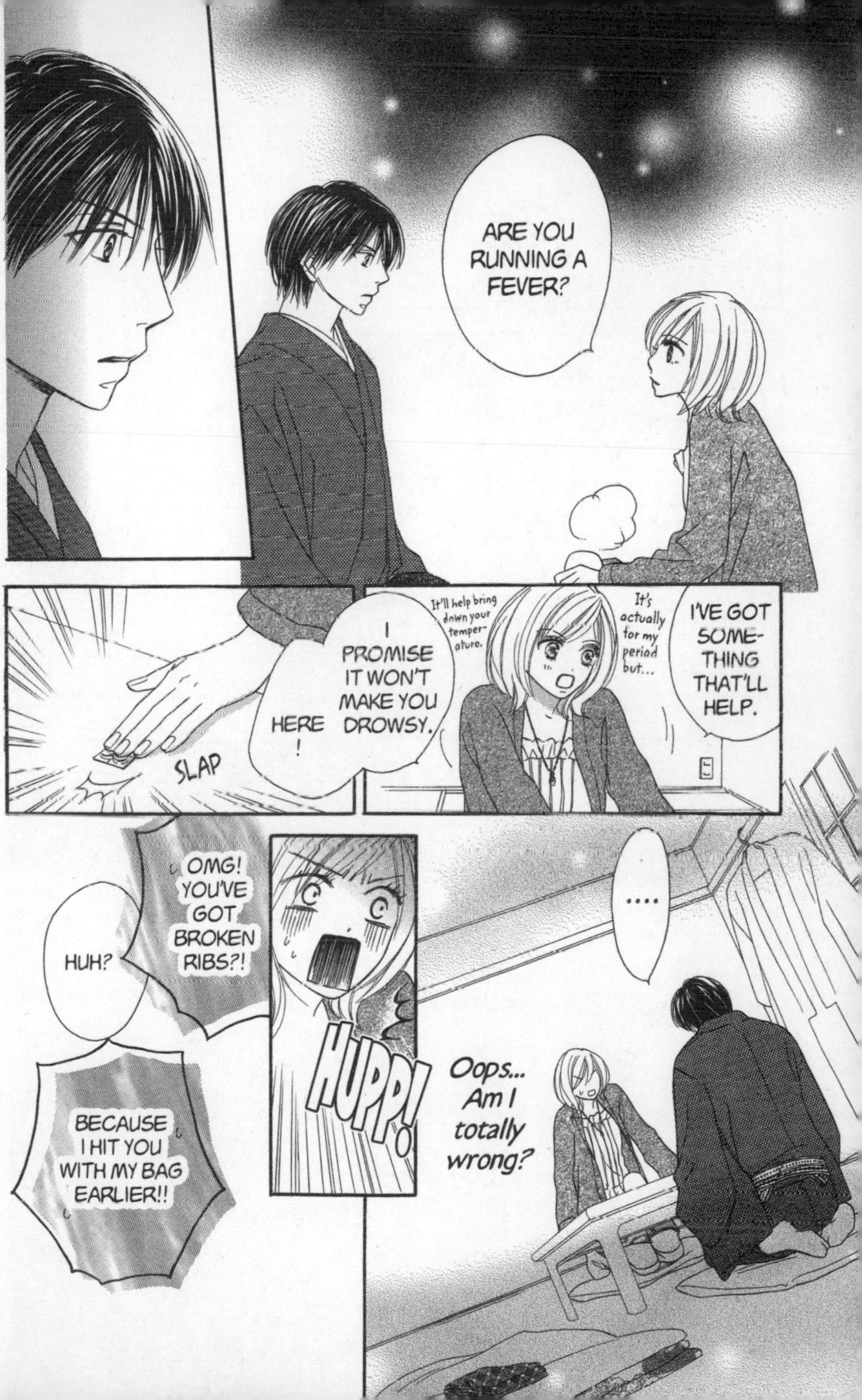
ARE YOU RUNNING A FEVER?
I'VE GOT SOMETHING THAT'LL HELP.
It's actually for my period but...
It'll help bring down your temperature.
I PROMISE IT WON'T MAKE YOU DROWSY.
HERE!
SLAP
....
Oops... Am I totally wrong?
HUPP!
OMG! YOU'VE GOT BROKEN RIBS?!
HUH?
BECAUSE I HIT YOU WITH MY BAG EARLIER!!

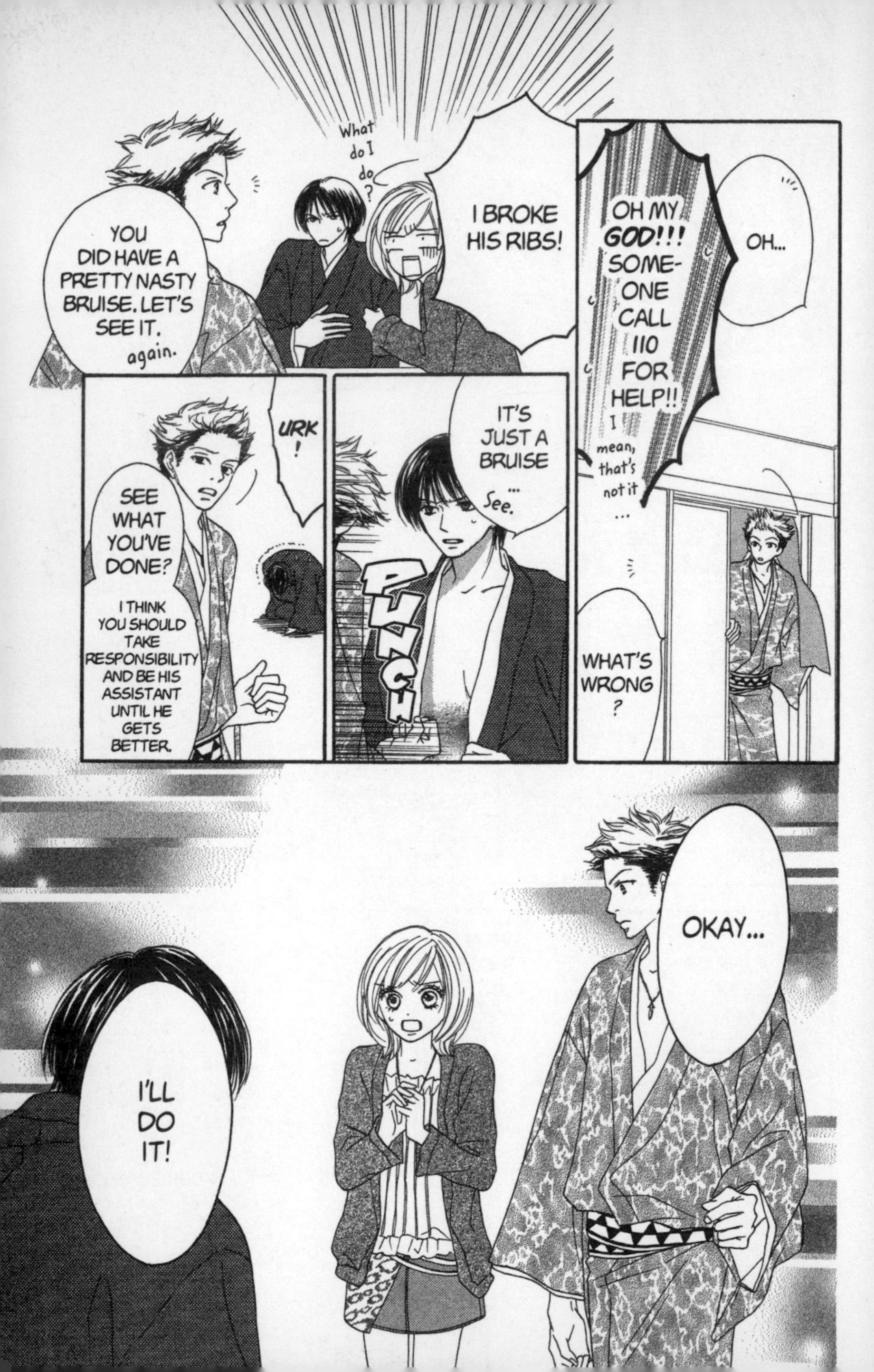
OH...
OH MY GOD!!! SOME-ONE CALL 110 FOR HELP!!
I mean, that's not it...
WHAT'S WRONG?
I BROKE HIS RIBS!
What do I do?
YOU DID HAVE A PRETTY NASTY BRUISE. LET'S SEE IT.
again.
IT'S JUST A BRUISE...
See.
PUNCH
URK!
SEE WHAT YOU'VE DONE?
I THINK YOU SHOULD TAKE RESPONSIBILITY AND BE HIS ASSISTANT UNTIL HE GETS BETTER.
OKAY...
I'LL DO IT!

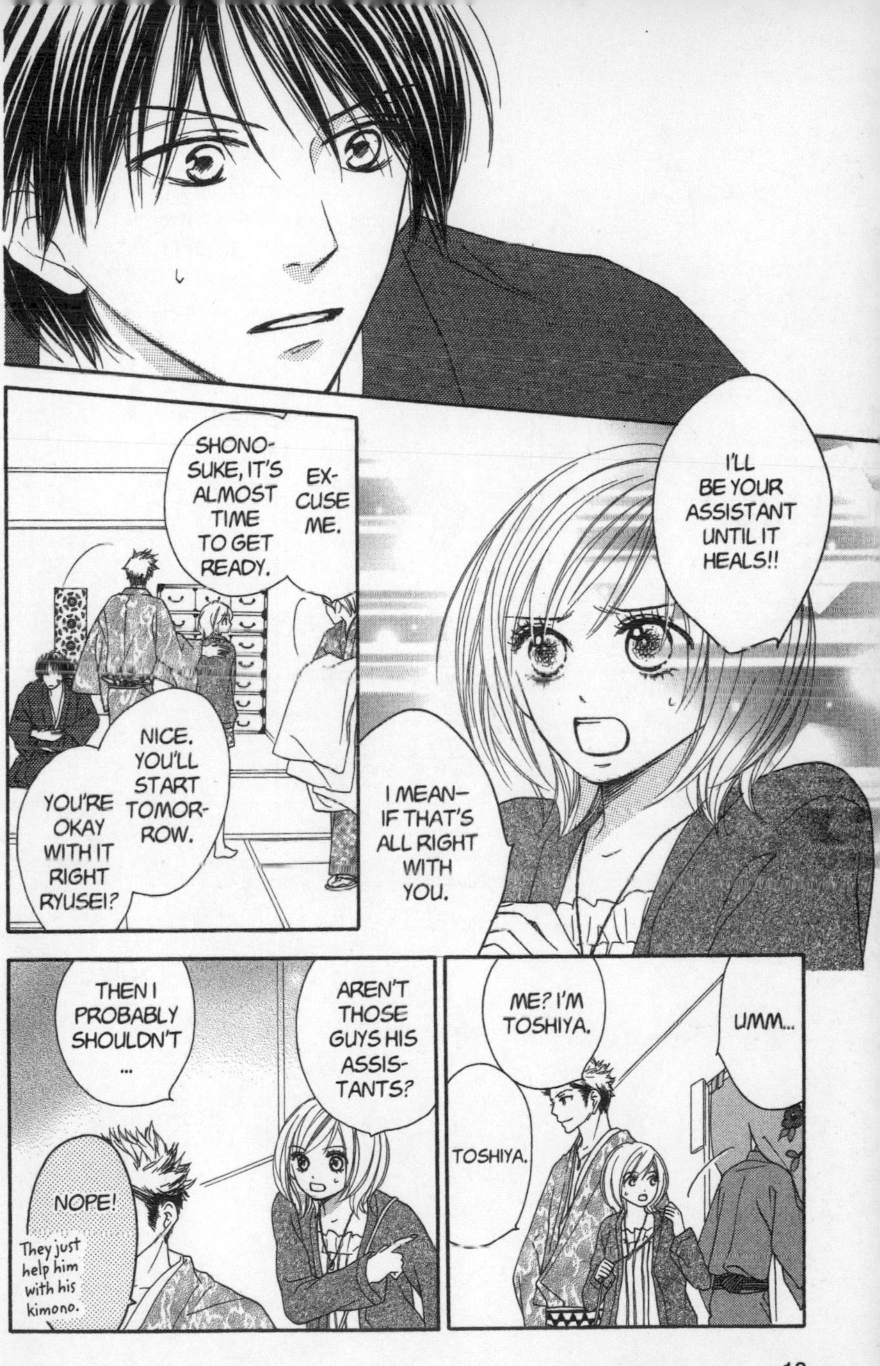
I'LL BE YOUR ASSISTANT UNTIL IT HEALS!!
I MEAN—IF THAT'S ALL RIGHT WITH YOU.
EX-CUSE ME.
SHONO-SUKE, IT'S ALMOST TIME TO GET READY.
NICE. YOU'LL START TOMOR-ROW.
YOU'RE OKAY WITH IT RIGHT RYUSEI?
UMM...
ME? I'M TOSHIYA.
TOSHIYA.
AREN'T THOSE GUYS HIS ASSIS-TANTS?
THEN I PROBABLY SHOULDN'T ...
NOPE!
They just help him with his kimono.

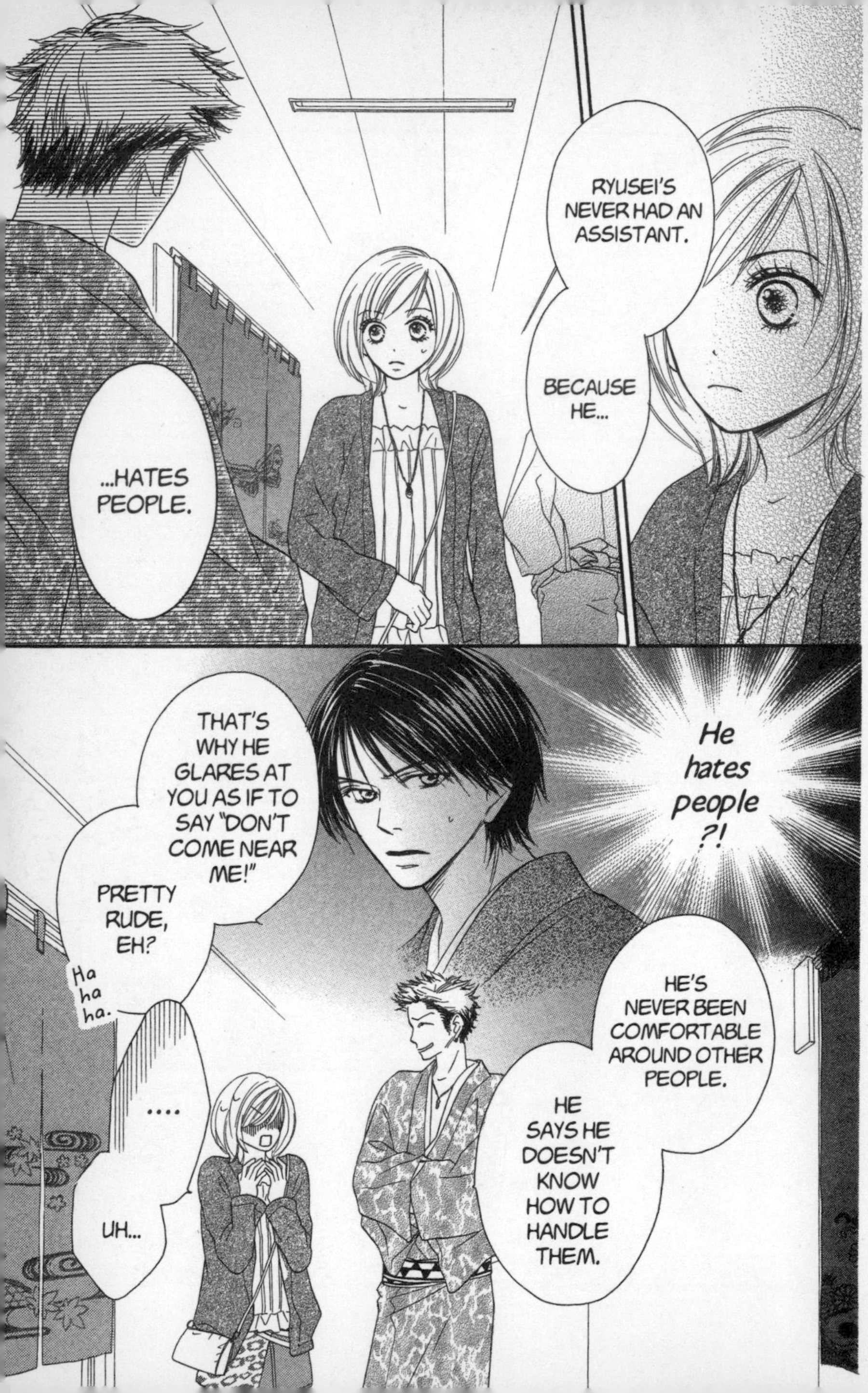
RYUSEI'S NEVER HAD AN ASSISTANT.
BECAUSE HE...
...HATES PEOPLE.
He hates people?!
THAT'S WHY HE GLARES AT YOU AS IF TO SAY "DON'T COME NEAR ME!"
PRETTY RUDE, EH?
Ha ha ha.
HE'S NEVER BEEN COMFORTABLE AROUND OTHER PEOPLE.
HE SAYS HE DOESN'T KNOW HOW TO HANDLE THEM.
....
UH...

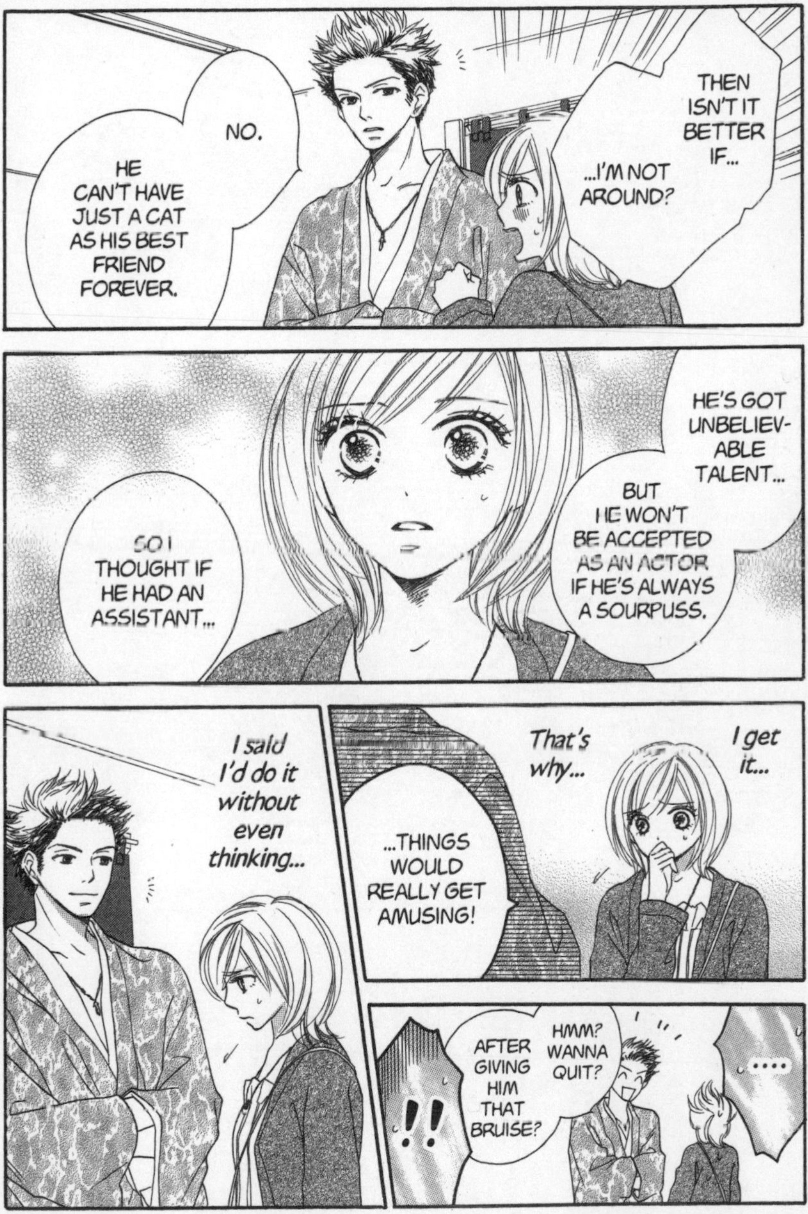
THEN ISN'T IT BETTER IF...
...I'M NOT AROUND?
NO.
HE CAN'T HAVE JUST A CAT AS HIS BEST FRIEND FOREVER.
HE'S GOT UNBELIEV-ABLE TALENT...
BUT HE WON'T BE ACCEPTED AS AN ACTOR IF HE'S ALWAYS A SOURPUSS.
SO I THOUGHT IF HE HAD AN ASSISTANT...
I get it...
That's why...
...THINGS WOULD REALLY GET AMUSING!
....
HMM? WANNA QUIT?
AFTER GIVING HIM THAT BRUISE?
!!
I said I'd do it without even thinking...

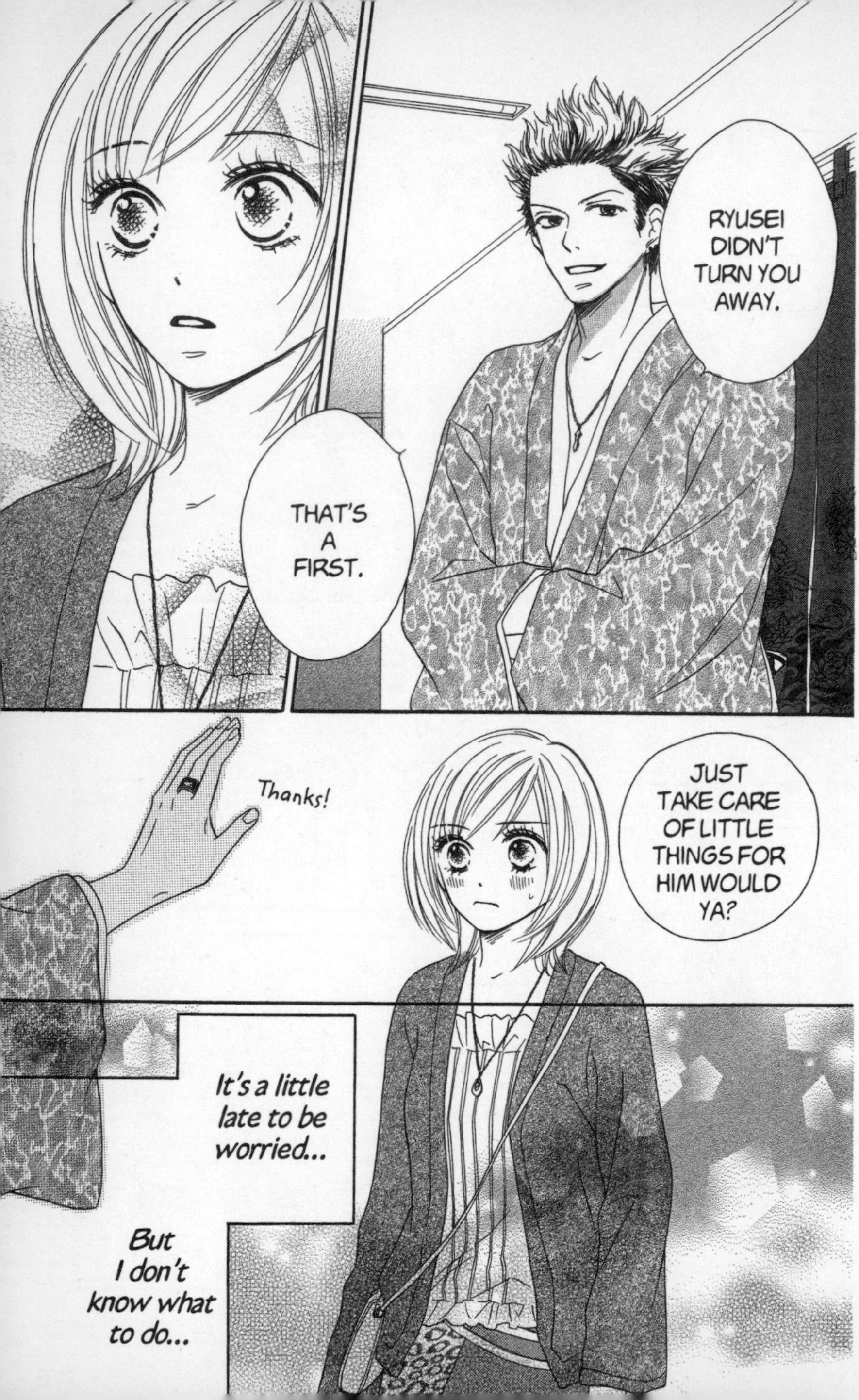
RYUSEI DIDN'T TURN YOU AWAY.
THAT'S A FIRST.
JUST TAKE CARE OF LITTLE THINGS FOR HIM WOULD YA?
Thanks!
It's a little late to be worried...
But I don't know what to do...

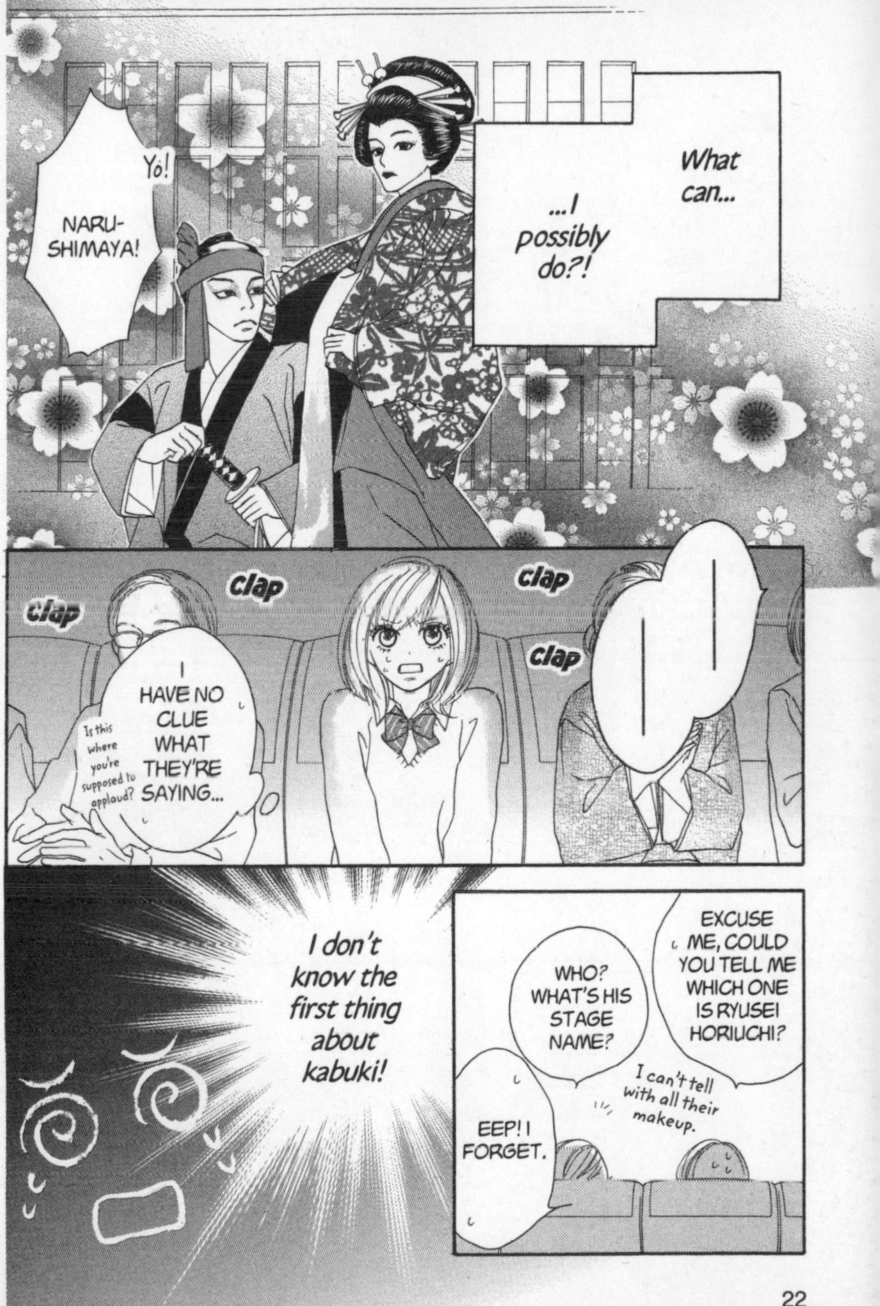
What can...
...I possibly do?!
Yo!
NARU-SHIMAYA!
Clap
Clap
Clap
clap
I HAVE NO CLUE WHAT THEY'RE SAYING...
Is this where you're supposed to applaud?
EXCUSE ME, COULD YOU TELL ME WHICH ONE IS RYUSEI HORIUCHI?
WHO? WHAT'S HIS STAGE NAME?
I can't tell with all their makeup.
EEP! I FORGET.
I don't know the first thing about kabuki!

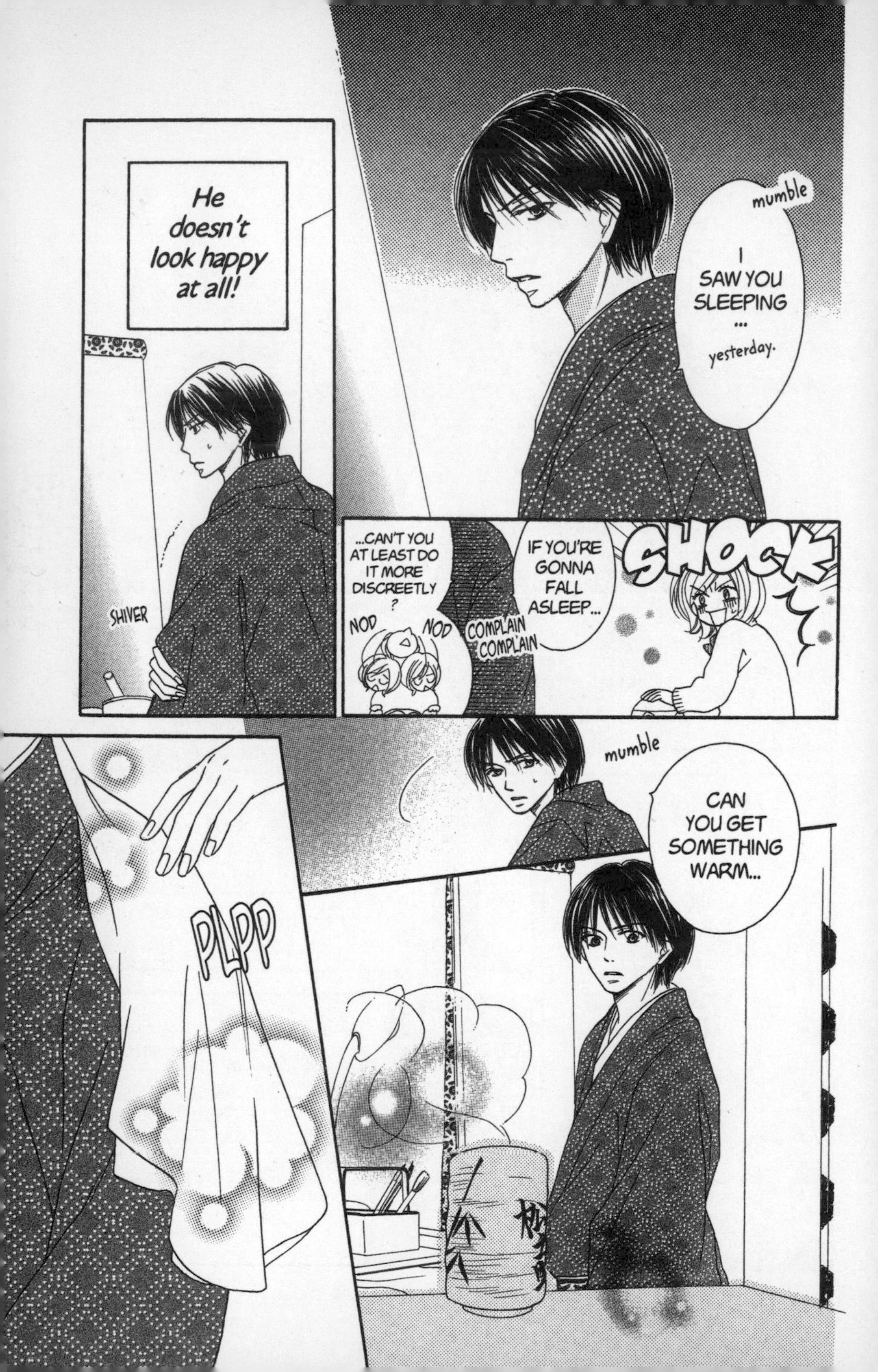
mumble
I SAW YOU SLEEPING ... yesterday.
SHOCK
IF YOU'RE GONNA FALL ASLEEP...
COMPLAIN COMPLAIN
...CAN'T YOU AT LEAST DO IT MORE DISCREETLY?
NOD NOD
He doesn't look happy at all!
SHIVER
mumble
CAN YOU GET SOMETHING WARM...
PLPP

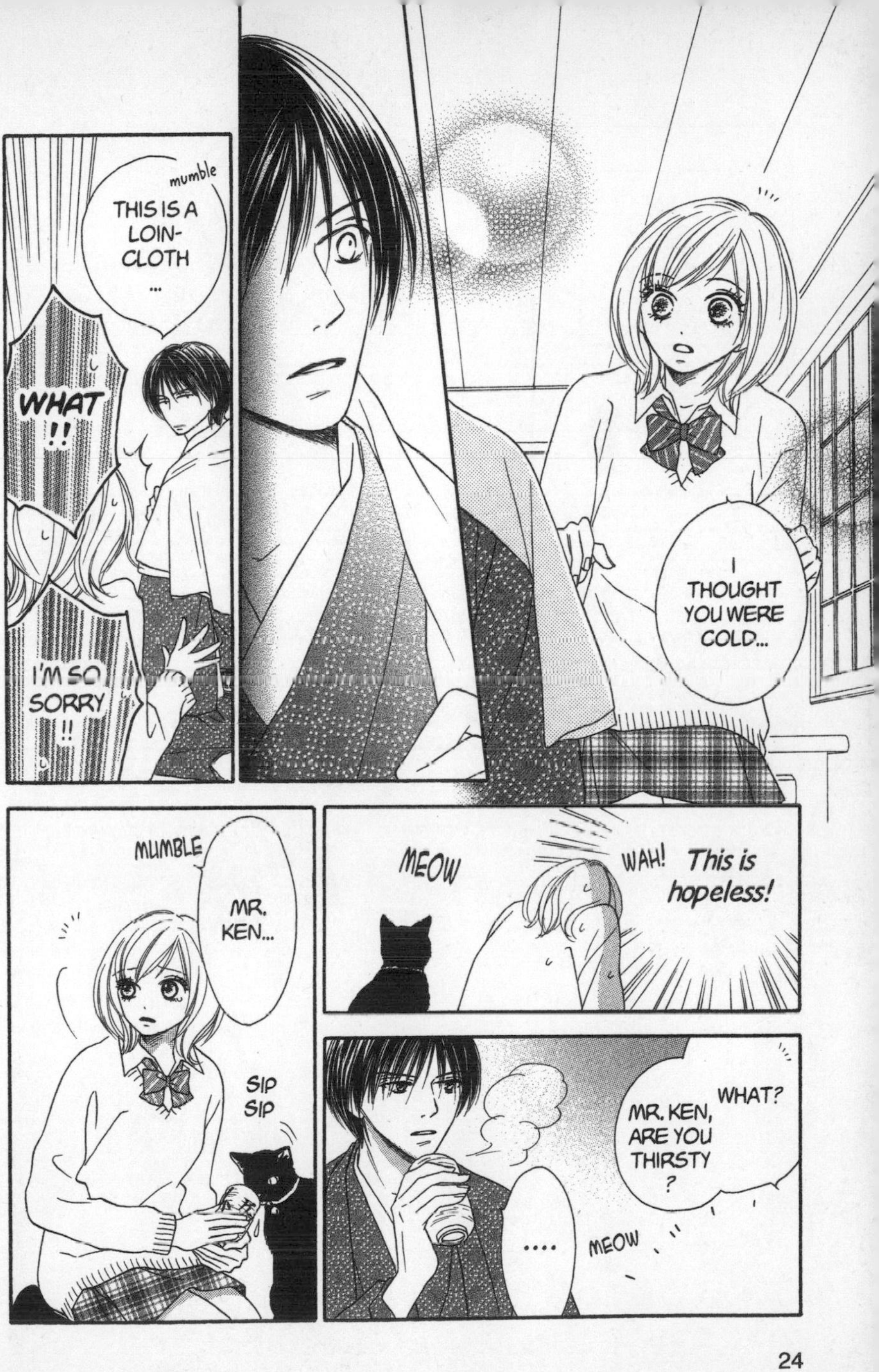
I THOUGHT YOU WERE COLD...
mumble
THIS IS A LOIN-CLOTH ...
WHAT !!
I'M SO SORRY !!
WAH! This is hopeless!
MEOW
WHAT?
MR. KEN, ARE YOU THIRSTY ?
....
MEOW
MUMBLE
MR. KEN...
SIP SIP

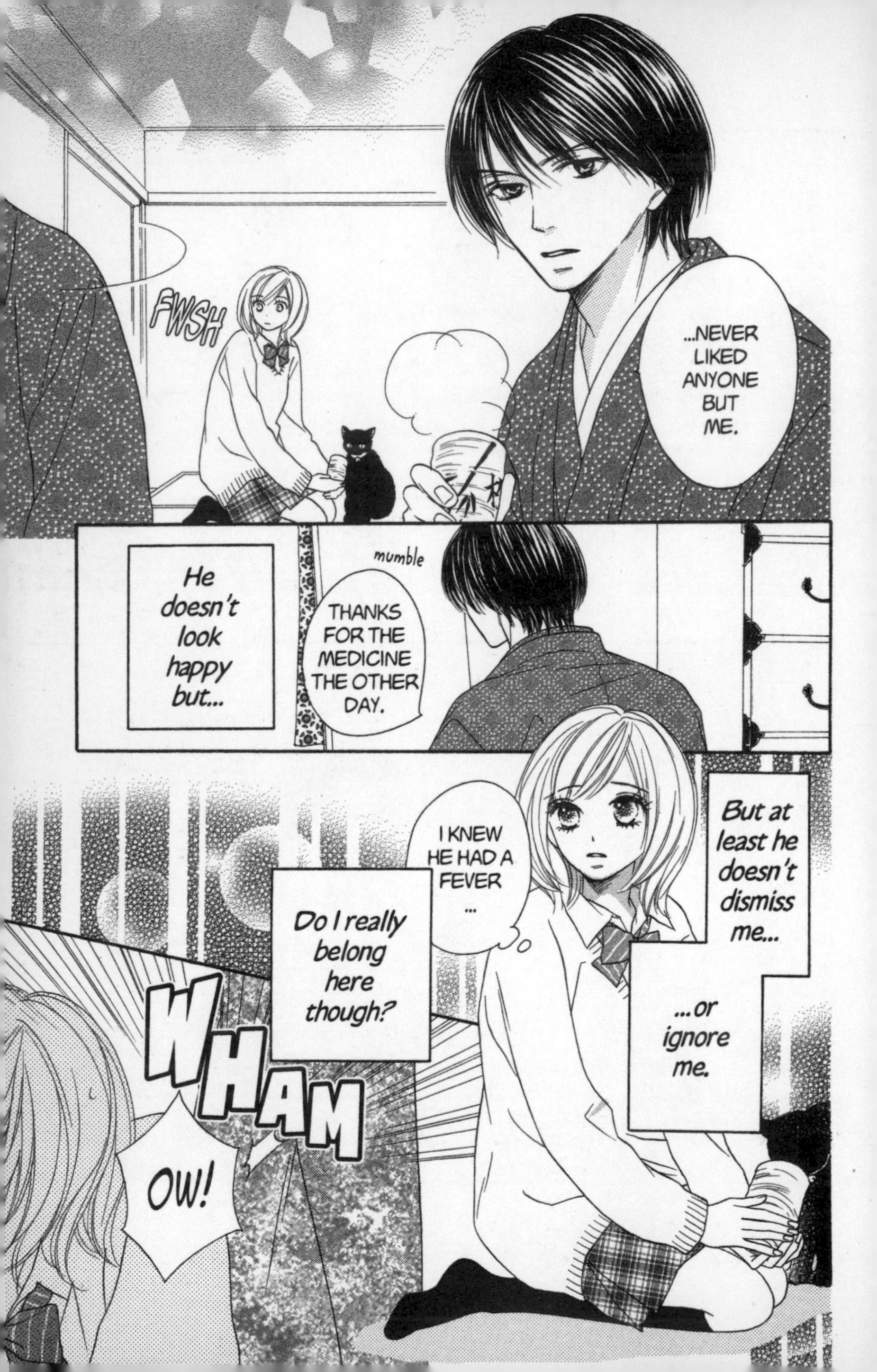
...NEVER LIKED ANYONE BUT ME.
FWSH
mumble
THANKS FOR THE MEDICINE THE OTHER DAY.
He doesn't look happy but...
But at least he doesn't dismiss me...
...or ignore me.
I KNEW HE HAD A FEVER ...
Do I really belong here though?
WHAM
OW!

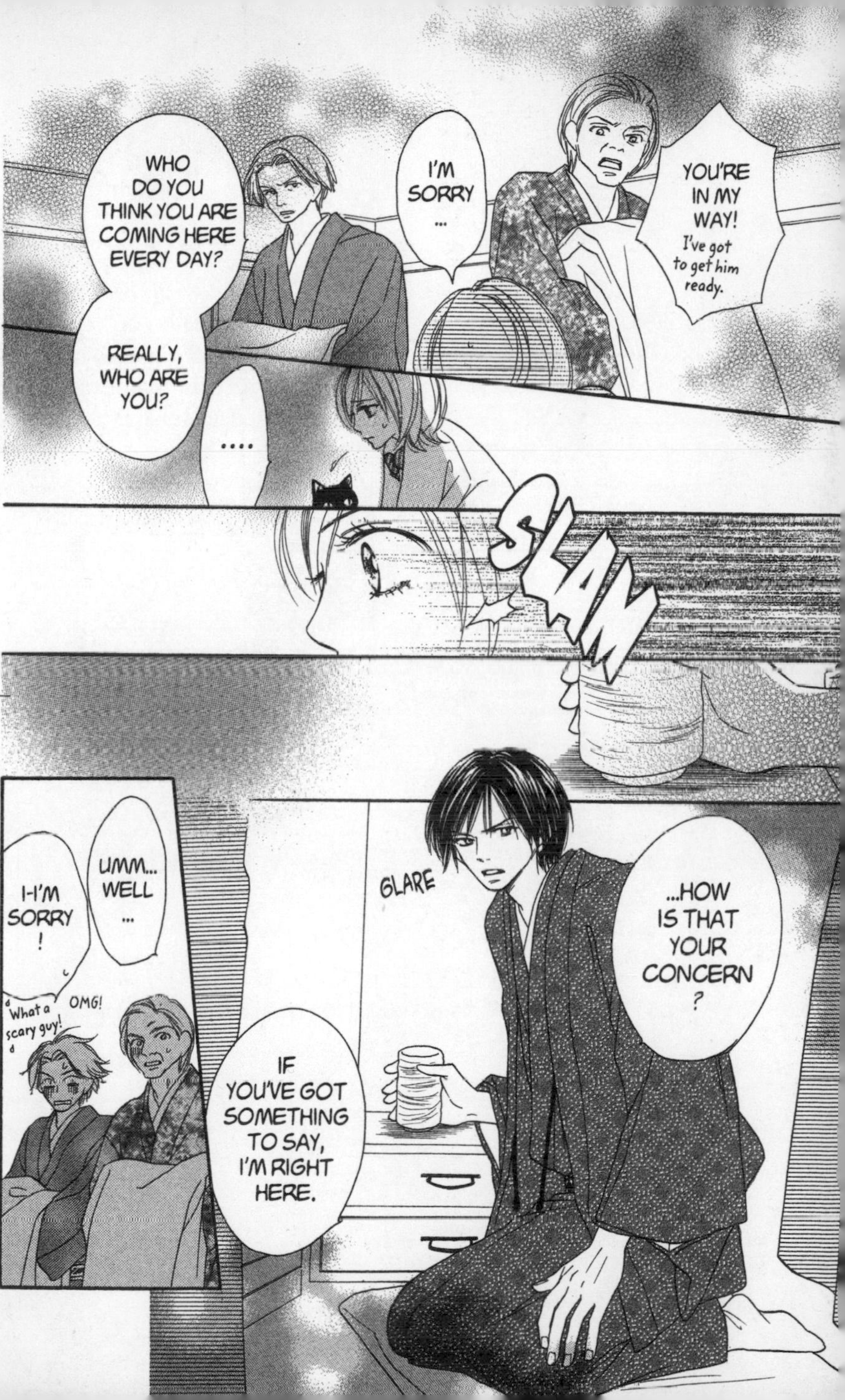
YOU'RE IN MY WAY!
I've got to get him ready.
I'M SORRY ...
WHO DO YOU THINK YOU ARE COMING HERE EVERY DAY?
REALLY, WHO ARE YOU?
....
SLAM
...HOW IS THAT YOUR CONCERN?
GLARE
IF YOU'VE GOT SOMETHING TO SAY, I'M RIGHT HERE.
UMM... WELL ...
I-I'M SORRY!
OMG!
What a scary guy!

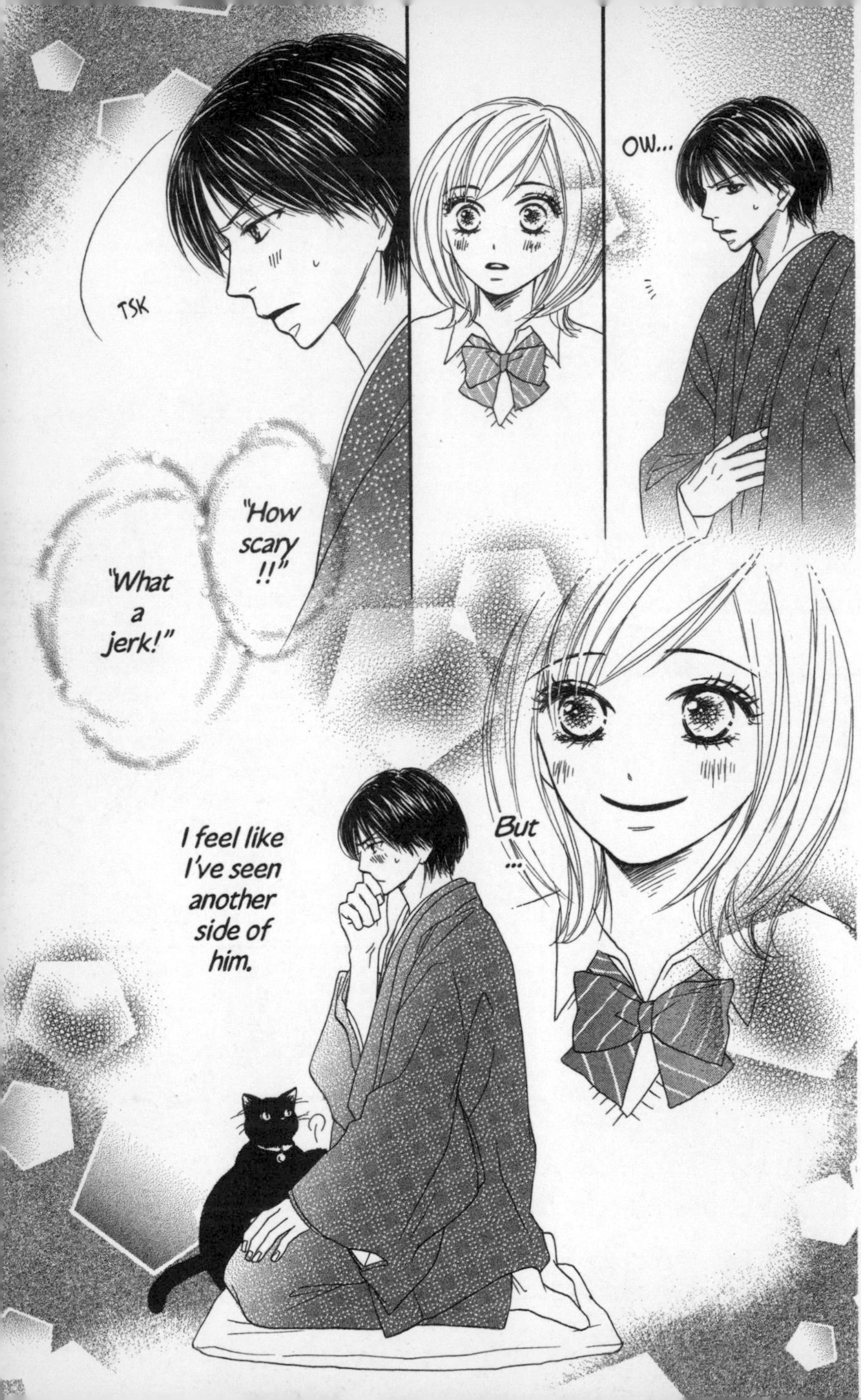
OW...
TSK
"How scary!!"
"What a jerk!"
But ...
I feel like I've seen another side of him.

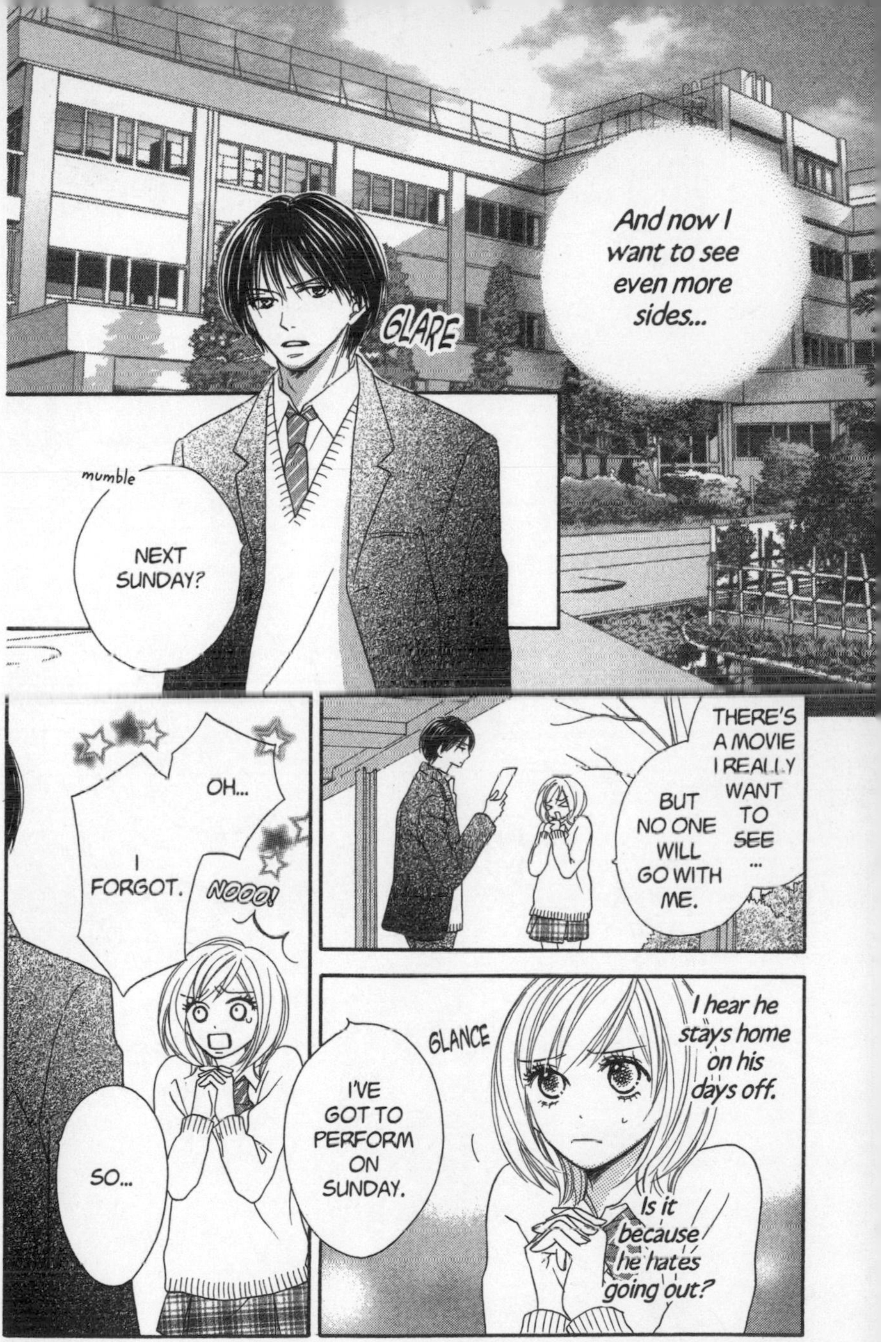
And now I want to see even more sides...
GLARE
mumble
NEXT SUNDAY?
THERE'S A MOVIE I REALLY WANT TO SEE...
BUT NO ONE WILL GO WITH ME.
I hear he stays home on his days off.
GLANCE
Is it because he hates going out?
OH... I FORGOT.
NOOO!
I'VE GOT TO PERFORM ON SUNDAY.
SO...

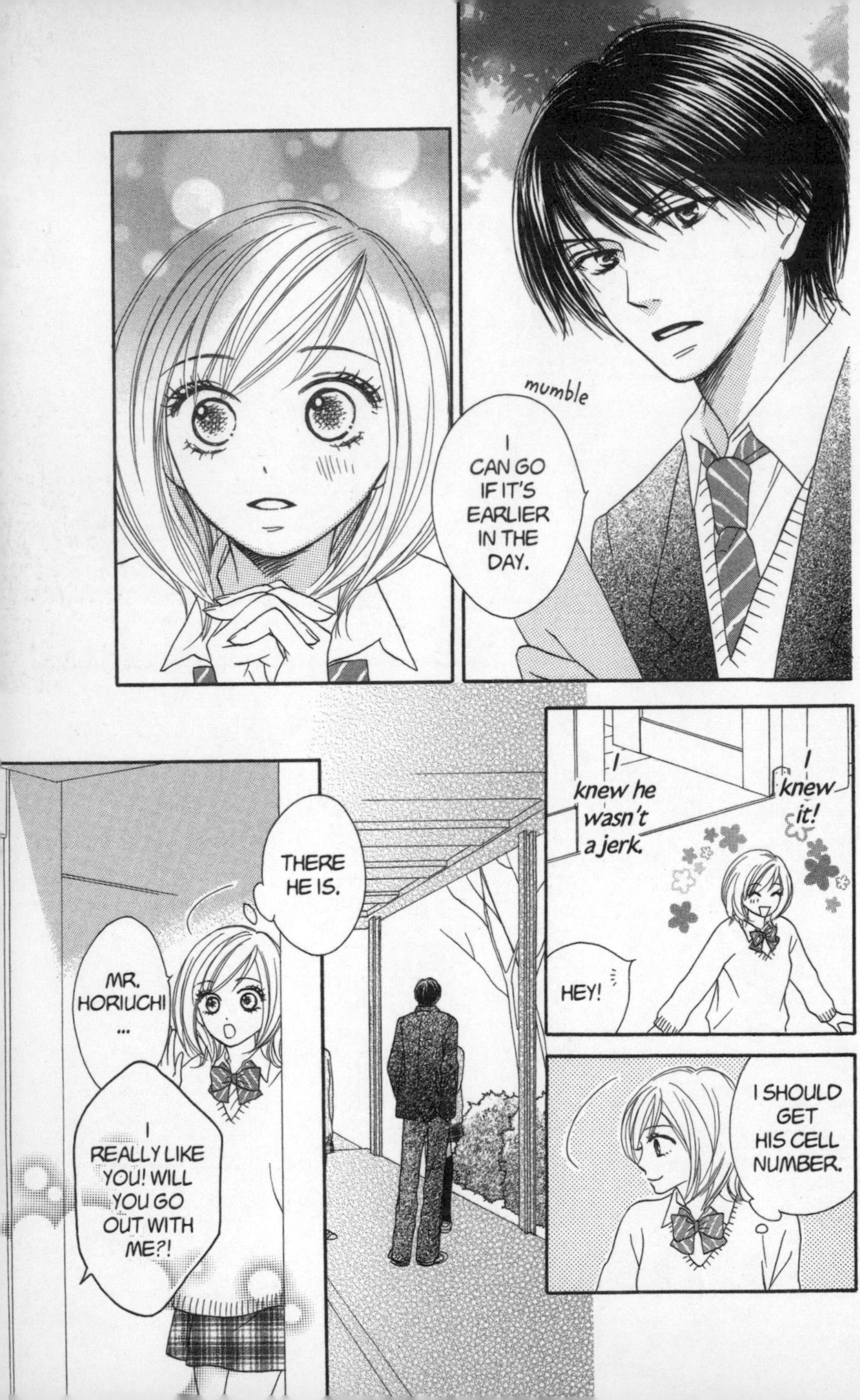
mumble
I CAN GO IF IT'S EARLIER IN THE DAY.
I knew it!
I knew he wasn't a jerk.
HEY!
I SHOULD GET HIS CELL NUMBER.
THERE HE IS.
MR. HORIUCHI ...
I REALLY LIKE YOU! WILL YOU GO OUT WITH ME?!

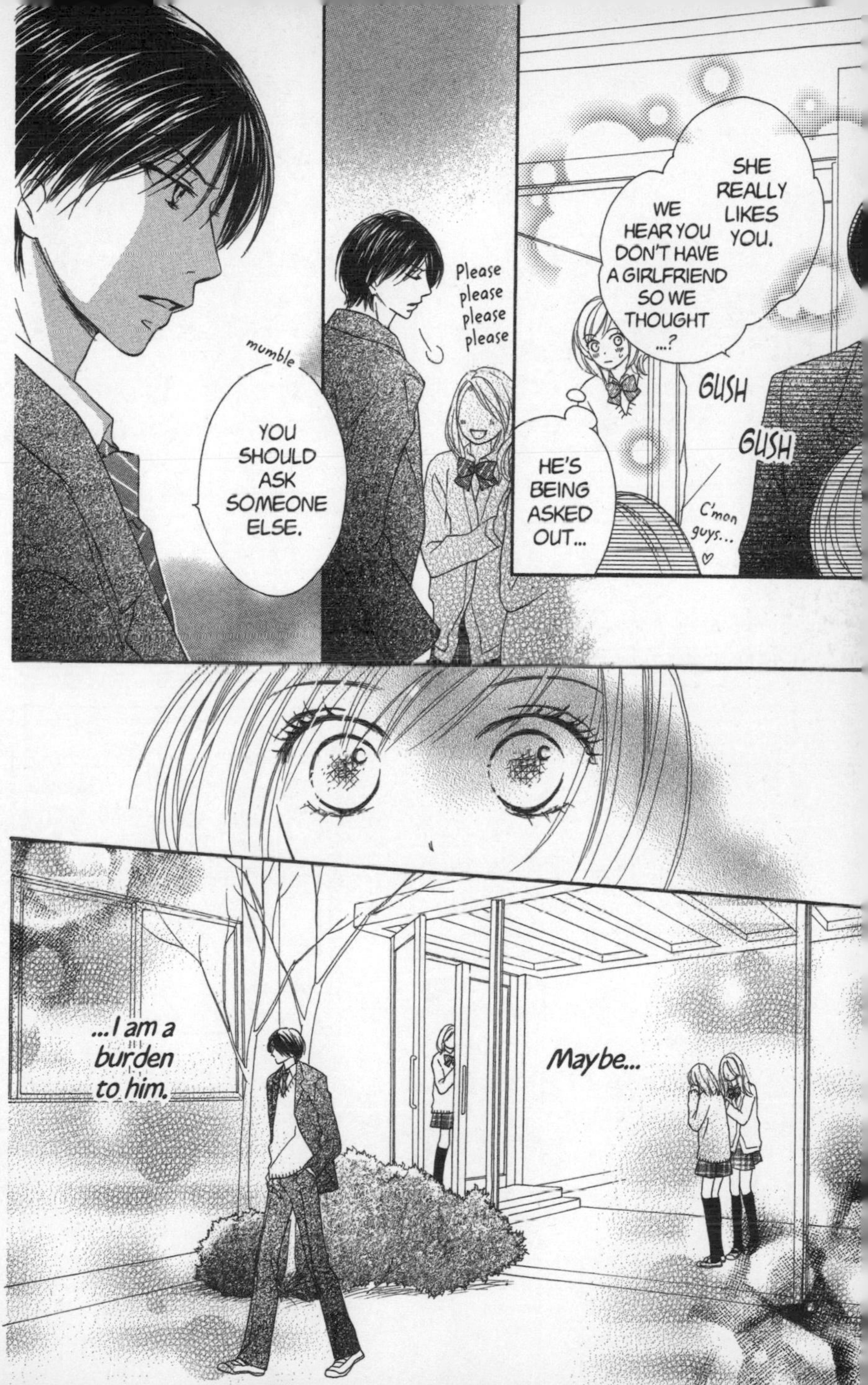
SHE REALLY LIKES YOU.
WE HEAR YOU DON'T HAVE A GIRLFRIEND SO WE THOUGHT ...?
GUSH
GUSH
HE'S BEING ASKED OUT...
C'mon guys... ♡
Please please please please
mumble
YOU SHOULD ASK SOMEONE ELSE.
Maybe...
...I am a burden to him.

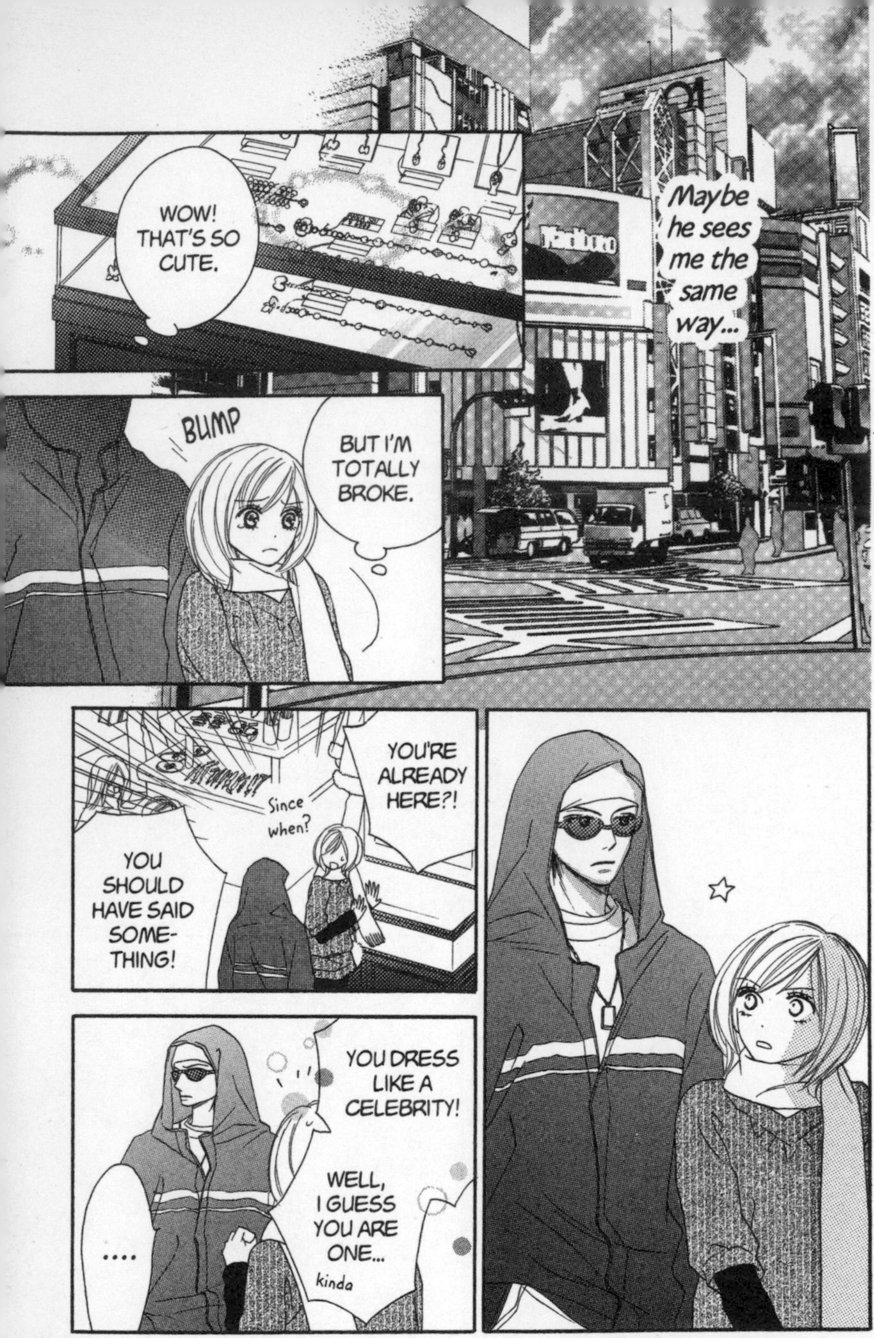
Maybe he sees me the same way...
WOW! THAT'S SO CUTE.
BUT I'M TOTALLY BROKE.
BUMP
YOU'RE ALREADY HERE?!
Since when?
YOU SHOULD HAVE SAID SOME-THING!
YOU DRESS LIKE A CELEBRITY!
WELL, I GUESS YOU ARE ONE...
kinda
....

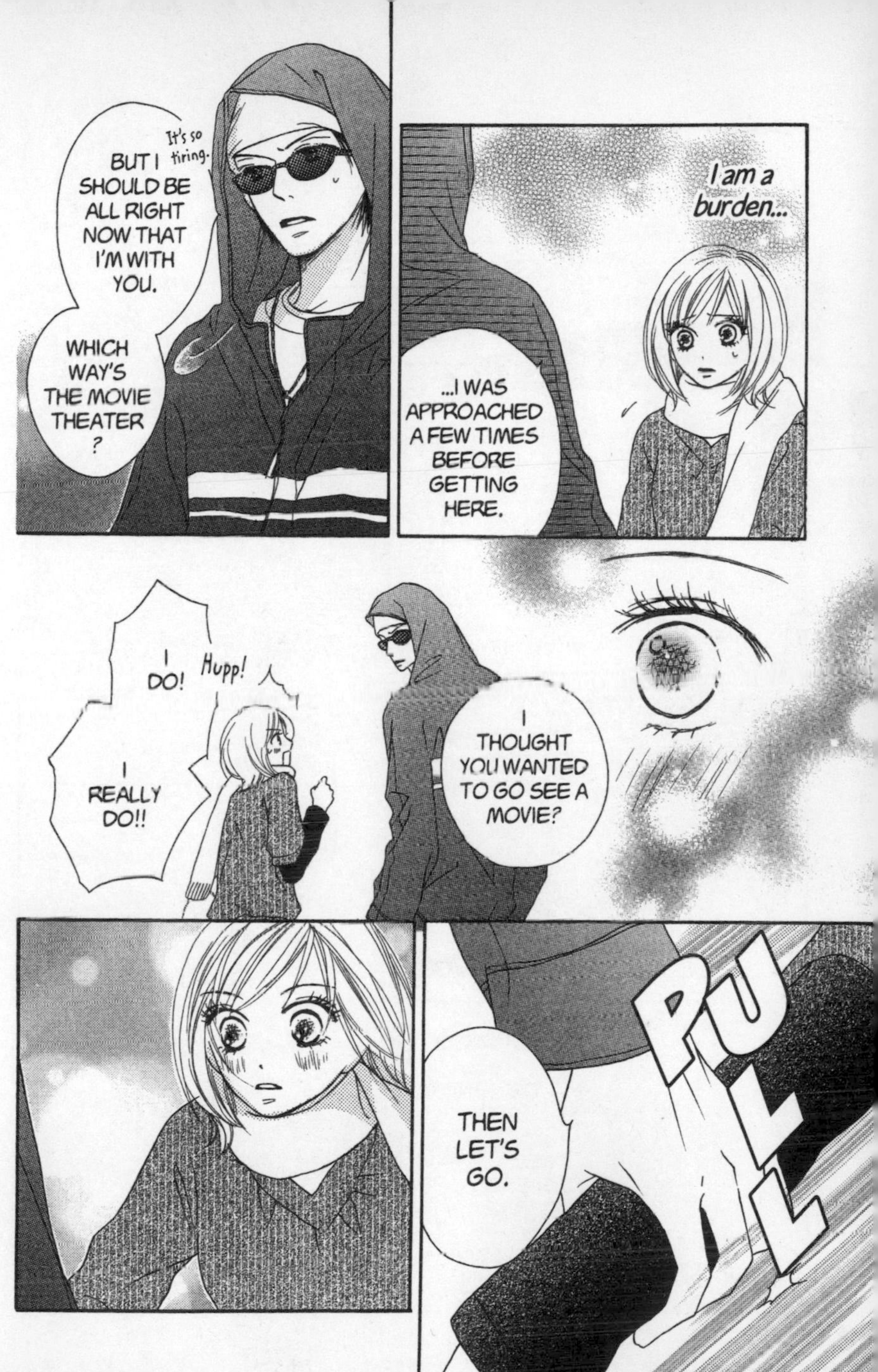
I am a burden...
...I WAS APPROACHED A FEW TIMES BEFORE GETTING HERE.
It's so tiring.
BUT I SHOULD BE ALL RIGHT NOW THAT I'M WITH YOU.
WHICH WAY'S THE MOVIE THEATER?
I THOUGHT YOU WANTED TO GO SEE A MOVIE?
Hupp!
I DO!
I REALLY DO!!
PULL
THEN LET'S GO.

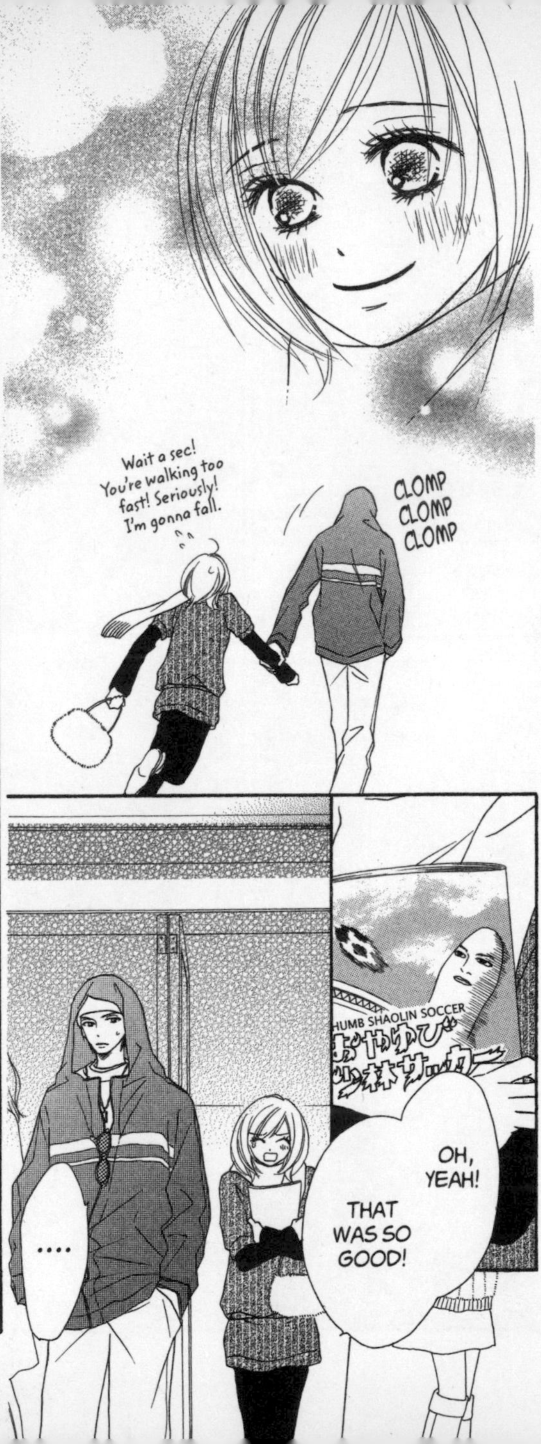
CLOMP
CLOMP
CLOMP
Wait a sec! You're walking too fast! Seriously! I'm gonna fall.
HUMB SHAOLIN SOCCER
OH, YEAH!
THAT WAS SO GOOD!
....

KANO

I'M IN LOVE WITH A KABUKI ACTOR NAMED KATAOKA NIZAEMON XV. (I'VE LIKED HIM EVEN BEFORE I STARTED WATCHING KABUKI.) HIS REAL NAME IS TAKAO-SAN. I USED A DIFFERENT KANJI TO WRITE *TAKAO* AT FIRST BUT...

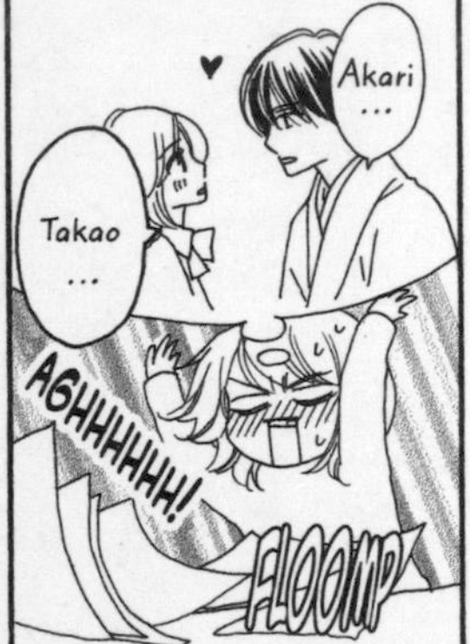
Akari
...
Takao
...
AGHHHHHH!
FLOOMP

...I COULDN'T. HE HAD BEEN WORKING UNDER HIS REAL NAME UNTIL A FEW YEARS AGO SO I GUESS THAT IMAGE STUCK WITH ME PRETTY STRONGLY. SO I DECIDED TO READ THE KANJI I CAME UP WITH DIFFERENTLY AND THUS THE NAME *RYUSEI*. JUST AS WELL...

I MET NIZAEMON-SAN ON VACATION BY RANDOM CHANCE IN THE PAST.

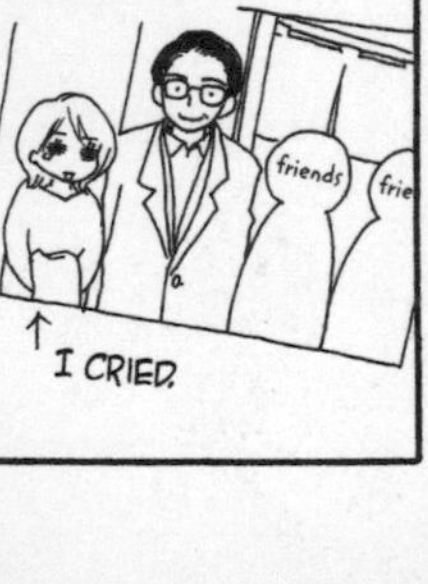
friends
frie
I CRIED.

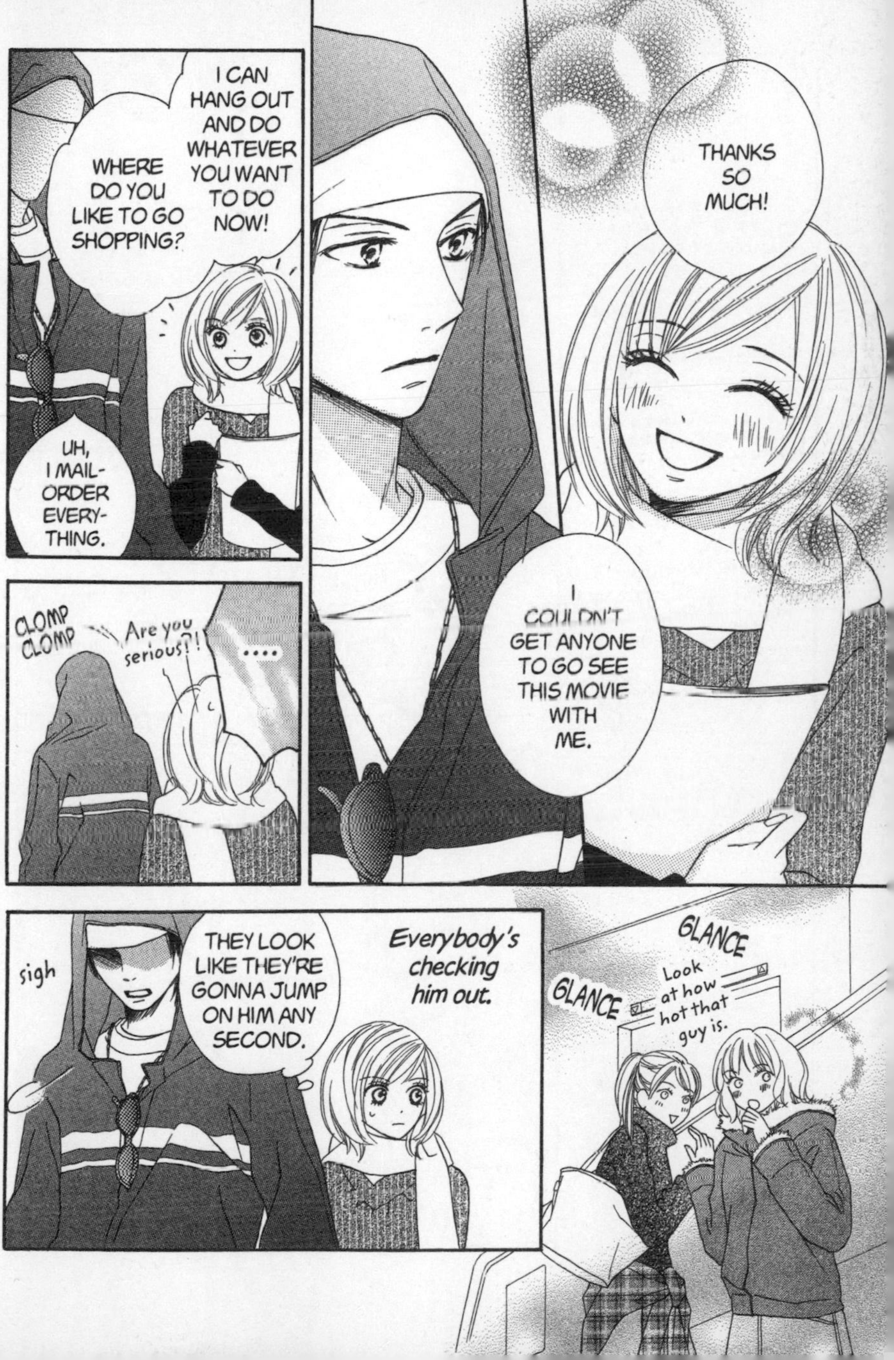
THANKS SO MUCH!
I COULDN'T GET ANYONE TO GO SEE THIS MOVIE WITH ME.
I CAN HANG OUT AND DO WHATEVER YOU WANT TO DO NOW!
WHERE DO YOU LIKE TO GO SHOPPING?
UH, I MAIL-ORDER EVERY-THING.
....
Are you serious?!
CLOMP CLOMP
GLANCE
Look at how hot that guy is.
GLANCE
Everybody's checking him out.
THEY LOOK LIKE THEY'RE GONNA JUMP ON HIM ANY SECOND.
sigh

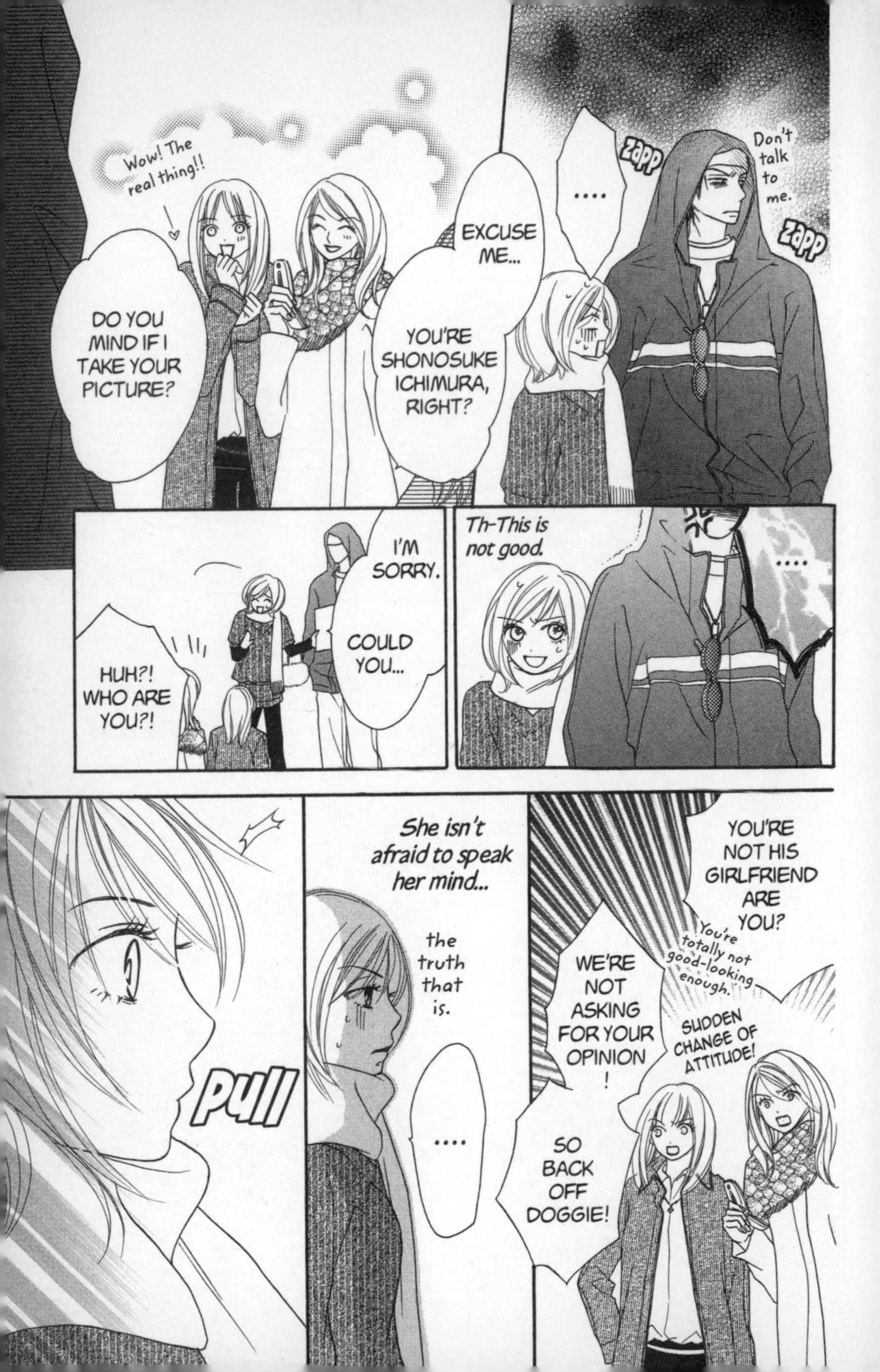
Don't talk to me.
ZAPP
....
ZAPP
EXCUSE ME...
YOU'RE SHONOSUKE ICHIMURA, RIGHT?
Wow! The real thing!!
DO YOU MIND IF I TAKE YOUR PICTURE?
Th-This is not good.
....
I'M SORRY.
COULD YOU...
HUH?! WHO ARE YOU?!
YOU'RE NOT HIS GIRLFRIEND ARE YOU?
You're totally not good-looking enough.
WE'RE NOT ASKING FOR YOUR OPINION!
SUDDEN CHANGE OF ATTITUDE!
SO BACK OFF DOGGIE!
She isn't afraid to speak her mind...
the truth that is.
....
PULL

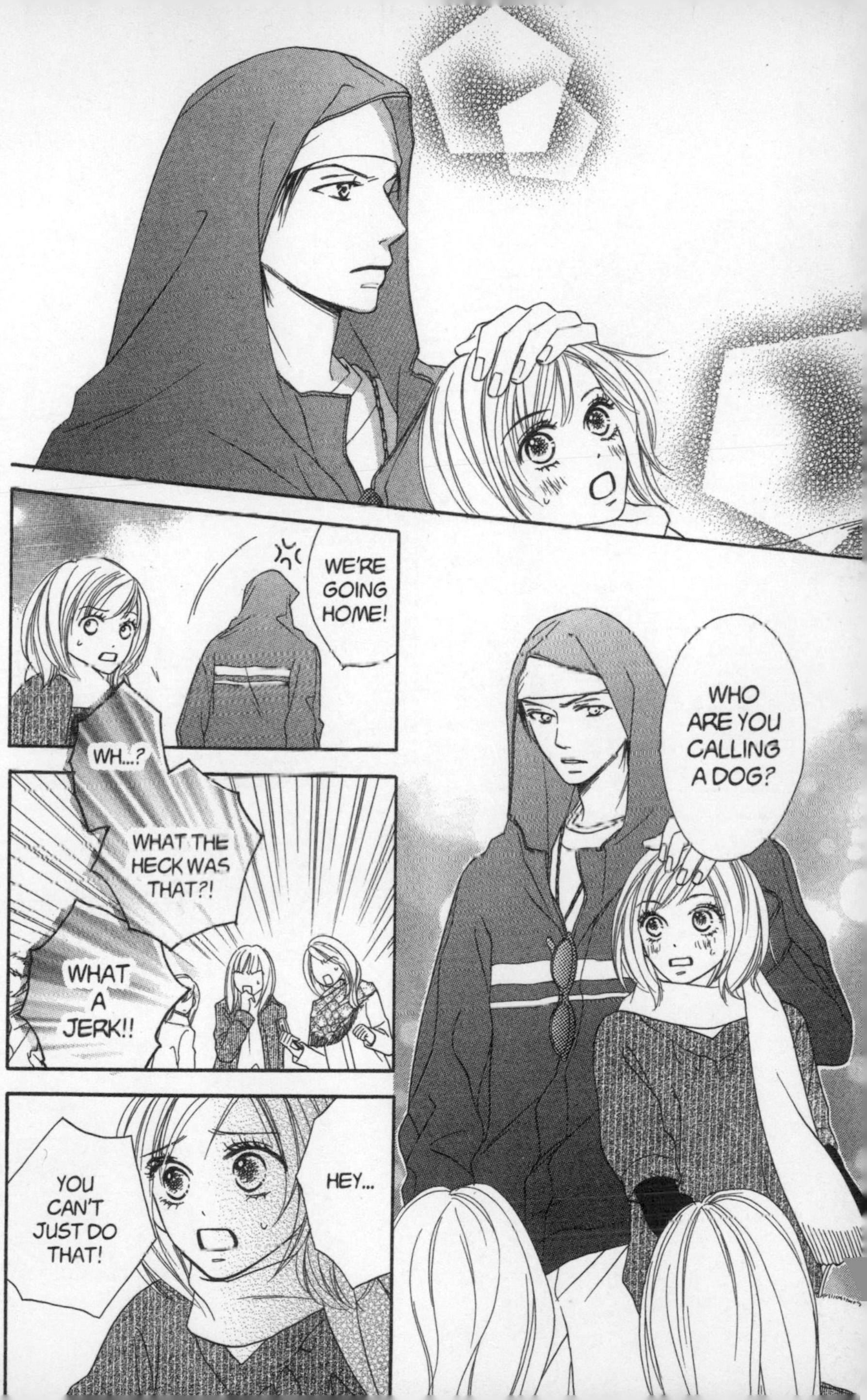
WHO ARE YOU CALLING A DOG?
WE'RE GOING HOME!
WH...?
WHAT THE HECK WAS THAT?!
WHAT A JERK!!
HEY...
YOU CAN'T JUST DO THAT!

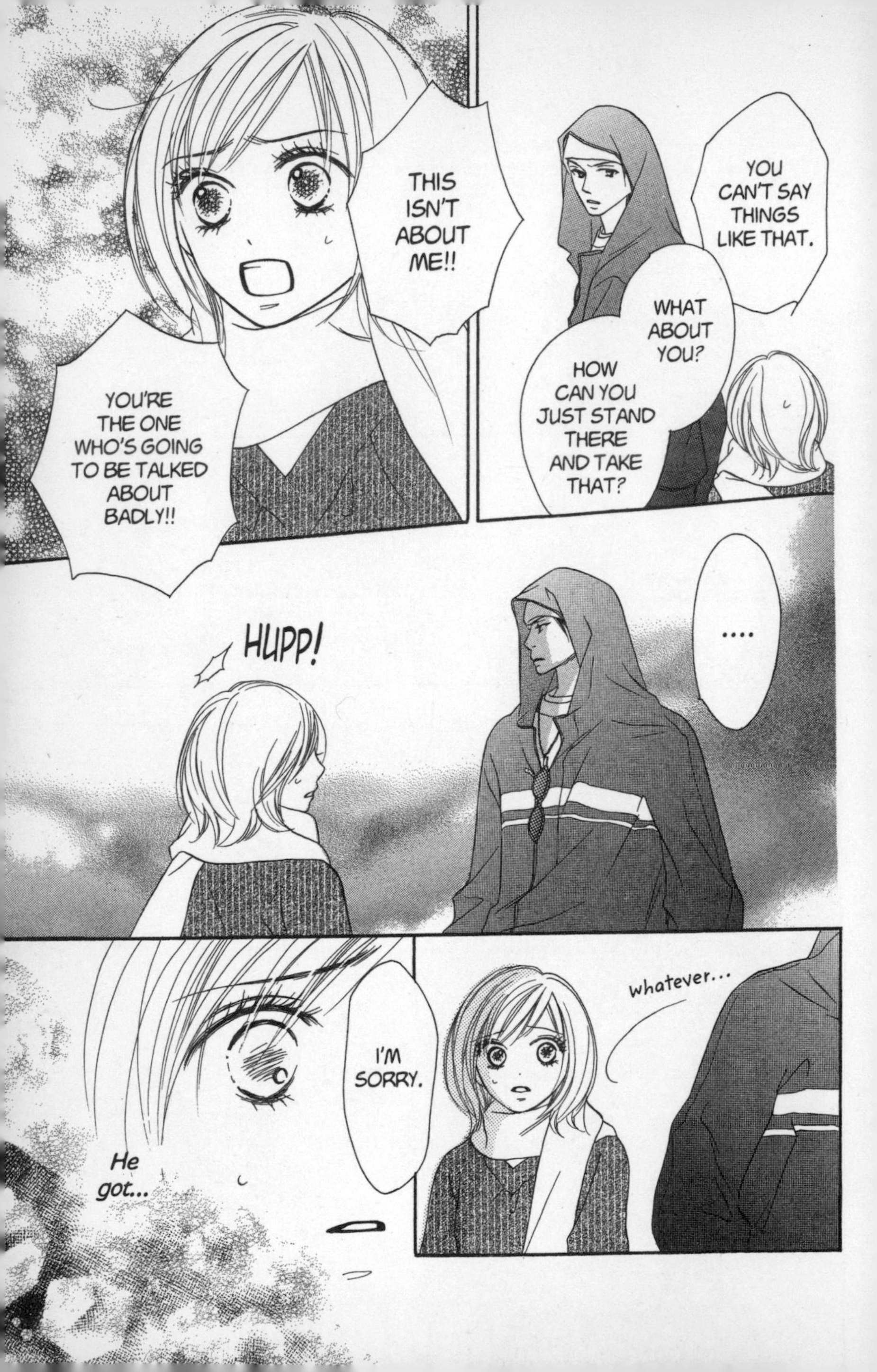
YOU CAN'T SAY THINGS LIKE THAT.
WHAT ABOUT YOU?
HOW CAN YOU JUST STAND THERE AND TAKE THAT?
THIS ISN'T ABOUT ME!!
YOU'RE THE ONE WHO'S GOING TO BE TALKED ABOUT BADLY!!
....
HUPP!
whatever...
I'M SORRY.
He got...

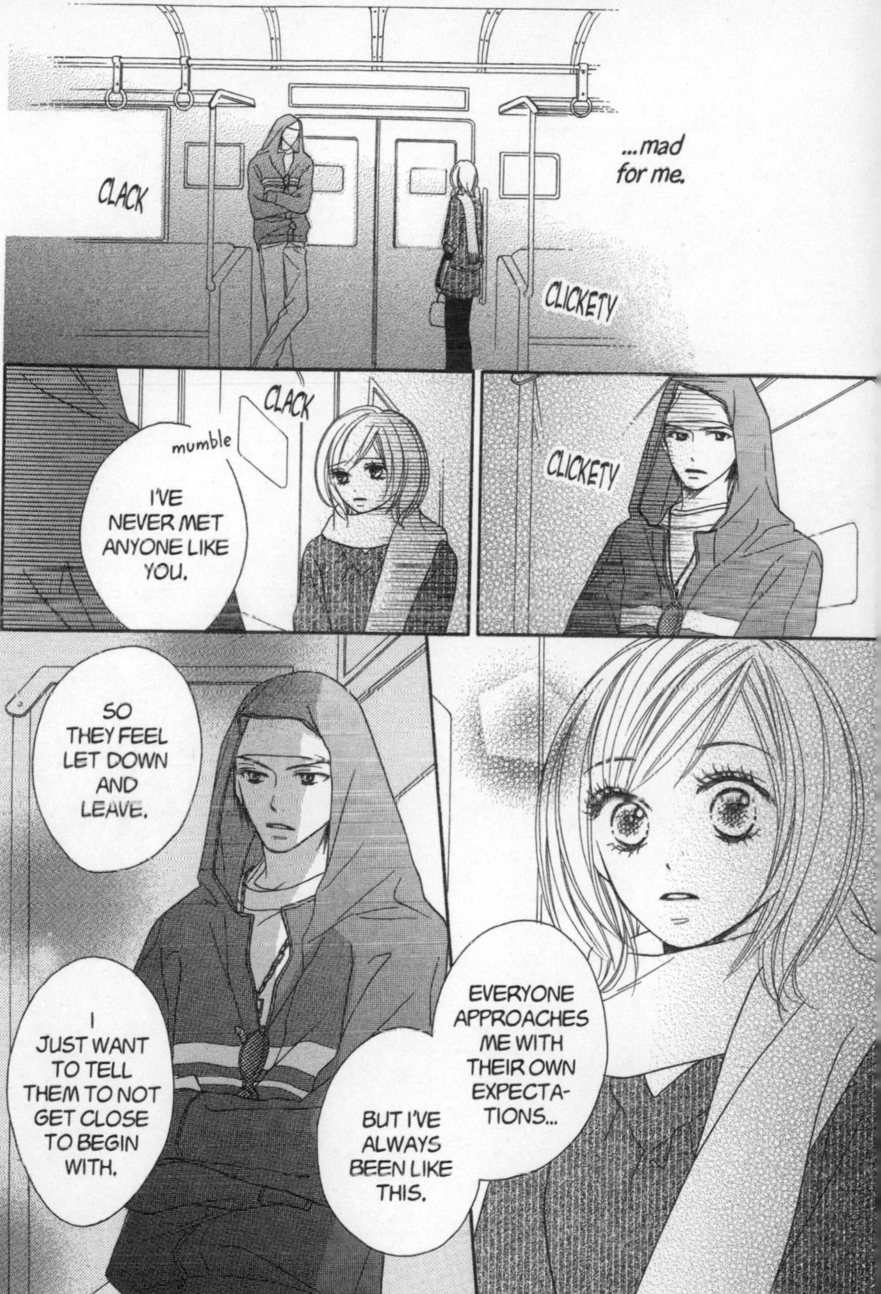
...mad for me.
CLACK
CLICKETY
CLICKETY
CLACK
mumble
I'VE NEVER MET ANYONE LIKE YOU.
EVERYONE APPROACHES ME WITH THEIR OWN EXPECTA-TIONS...
BUT I'VE ALWAYS BEEN LIKE THIS.
SO THEY FEEL LET DOWN AND LEAVE.
I JUST WANT TO TELL THEM TO NOT GET CLOSE TO BEGIN WITH.

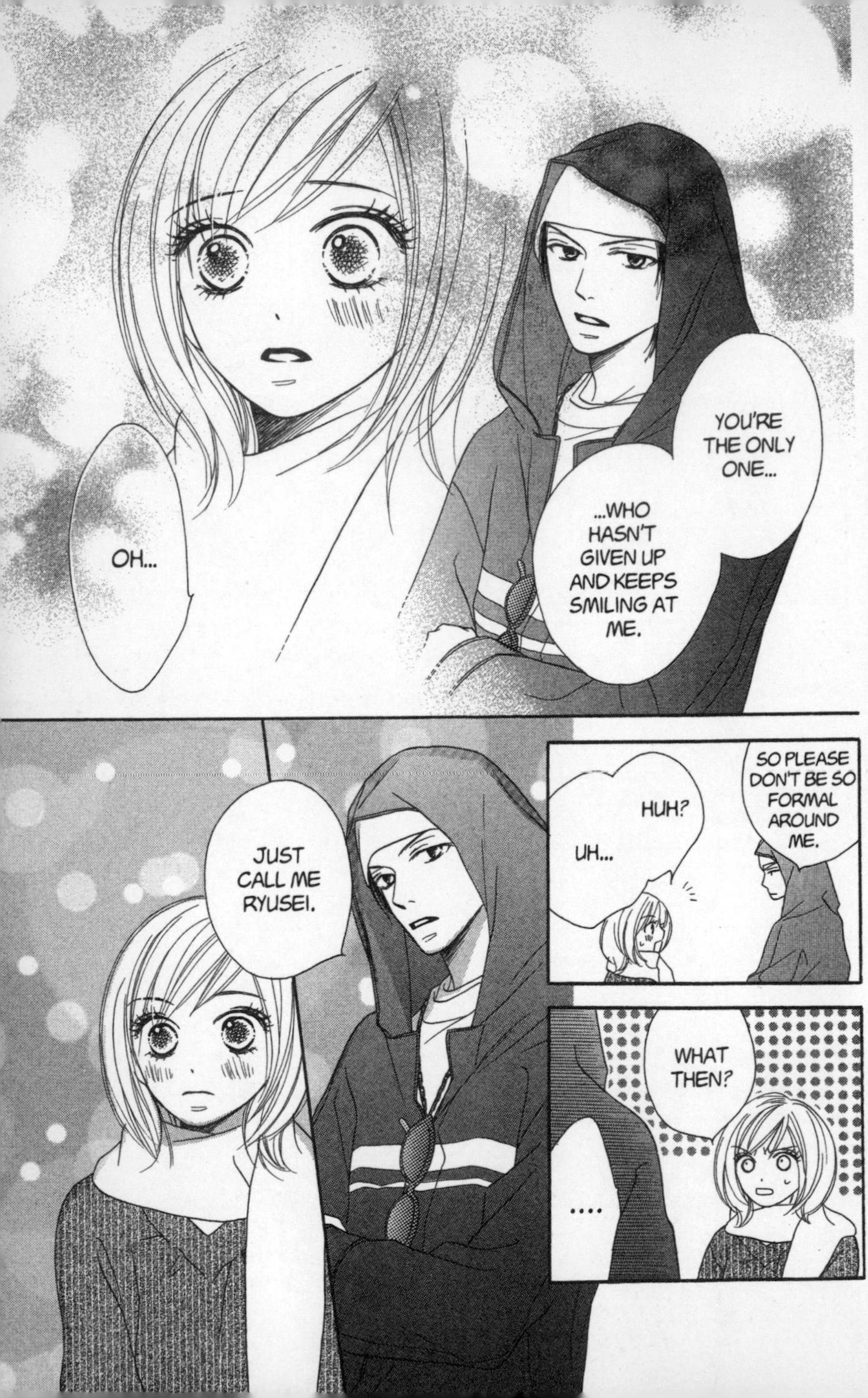
YOU'RE THE ONLY ONE...
...WHO HASN'T GIVEN UP AND KEEPS SMILING AT ME.
OH...
SO PLEASE DON'T BE SO FORMAL AROUND ME.
HUH?
UH...
WHAT THEN?
....
JUST CALL ME RYUSEI.

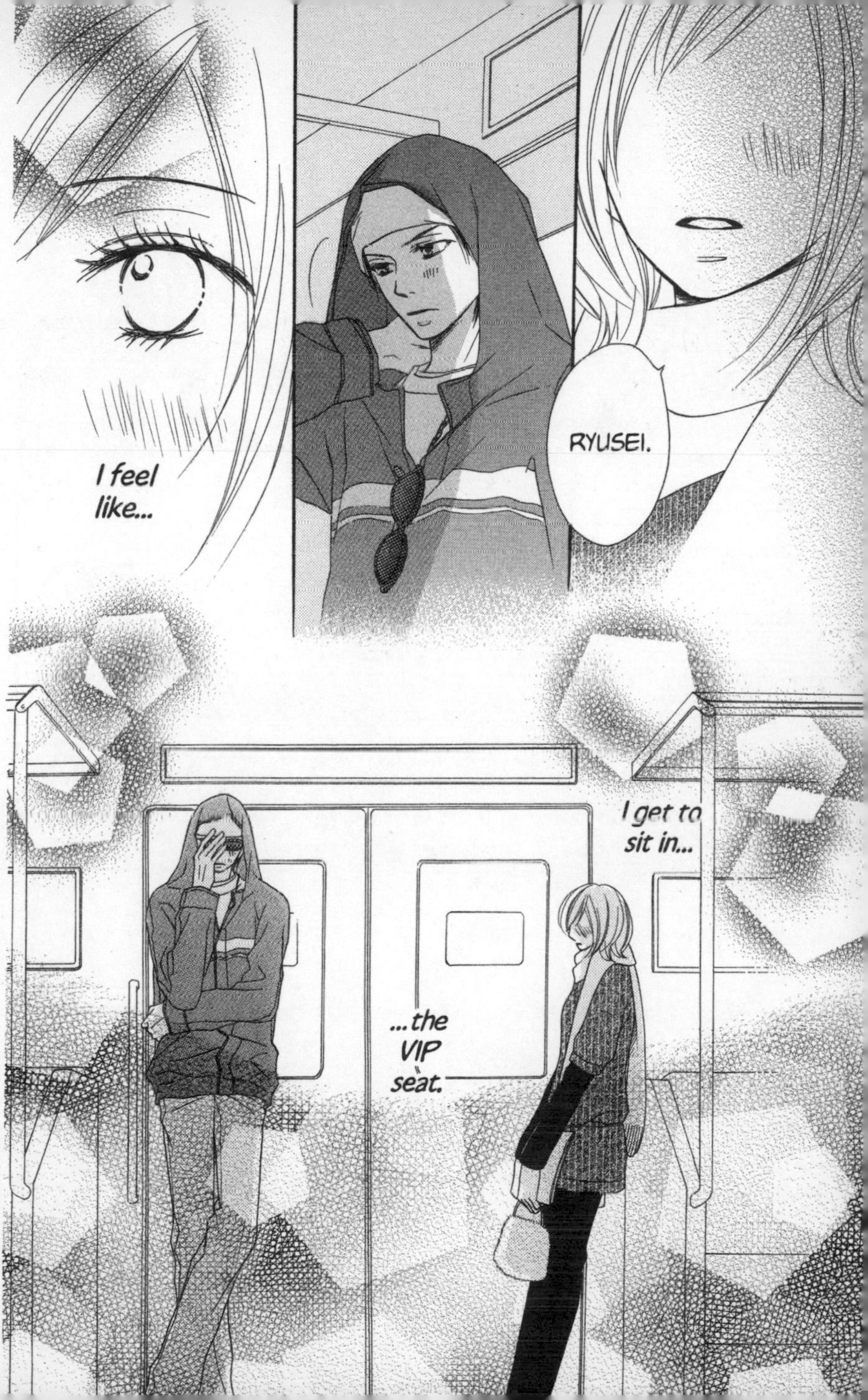
RYUSEI.
I feel like...
I get to sit in...
...the VIP seat.

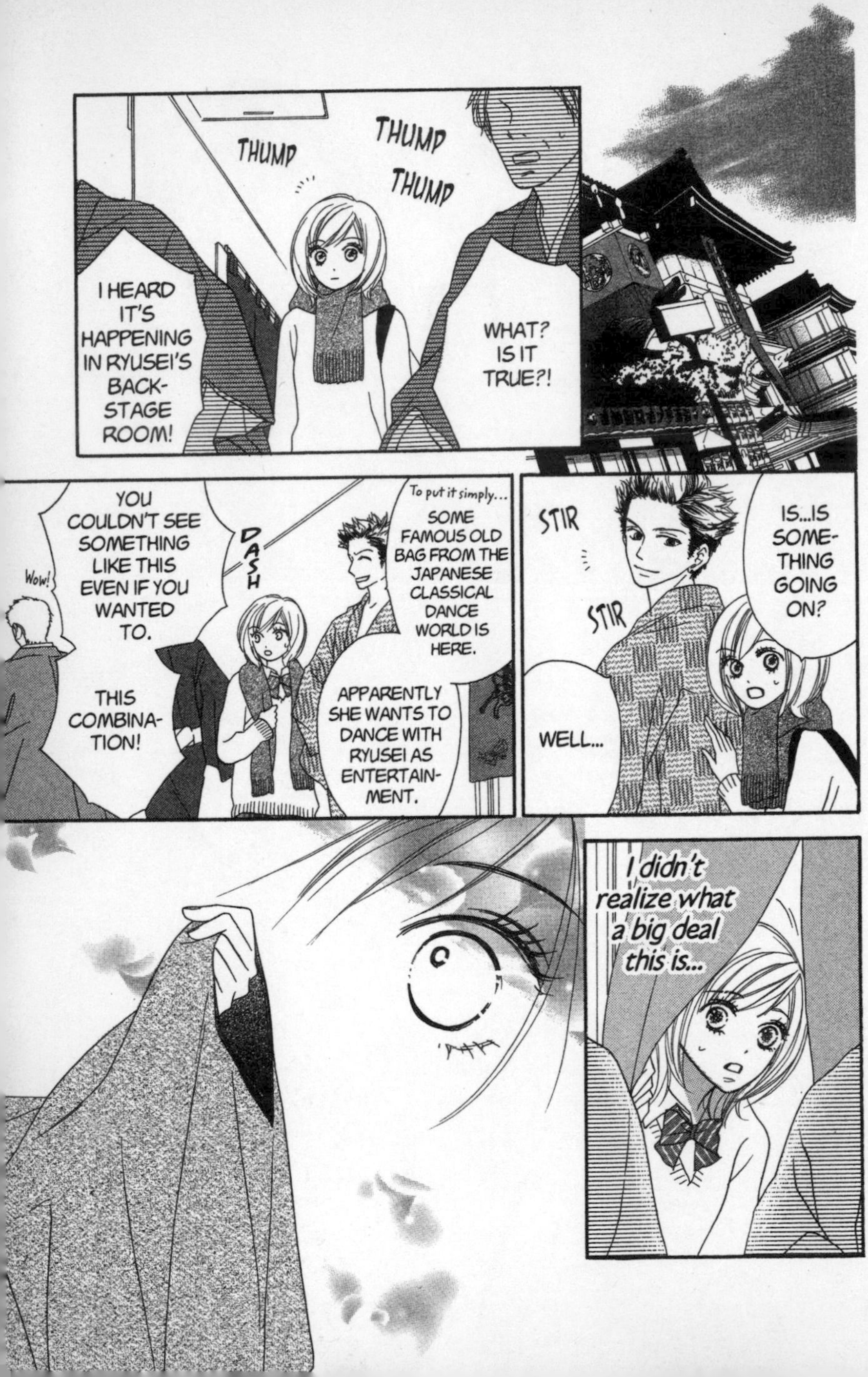
THUMP
THUMP
WHAT? IS IT TRUE?!
THUMP
I HEARD IT'S HAPPENING IN RYUSEI'S BACK-STAGE ROOM!
IS...IS SOME-THING GOING ON?
STIR
STIR
WELL...
To put it simply...
SOME FAMOUS OLD BAG FROM THE JAPANESE CLASSICAL DANCE WORLD IS HERE.
APPARENTLY SHE WANTS TO DANCE WITH RYUSEI AS ENTERTAIN-MENT.
DASH
YOU COULDN'T SEE SOMETHING LIKE THIS EVEN IF YOU WANTED TO.
Wow!
THIS COMBINA-TION!
I didn't realize what a big deal this is...

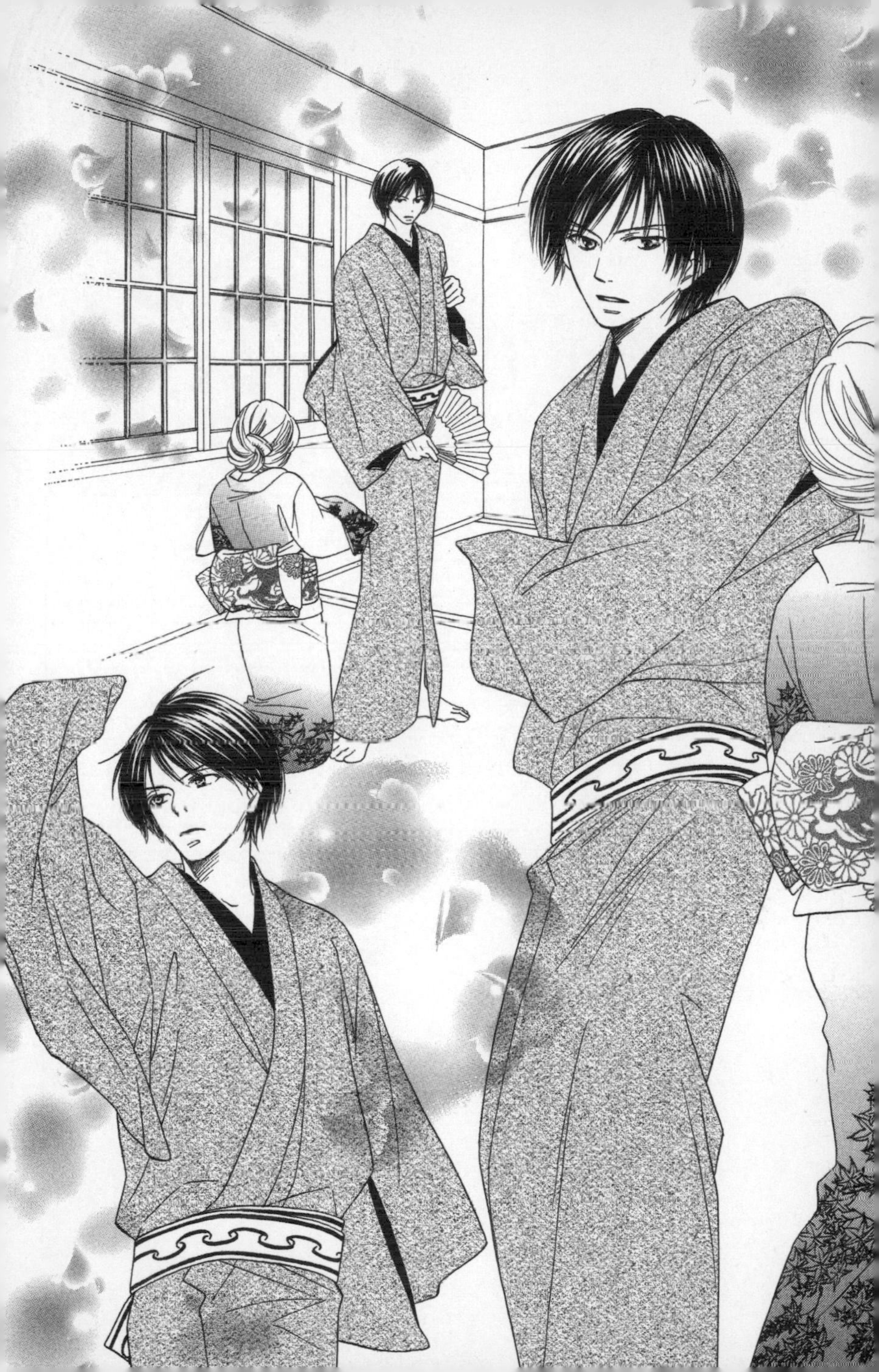

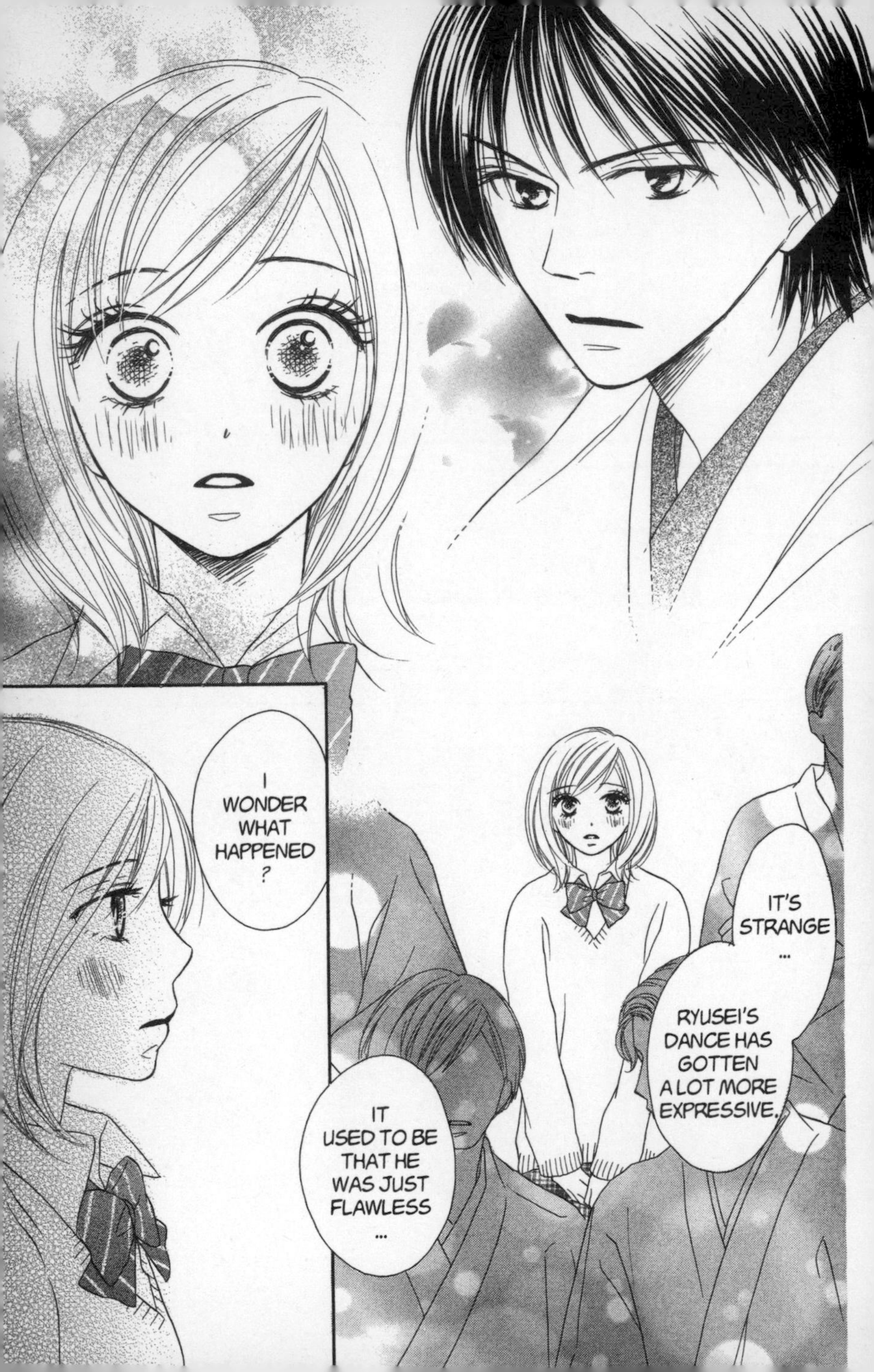
IT'S STRANGE ...
RYUSEI'S DANCE HAS GOTTEN A LOT MORE EXPRESSIVE.
IT USED TO BE THAT HE WAS JUST FLAWLESS ...
I WONDER WHAT HAPPENED?

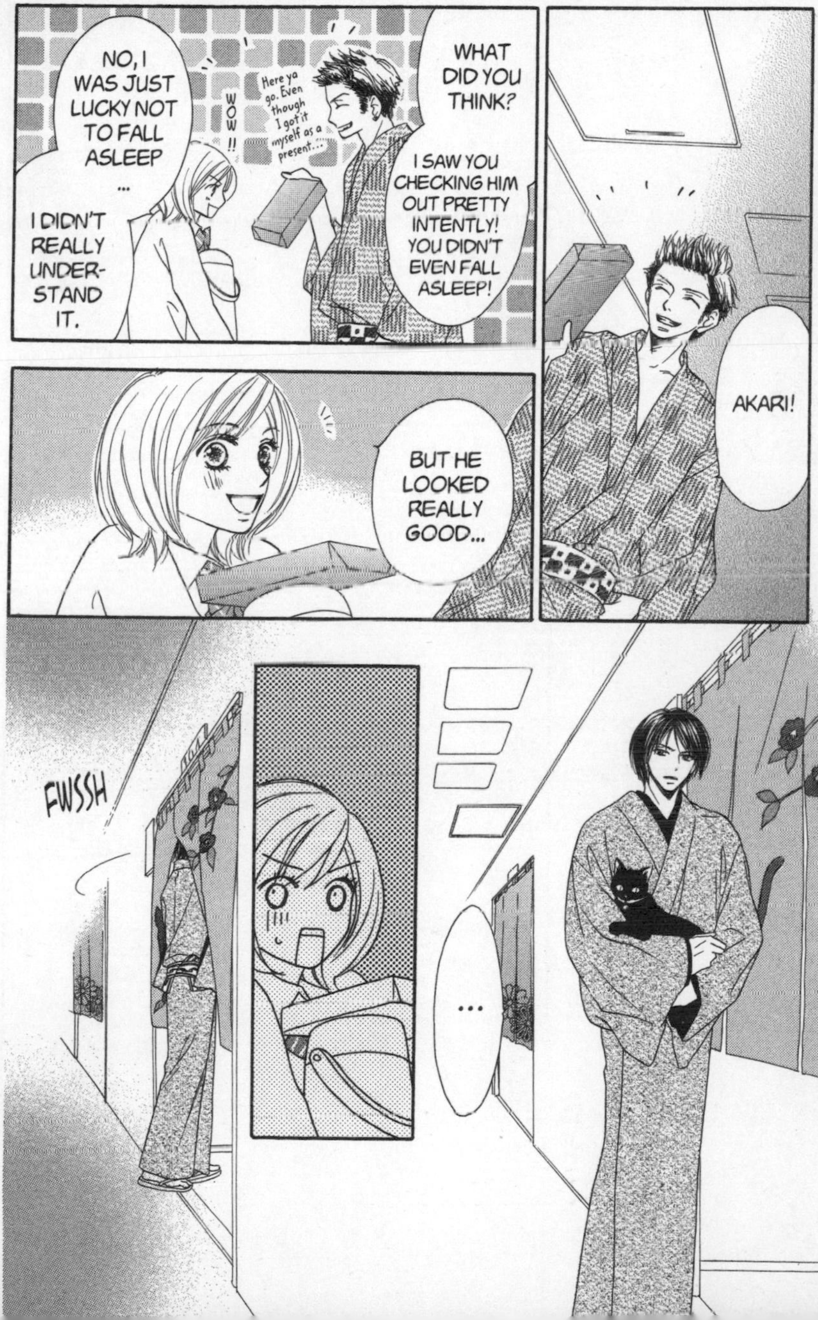
AKARI!
WHAT DID YOU THINK?
I SAW YOU CHECKING HIM OUT PRETTY INTENTLY! YOU DIDN'T EVEN FALL ASLEEP!
Here ya go. Even though I got it myself as a present...
WOW!!
NO, I WAS JUST LUCKY NOT TO FALL ASLEEP
...
I DIDN'T REALLY UNDERSTAND IT.
BUT HE LOOKED REALLY GOOD...
...
FWSSH

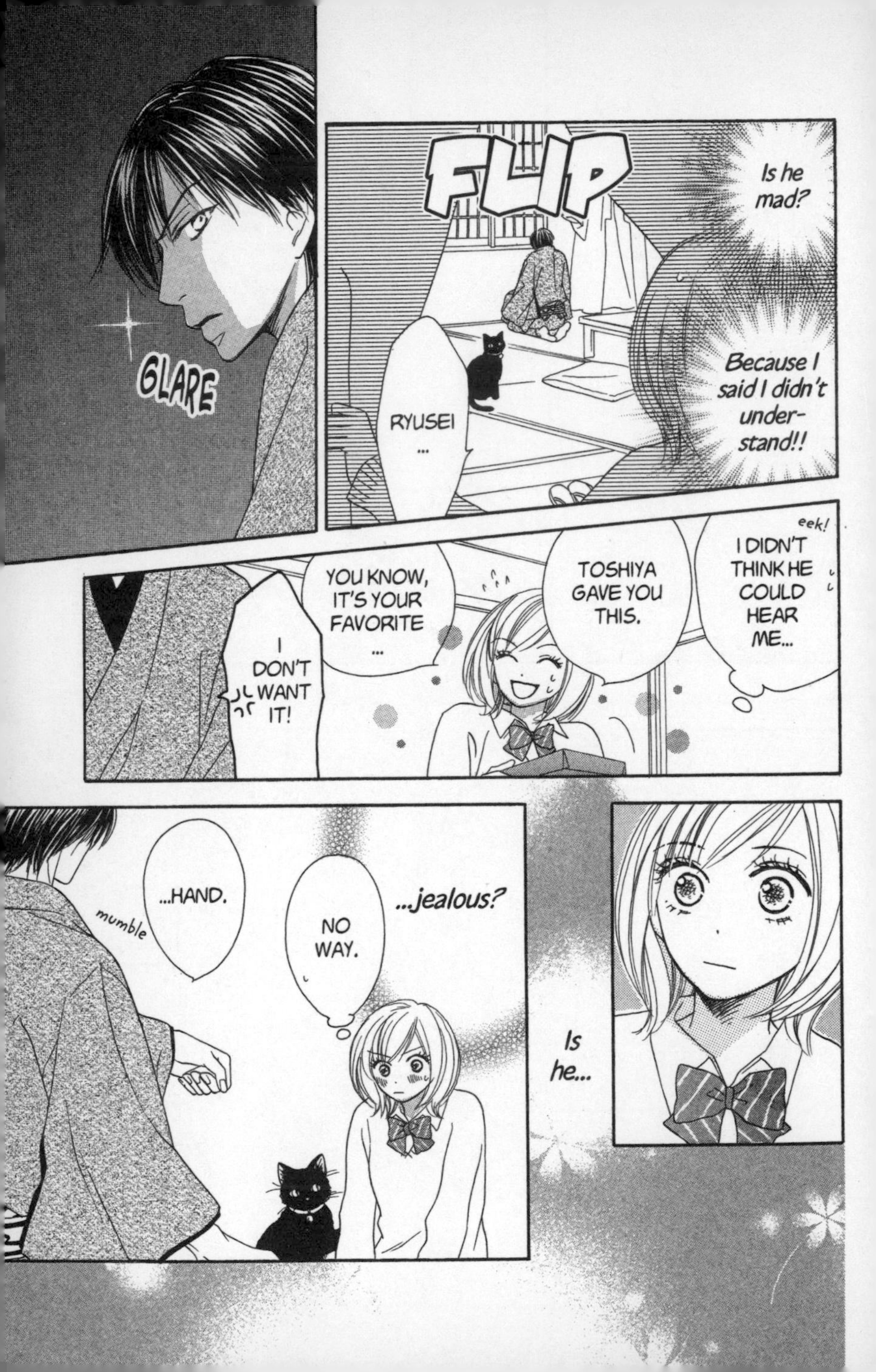
FLIP
Is he mad?
Because I said I didn't under-stand!!
RYUSEI ...
GLARE
eek!
I DIDN'T THINK HE COULD HEAR ME...
TOSHIYA GAVE YOU THIS.
YOU KNOW, IT'S YOUR FAVORITE ...
I DON'T WANT IT!
Is he...
...jealous?
NO WAY.
...HAND.
mumble

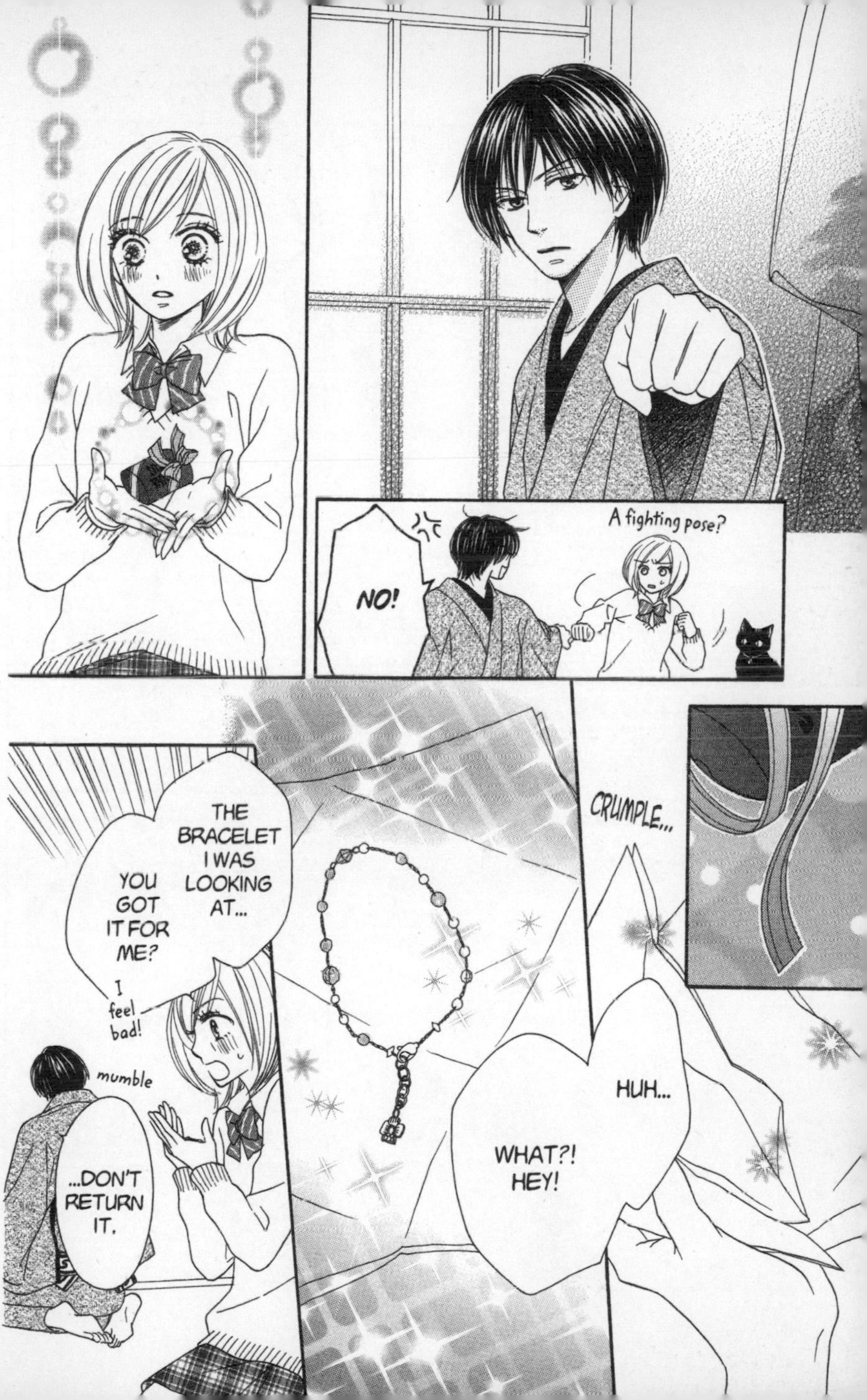
A fighting pose?
NO!
CRUMPLE...
HUH...
WHAT?! HEY!
THE BRACELET I WAS LOOKING AT...
YOU GOT IT FOR ME?
I feel bad!
mumble
...DON'T RETURN IT.

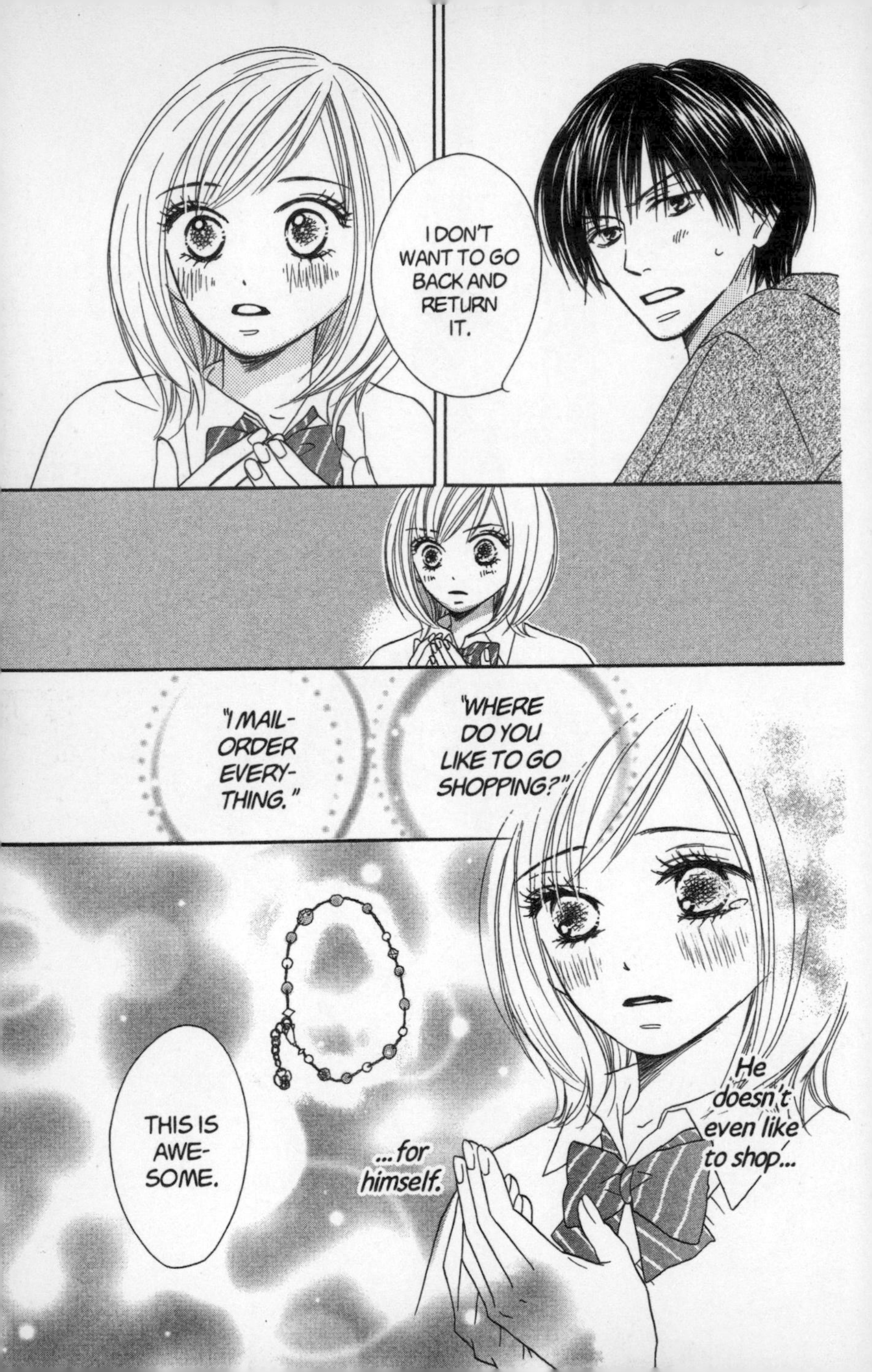
I DON'T WANT TO GO BACK AND RETURN IT.
"WHERE DO YOU LIKE TO GO SHOPPING?"
"I MAIL-ORDER EVERY-THING."
He doesn't even like to shop...
...for himself.
THIS IS AWE-SOME.

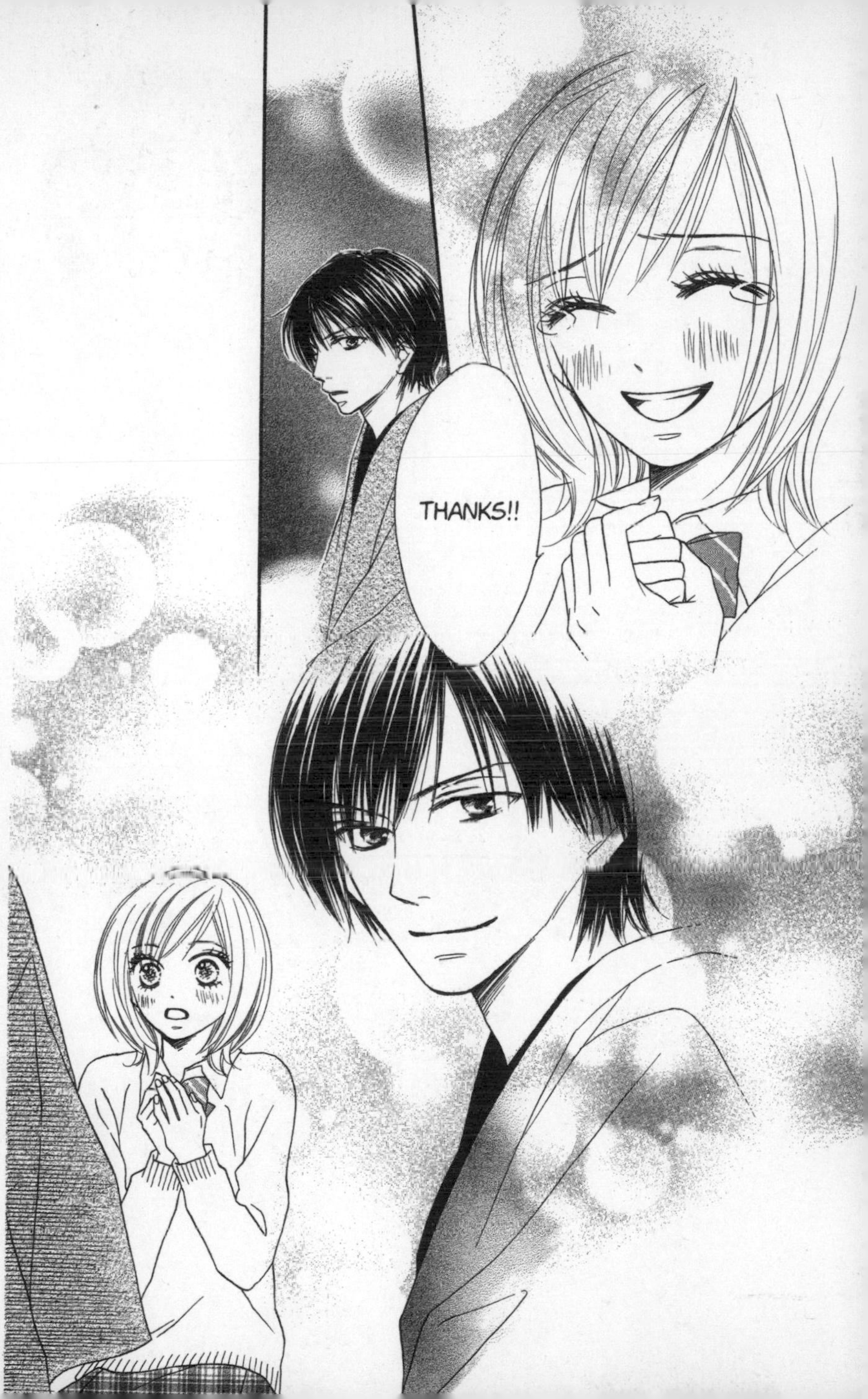
THANKS!!

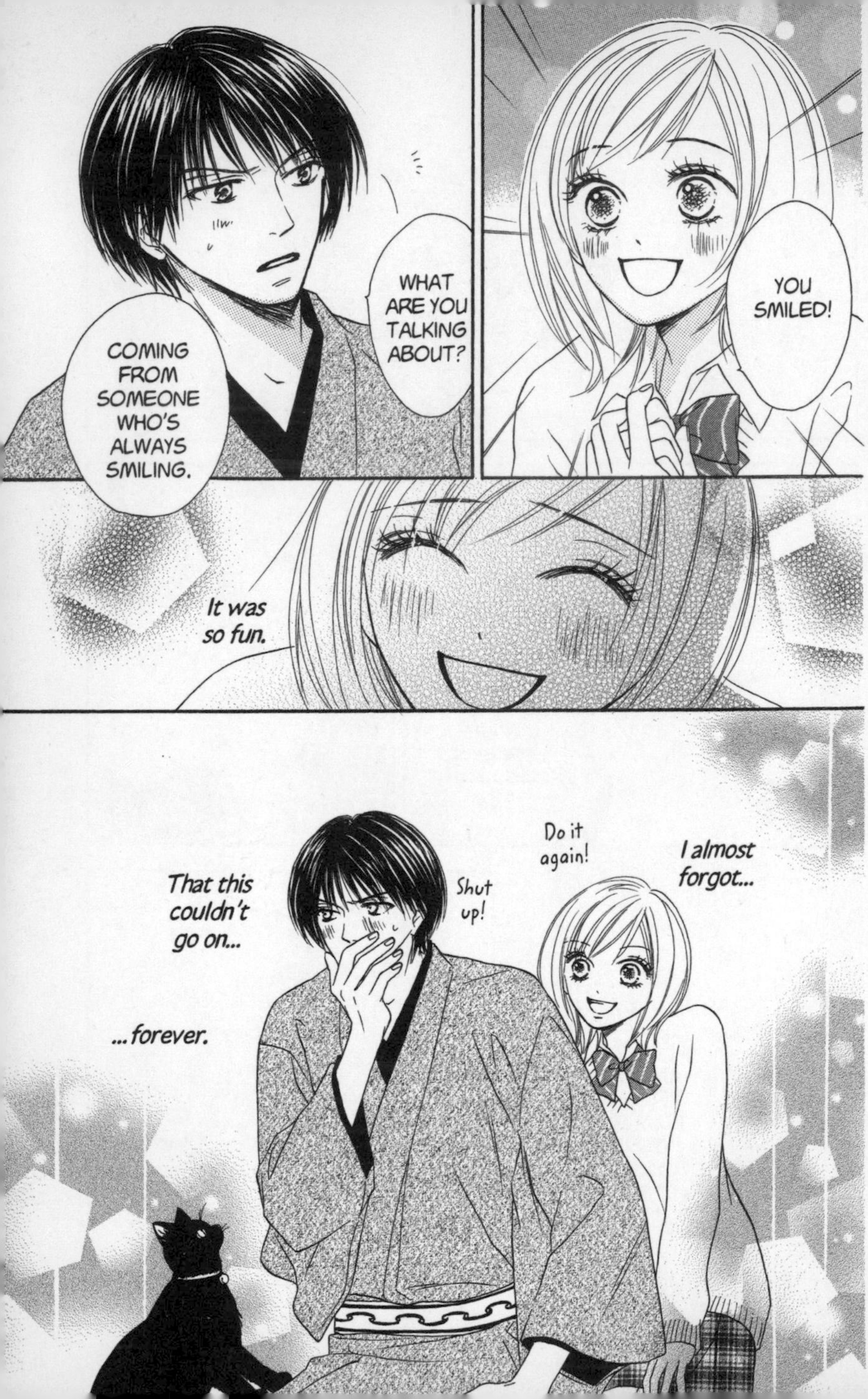
YOU SMILED!
WHAT ARE YOU TALKING ABOUT?
COMING FROM SOMEONE WHO'S ALWAYS SMILING.
It was so fun.
I almost forgot...
Do it again!
Shut up!
That this couldn't go on...
...forever.

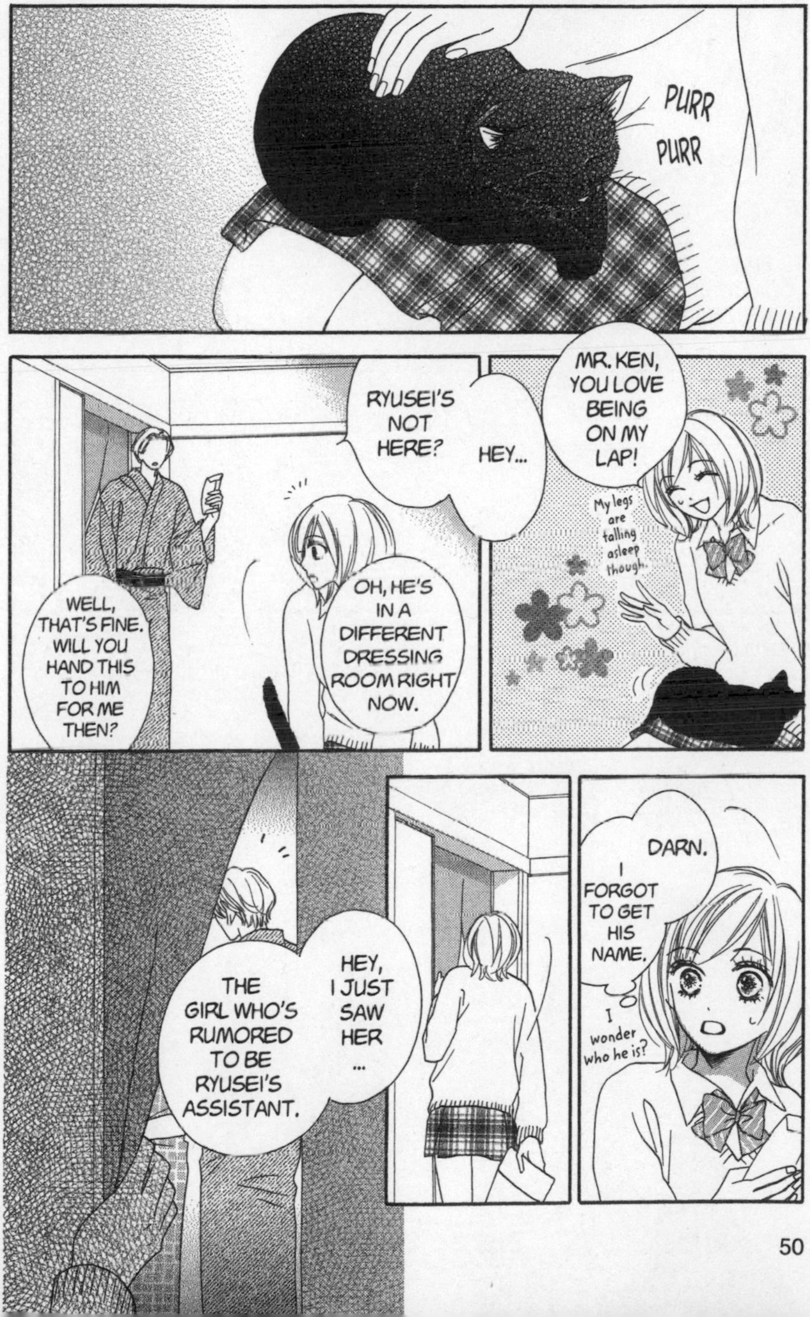
PURR
PURR
MR. KEN, YOU LOVE BEING ON MY LAP!
My legs are falling asleep though.
HEY...
RYUSEI'S NOT HERE?
OH, HE'S IN A DIFFERENT DRESSING ROOM RIGHT NOW.
WELL, THAT'S FINE. WILL YOU HAND THIS TO HIM FOR ME THEN?
DARN.
I FORGOT TO GET HIS NAME.
I wonder who he is?
HEY, I JUST SAW HER...
THE GIRL WHO'S RUMORED TO BE RYUSEI'S ASSISTANT.

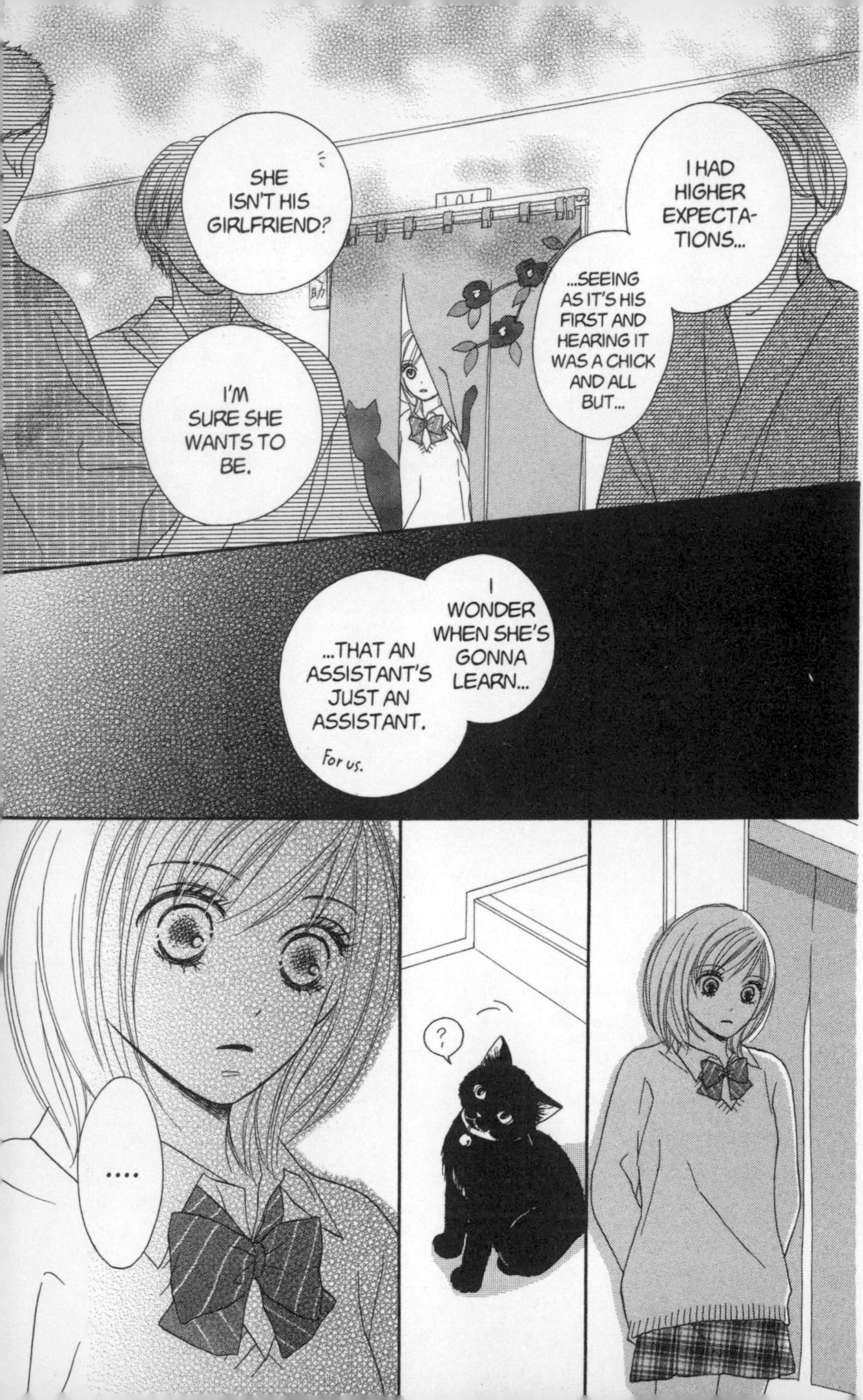
I HAD HIGHER EXPECTATIONS...
...SEEING AS IT'S HIS FIRST AND HEARING IT WAS A CHICK AND ALL BUT...
SHE ISN'T HIS GIRLFRIEND?
I'M SURE SHE WANTS TO BE.
I WONDER WHEN SHE'S GONNA LEARN...
...THAT AN ASSISTANT'S JUST AN ASSISTANT.
For us.
?
....

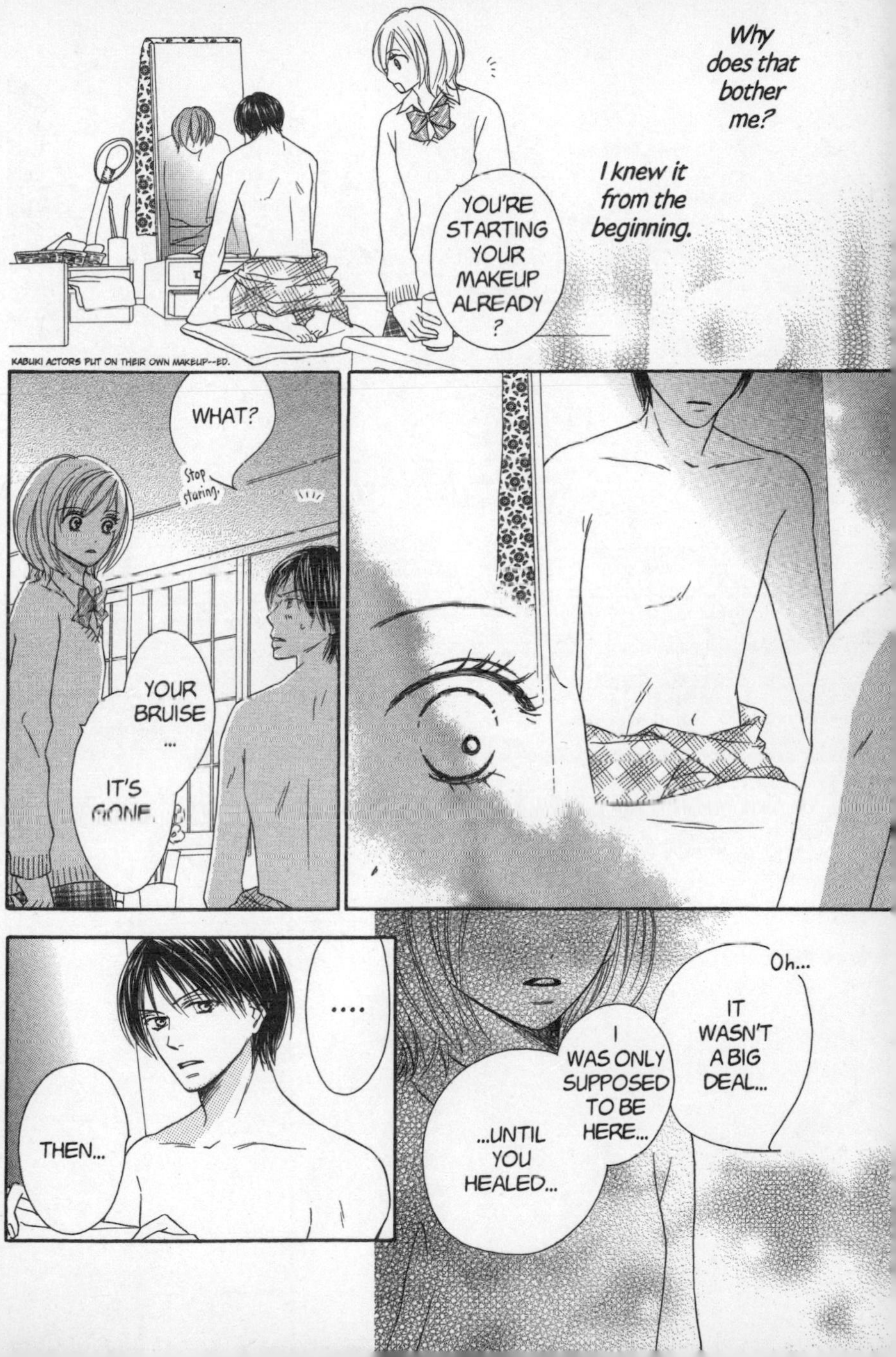
Why does that bother me?
I knew it from the beginning.
YOU'RE STARTING YOUR MAKEUP ALREADY?
KABUKI ACTORS PUT ON THEIR OWN MAKEUP--ED.
WHAT?
Stop staring.
YOUR BRUISE... IT'S GONE.
Oh...
IT WASN'T A BIG DEAL...
I WAS ONLY SUPPOSED TO BE HERE...
...UNTIL YOU HEALED...
....
THEN...

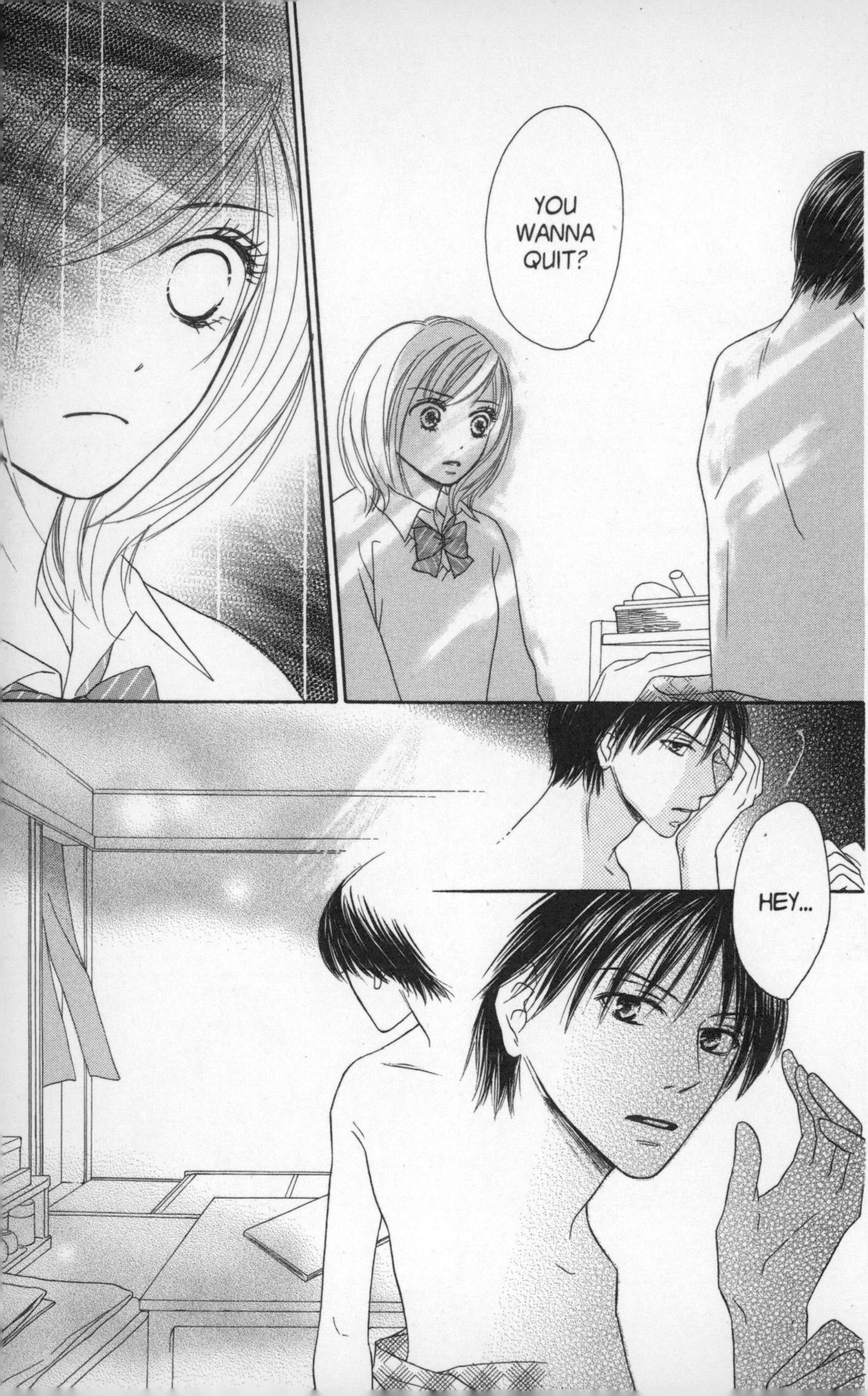
YOU WANNA QUIT?
HEY...

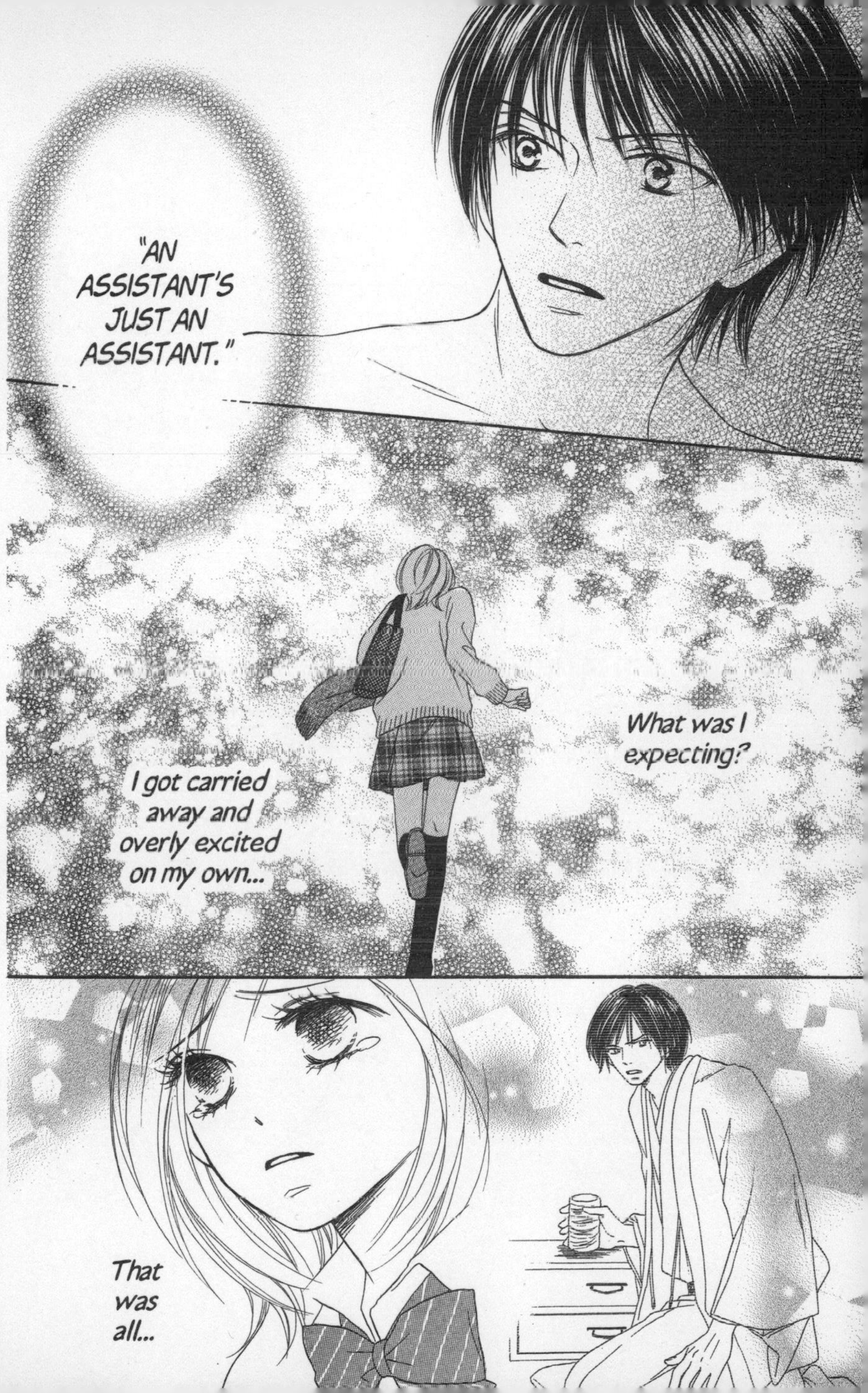
"AN ASSISTANT'S JUST AN ASSISTANT."
What was I expecting?
I got carried away and overly excited on my own...
That was all...

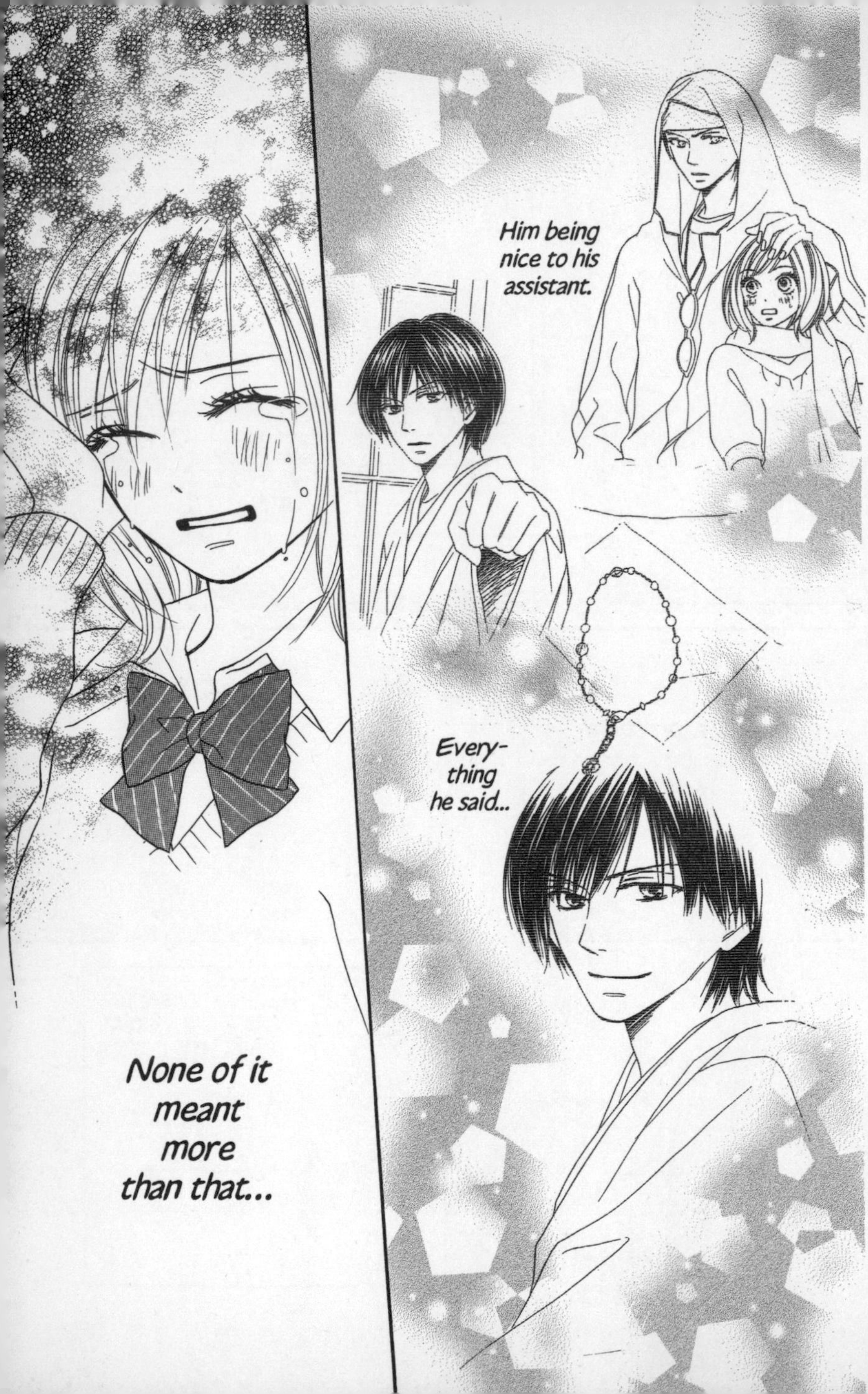
Him being nice to his assistant.
Every-thing he said...
None of it meant more than that...

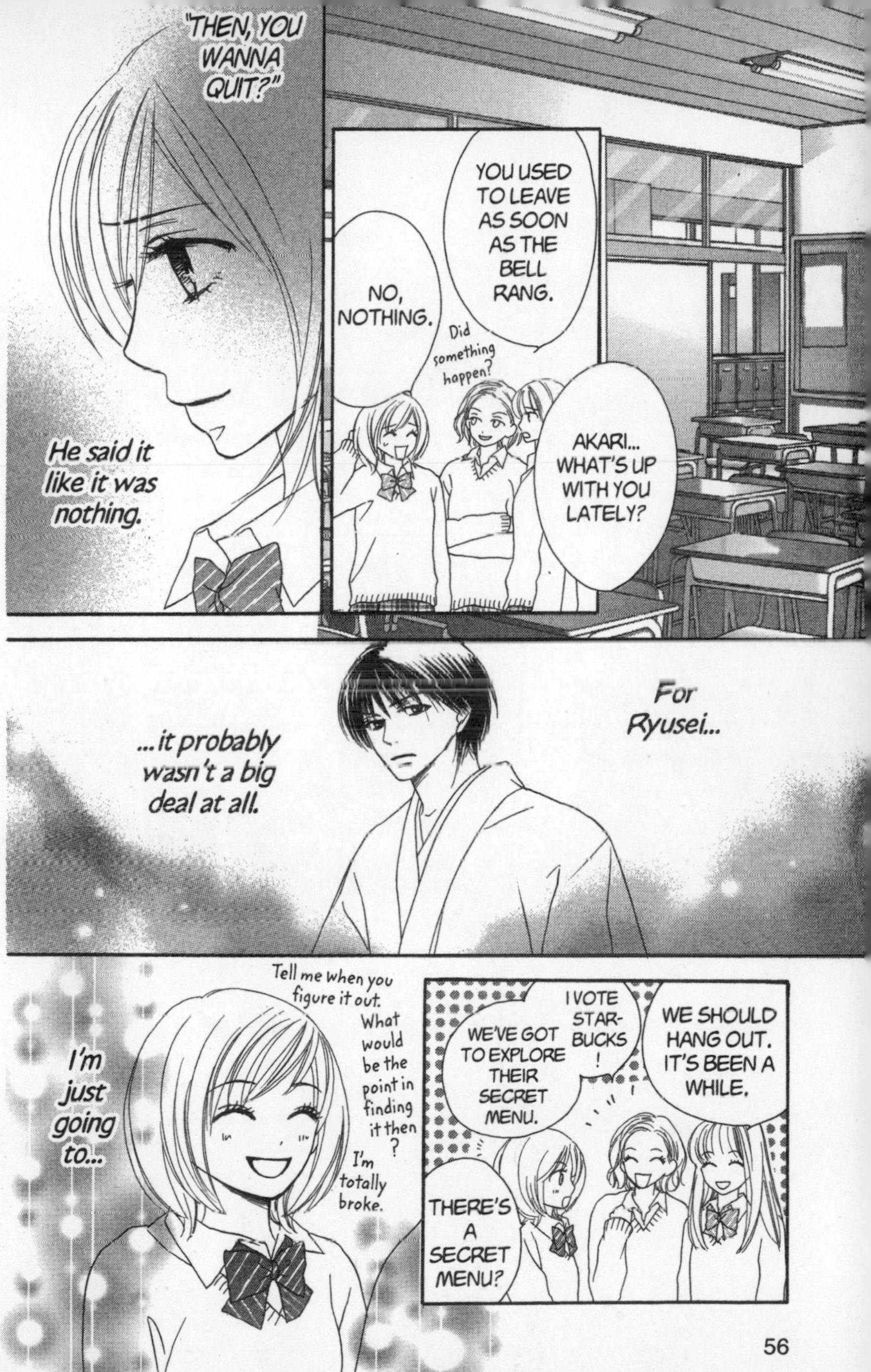
AKARI... WHAT'S UP WITH YOU LATELY?
YOU USED TO LEAVE AS SOON AS THE BELL RANG.
Did something happen?
NO, NOTHING.
"THEN, YOU WANNA QUIT?"
He said it like it was nothing.
For Ryusei...
...it probably wasn't a big deal at all.
WE SHOULD HANG OUT. IT'S BEEN A WHILE.
I VOTE STARBUCKS!
WE'VE GOT TO EXPLORE THEIR SECRET MENU.
THERE'S A SECRET MENU?
Tell me when you figure it out.
What would be the point in finding it then?
I'm totally broke.
I'm just going to...

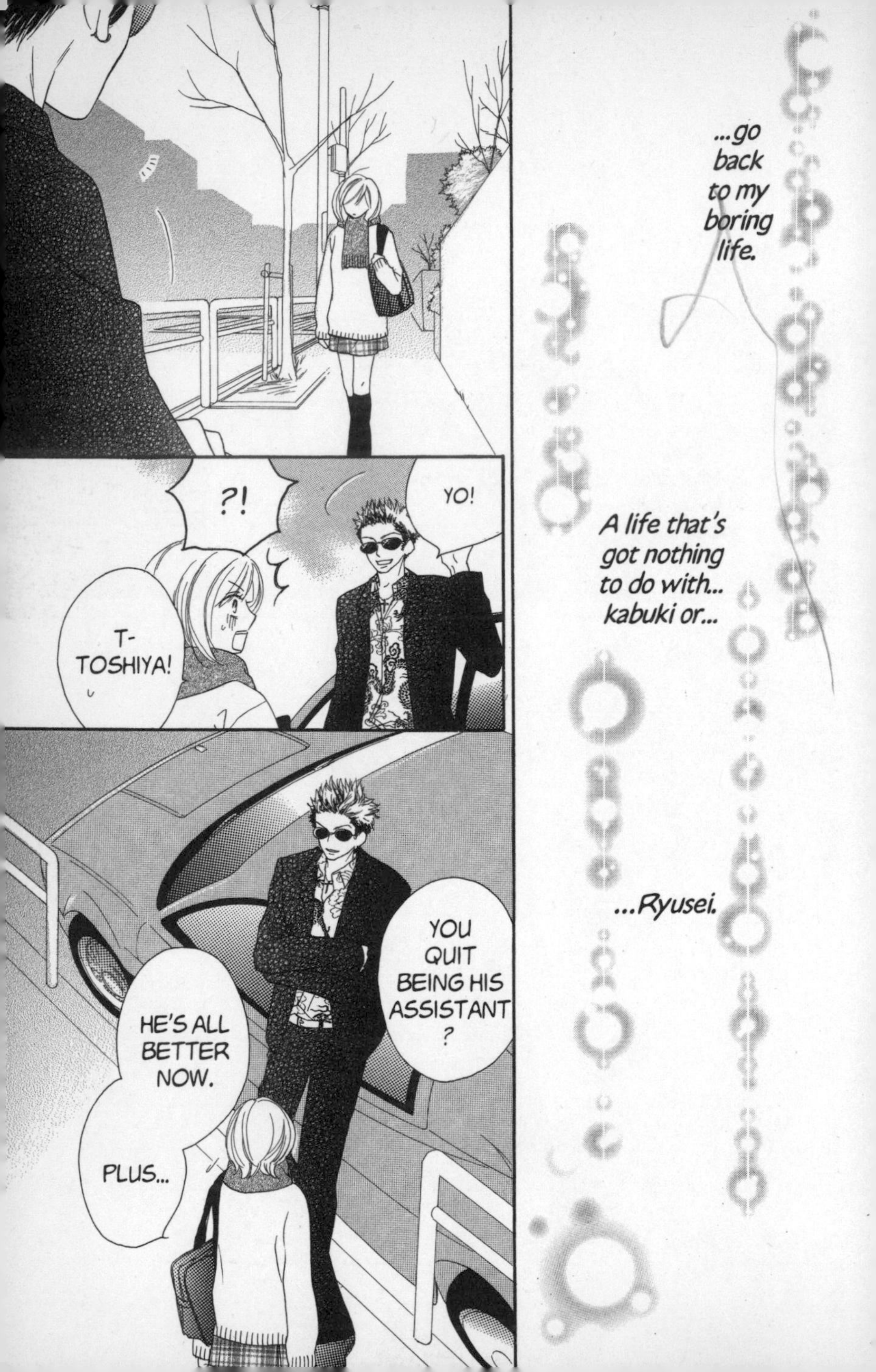
...go back to my boring life.
A life that's got nothing to do with... kabuki or...
...Ryusei.
YO!
?!
T-TOSHIYA!
YOU QUIT BEING HIS ASSISTANT?
HE'S ALL BETTER NOW.
PLUS...

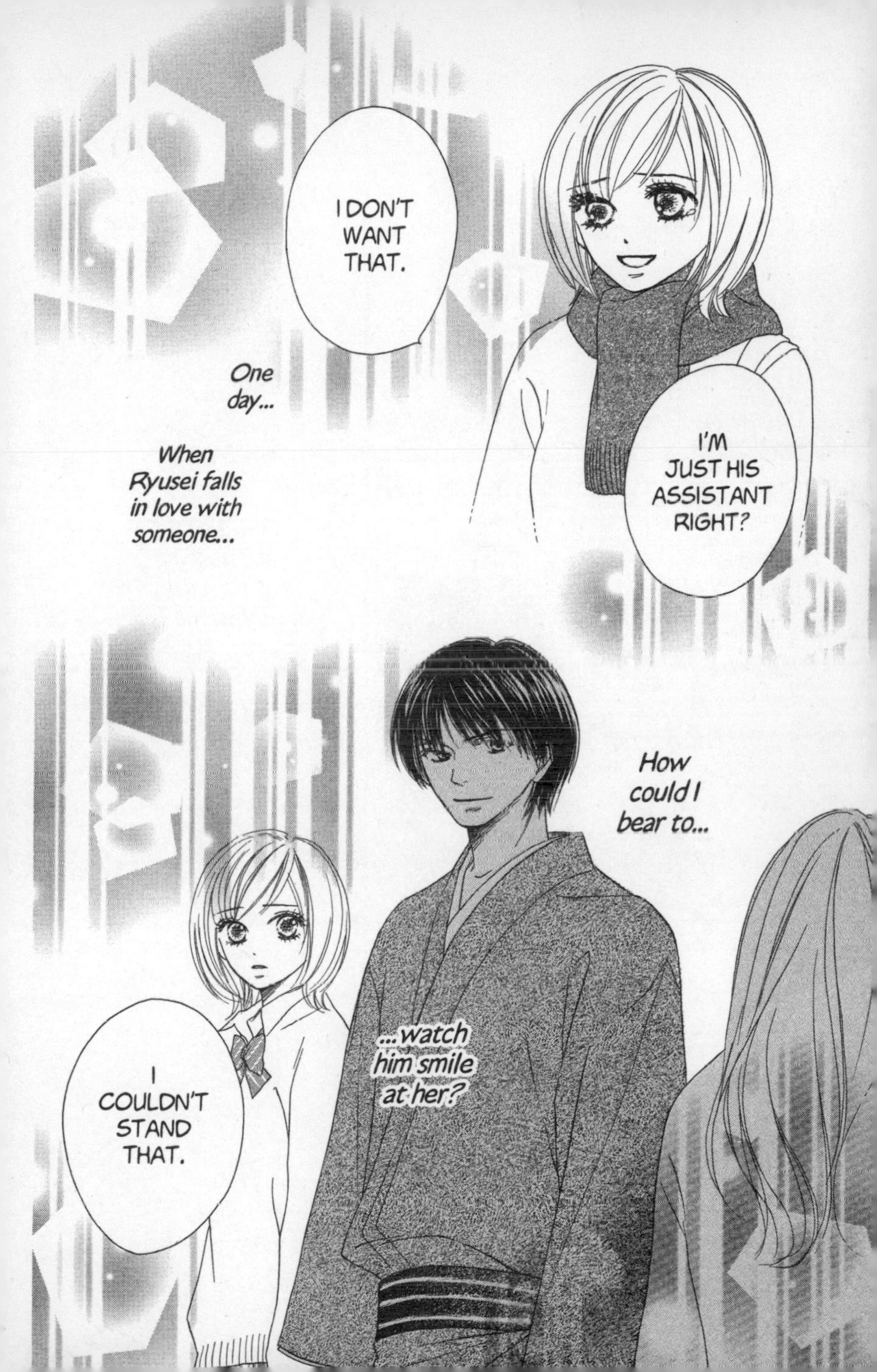

I'M JUST HIS ASSISTANT RIGHT?
One day...
When Ryusei falls in love with someone...
I DON'T WANT THAT.
How could I bear to...
...watch him smile at her?
I COULDN'T STAND THAT.

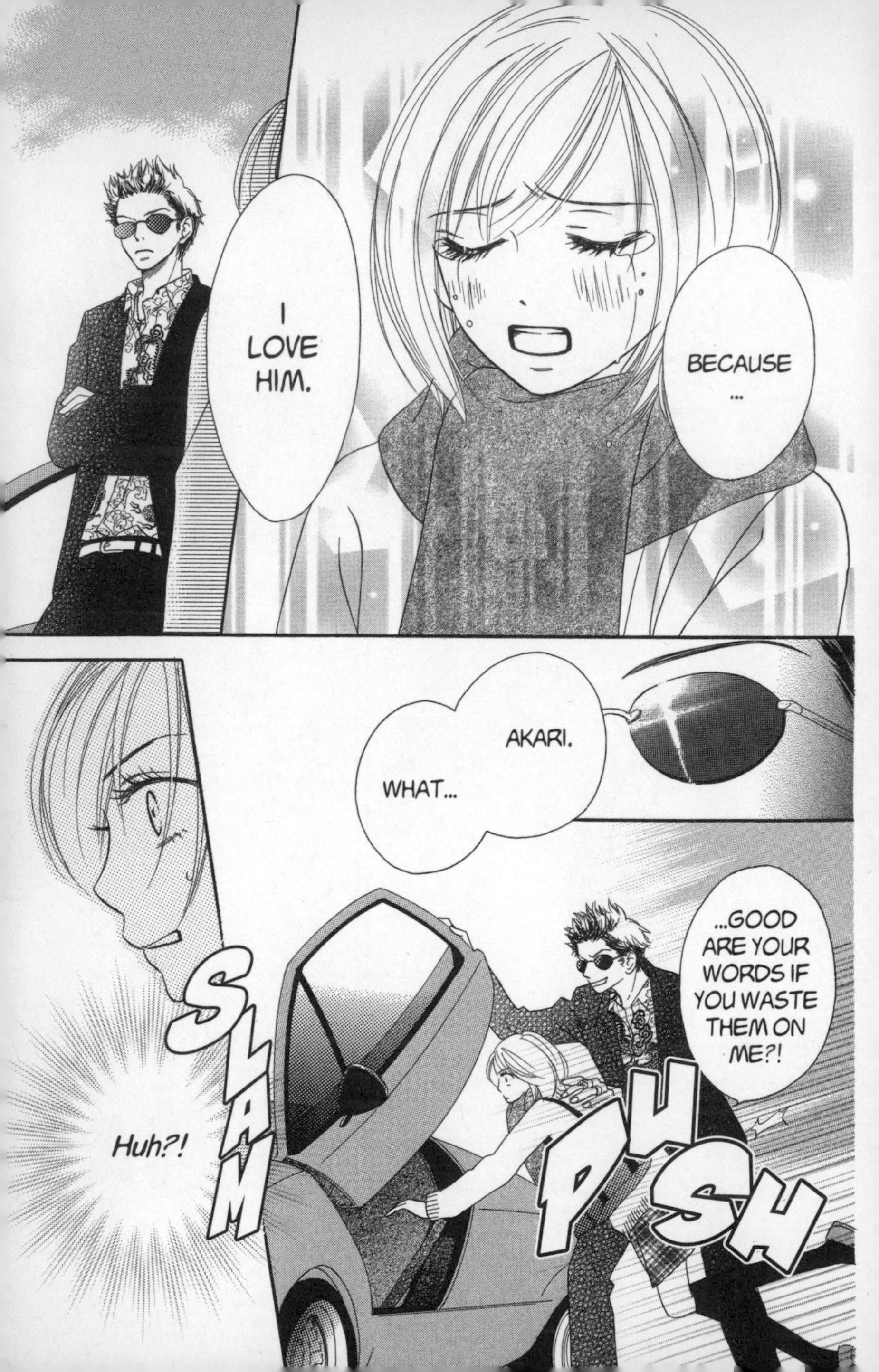
BECAUSE ...
I LOVE HIM.
AKARI. WHAT...
...GOOD ARE YOUR WORDS IF YOU WASTE THEM ON ME?!
PUSH
SLAM
Huh?!

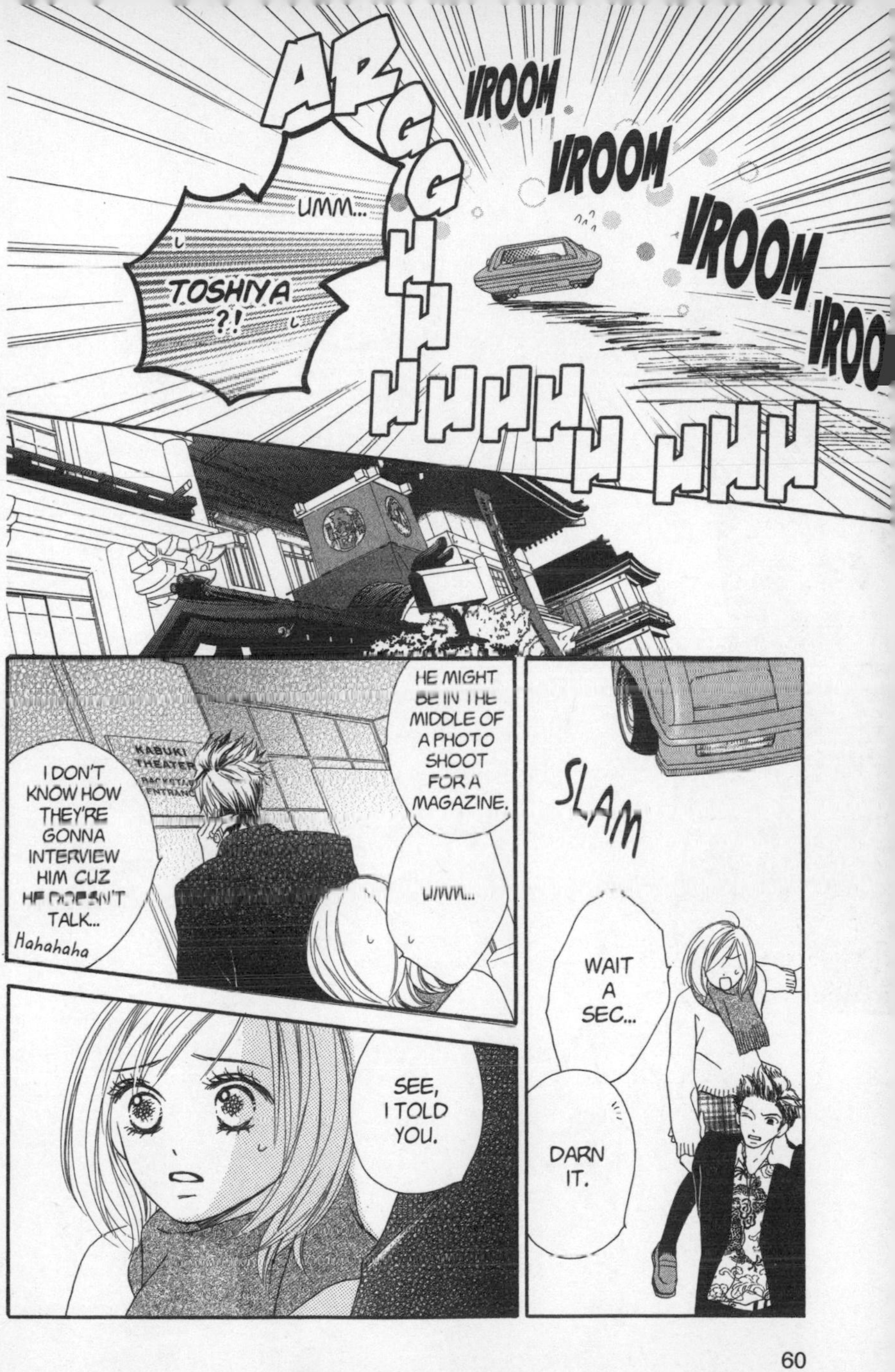
VROOM
VROOM
VROOM
VROO
ARGGHHHHHHHH HHHH
UMM...
TOSHIYA ?!
SLAM
WAIT A SEC...
DARN IT.
HE MIGHT BE IN THE MIDDLE OF A PHOTO SHOOT FOR A MAGAZINE.
UMM...
KABUKI THEATER
I DON'T KNOW HOW THEY'RE GONNA INTERVIEW HIM CUZ HE DOESN'T TALK...
Hahahaha
SEE, I TOLD YOU.

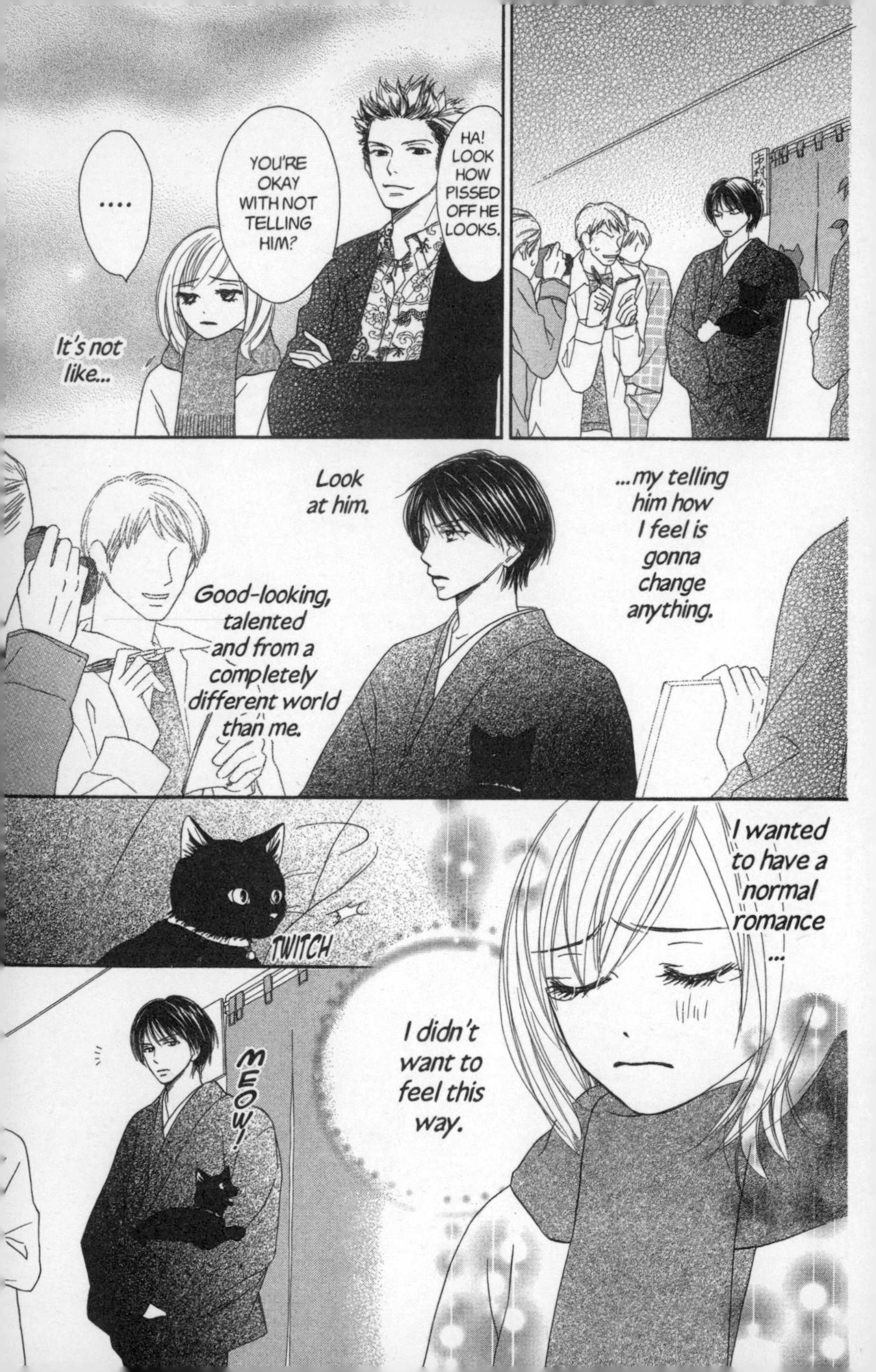
HA! LOOK HOW PISSED OFF HE LOOKS.
YOU'RE OKAY WITH NOT TELLING HIM?
....
It's not like...
...my telling him how I feel is gonna change anything.
Look at him.
Good-looking, talented and from a completely different world than me.
I wanted to have a normal romance...
I didn't want to feel this way.
TWITCH
MEOW!

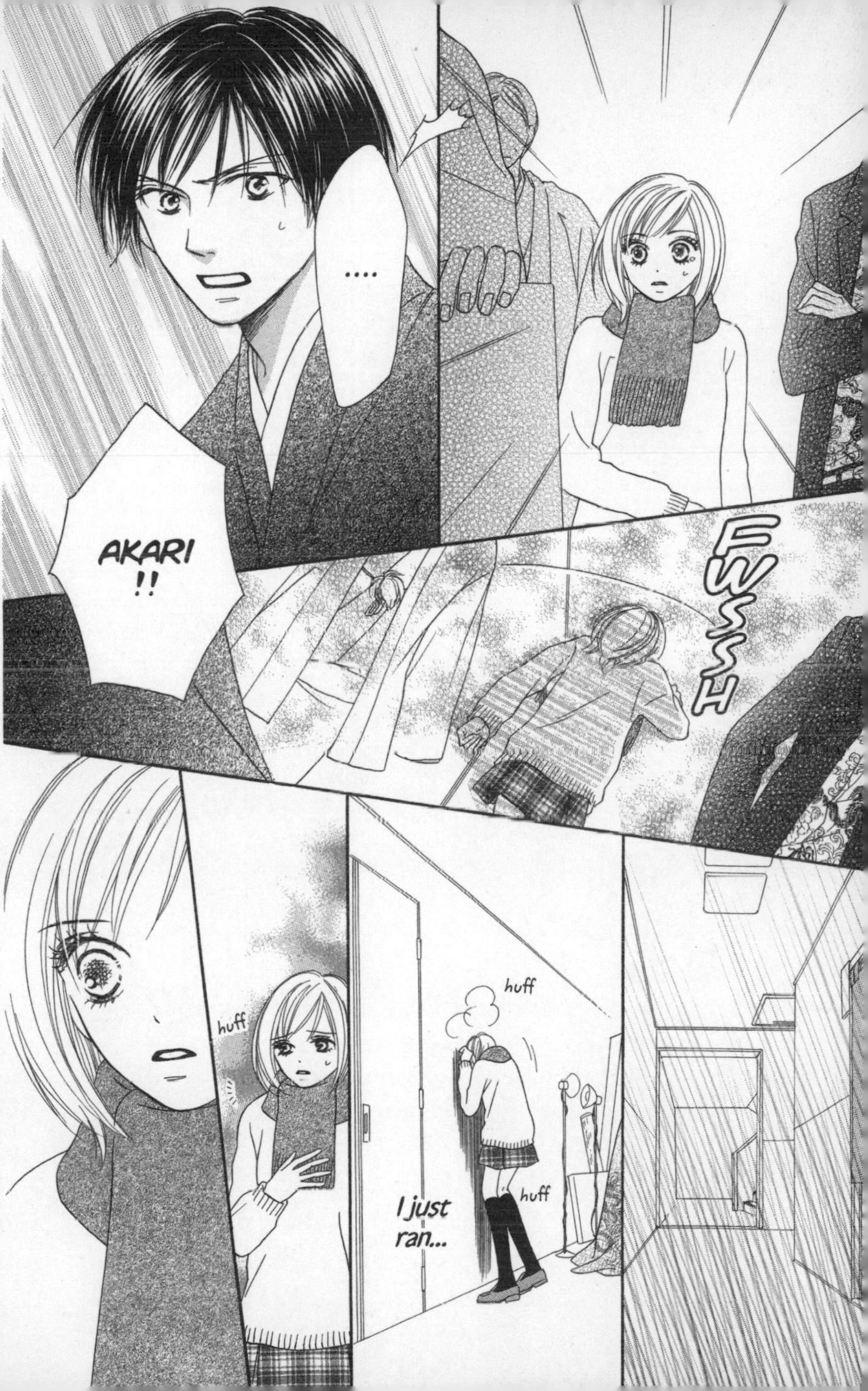
....
AKARI !!
FWSSH
huff
huff
I just ran...
huff

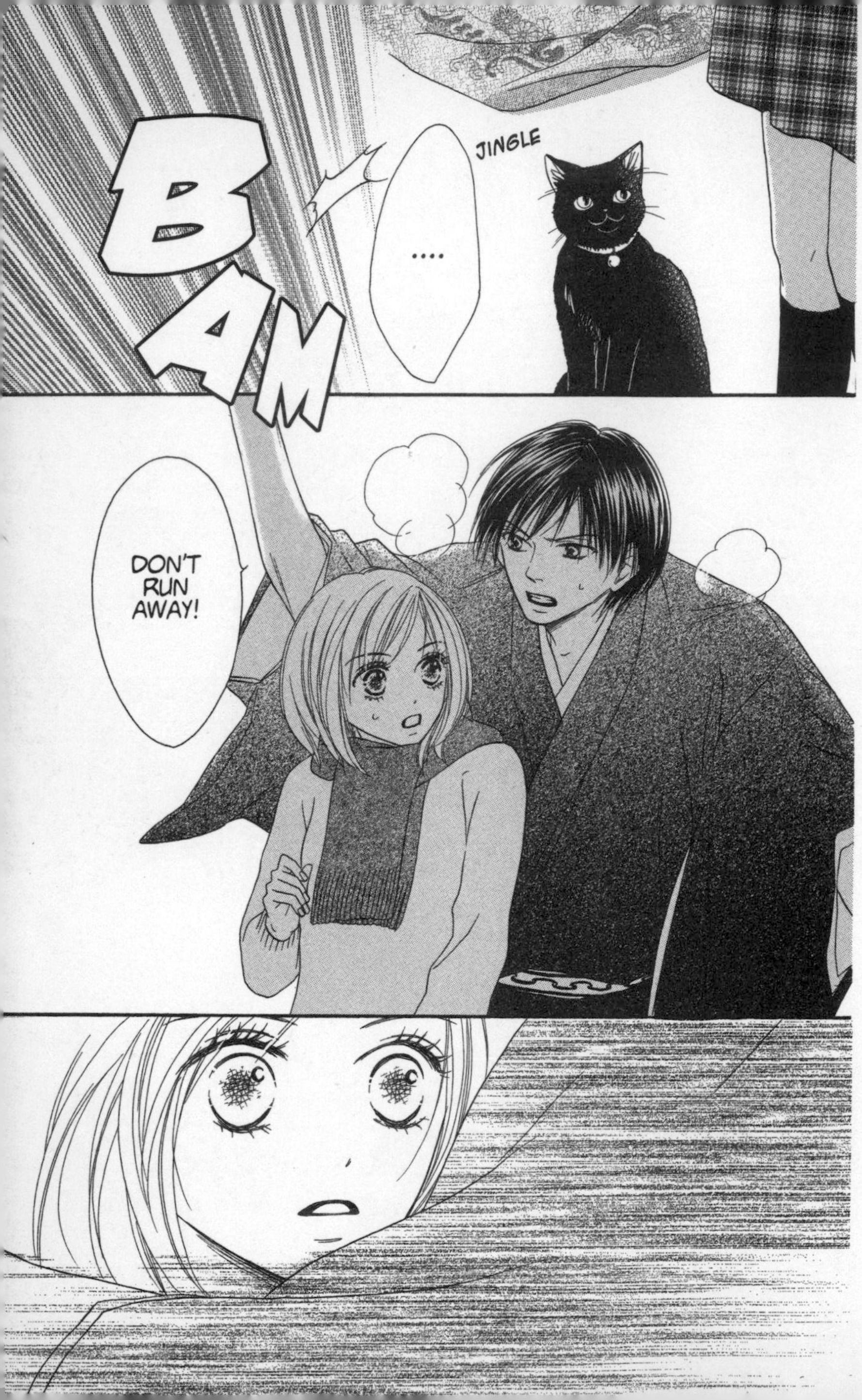
JINGLE
....
BAM
DON'T RUN AWAY!

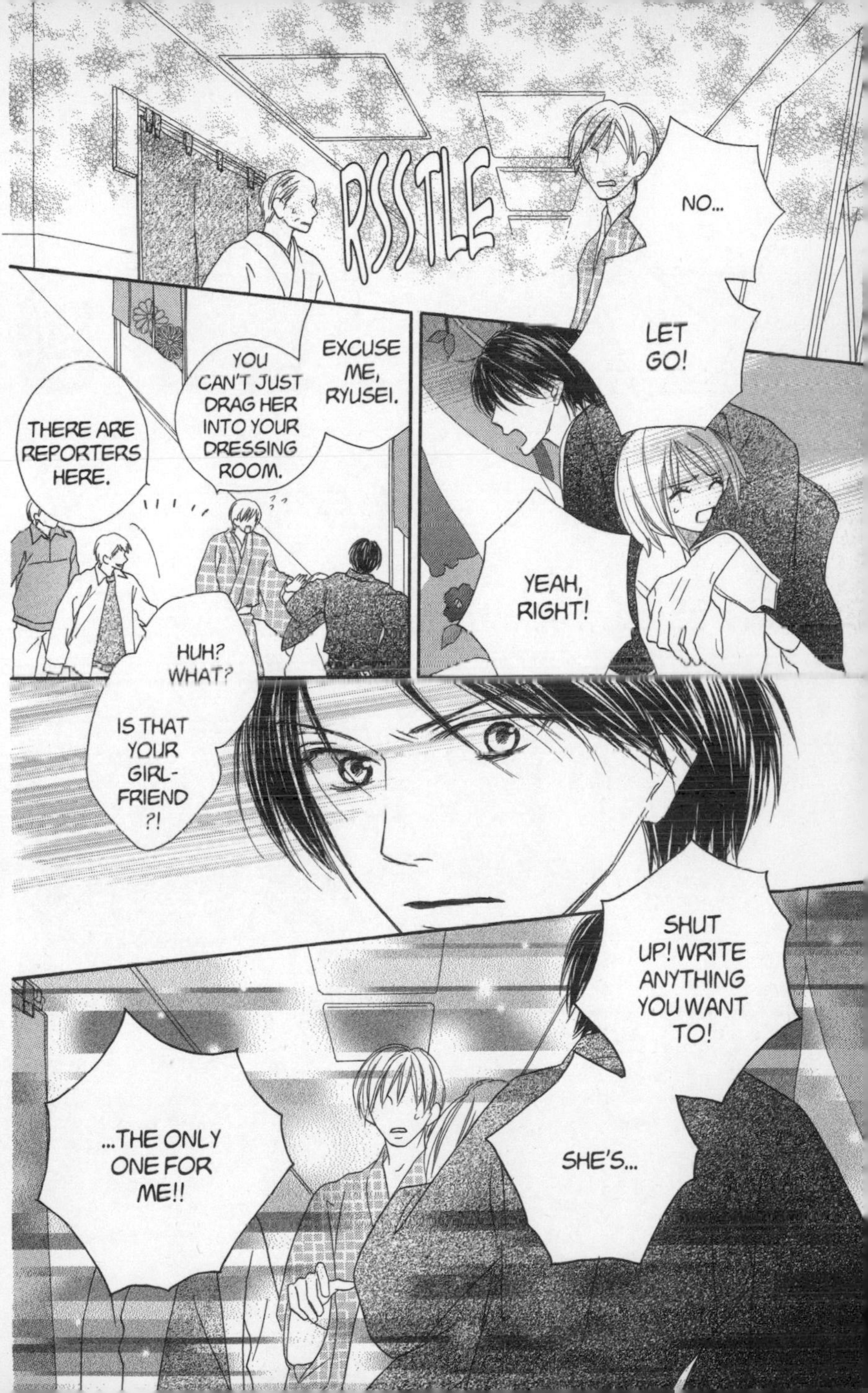
NO...
RSSTLE
LET GO!
YEAH, RIGHT!
EXCUSE ME, RYUSEI.
YOU CAN'T JUST DRAG HER INTO YOUR DRESSING ROOM.
THERE ARE REPORTERS HERE.
HUH? WHAT?
IS THAT YOUR GIRL-FRIEND ?!
SHUT UP! WRITE ANYTHING YOU WANT TO!
SHE'S...
...THE ONLY ONE FOR ME!!

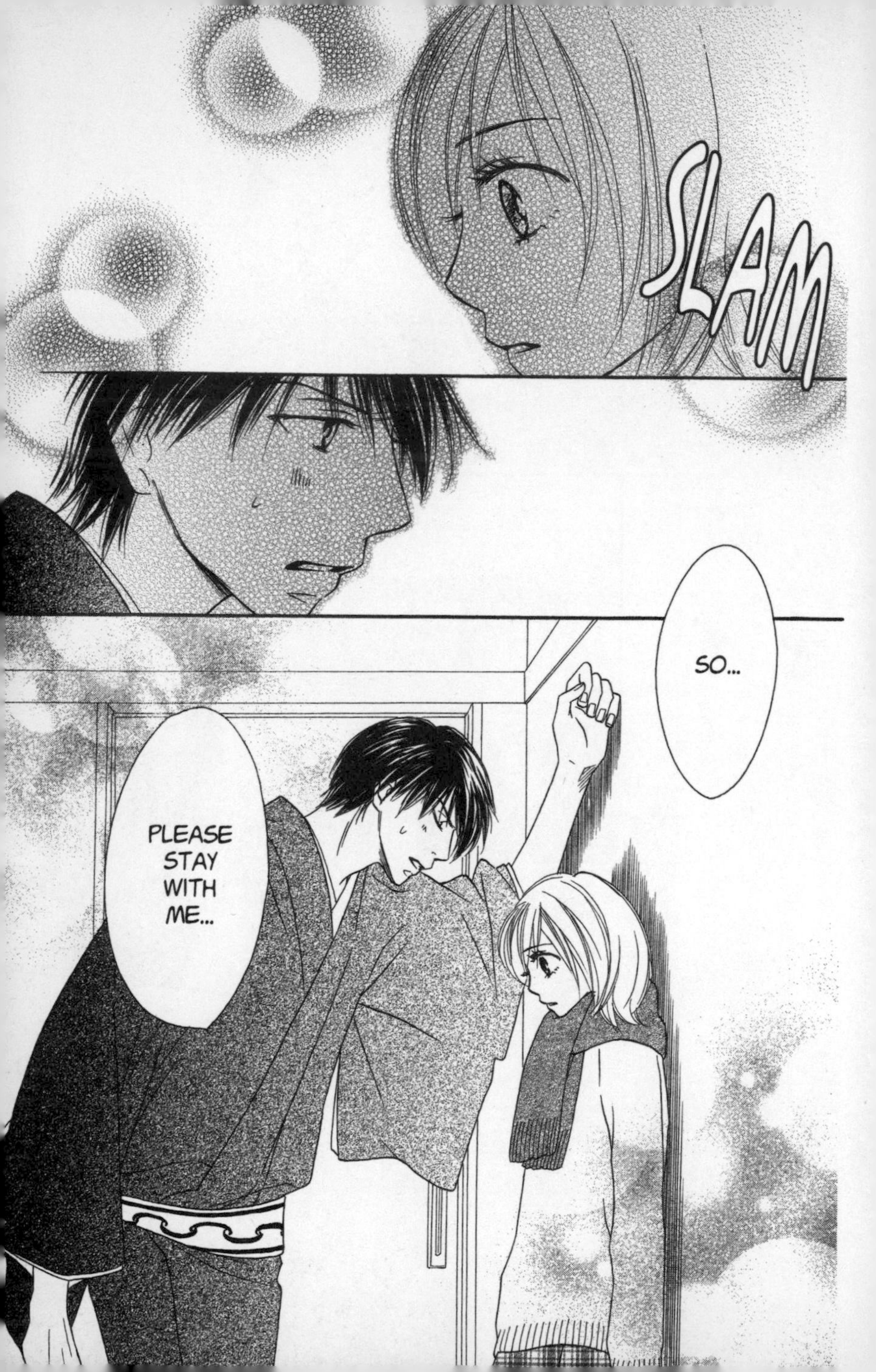
SLAM
SO...
PLEASE STAY WITH ME...

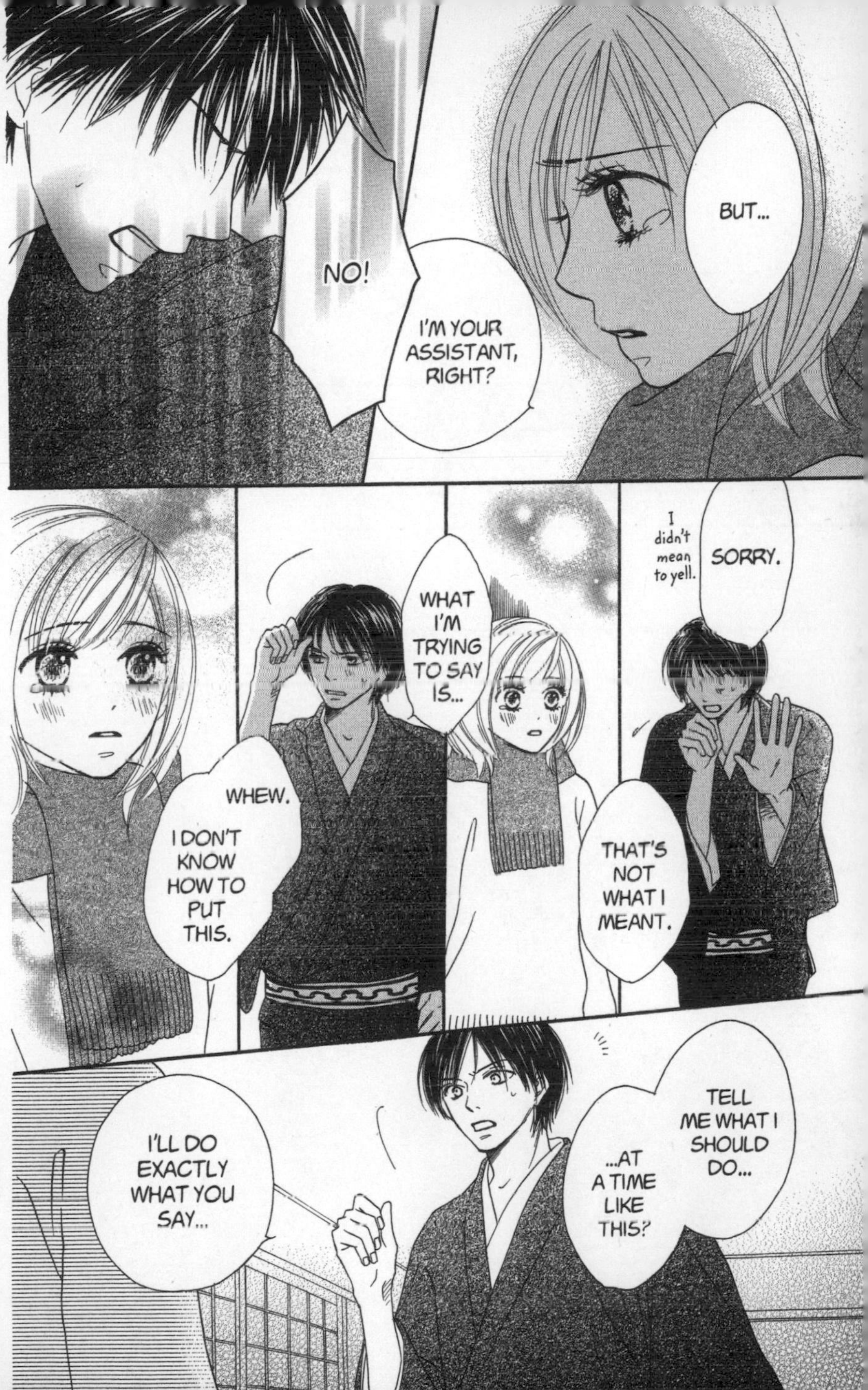
BUT...
I'M YOUR ASSISTANT, RIGHT?
NO!
SORRY.
I didn't mean to yell.
THAT'S NOT WHAT I MEANT.
WHAT I'M TRYING TO SAY IS...
WHEW.
I DON'T KNOW HOW TO PUT THIS.
TELL ME WHAT I SHOULD DO...
...AT A TIME LIKE THIS?
I'LL DO EXACTLY WHAT YOU SAY...

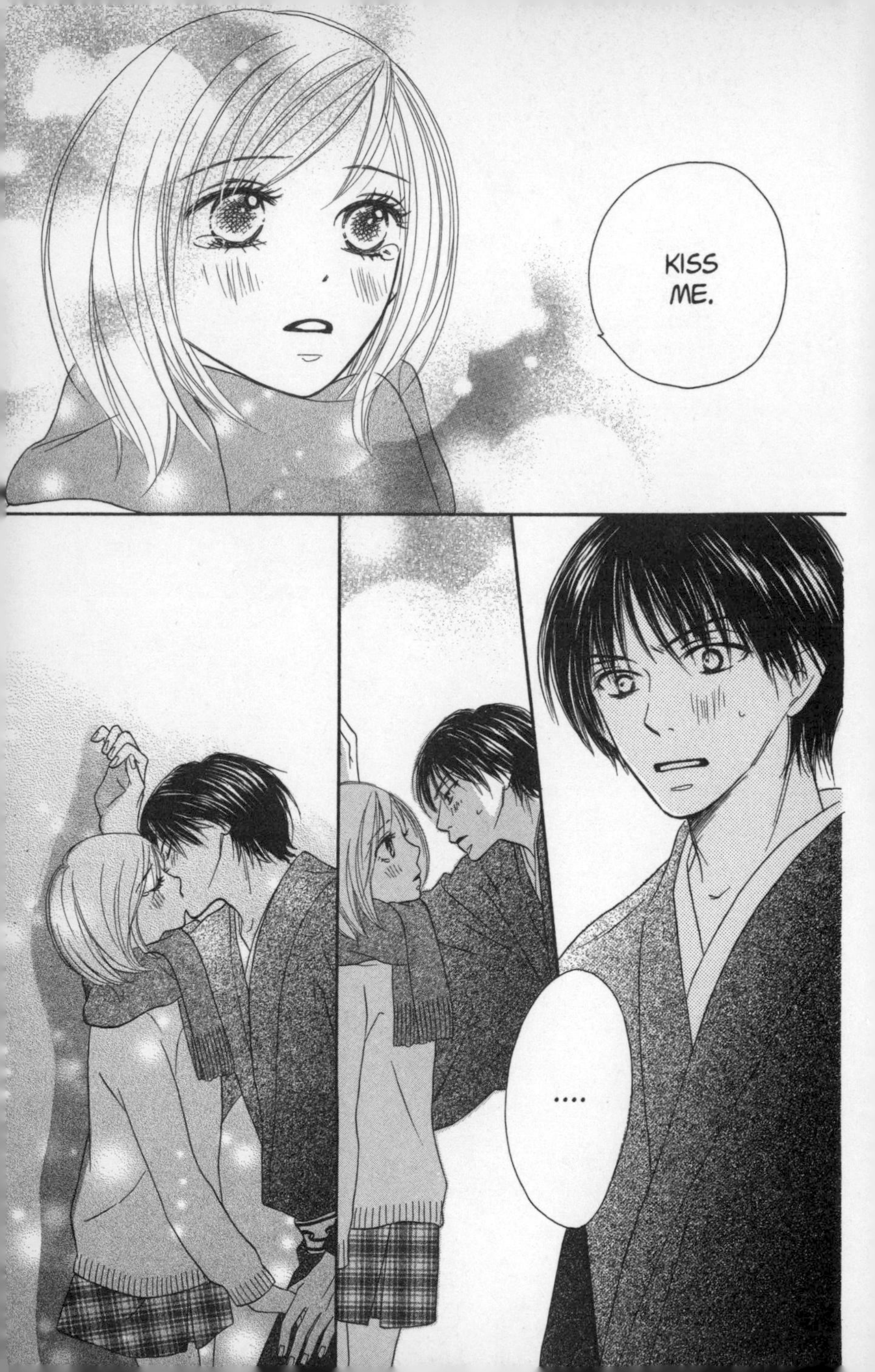
KISS ME.
....

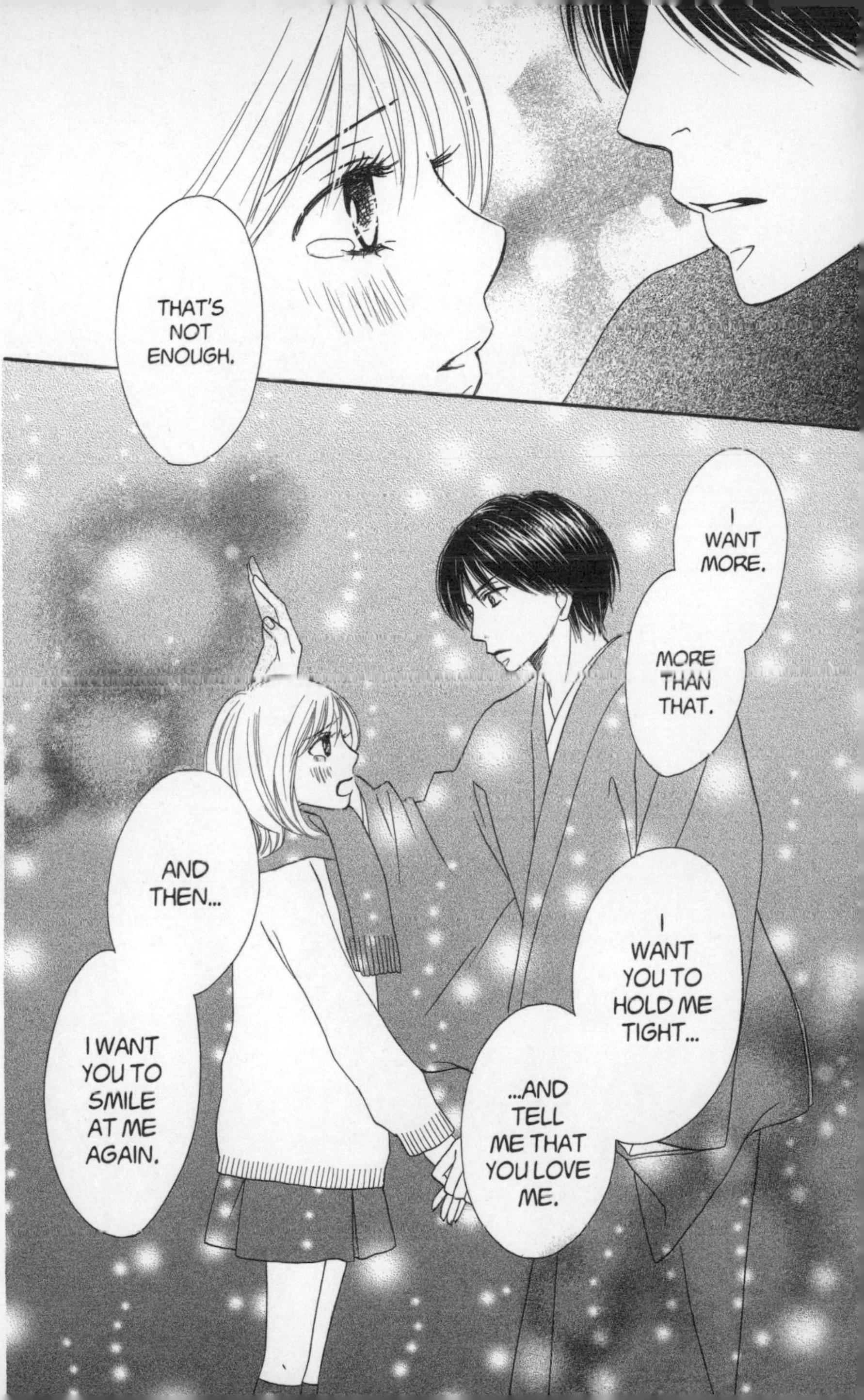
THAT'S NOT ENOUGH.
I WANT MORE.
MORE THAN THAT.
I WANT YOU TO HOLD ME TIGHT...
...AND TELL ME THAT YOU LOVE ME.
AND THEN...
I WANT YOU TO SMILE AT ME AGAIN.

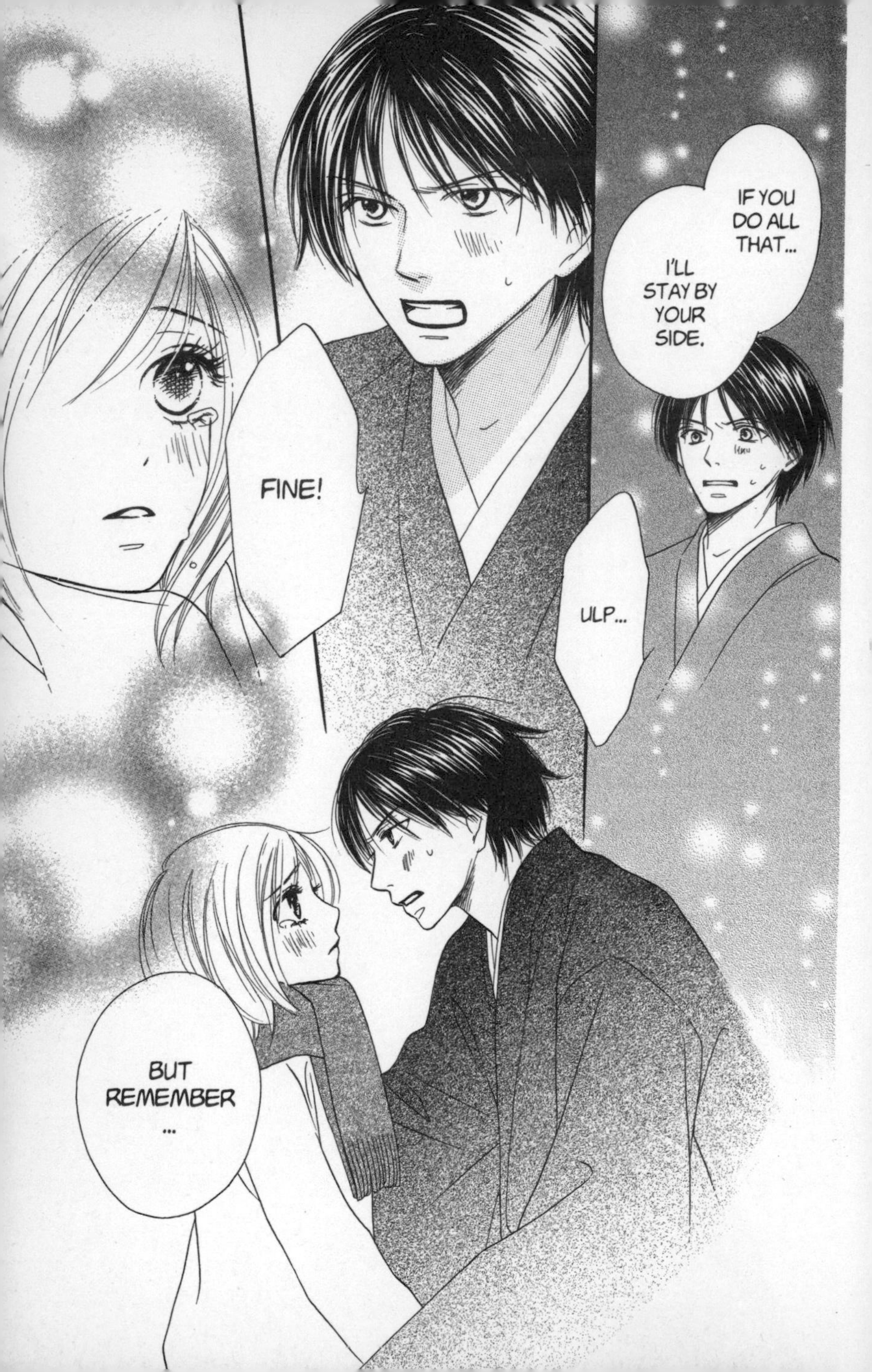
IF YOU DO ALL THAT... I'LL STAY BY YOUR SIDE.
ULP...
FINE!
BUT REMEMBER ...

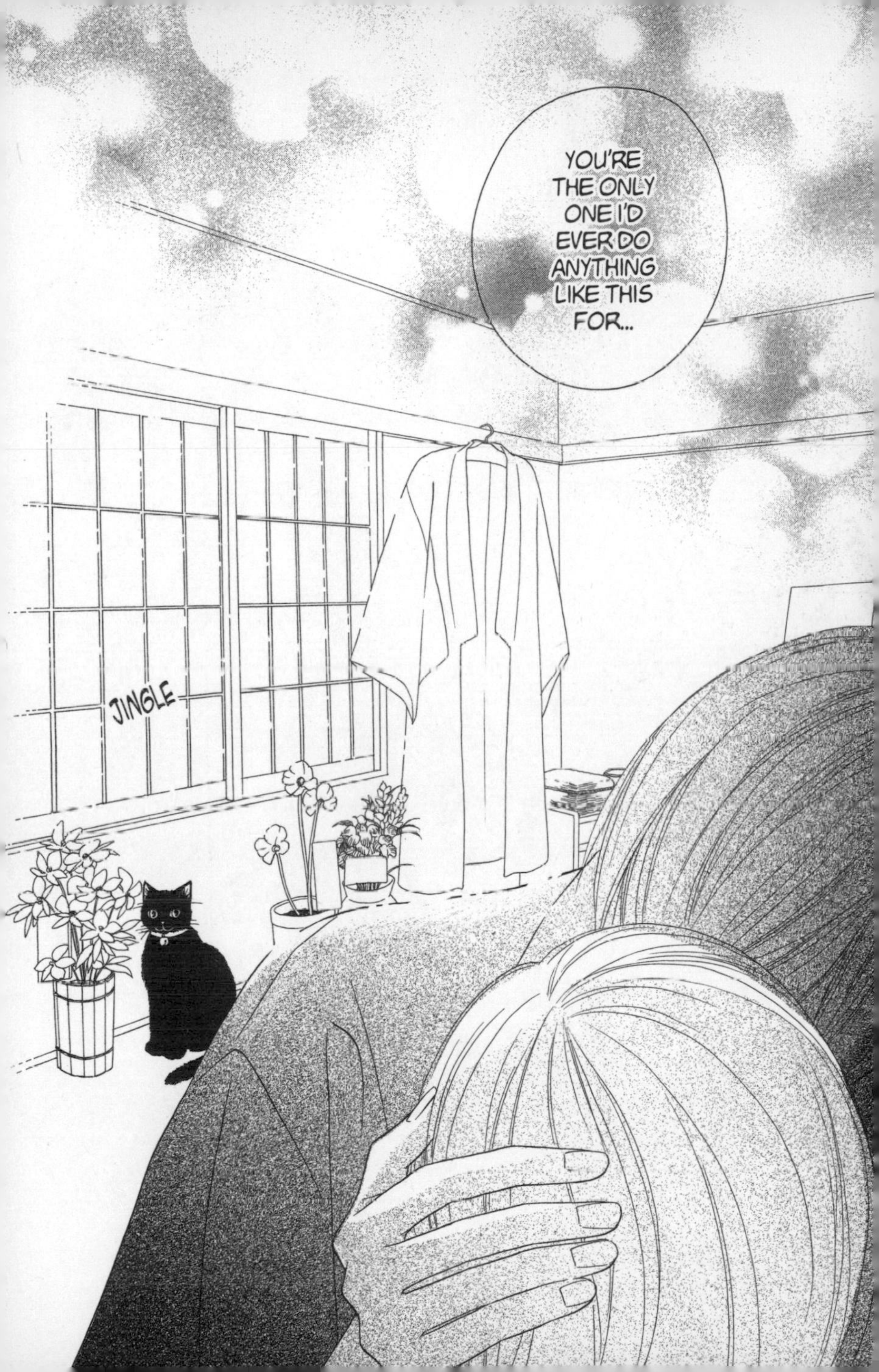
YOU'RE THE ONLY ONE I'D EVER DO ANYTHING LIKE THIS FOR...
JINGLE

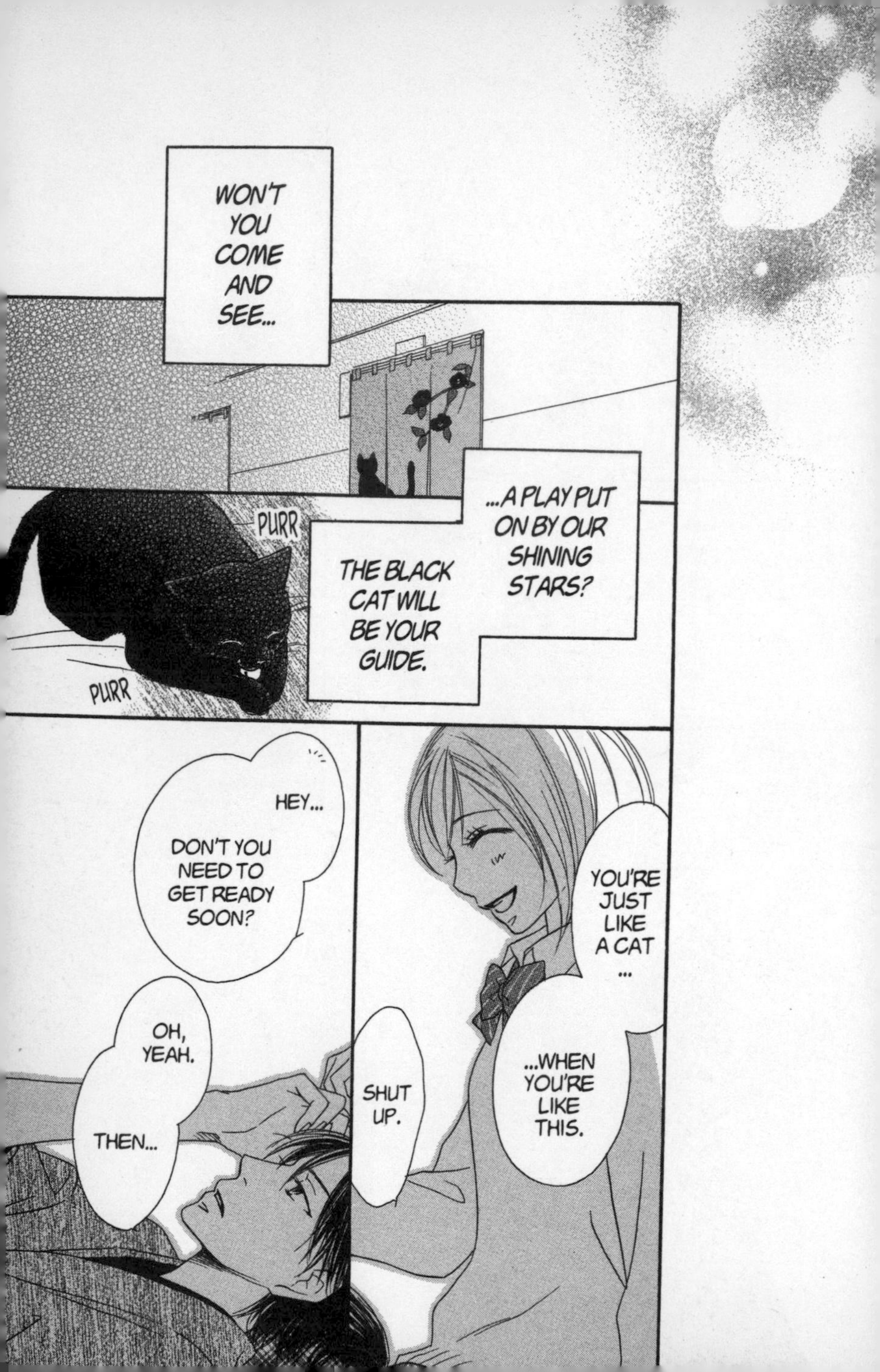
WON'T YOU COME AND SEE...
...A PLAY PUT ON BY OUR SHINING STARS?
PURR
THE BLACK CAT WILL BE YOUR GUIDE.
PURR
YOU'RE JUST LIKE A CAT ...
...WHEN YOU'RE LIKE THIS.
SHUT UP.
HEY...
DON'T YOU NEED TO GET READY SOON?
OH, YEAH.
THEN...

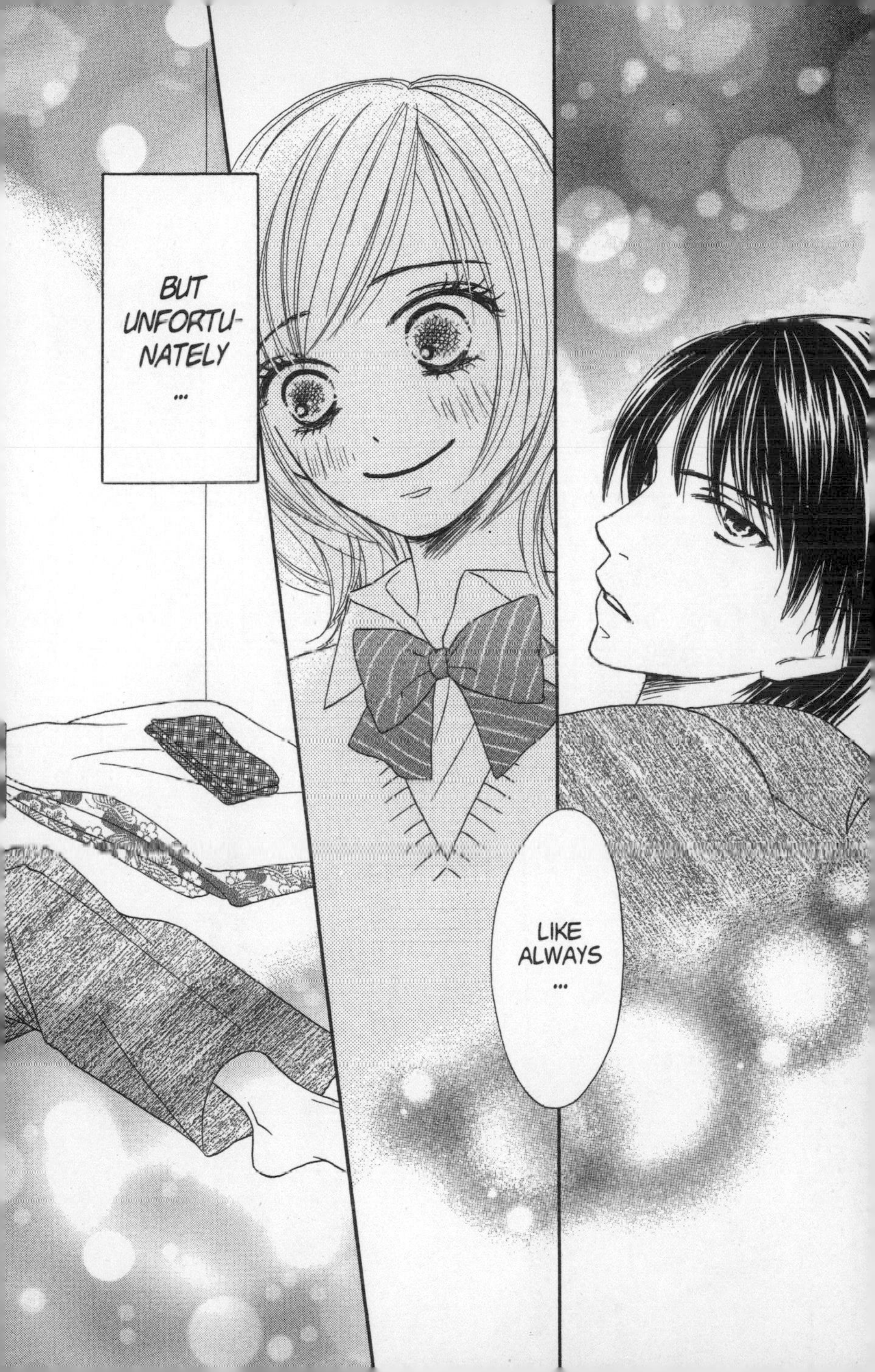
LIKE ALWAYS ...
BUT UNFORTUNATELY ...

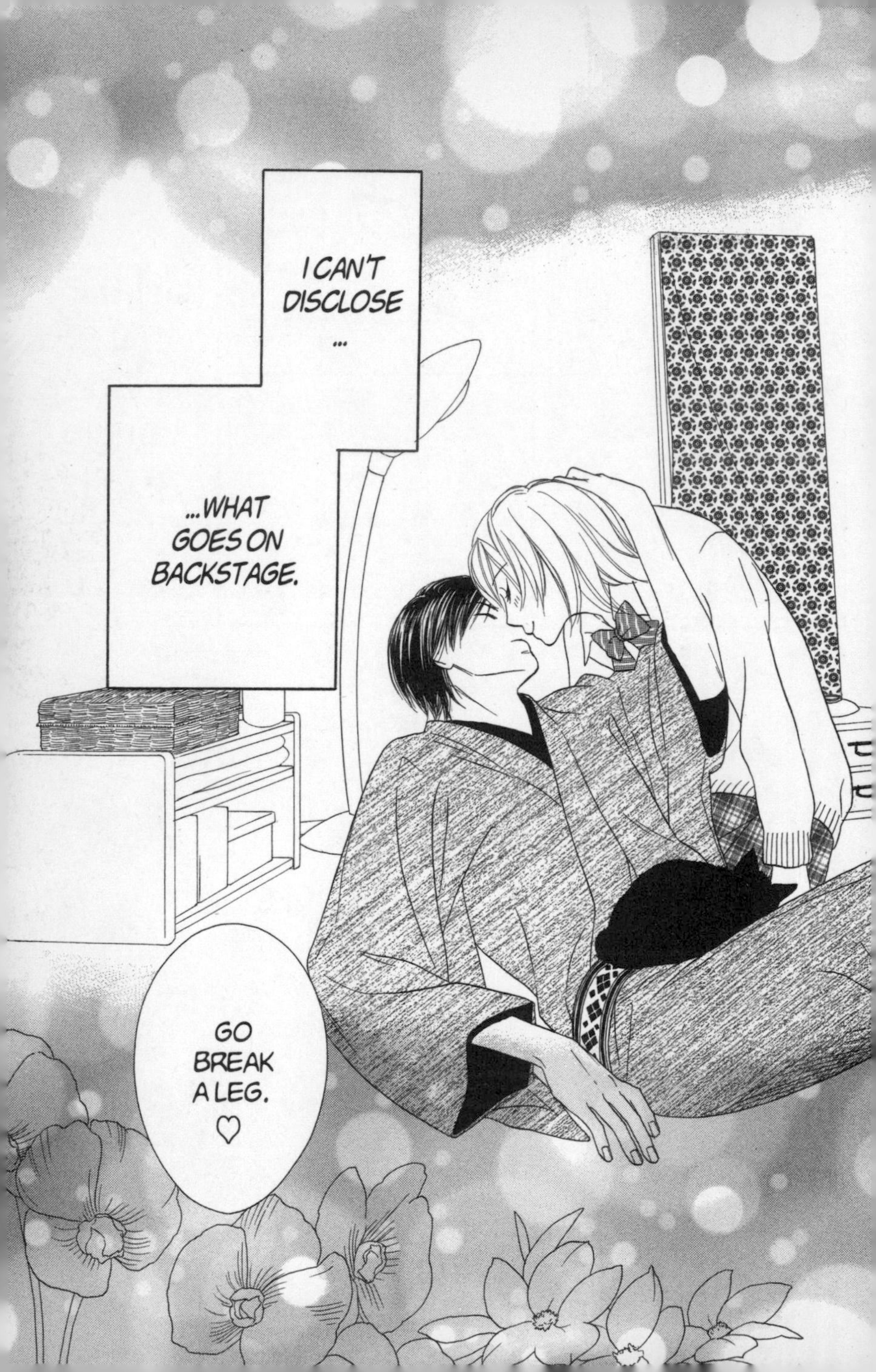
I CAN'T DISCLOSE ...
...WHAT GOES ON BACKSTAGE.
GO BREAK A LEG. ♡

Backstage at Backstage Prince: Part 1

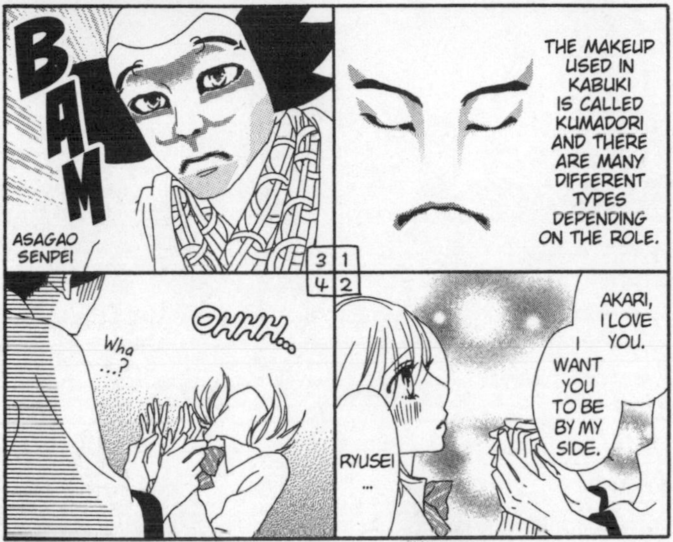
THE MAKEUP USED IN KABUKI IS CALLED KUMADORI AND THERE ARE MANY DIFFERENT TYPES DEPENDING ON THE ROLE.
AKARI, I LOVE YOU.
I WANT YOU TO BE BY MY SIDE.
RYUSEI ...
BAM
ASAGAO SENPEI
OHHH...
Wha ...?

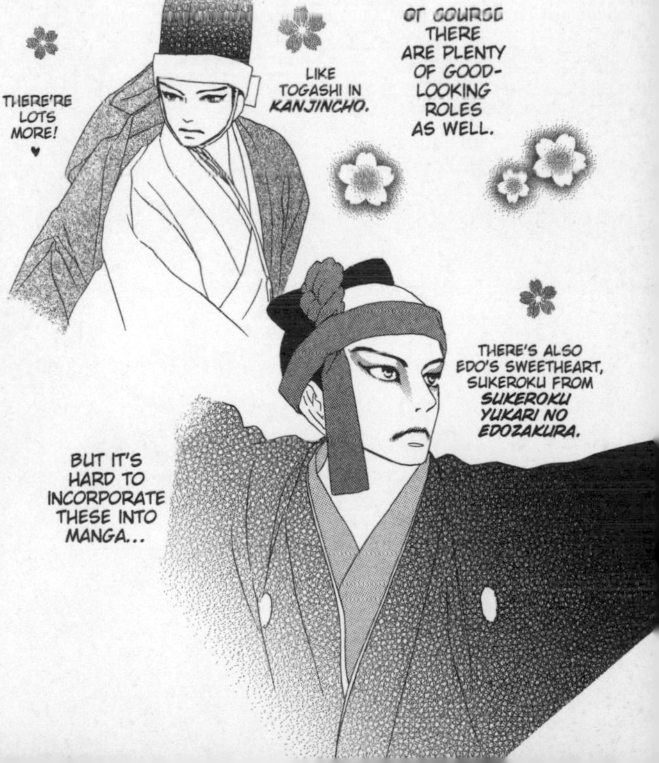
OF COURSE THERE ARE PLENTY OF GOOD-LOOKING ROLES AS WELL.
LIKE TOGASHI IN *KANJINCHO*.
THERE'RE LOTS MORE! ♥
THERE'S ALSO EDO'S SWEETHEART, SUKEROKU FROM *SUKEROKU YUKARI NO EDOZAKURA*.
BUT IT'S HARD TO INCORPORATE THESE INTO MANGA...

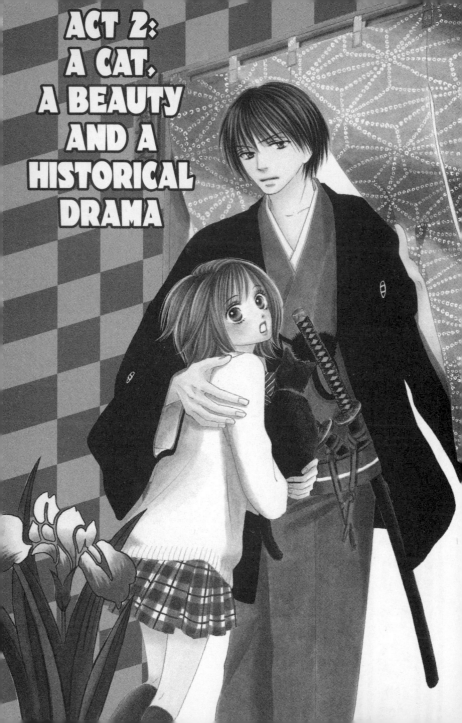

ACT 2:
A CAT,
A BEAUTY
AND A
HISTORICAL
DRAMA

Backstage at Backstage Prince: Part 2

RYUSEI'S PRIVATE CLOTHES ARE
KIMONOS, HIS PRACTICE OUTFITS ARE
YUKATAS AND HE WEARS NORMAL
CLOTHES WHEN HE'S OUT AND ABOUT...

THAT WAS JUST WHAT ENDED UP
HAPPENING IN THE PROCESS OF DRAWING
THIS PIECE. I REALIZE IT'S A LITTLE WEIRD
THAT HIS PRIVATE CLOTHES ARE KIMONOS...

I HAD TO PRACTICE DRAWING KIMONOS.

HE LOOKS LIKE SOME WEIRD CHARACTER
FROM AN OLD TV SHOW...

I'M GETTING
OLD...

What a
weird chap ♪

Such a
weird chap
♪

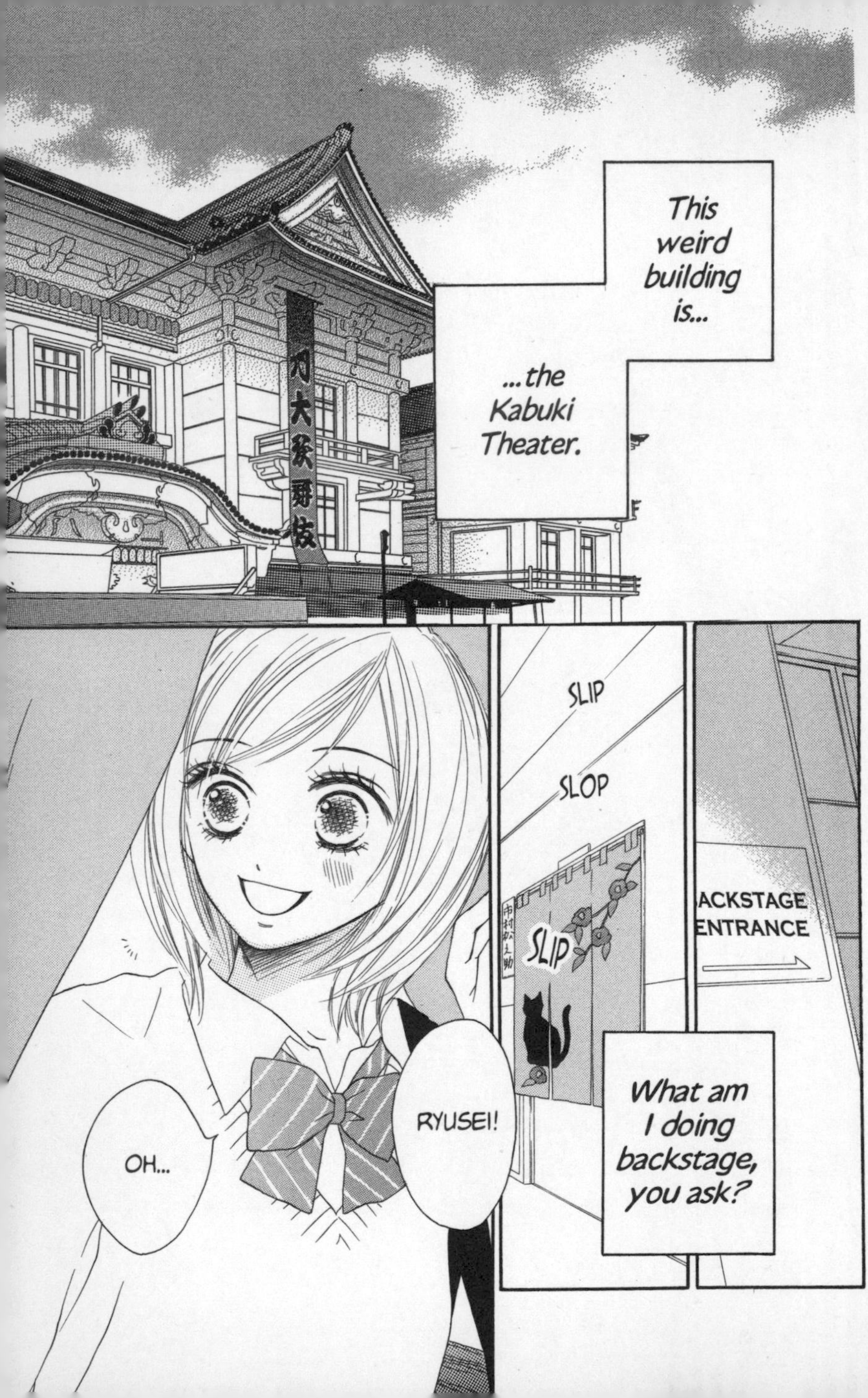
This weird building is...
...the Kabuki Theater.
ACKSTAGE ENTRANCE
What am I doing backstage, you ask?
SLIP
SLOP
SLIP
RYUSEI!
OH...

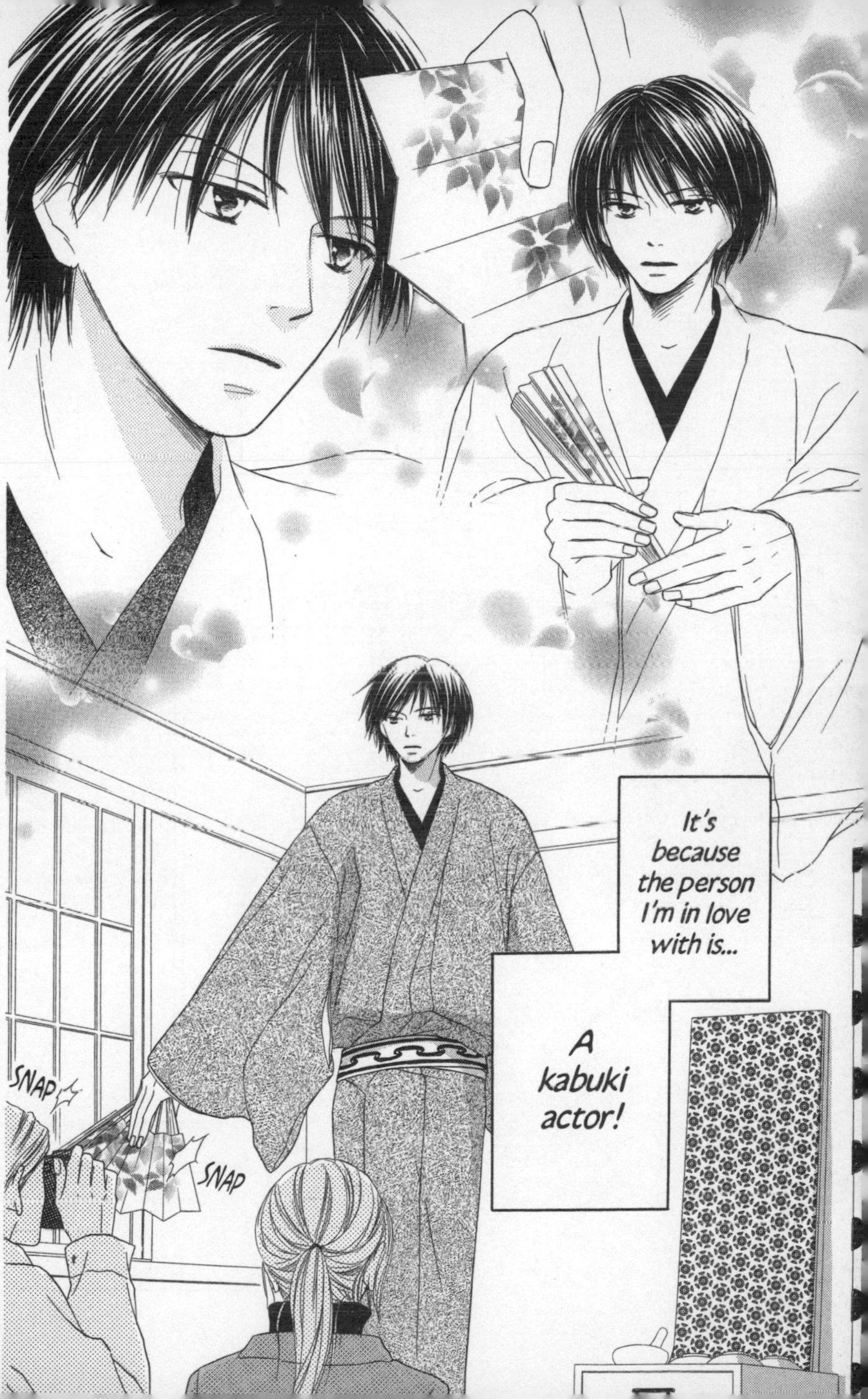
It's because the person I'm in love with is...
A kabuki actor!
SNAP
SNAP

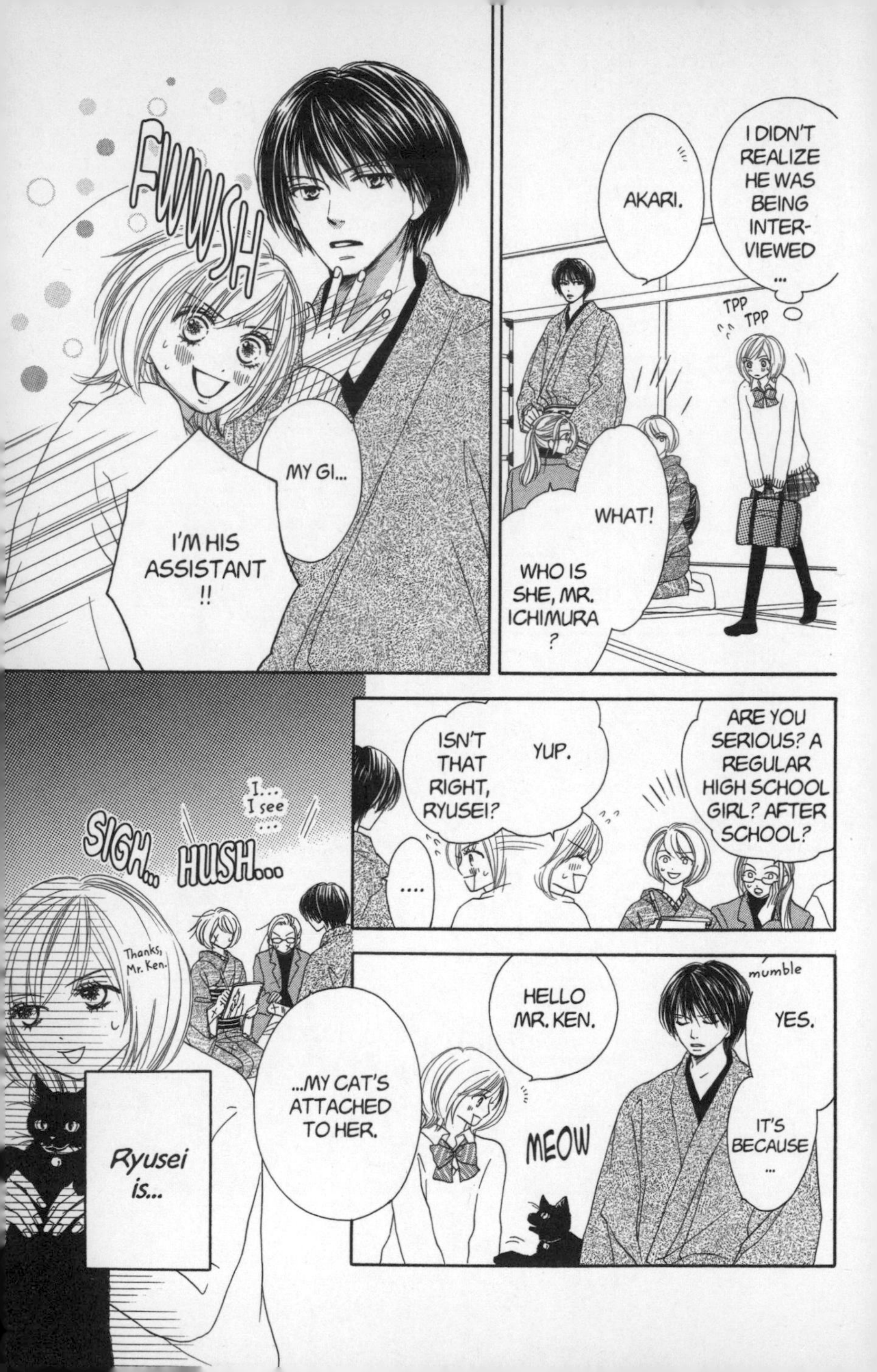
I DIDN'T REALIZE HE WAS BEING INTER-VIEWED ...
AKARI.
TPP TPP
WHAT!
WHO IS SHE, MR. ICHIMURA?
FWUSH
MY GI...
I'M HIS ASSISTANT!!
ARE YOU SERIOUS? A REGULAR HIGH SCHOOL GIRL? AFTER SCHOOL?
YUP.
ISN'T THAT RIGHT, RYUSEI?
....
mumble
YES.
HELLO MR. KEN.
IT'S BECAUSE ...
MEOW
...MY CAT'S ATTACHED TO HER.
I... I see...
SIGH... HUSH...
Thanks, Mr. Ken.
Ryusei is...

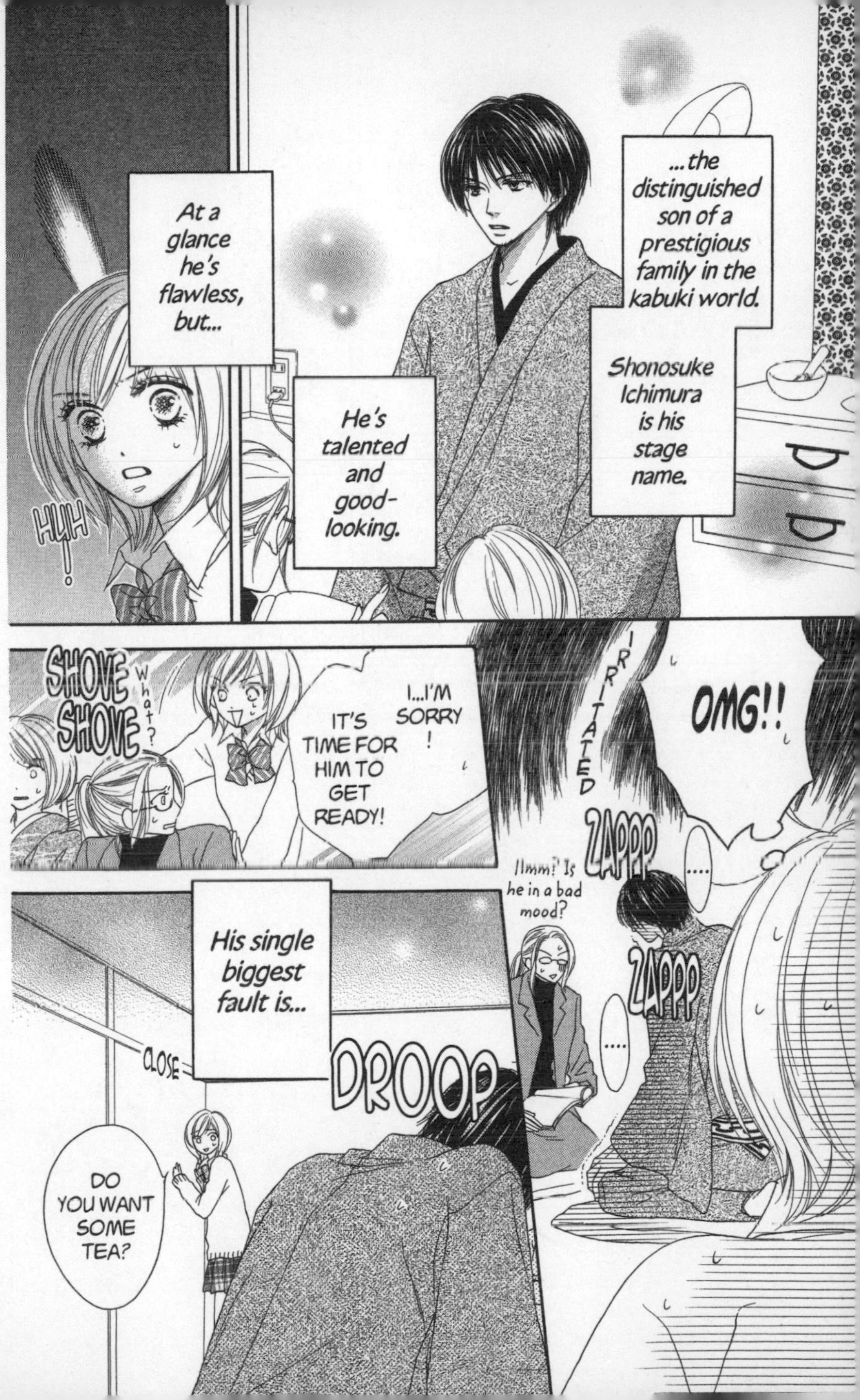
...the distinguished son of a prestigious family in the kabuki world.
Shonosuke Ichimura is his stage name.
He's talented and good-looking.
At a glance he's flawless, but...
HUH!
IRRITATED
OMG!!
I...I'M SORRY!
IT'S TIME FOR HIM TO GET READY!
SHOVE SHOVE
what?
ZAPPP
....
Hmm? Is he in a bad mood?
ZAPPP
....
His single biggest fault is...
DROOP
CLOSE
DO YOU WANT SOME TEA?

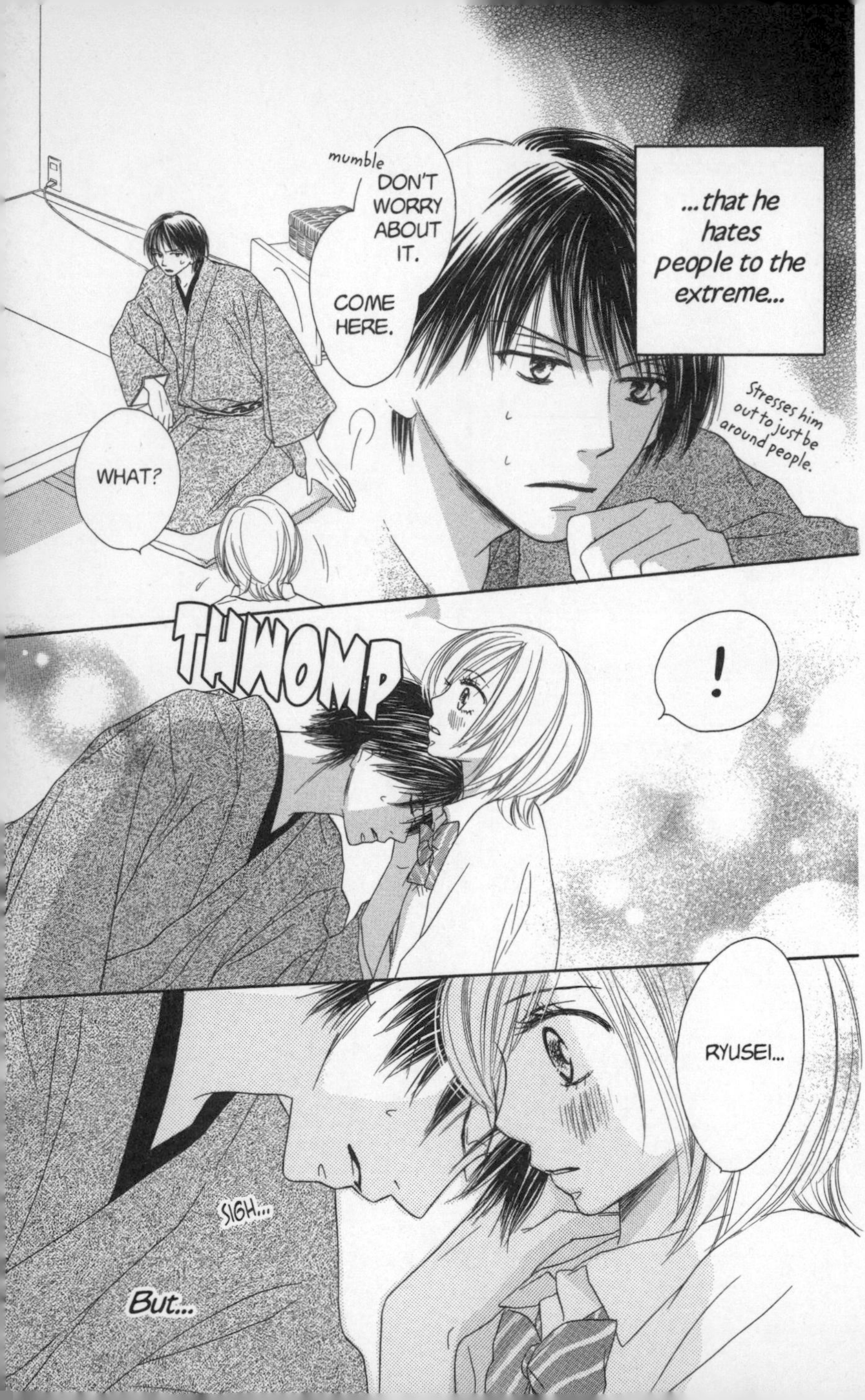
...that he hates people to the extreme...
mumble
DON'T WORRY ABOUT IT.
COME HERE.
Stresses him out to just be around people.
WHAT?
!
THWOMP
RYUSEI...
SIGH...
But...

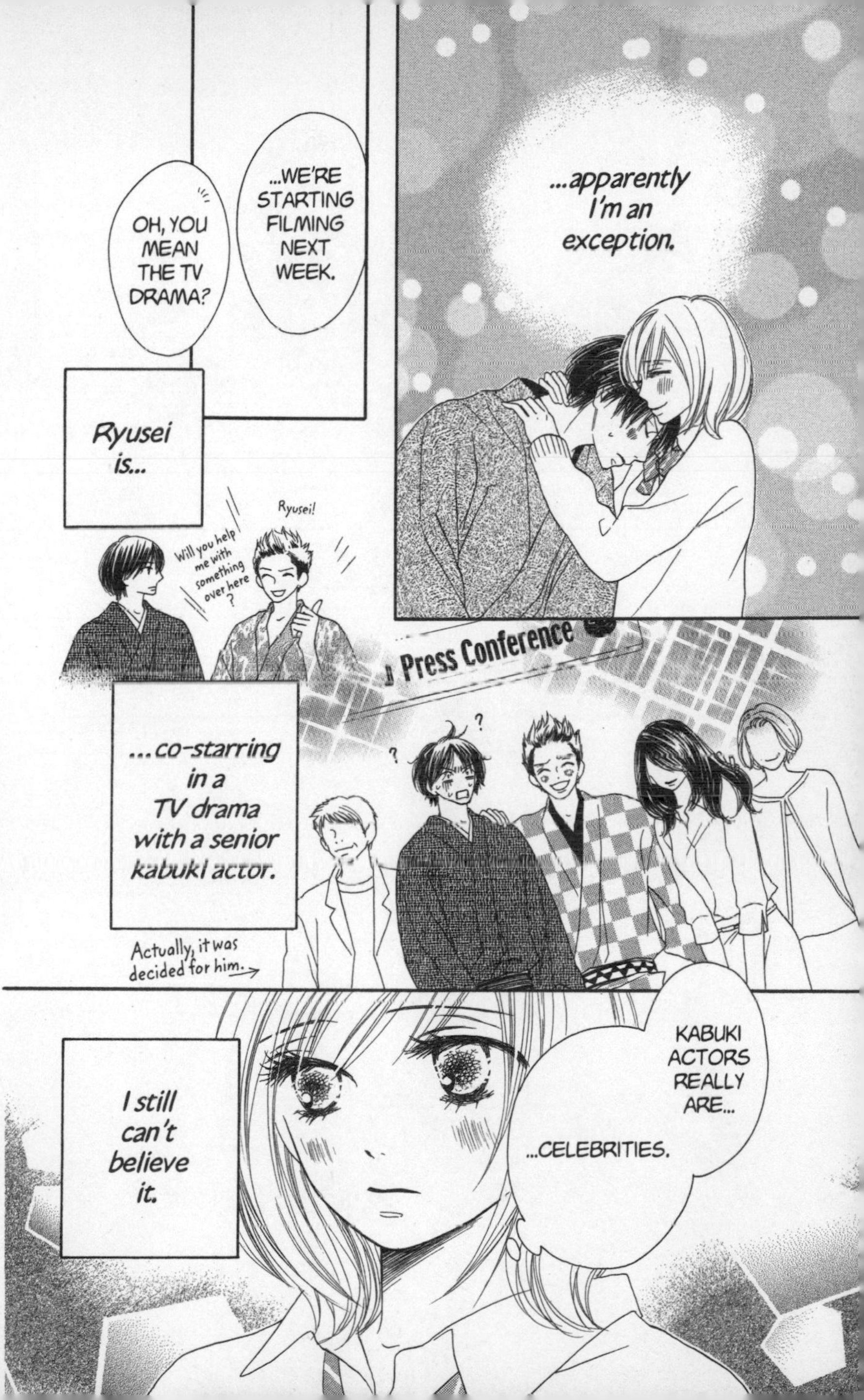
...apparently I'm an exception.
...WE'RE STARTING FILMING NEXT WEEK.
OH, YOU MEAN THE TV DRAMA?
Ryusei is...
Ryusei!
Will you help me with something over here?
Press Conference
...co-starring in a TV drama with a senior kabuki actor.
Actually, it was decided for him.
KABUKI ACTORS REALLY ARE...
...CELEBRITIES.
I still can't believe it.

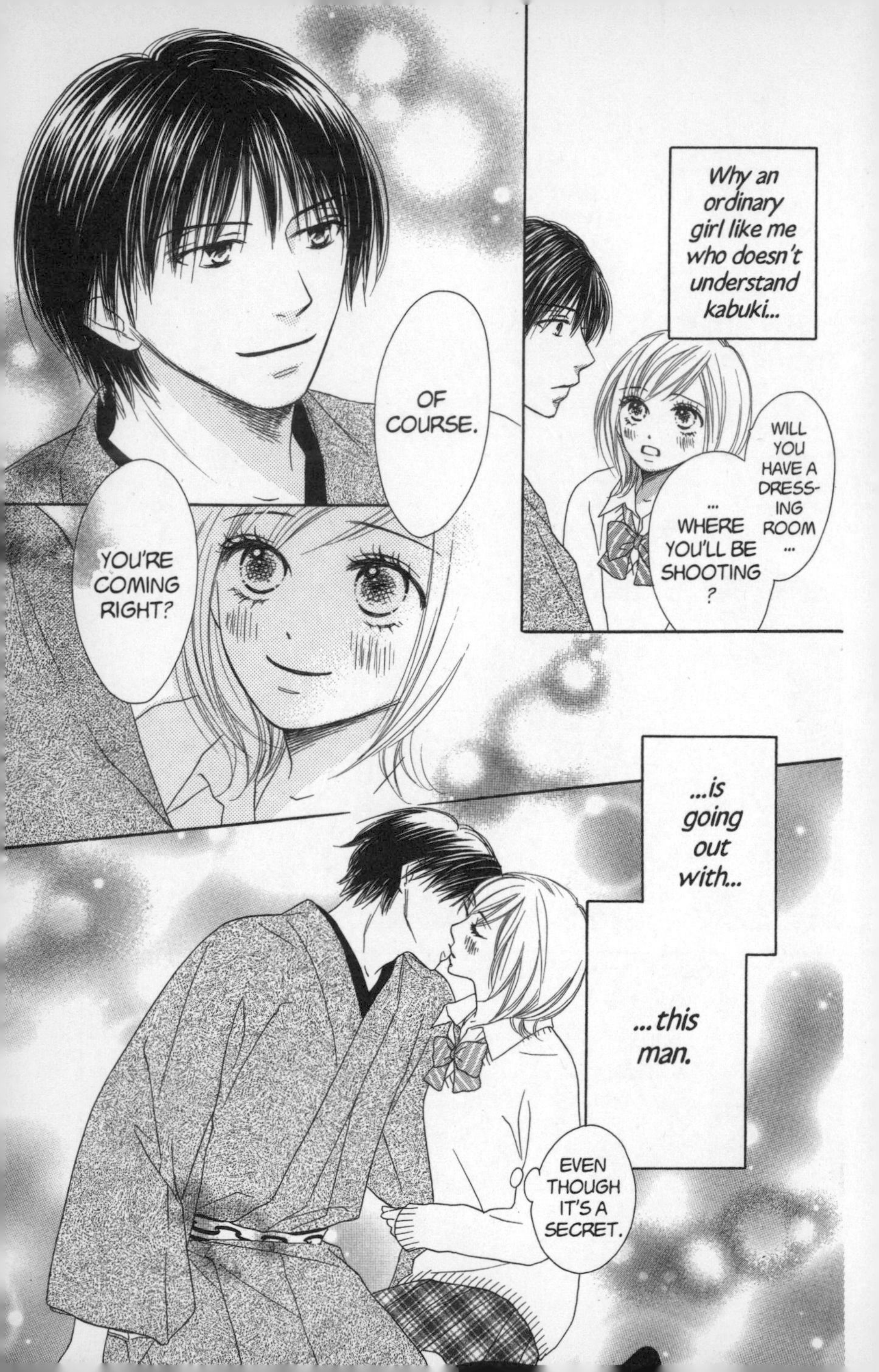
Why an ordinary girl like me who doesn't understand kabuki...
WILL YOU HAVE A DRESSING-ROOM ...
... WHERE YOU'LL BE SHOOTING ?
OF COURSE.
YOU'RE COMING RIGHT?
...is going out with...
...this man.
EVEN THOUGH IT'S A SECRET.

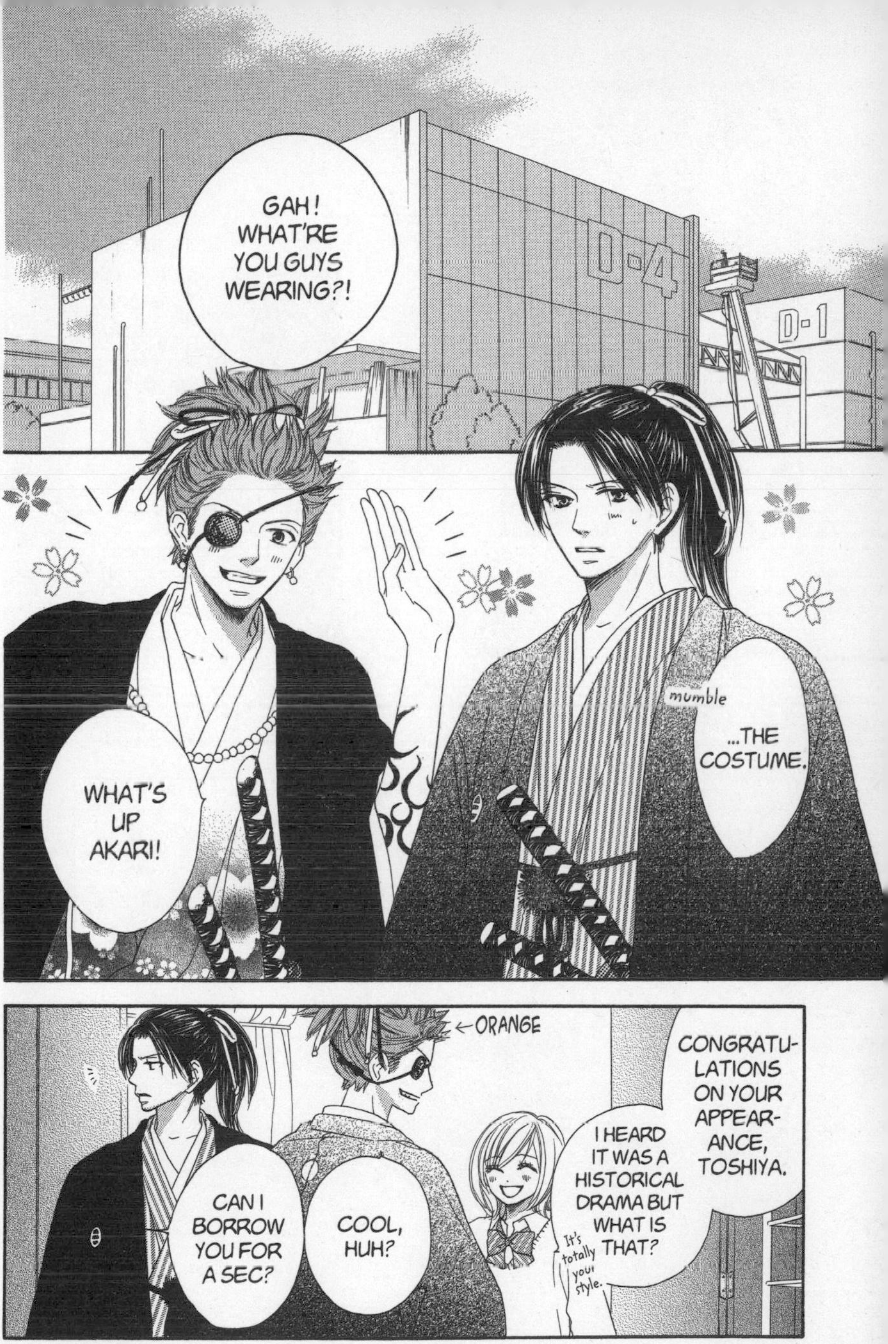
GAH! WHAT'RE YOU GUYS WEARING?!
mumble
...THE COSTUME.
WHAT'S UP AKARI!
CONGRATU-LATIONS ON YOUR APPEAR-ANCE, TOSHIYA.
← ORANGE
I HEARD IT WAS A HISTORICAL DRAMA BUT WHAT IS THAT?
It's totally your style.
COOL, HUH?
CAN I BORROW YOU FOR A SEC?

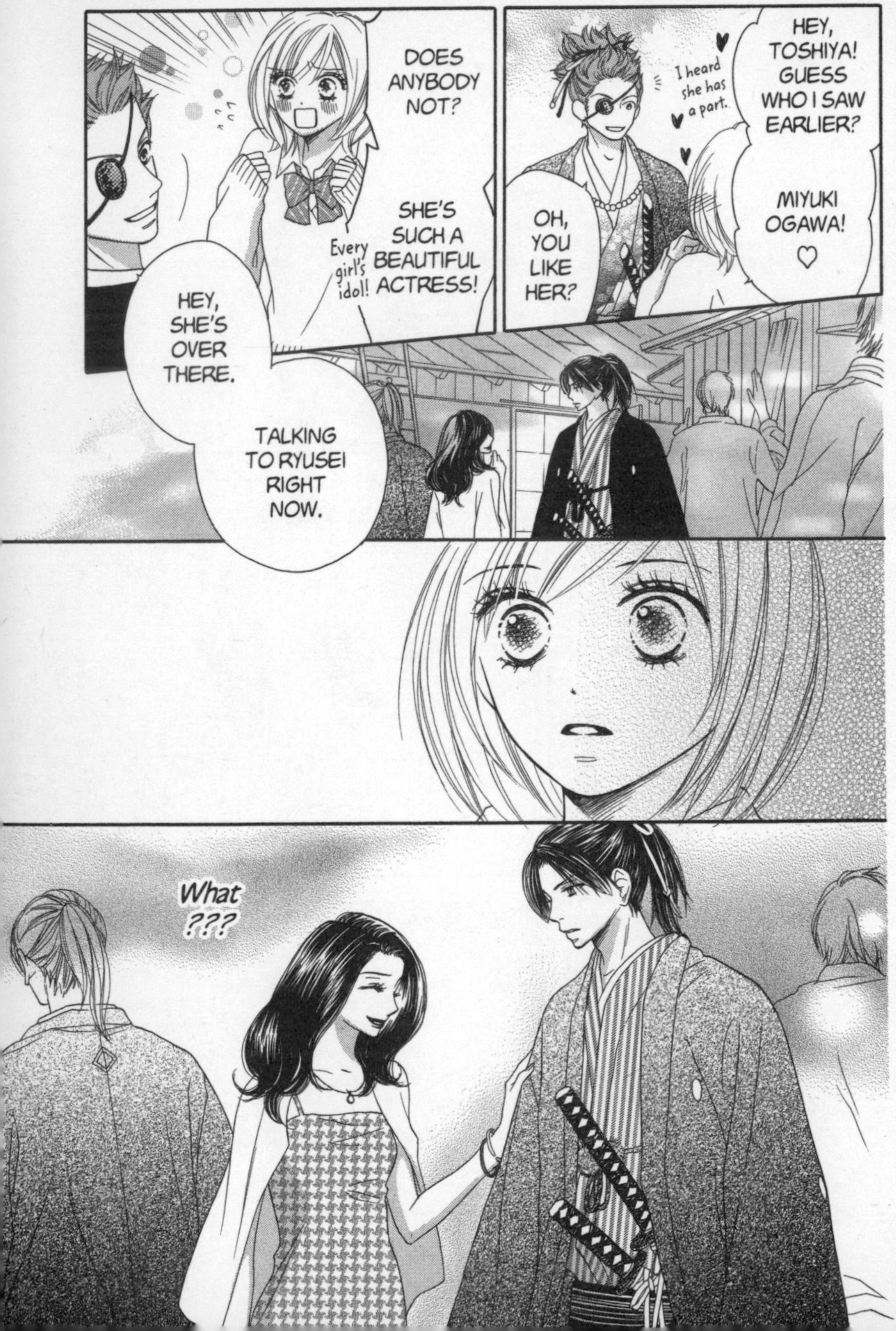
HEY, TOSHIYA! GUESS WHO I SAW EARLIER?
I heard she has a part.
MIYUKI OGAWA! ♡
OH, YOU LIKE HER?
DOES ANYBODY NOT?
SHE'S SUCH A BEAUTIFUL ACTRESS!
Every girl's idol!
HEY, SHE'S OVER THERE.
TALKING TO RYUSEI RIGHT NOW.
What ???

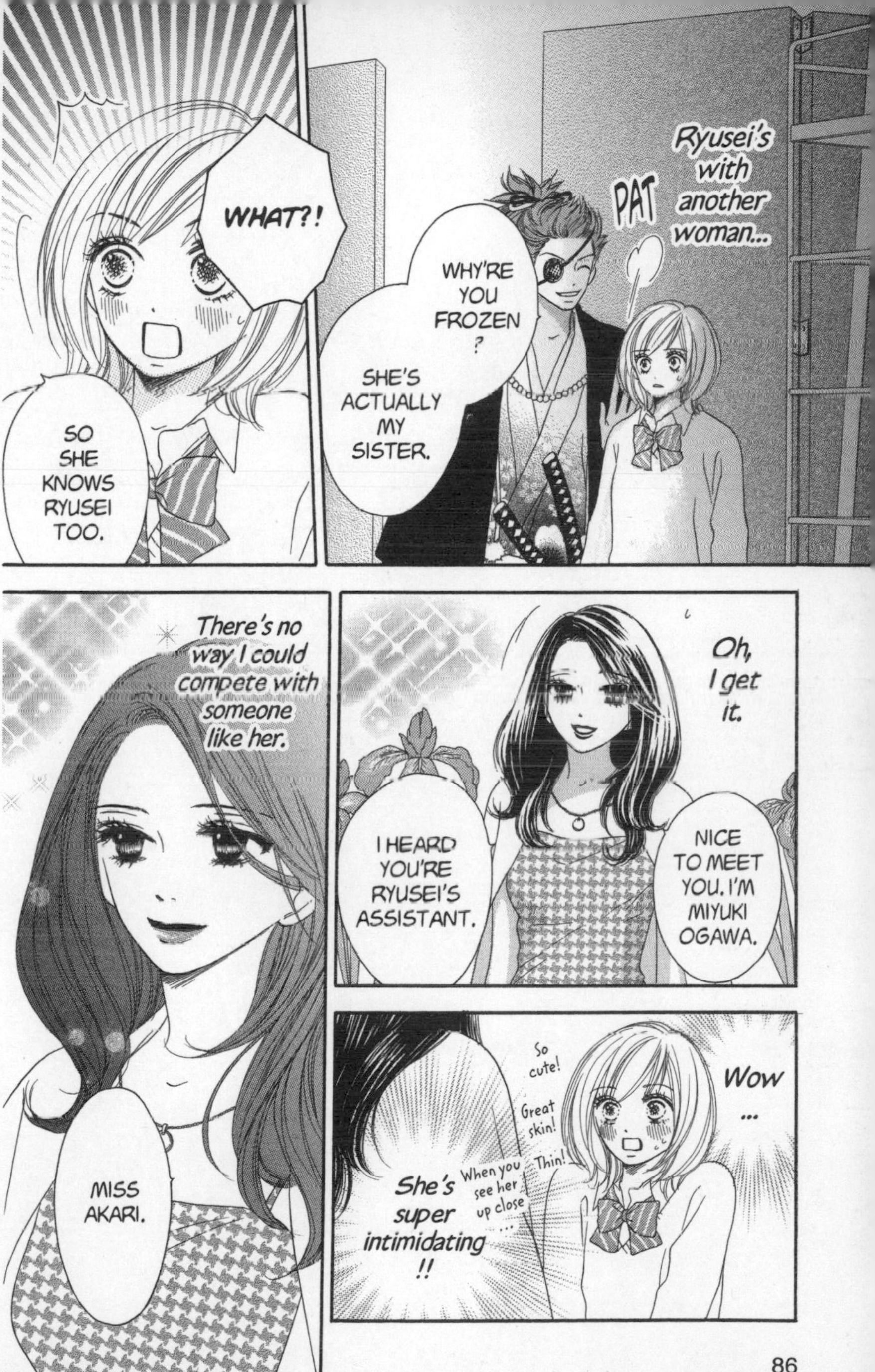

Ryusei's with another woman...
PAT
WHY'RE YOU FROZEN?
SHE'S ACTUALLY MY SISTER.
WHAT?!
SO SHE KNOWS RYUSEI TOO.
Oh, I get it.
NICE TO MEET YOU. I'M MIYUKI OGAWA.
I HEARD YOU'RE RYUSEI'S ASSISTANT.
Wow...
So cute!
Great skin!
Thin!
When you see her up close...
She's super intimidating!!
There's no way I could compete with someone like her.
MISS AKARI.

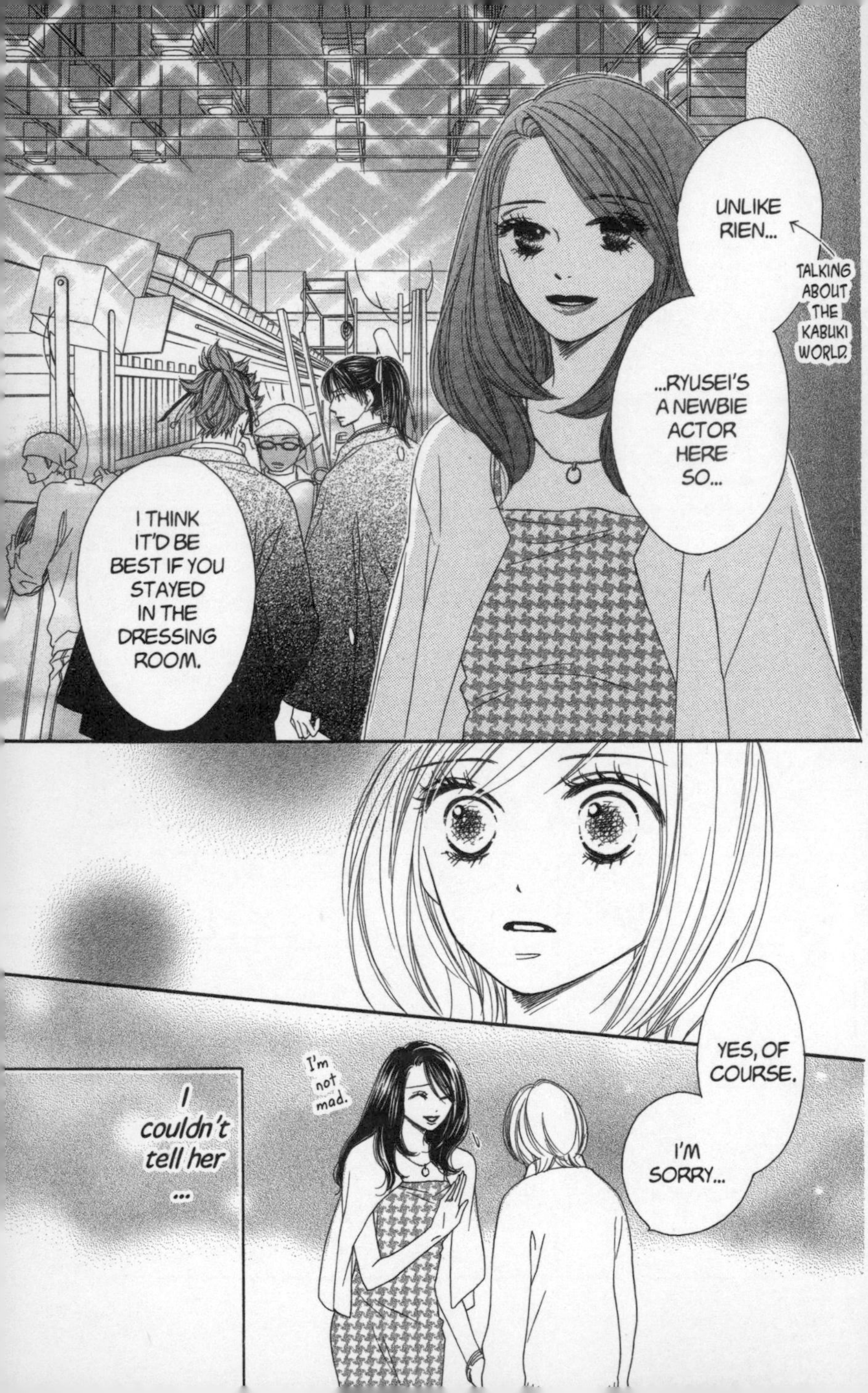
UNLIKE RIEN...
TALKING ABOUT THE KABUKI WORLD.
...RYUSEI'S A NEWBIE ACTOR HERE SO...
I THINK IT'D BE BEST IF YOU STAYED IN THE DRESSING ROOM.
YES, OF COURSE.
I'M SORRY...
I'm not mad.
I couldn't tell her ...

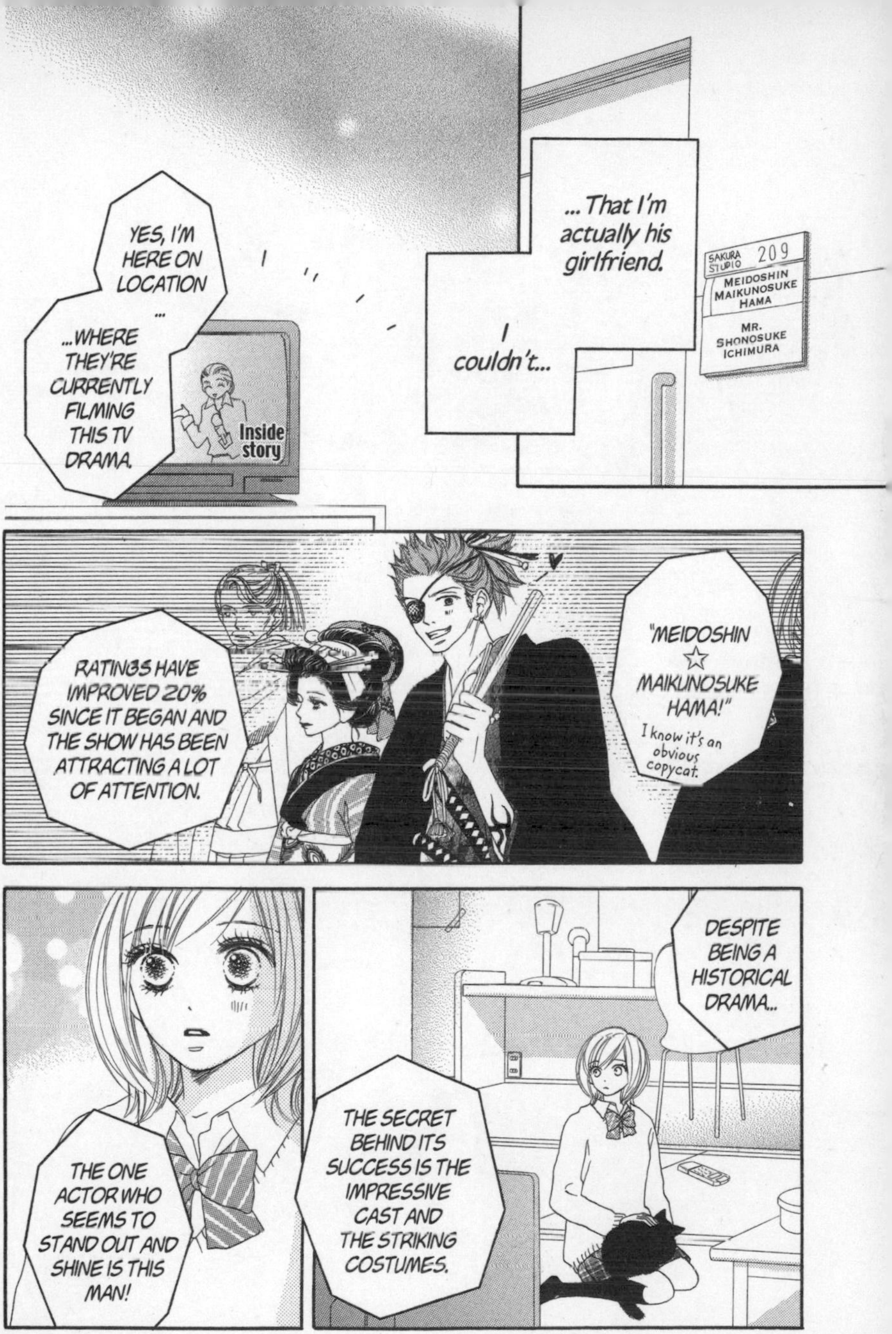
...That I'm actually his girlfriend.
I couldn't...
SAKURA STUDIO 209
MEIDOSHIN MAIKUNOSUKE HAMA
MR. SHONOSUKE ICHIMURA
YES, I'M HERE ON LOCATION ...
...WHERE THEY'RE CURRENTLY FILMING THIS TV DRAMA.
Inside story
"MEIDOSHIN ☆ MAIKUNOSUKE HAMA!"
I know it's an obvious copycat.
RATINGS HAVE IMPROVED 20% SINCE IT BEGAN AND THE SHOW HAS BEEN ATTRACTING A LOT OF ATTENTION.
DESPITE BEING A HISTORICAL DRAMA...
THE SECRET BEHIND ITS SUCCESS IS THE IMPRESSIVE CAST AND THE STRIKING COSTUMES.
THE ONE ACTOR WHO SEEMS TO STAND OUT AND SHINE IS THIS MAN!

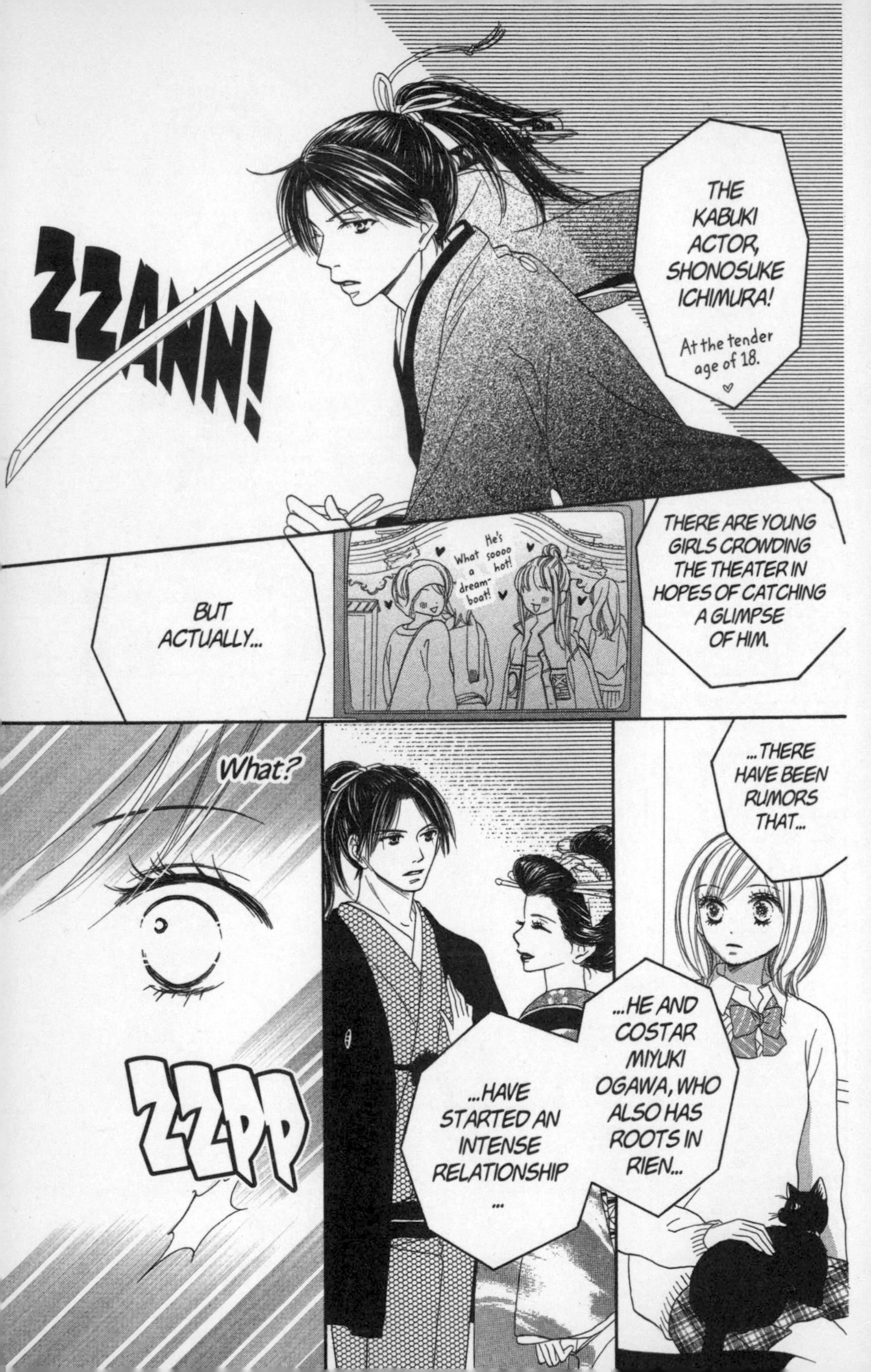
THE KABUKI ACTOR, SHONOSUKE ICHIMURA!
At the tender age of 18. ♥
ZZANN!
THERE ARE YOUNG GIRLS CROWDING THE THEATER IN HOPES OF CATCHING A GLIMPSE OF HIM.
He's soooo hot!
What a dream-boat!
BUT ACTUALLY...
...THERE HAVE BEEN RUMORS THAT...
...HE AND COSTAR MIYUKI OGAWA, WHO ALSO HAS ROOTS IN RIEN...
...HAVE STARTED AN INTENSE RELATIONSHIP ...
What?
ZZDP

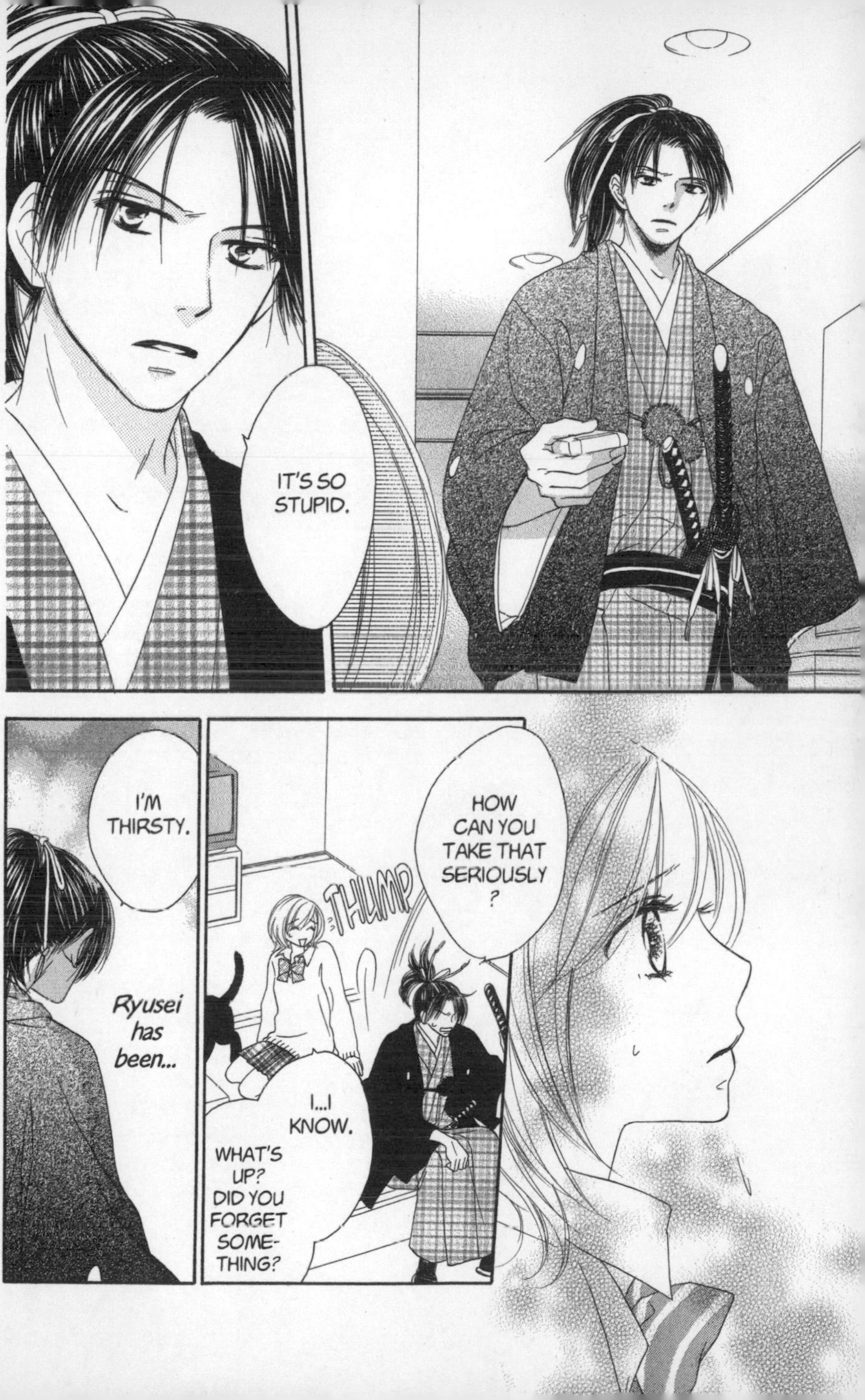
IT'S SO STUPID.
HOW CAN YOU TAKE THAT SERIOUSLY?
THUMP
I...I KNOW.
WHAT'S UP? DID YOU FORGET SOME-THING?
I'M THIRSTY.
Ryusei has been...

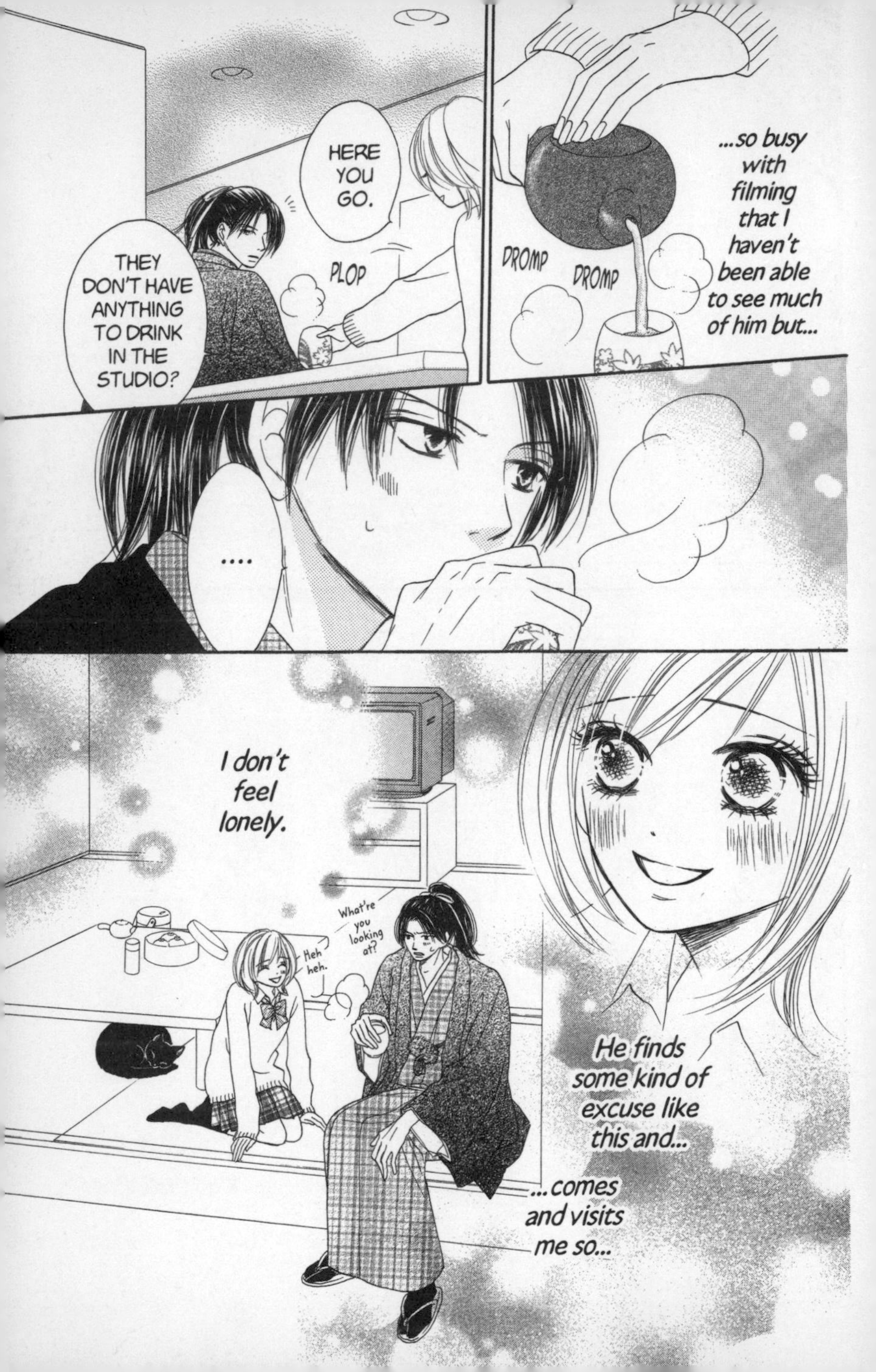

...so busy with filming that I haven't been able to see much of him but...
DROMP
DROMP
HERE YOU GO.
PLOP
THEY DON'T HAVE ANYTHING TO DRINK IN THE STUDIO?
....
He finds some kind of excuse like this and...
...comes and visits me so...
I don't feel lonely.
What're you looking at?
Heh heh.

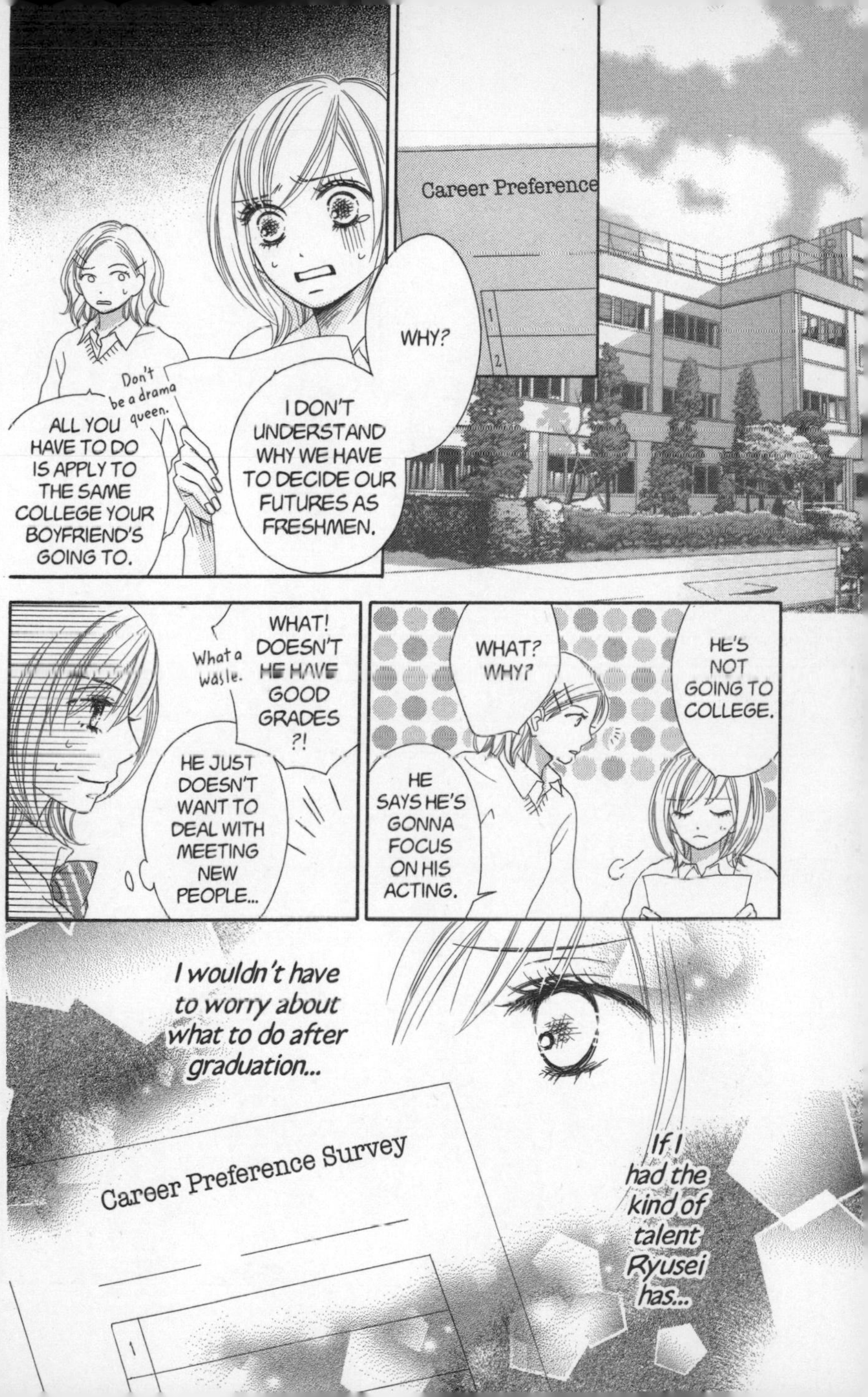
Career Preference
1
2
WHY?
I DON'T UNDERSTAND WHY WE HAVE TO DECIDE OUR FUTURES AS FRESHMEN.
ALL YOU HAVE TO DO IS APPLY TO THE SAME COLLEGE YOUR BOYFRIEND'S GOING TO.
Don't be a drama queen.
HE'S NOT GOING TO COLLEGE.
WHAT? WHY?
HE SAYS HE'S GONNA FOCUS ON HIS ACTING.
WHAT! DOESN'T HE HAVE GOOD GRADES?!
What a waste.
HE JUST DOESN'T WANT TO DEAL WITH MEETING NEW PEOPLE...
If I had the kind of talent Ryusei has...
I wouldn't have to worry about what to do after graduation...
Career Preference Survey
1

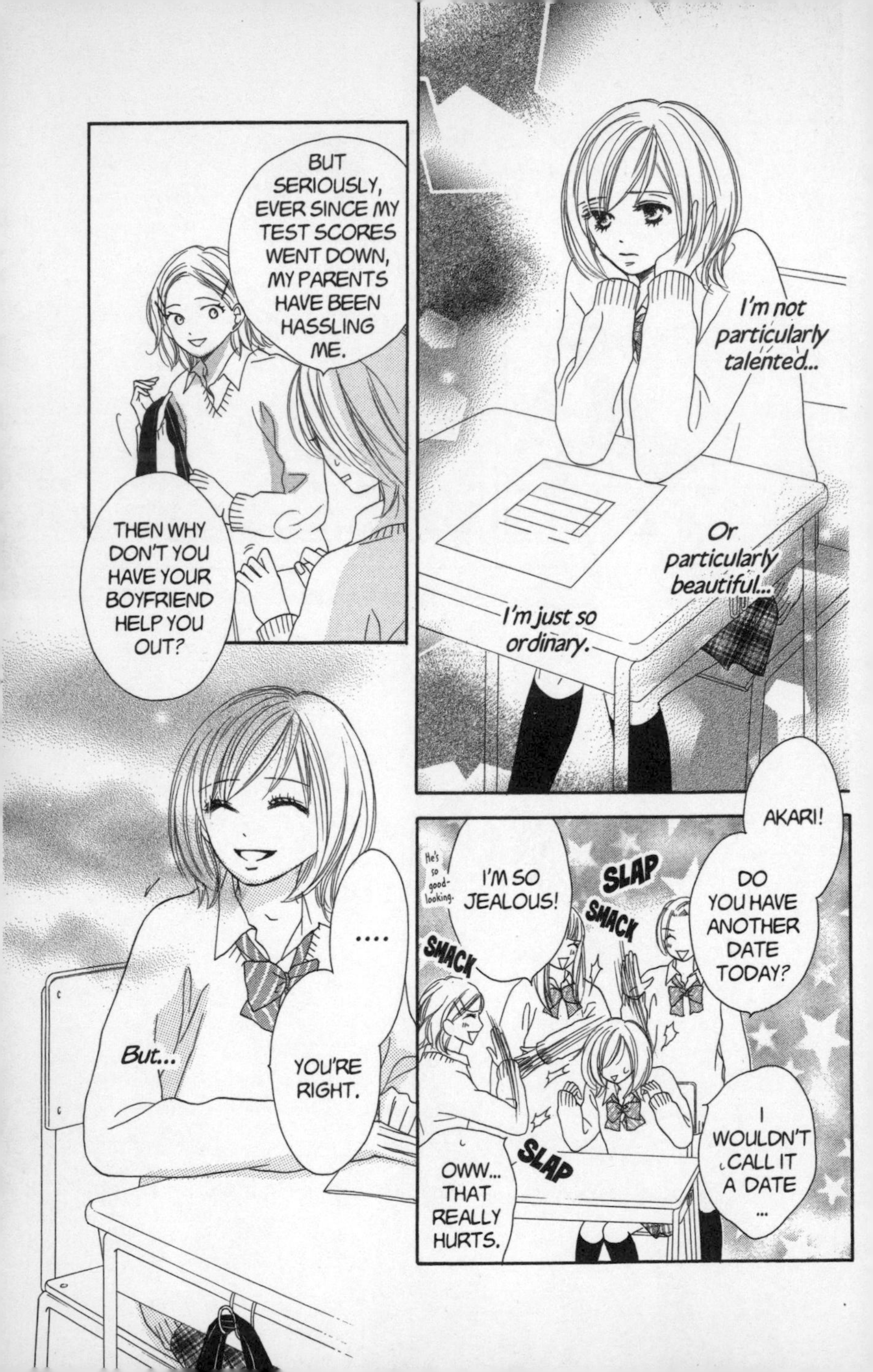
I'm not particularly talented...
Or particularly beautiful...
I'm just so ordinary.
AKARI!
DO YOU HAVE ANOTHER DATE TODAY?
I'M SO JEALOUS!
He's so good-looking.
SLAP
SMACK
SMACK
I WOULDN'T CALL IT A DATE ...
SLAP
OWW... THAT REALLY HURTS.
BUT SERIOUSLY, EVER SINCE MY TEST SCORES WENT DOWN, MY PARENTS HAVE BEEN HASSLING ME.
THEN WHY DON'T YOU HAVE YOUR BOYFRIEND HELP YOU OUT?
....
YOU'RE RIGHT.
But...

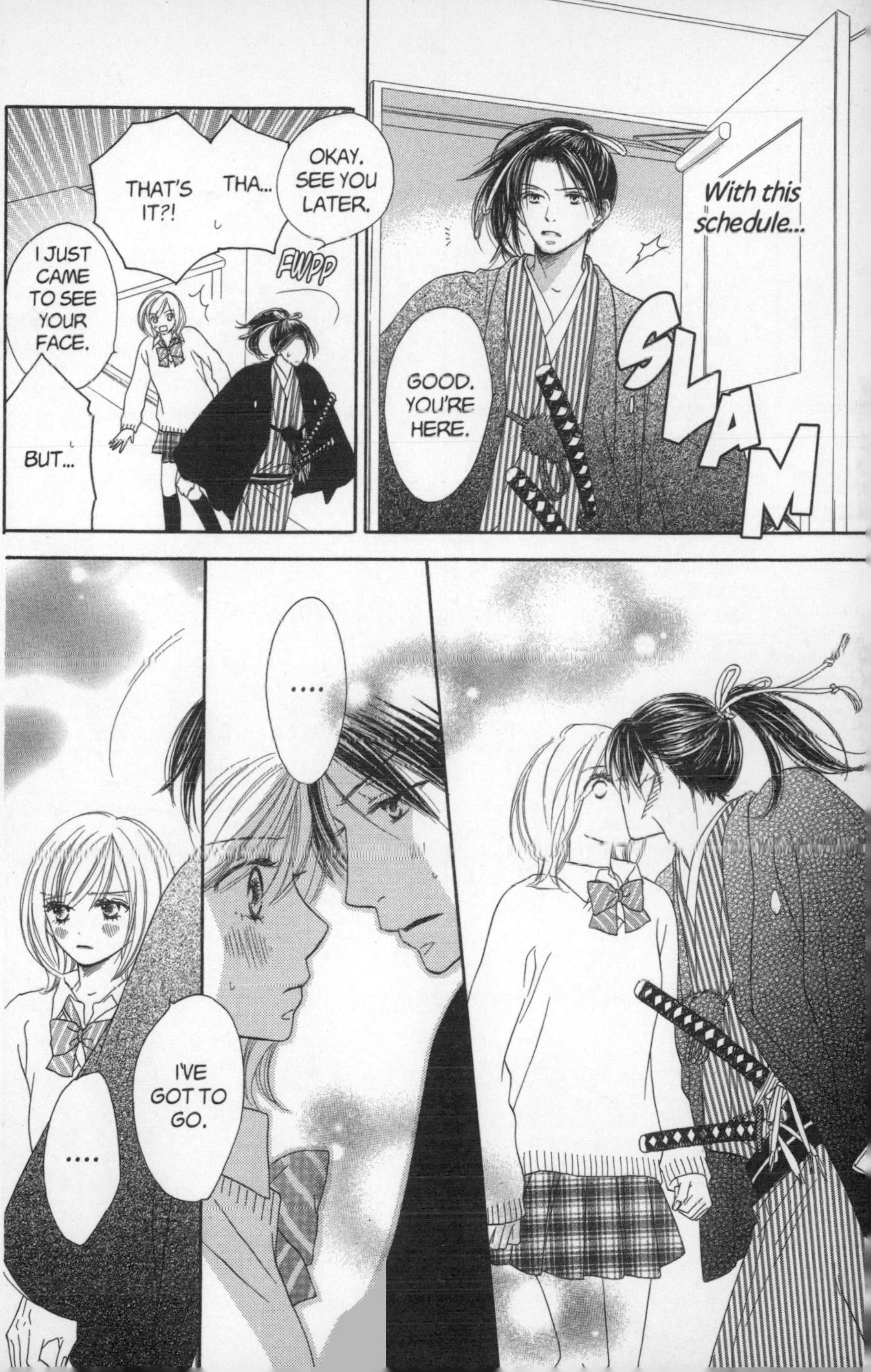
With this schedule...
SLAM
GOOD. YOU'RE HERE.
OKAY. SEE YOU LATER.
FWPP
THA...
THAT'S IT?!
I JUST CAME TO SEE YOUR FACE.
BUT...
....
I'VE GOT TO GO.
....

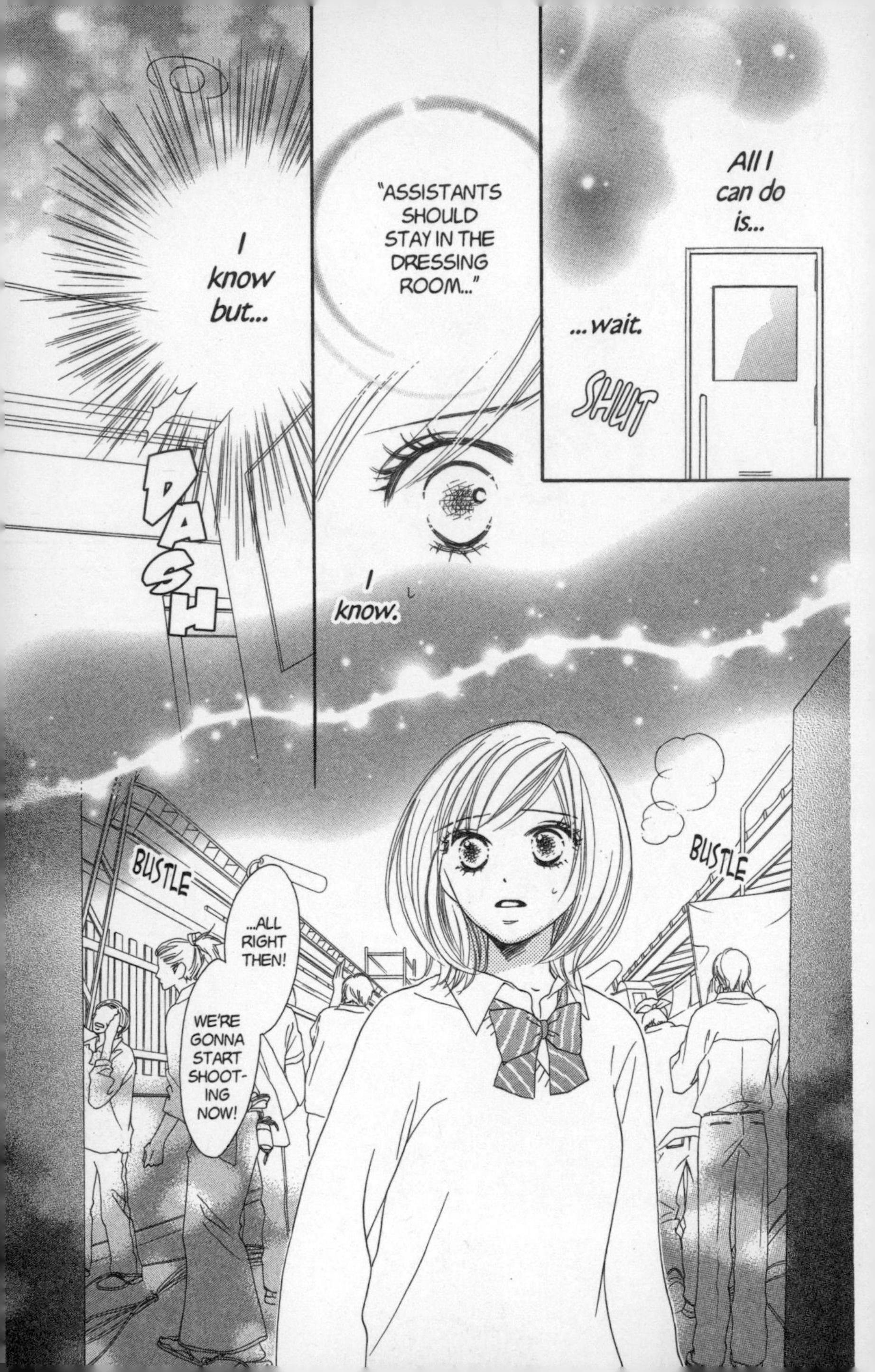
All I can do is...
...wait.
SHUT
"ASSISTANTS SHOULD STAY IN THE DRESSING ROOM..."
I know.
I know but...
DASH
BUSTLE
...ALL RIGHT THEN!
WE'RE GONNA START SHOOT-ING NOW!
BUSTLE

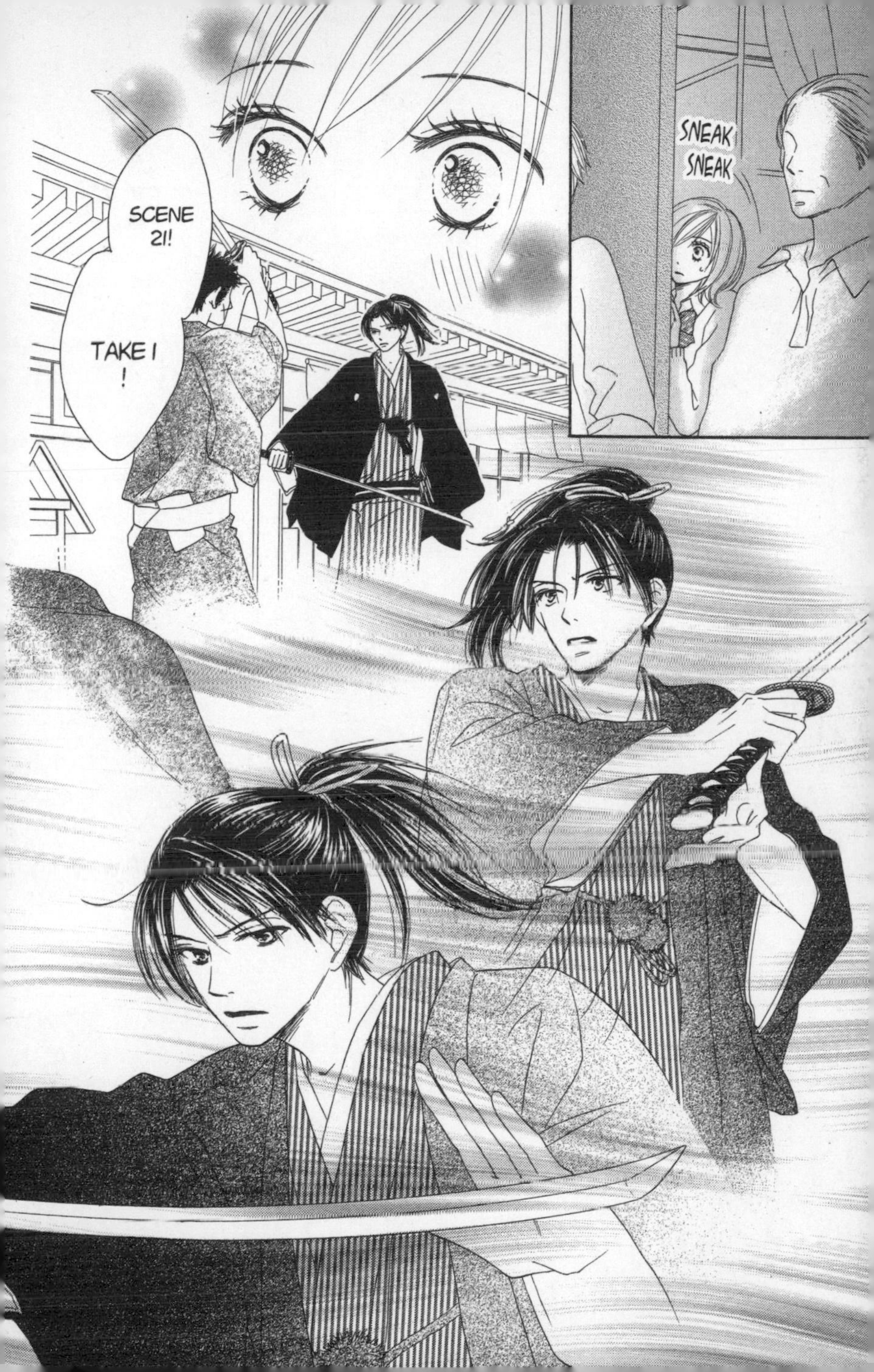
SNEAK SNEAK
SCENE 21!
TAKE 1!

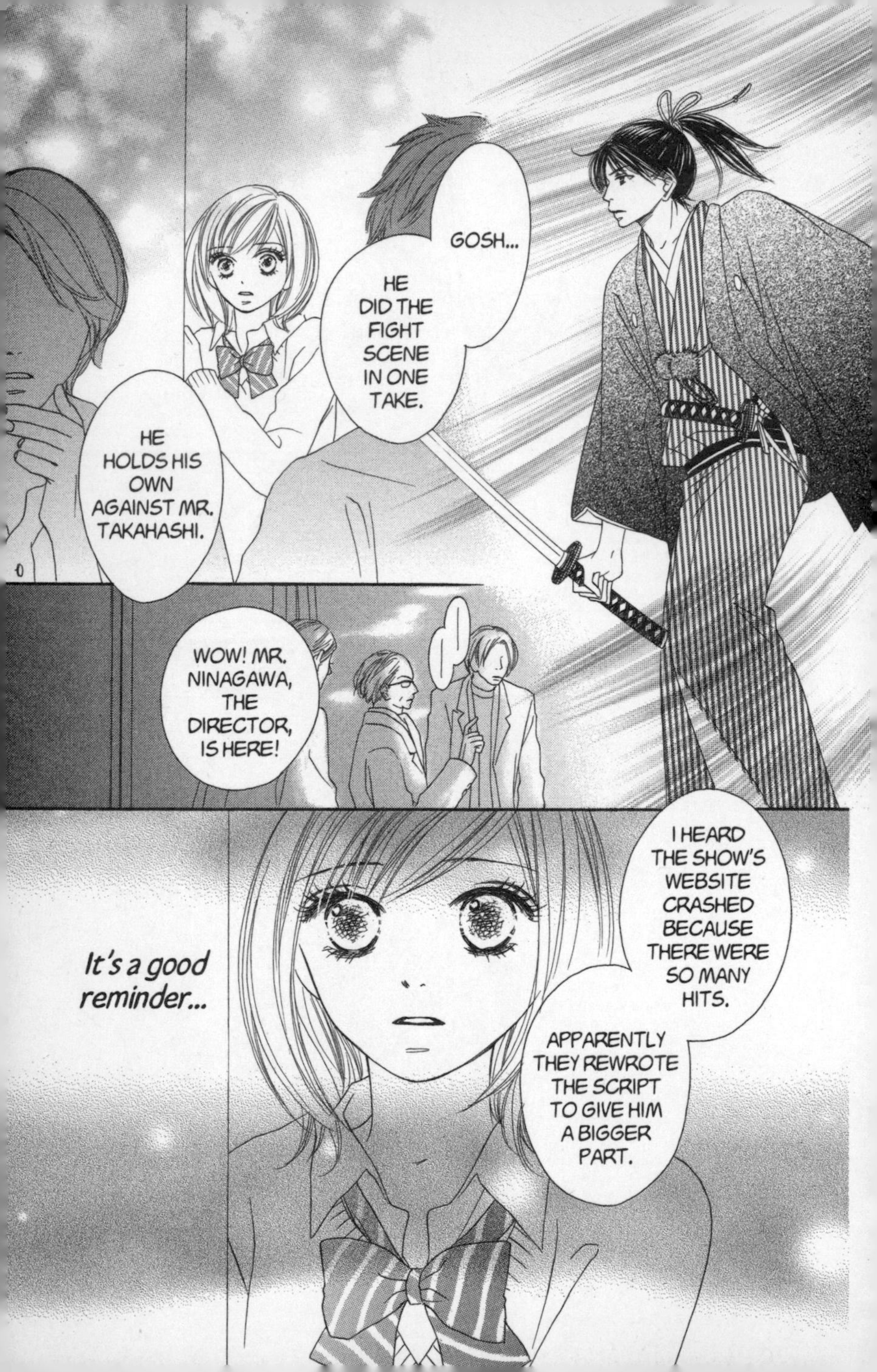
GOSH...
HE DID THE FIGHT SCENE IN ONE TAKE.
HE HOLDS HIS OWN AGAINST MR. TAKAHASHI.
!
WOW! MR. NINAGAWA, THE DIRECTOR, IS HERE!
I HEARD THE SHOW'S WEBSITE CRASHED BECAUSE THERE WERE SO MANY HITS.
APPARENTLY THEY REWROTE THE SCRIPT TO GIVE HIM A BIGGER PART.
It's a good reminder...

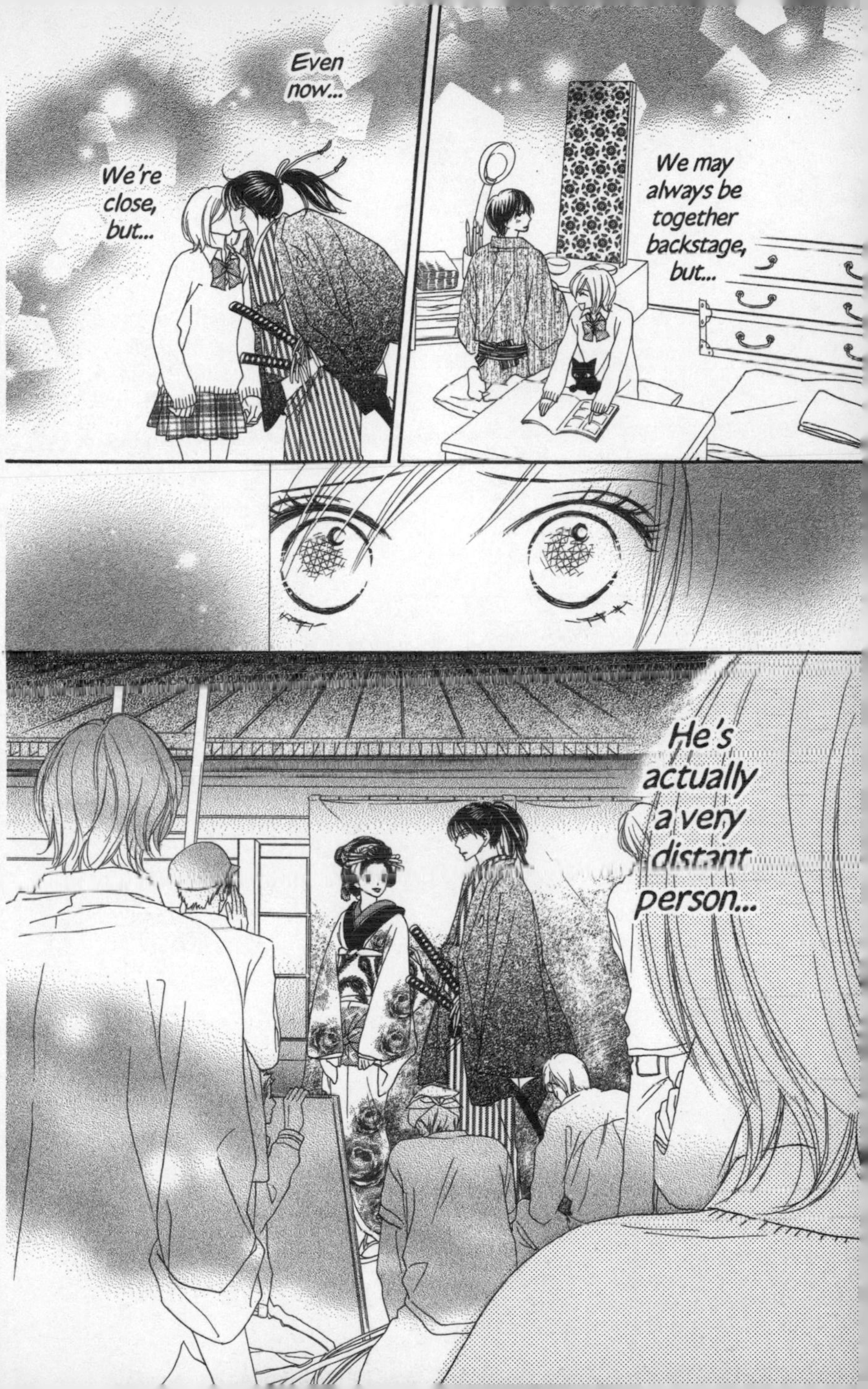
We may always be together backstage, but...
Even now...
We're close, but...
He's actually a very distant person...

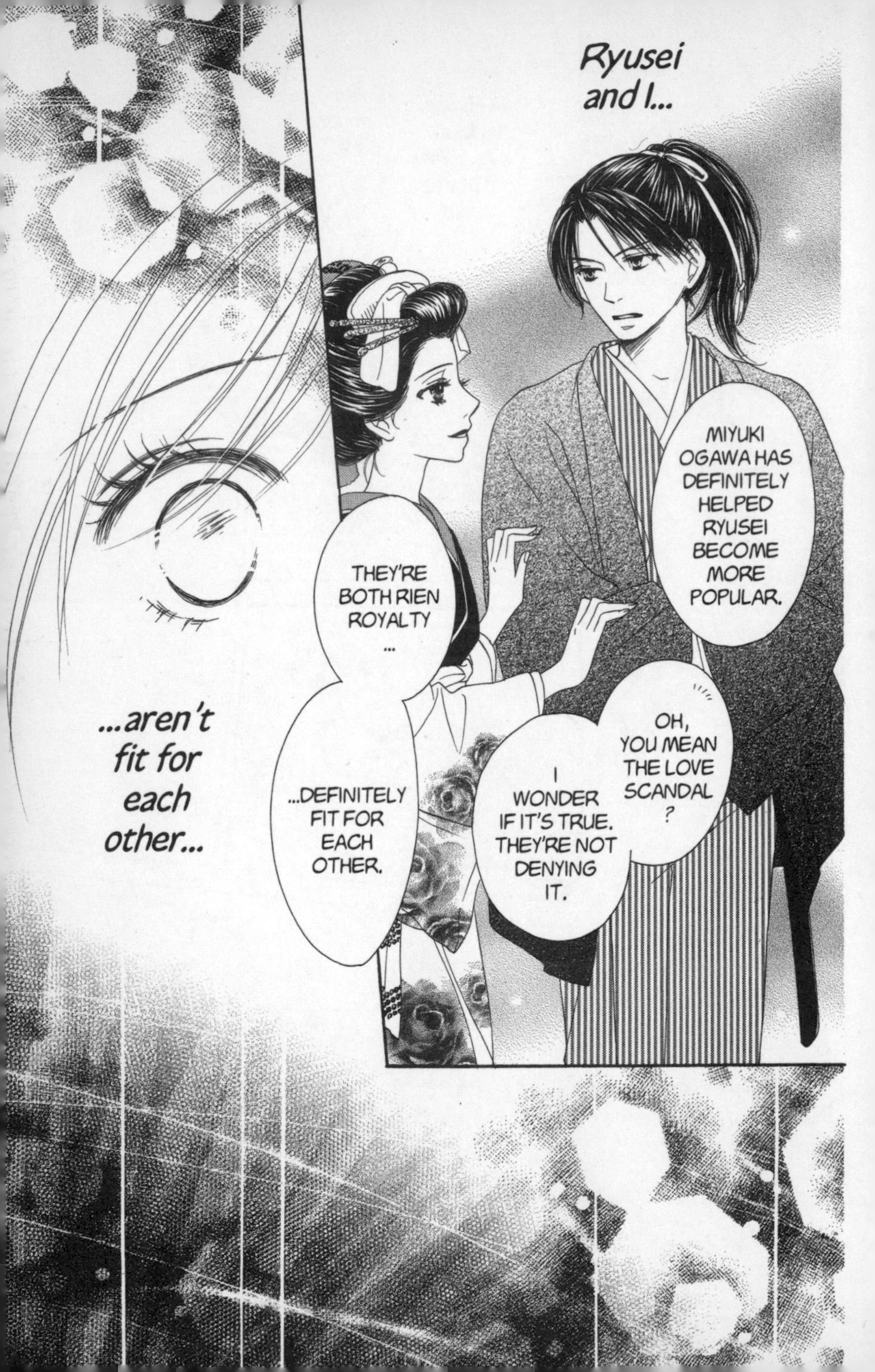
Ryusei and I...
MIYUKI OGAWA HAS DEFINITELY HELPED RYUSEI BECOME MORE POPULAR.
THEY'RE BOTH RIEN ROYALTY ...
...DEFINITELY FIT FOR EACH OTHER.
OH, YOU MEAN THE LOVE SCANDAL ?
I WONDER IF IT'S TRUE. THEY'RE NOT DENYING IT.
...aren't fit for each other...

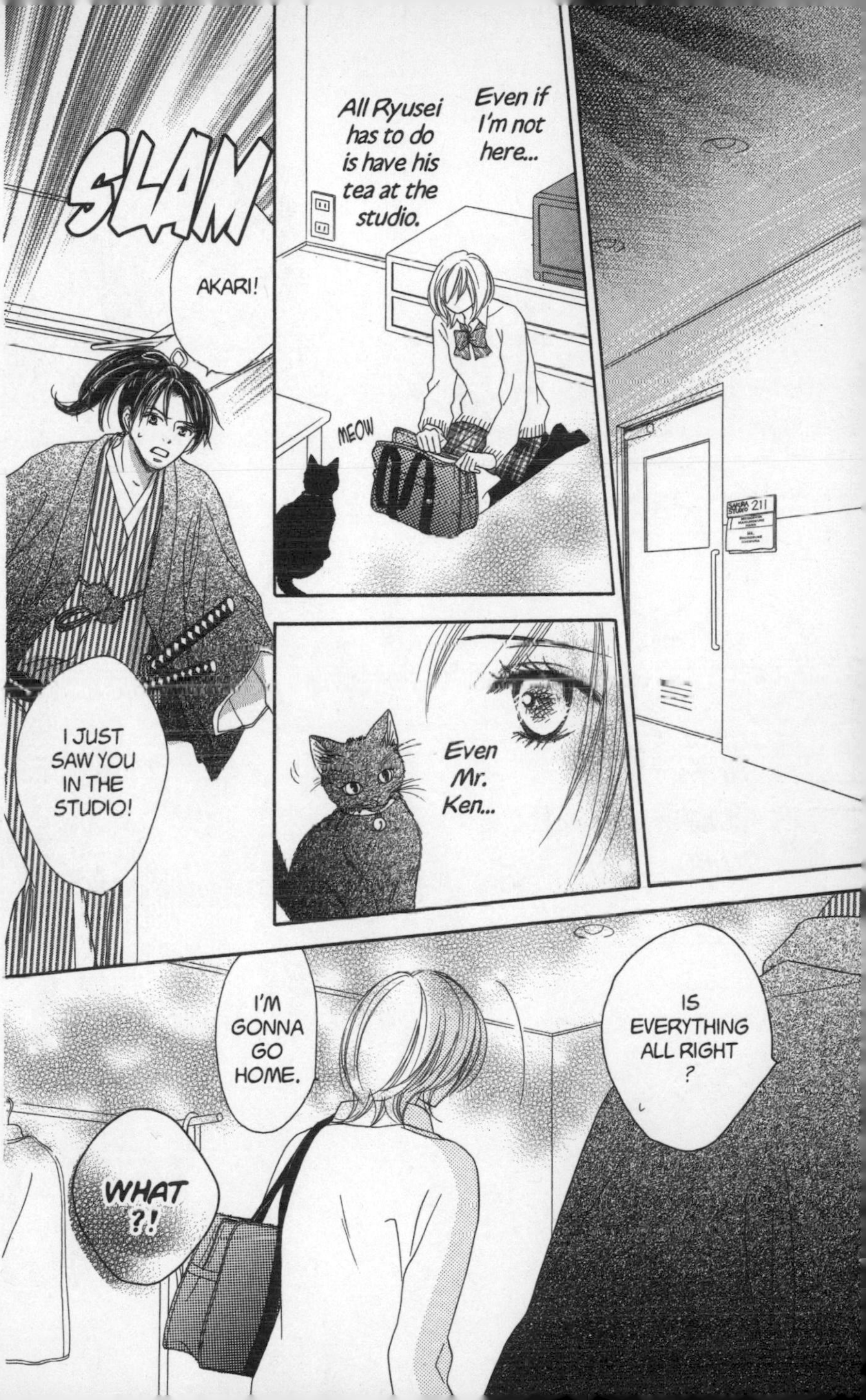

Even if I'm not here...
All Ryusei has to do is have his tea at the studio.
MEOW
Even Mr. Ken...
SLAM
AKARI!
I JUST SAW YOU IN THE STUDIO!
IS EVERYTHING ALL RIGHT?
I'M GONNA GO HOME.
WHAT?!

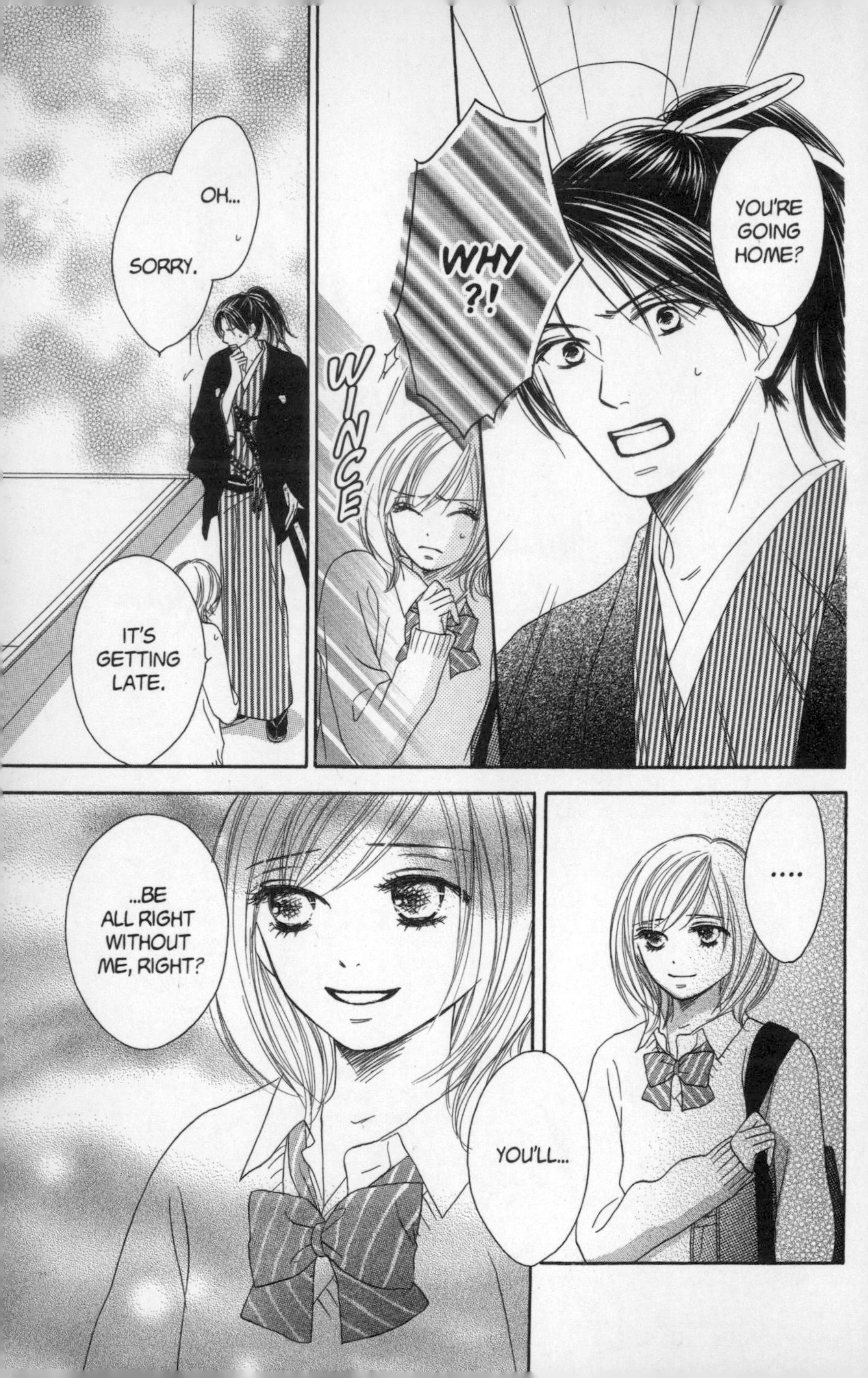
YOU'RE GOING HOME?
WHY?!
WINCE
OH... SORRY.
IT'S GETTING LATE.
....
YOU'LL...
...BE ALL RIGHT WITHOUT ME, RIGHT?

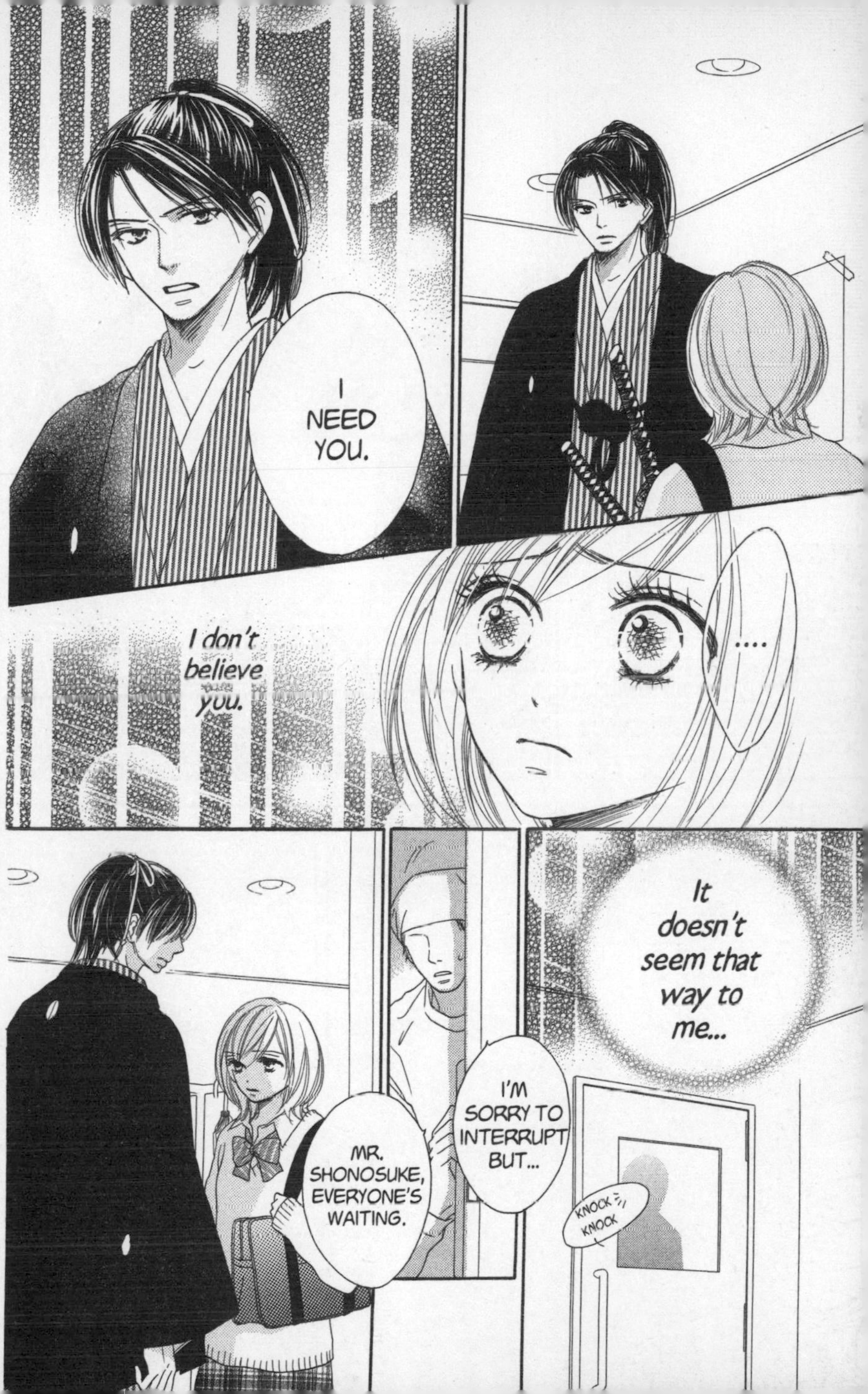
I NEED YOU.
....
I don't believe you.
It doesn't seem that way to me...
KNOCK KNOCK
I'M SORRY TO INTERRUPT BUT...
MR. SHONOSUKE, EVERYONE'S WAITING.

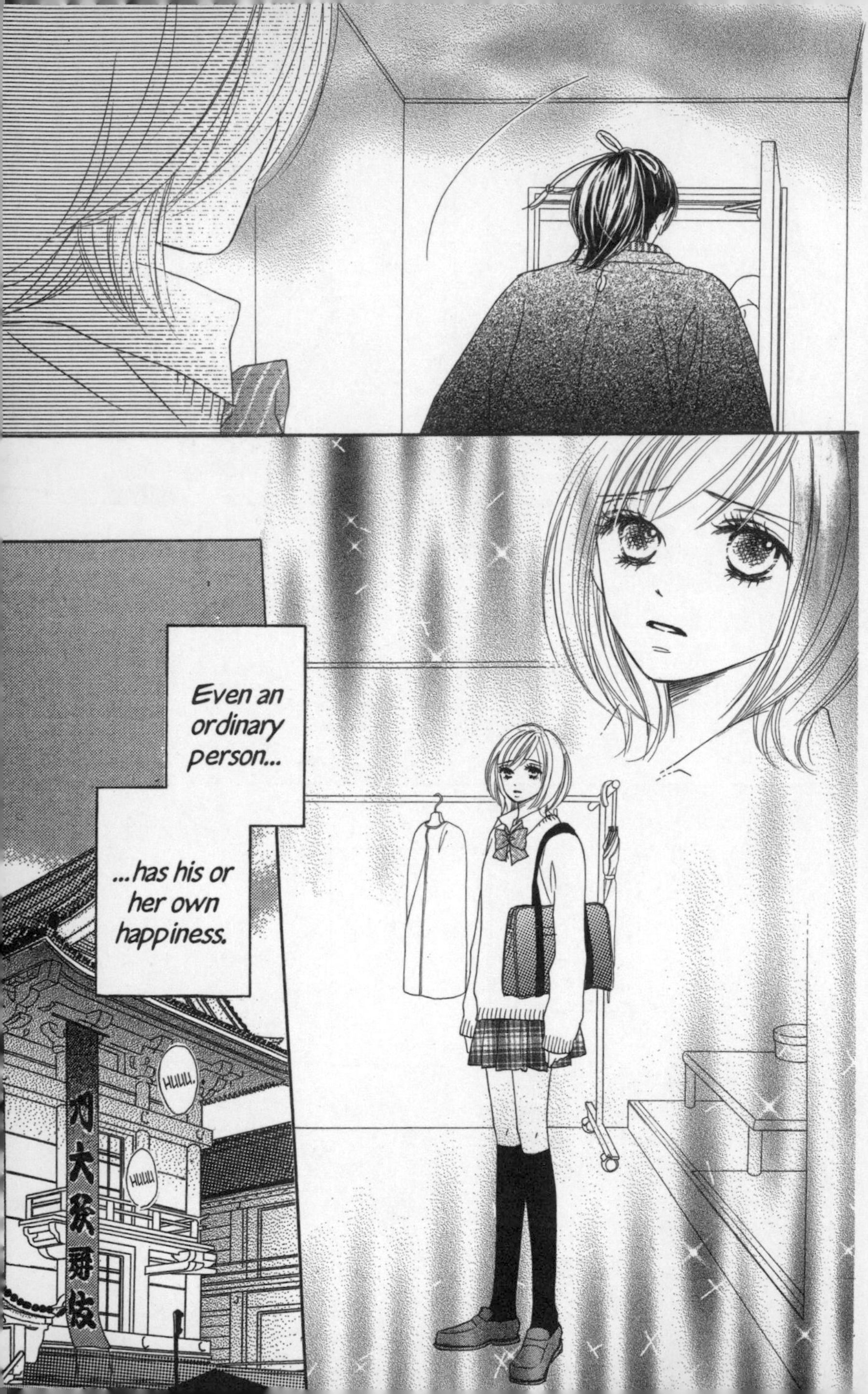
Even an ordinary person...
...has his or her own happiness.
HUUU.
HUUU

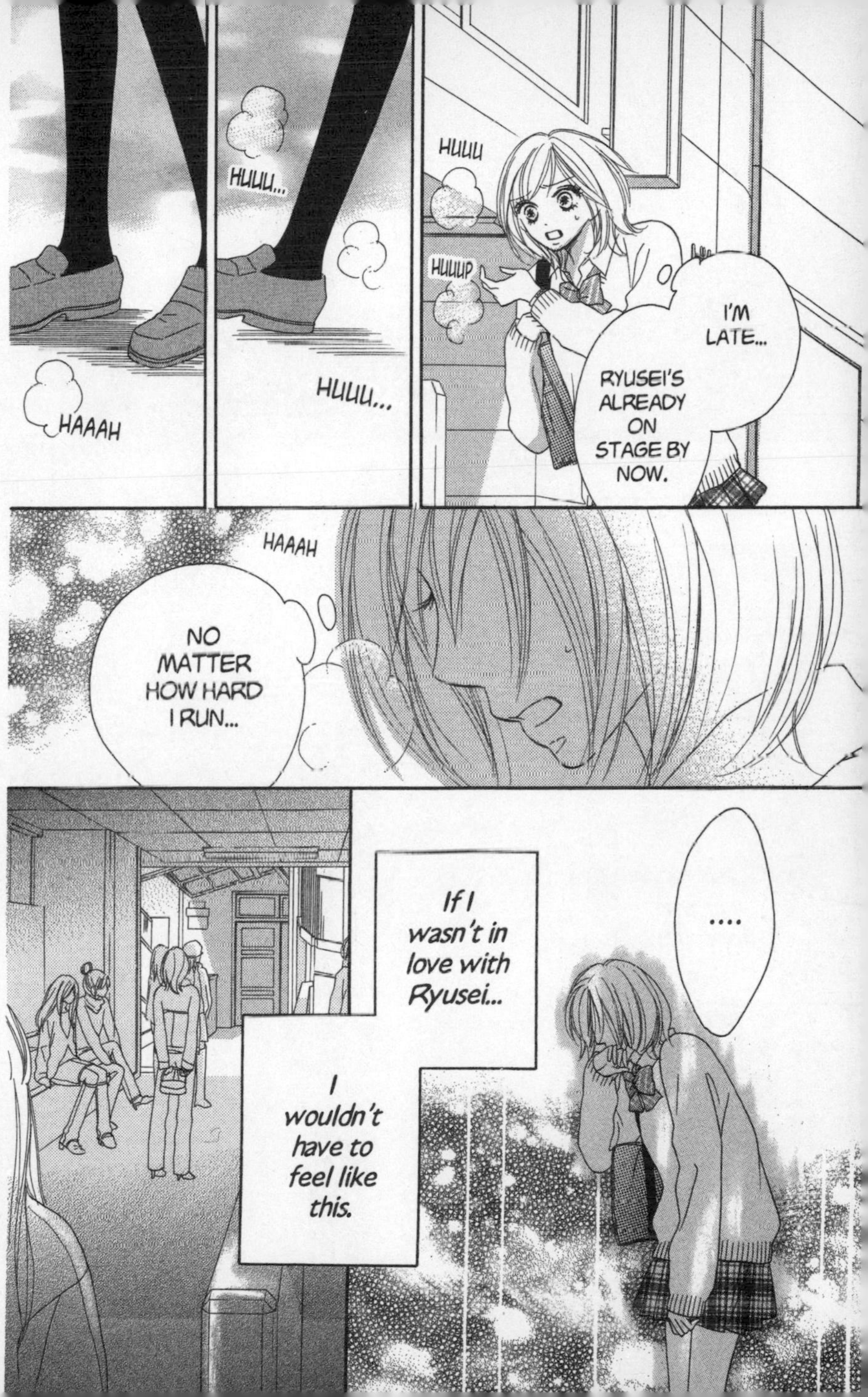
HUUU
HUUUP
I'M LATE...
RYUSEI'S ALREADY ON STAGE BY NOW.
HUUU...
HUUU...
HAAAH
HAAAH
NO MATTER HOW HARD I RUN...
....
If I wasn't in love with Ryusei...
I wouldn't have to feel like this.

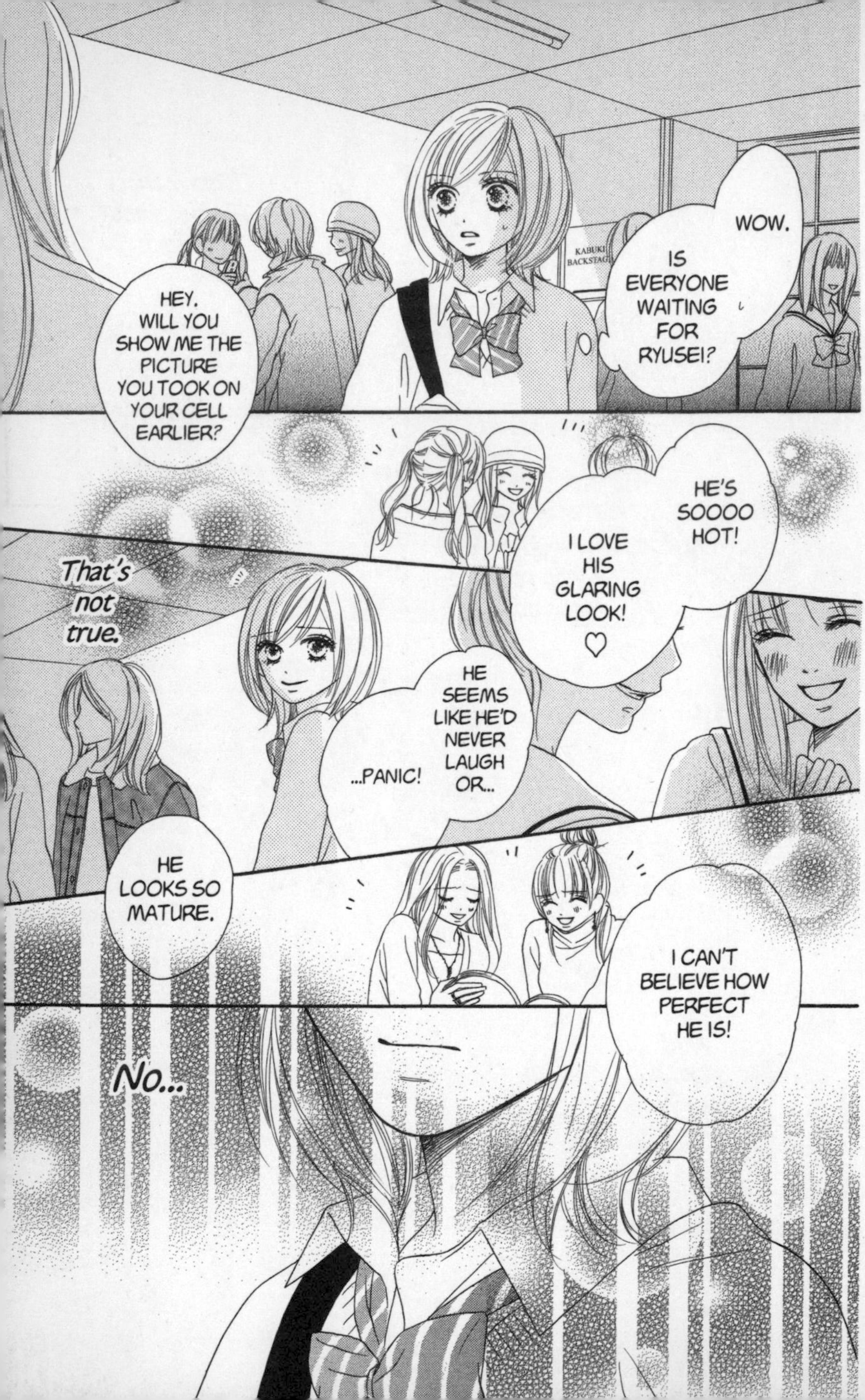

WOW.
IS EVERYONE WAITING FOR RYUSEI?
HEY. WILL YOU SHOW ME THE PICTURE YOU TOOK ON YOUR CELL EARLIER?
HE'S SOOOO HOT!
I LOVE HIS GLARING LOOK! ♡
HE SEEMS LIKE HE'D NEVER LAUGH OR...
...PANIC!
That's not true.
I CAN'T BELIEVE HOW PERFECT HE IS!
HE LOOKS SO MATURE.
No...

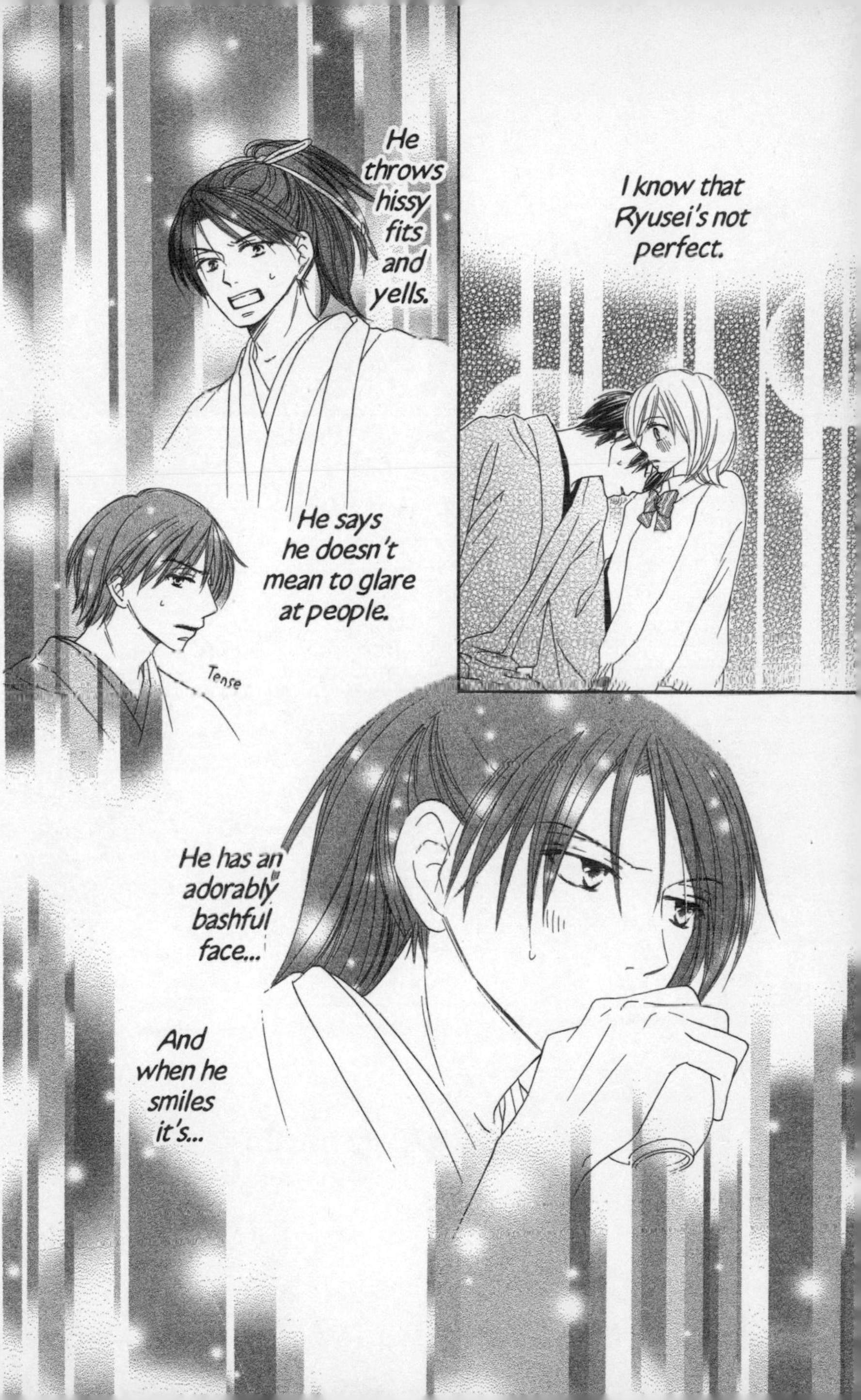
I know that Ryusei's not perfect.
He throws hissy fits and yells.
He says he doesn't mean to glare at people.
Tense
He has an adorably bashful face...
And when he smiles it's...

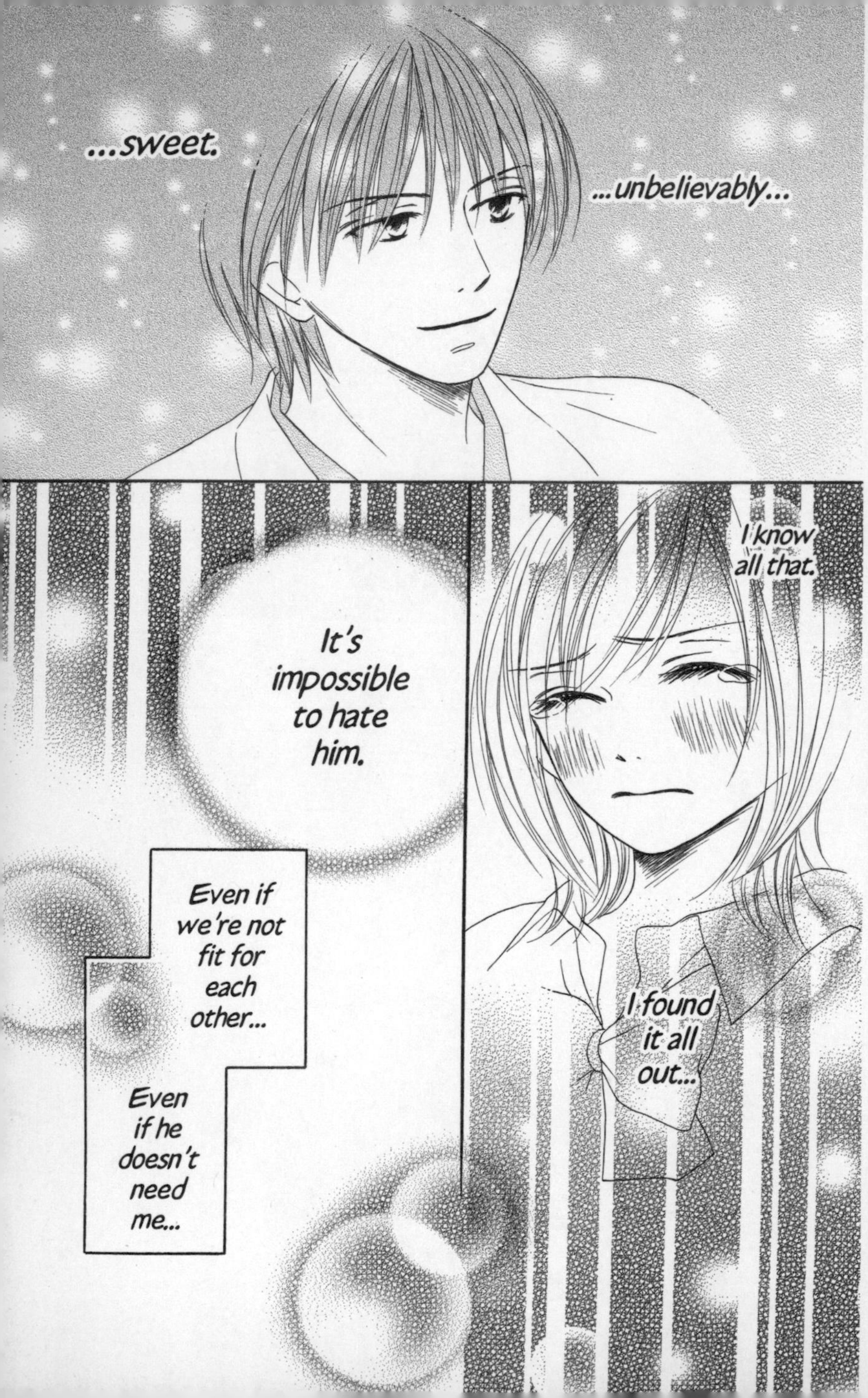
...unbelievably...
...sweet.
I know all that.
I found it all out...
It's impossible to hate him.
Even if we're not fit for each other...
Even if he doesn't need me...

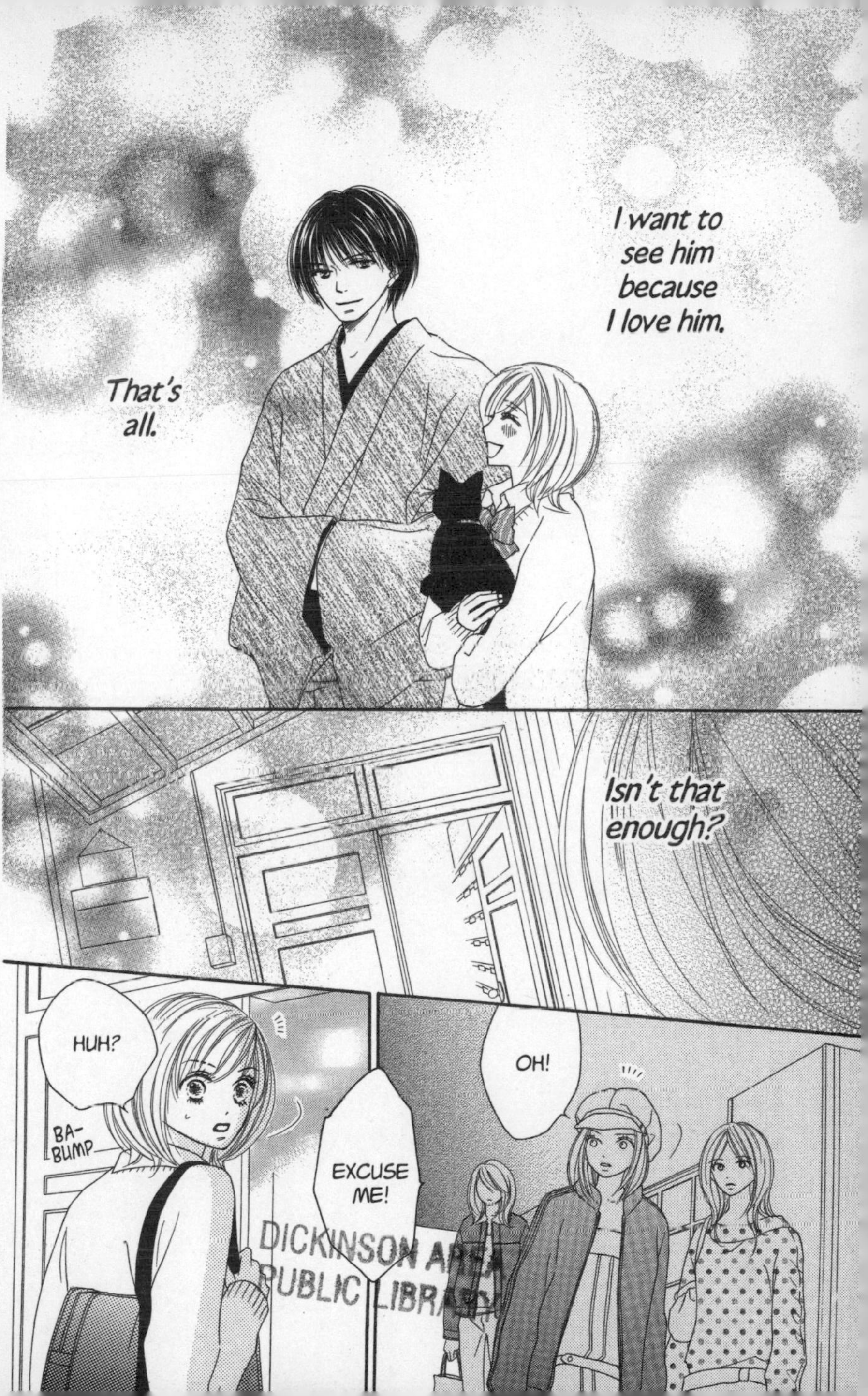
I want to see him because I love him.
That's all.
Isn't that enough?
OH!
EXCUSE ME!
HUH?
BA-BUMP
DICKINSON AREA
PUBLIC LIBRAR

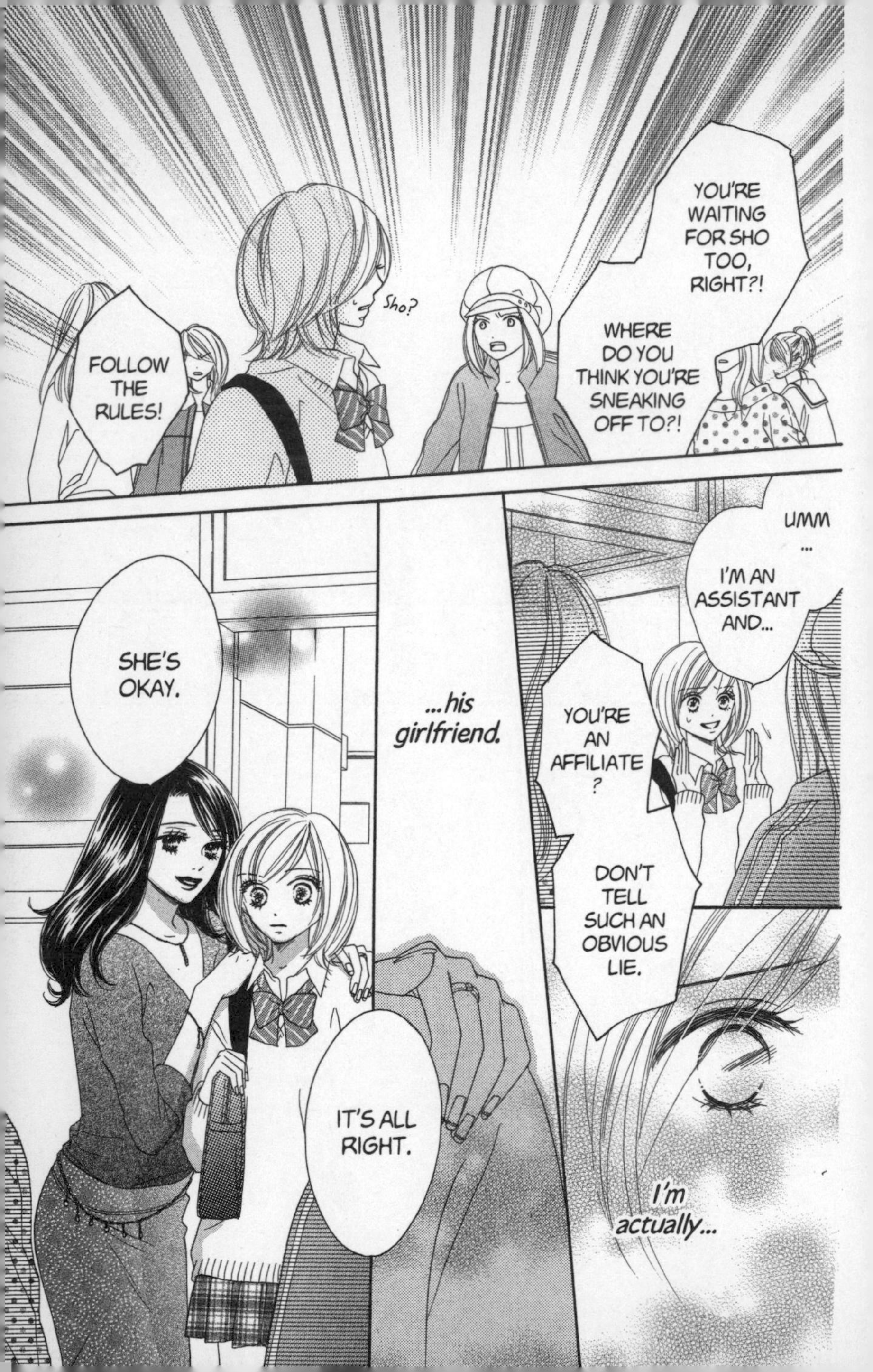
YOU'RE WAITING FOR SHO TOO, RIGHT?!
WHERE DO YOU THINK YOU'RE SNEAKING OFF TO?!
Sho?
FOLLOW THE RULES!
UMM ... I'M AN ASSISTANT AND...
YOU'RE AN AFFILIATE?
DON'T TELL SUCH AN OBVIOUS LIE.
I'm actually...
...his girlfriend.
SHE'S OKAY.
IT'S ALL RIGHT.

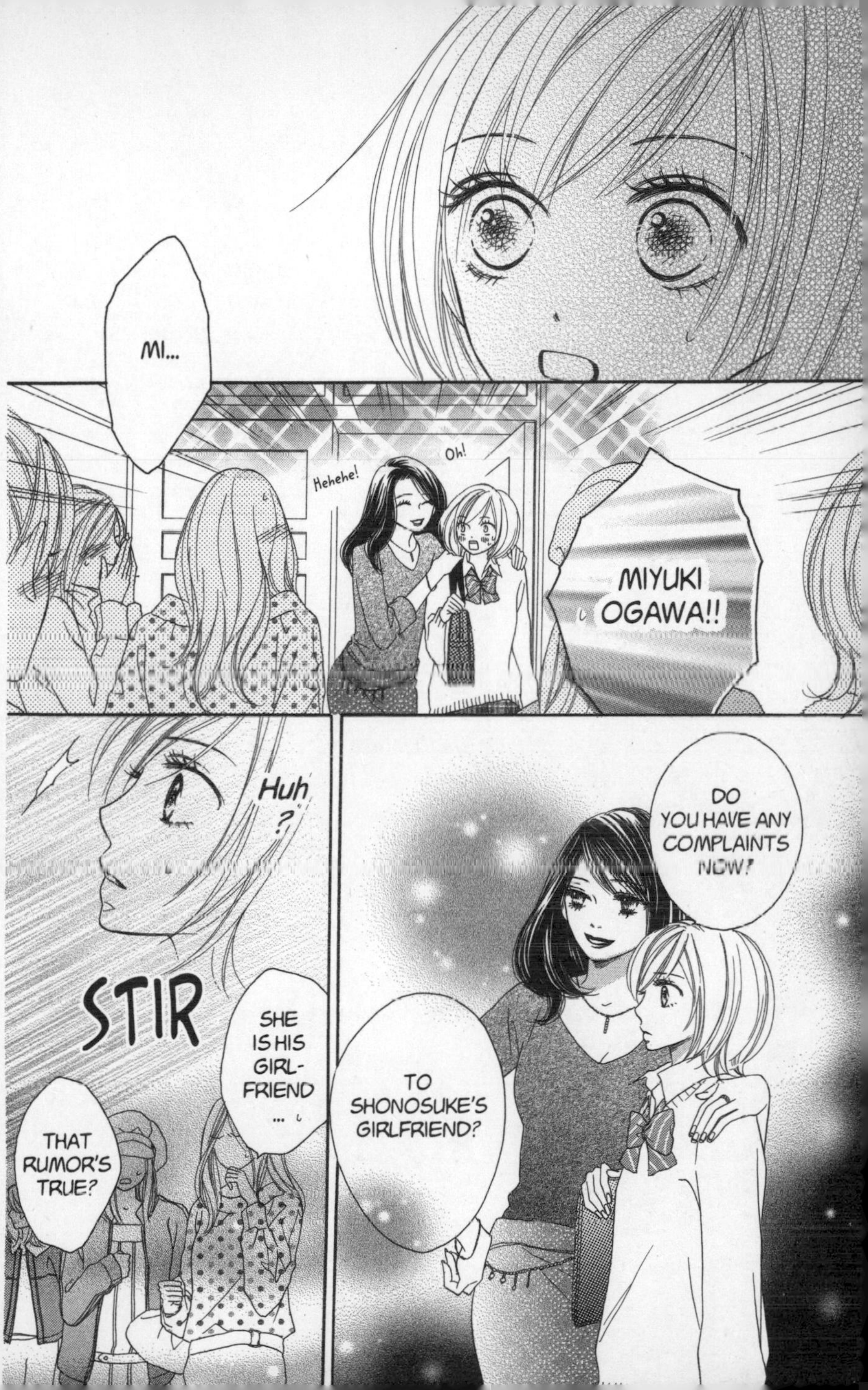
MI...
MIYUKI OGAWA!!
Oh!
Hehehe!
DO YOU HAVE ANY COMPLAINTS NOW?
TO SHONOSUKE'S GIRLFRIEND?
Huh?
STIR
SHE IS HIS GIRLFRIEND...
THAT RUMOR'S TRUE?

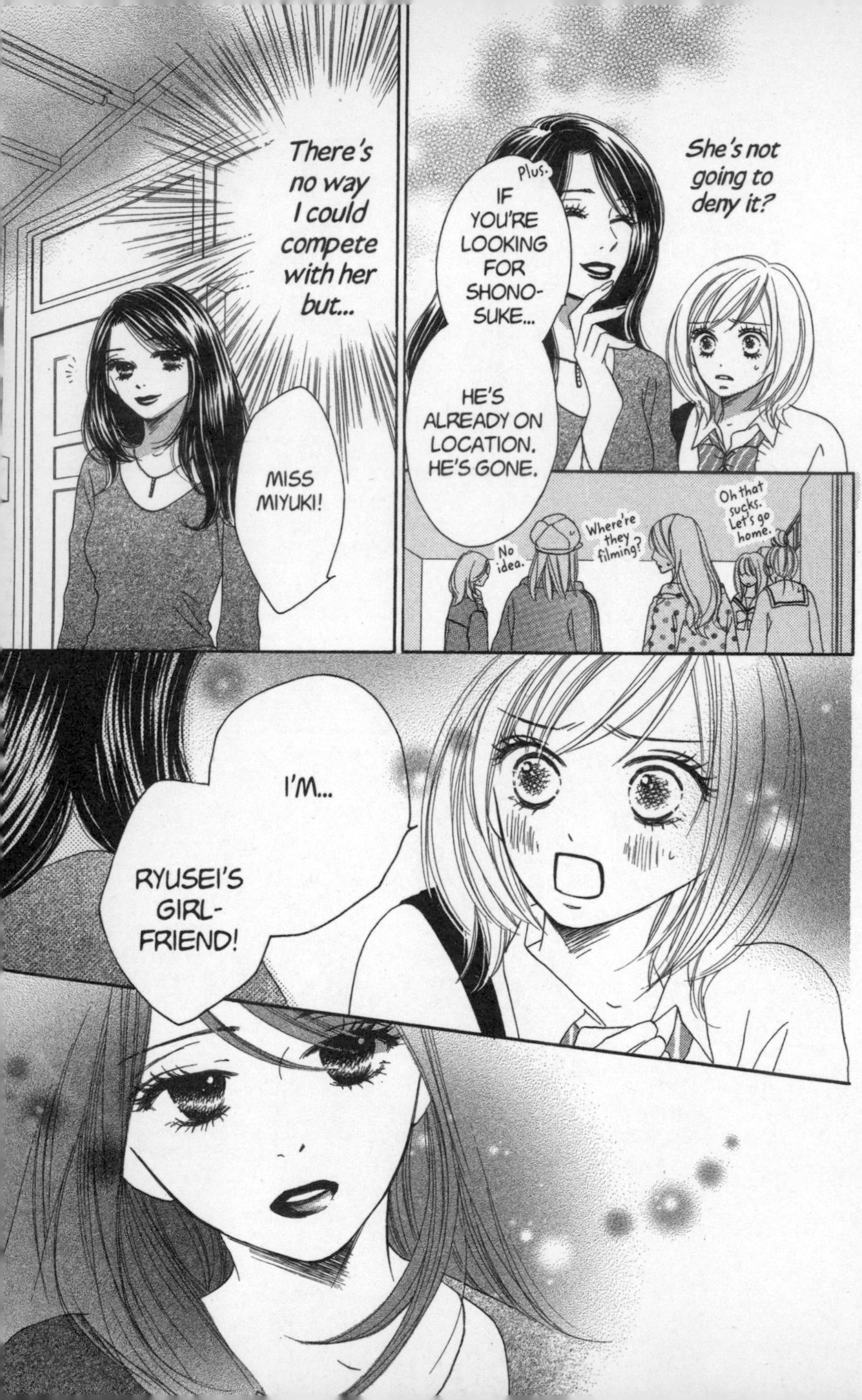
She's not going to deny it?
Plus.
IF YOU'RE LOOKING FOR SHONOSUKE...
HE'S ALREADY ON LOCATION. HE'S GONE.
Oh that sucks. Let's go home.
Where're they filming?
No idea.
There's no way I could compete with her but...
MISS MIYUKI!
I'M...
RYUSEI'S GIRLFRIEND!

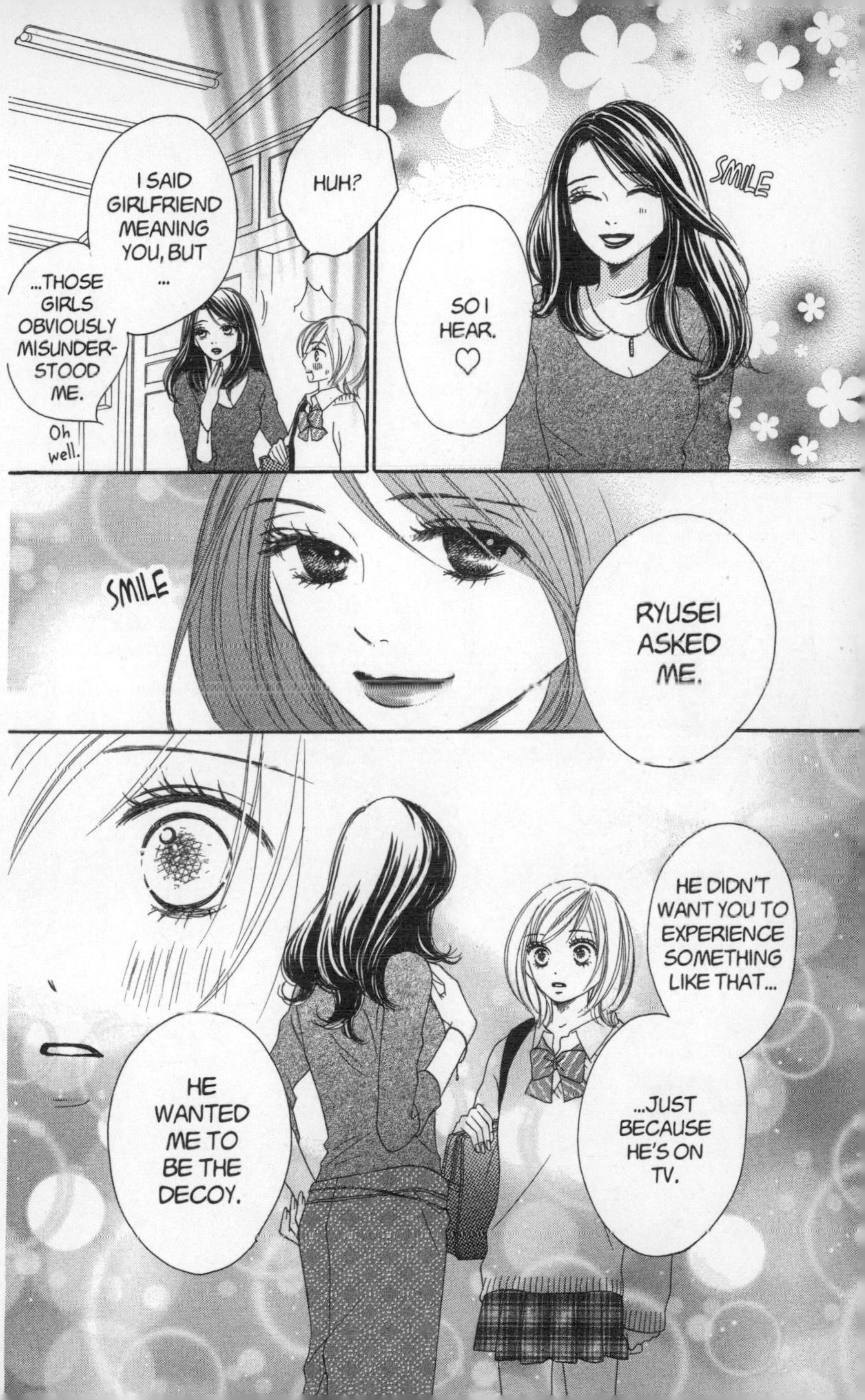
SMILE
SO I HEAR. ♡
HUH?
I SAID GIRLFRIEND MEANING YOU, BUT ...
...THOSE GIRLS OBVIOUSLY MISUNDERSTOOD ME.
Oh well.
RYUSEI ASKED ME.
SMILE
HE DIDN'T WANT YOU TO EXPERIENCE SOMETHING LIKE THAT...
...JUST BECAUSE HE'S ON TV.
HE WANTED ME TO BE THE DECOY.

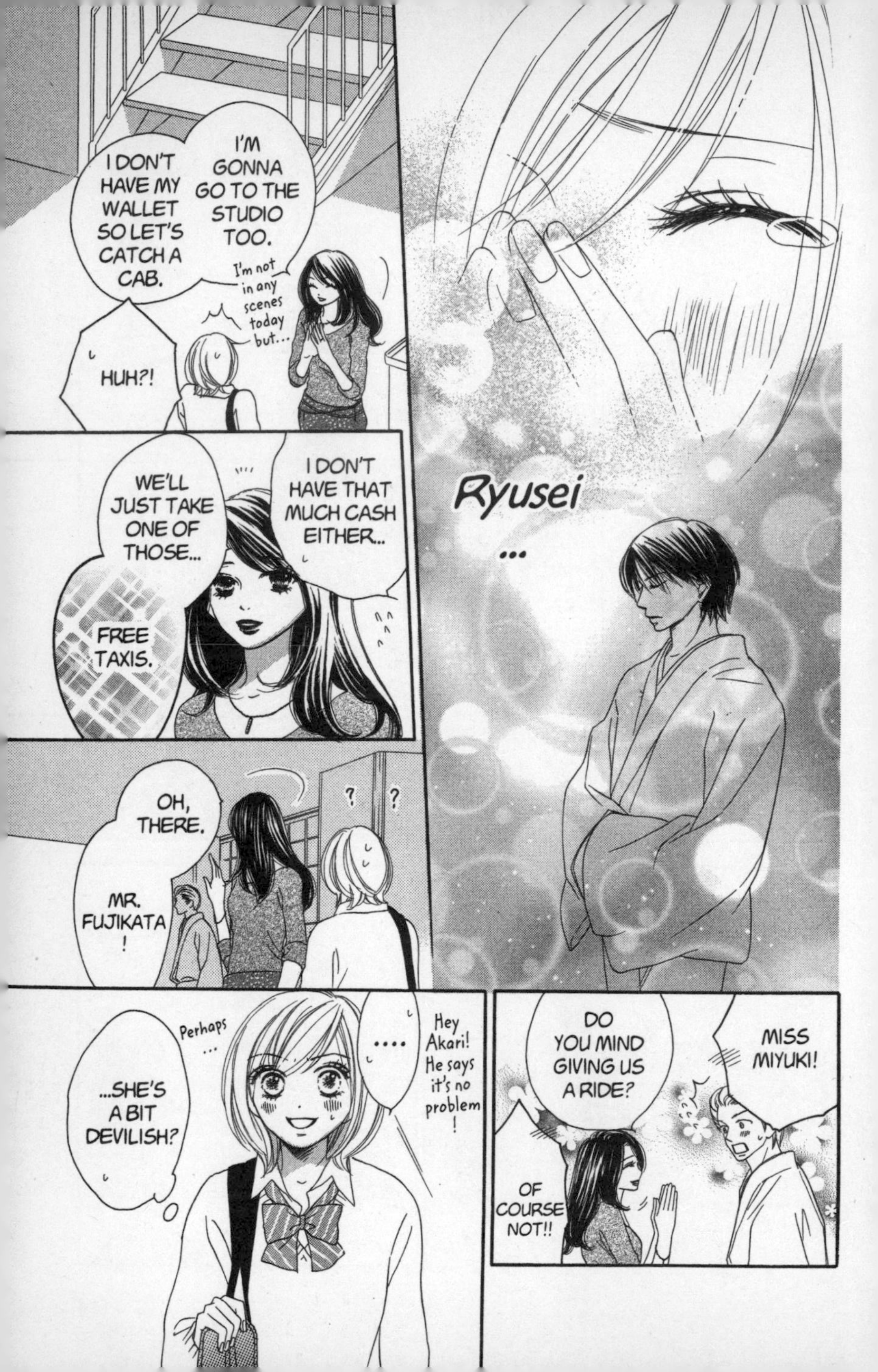
Ryusei ...
I'M GONNA GO TO THE STUDIO TOO.
I'm not in any scenes today but...
I DON'T HAVE MY WALLET SO LET'S CATCH A CAB.
HUH?!
I DON'T HAVE THAT MUCH CASH EITHER...
WE'LL JUST TAKE ONE OF THOSE...
FREE TAXIS.
OH, THERE.
MR. FUJIKATA!
MISS MIYUKI!
DO YOU MIND GIVING US A RIDE?
OF COURSE NOT!!
Hey Akari! He says it's no problem!
....
Perhaps...
...SHE'S A BIT DEVILISH?

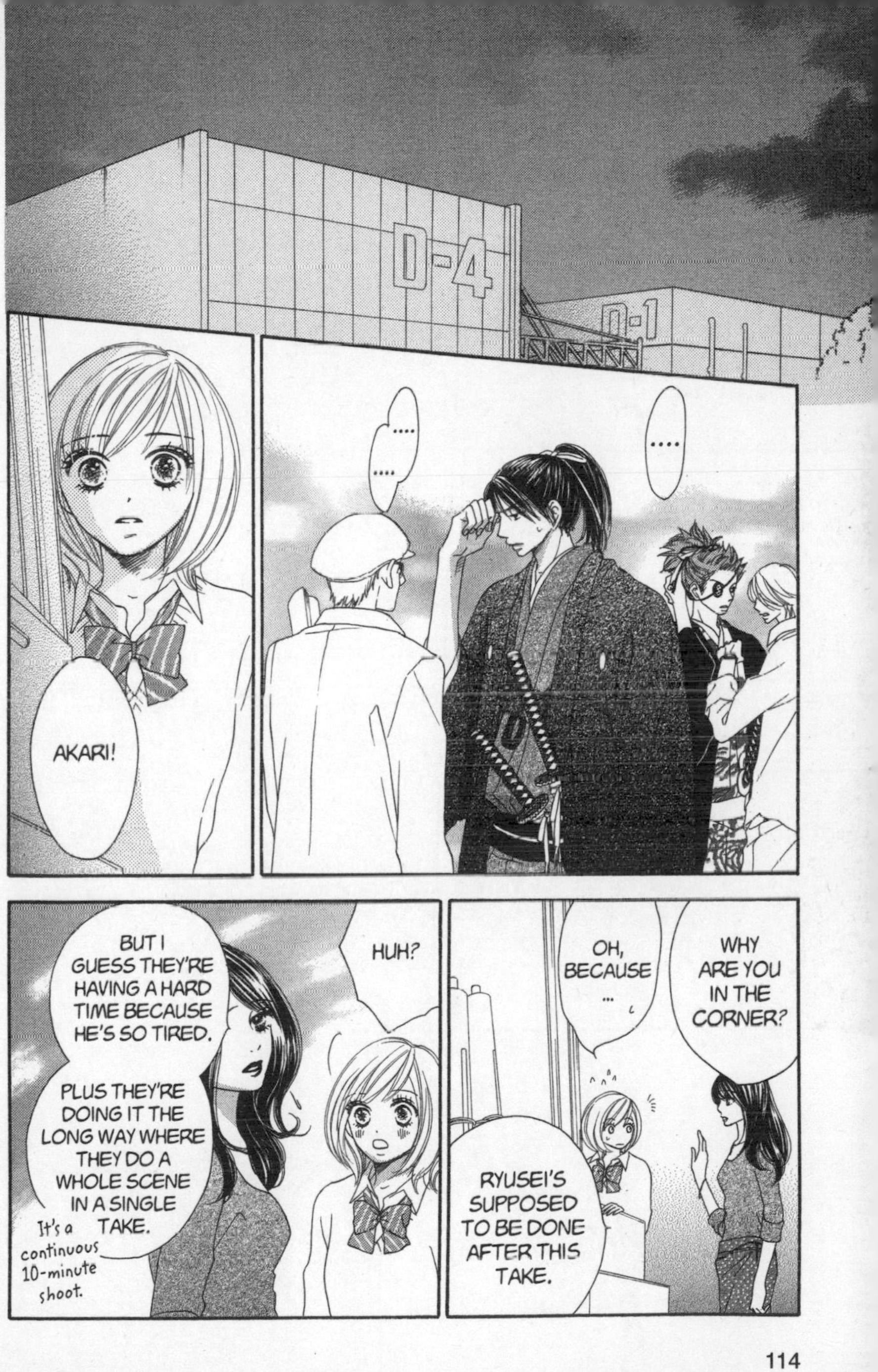
.....
.....
.....
AKARI!
WHY ARE YOU IN THE CORNER?
OH, BECAUSE ...
RYUSEI'S SUPPOSED TO BE DONE AFTER THIS TAKE.
HUH?
BUT I GUESS THEY'RE HAVING A HARD TIME BECAUSE HE'S SO TIRED.
PLUS THEY'RE DOING IT THE LONG WAY WHERE THEY DO A WHOLE SCENE IN A SINGLE TAKE.
It's a continuous 10-minute shoot.

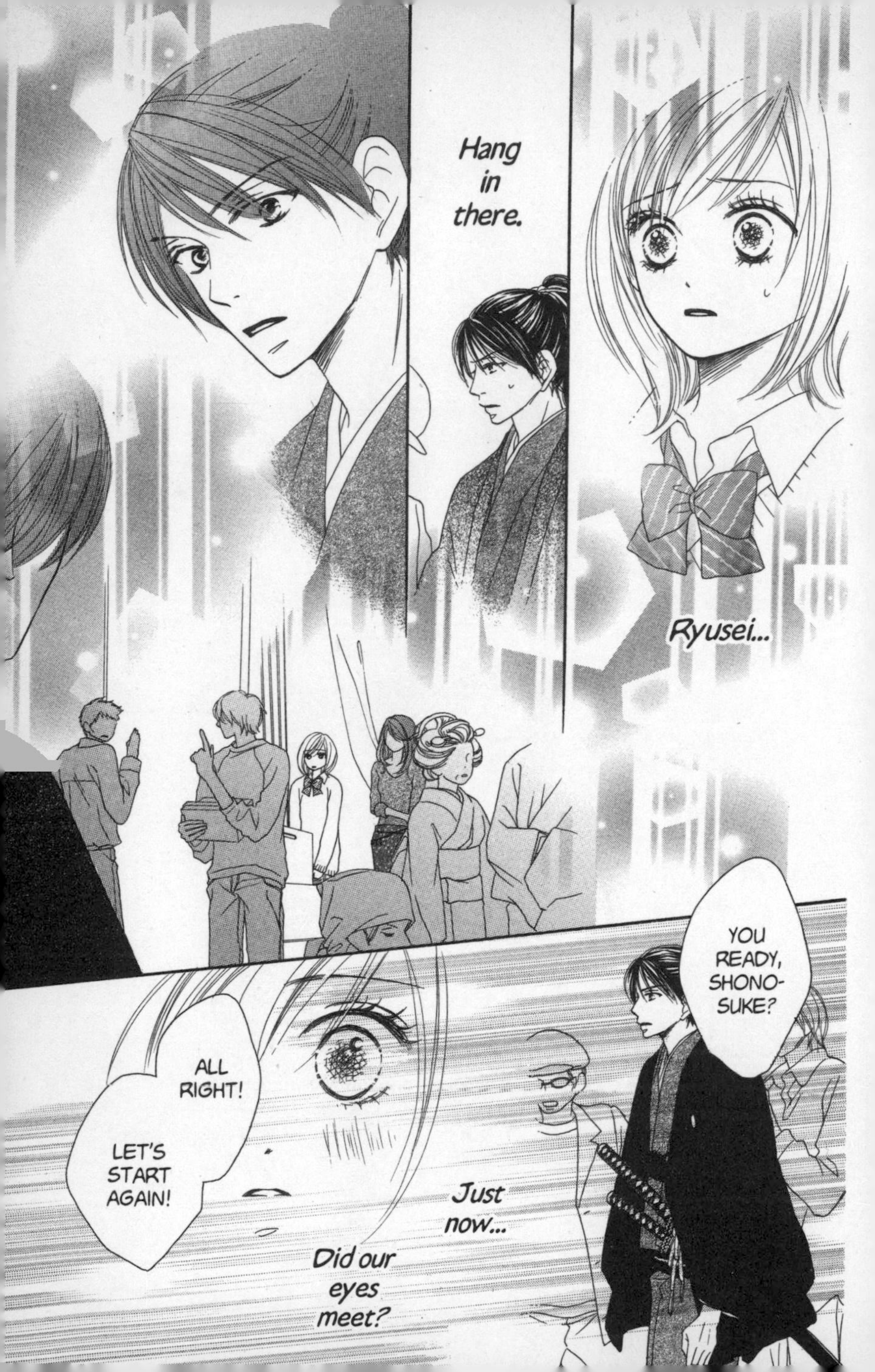
Ryusei...
Hang in there.
YOU READY, SHONOSUKE?
ALL RIGHT!
LET'S START AGAIN!
Just now...
Did our eyes meet?

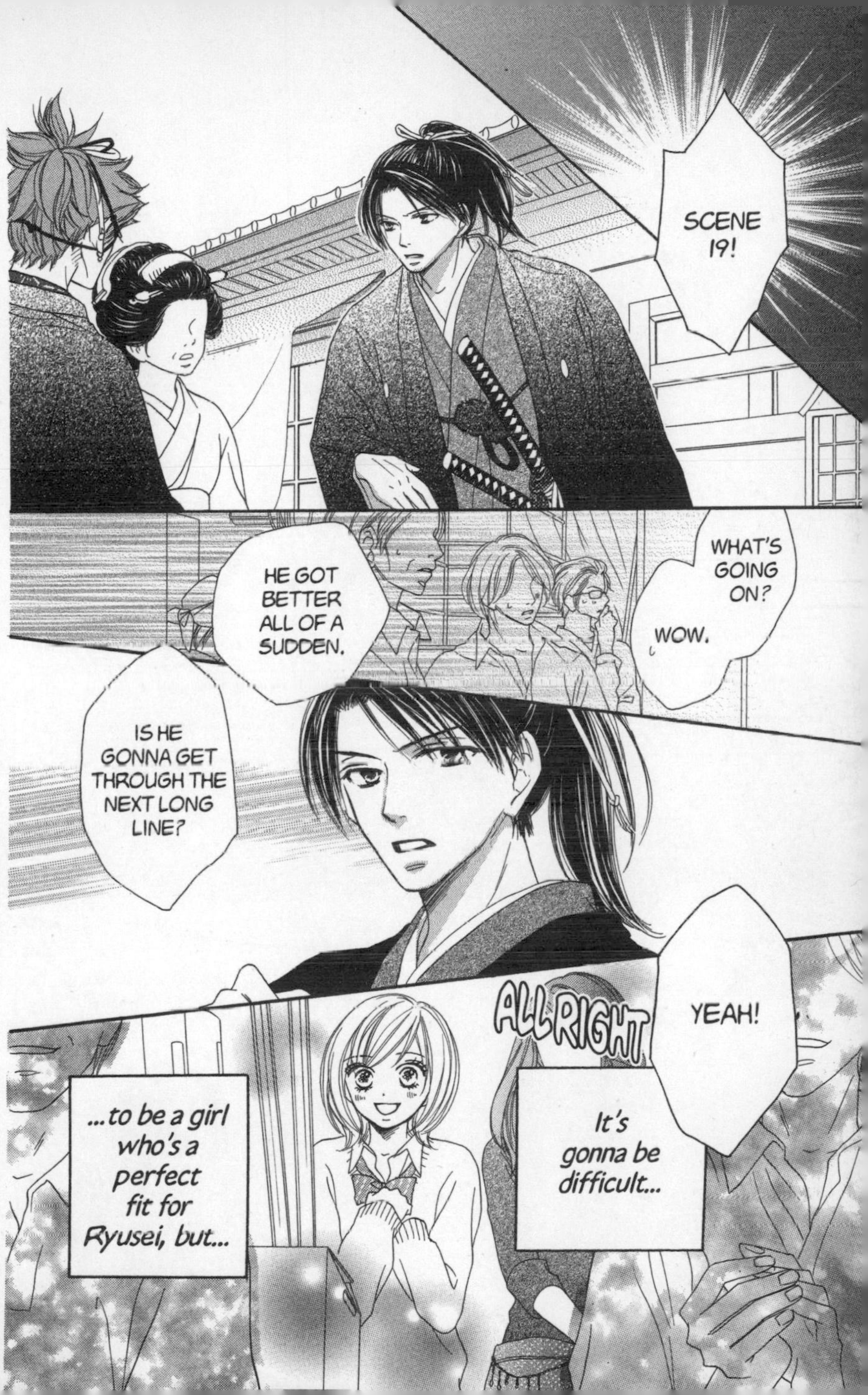
SCENE 19!
WHAT'S GOING ON?
WOW.
HE GOT BETTER ALL OF A SUDDEN.
IS HE GONNA GET THROUGH THE NEXT LONG LINE?
YEAH!
ALLRIGHT
It's gonna be difficult...
...to be a girl who's a perfect fit for Ryusei, but...

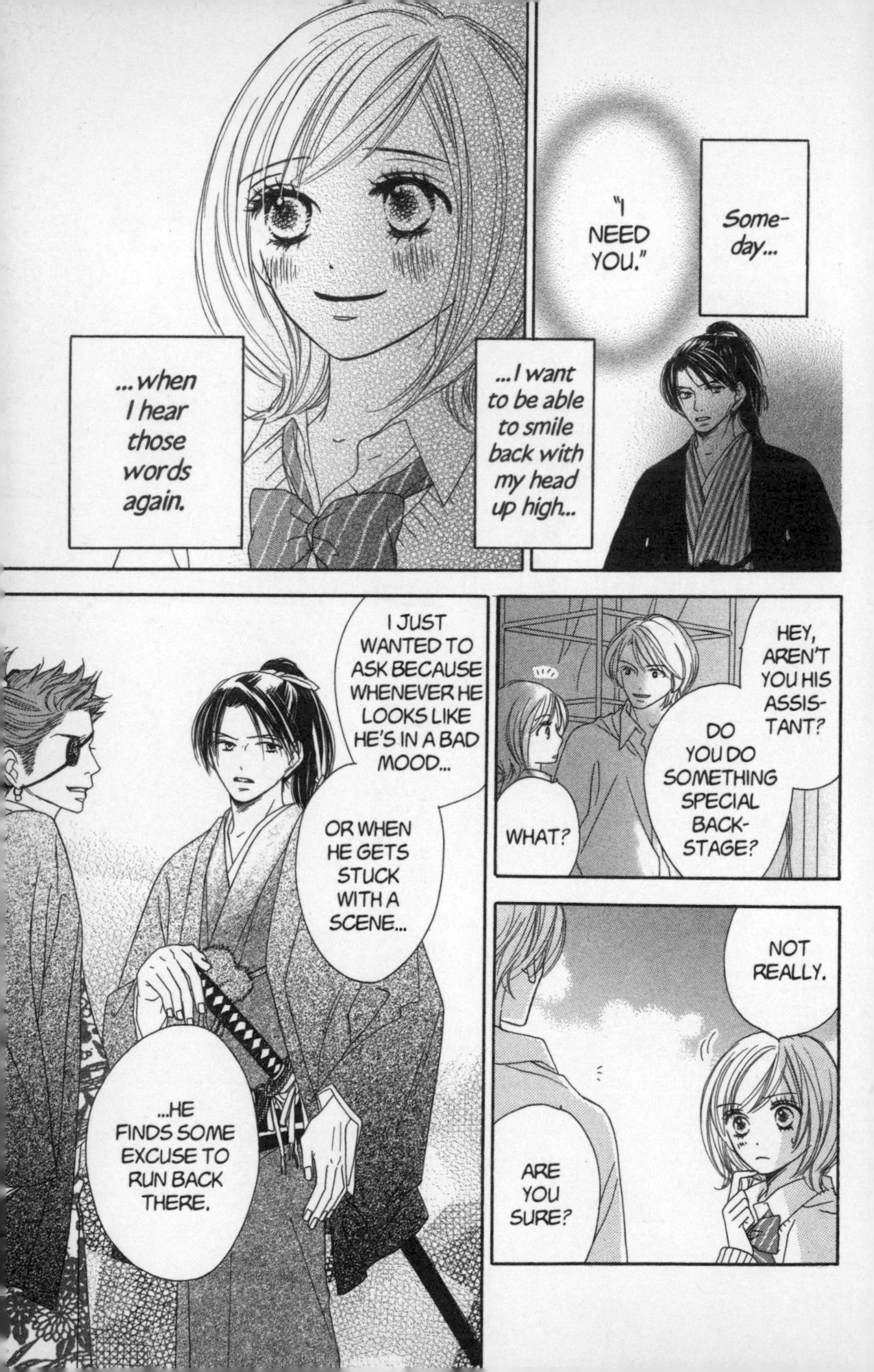
Some-day...
"I NEED YOU."
...I want to be able to smile back with my head up high...
...when I hear those words again.
HEY, AREN'T YOU HIS ASSIS-TANT?
DO YOU DO SOMETHING SPECIAL BACK-STAGE?
WHAT?
NOT REALLY.
ARE YOU SURE?
I JUST WANTED TO ASK BECAUSE WHENEVER HE LOOKS LIKE HE'S IN A BAD MOOD...
OR WHEN HE GETS STUCK WITH A SCENE...
...HE FINDS SOME EXCUSE TO RUN BACK THERE.

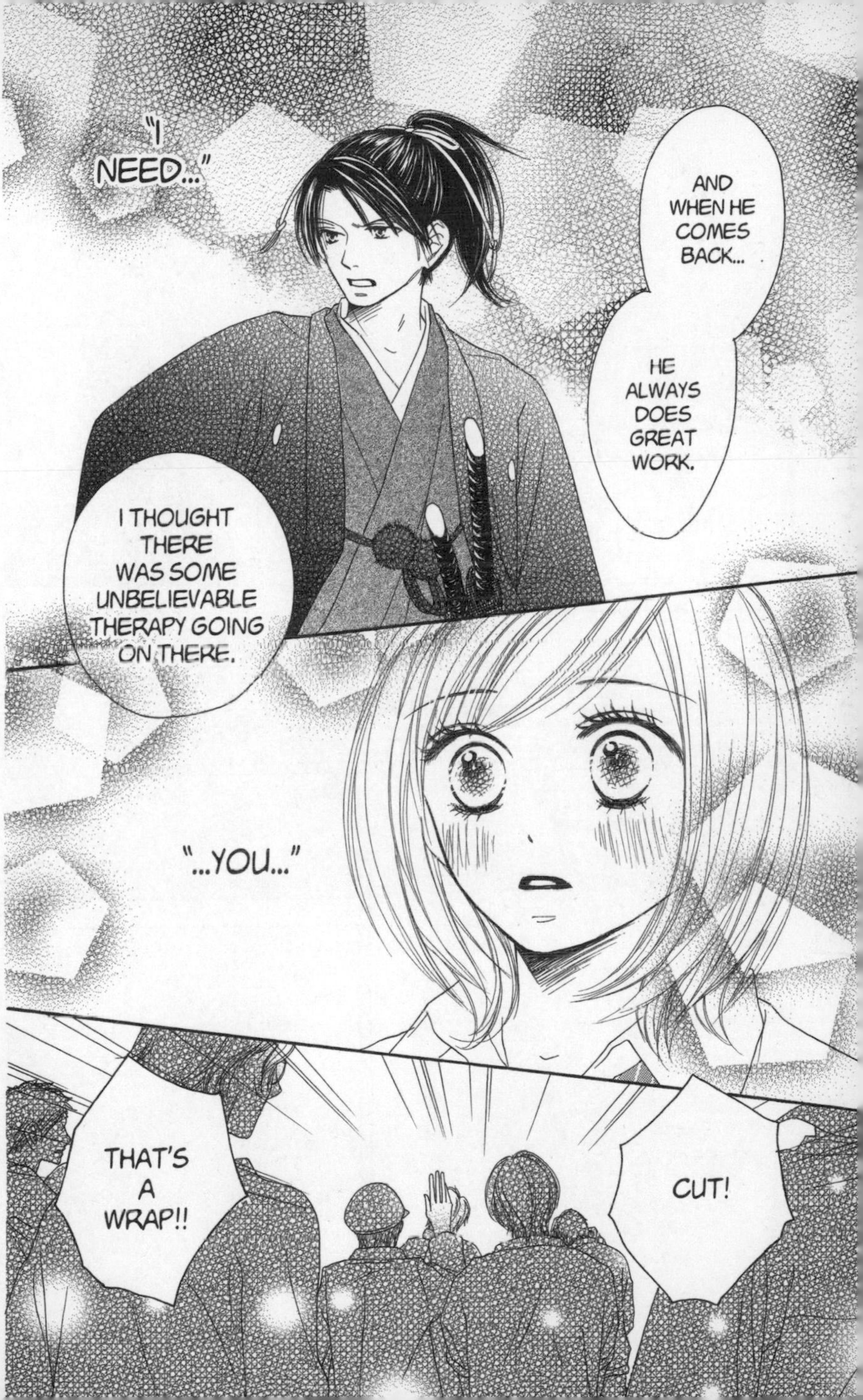
AND WHEN HE COMES BACK...
HE ALWAYS DOES GREAT WORK.
"I NEED..."
I THOUGHT THERE WAS SOME UNBELIEVABLE THERAPY GOING ON THERE.
"...YOU..."
CUT!
THAT'S A WRAP!!

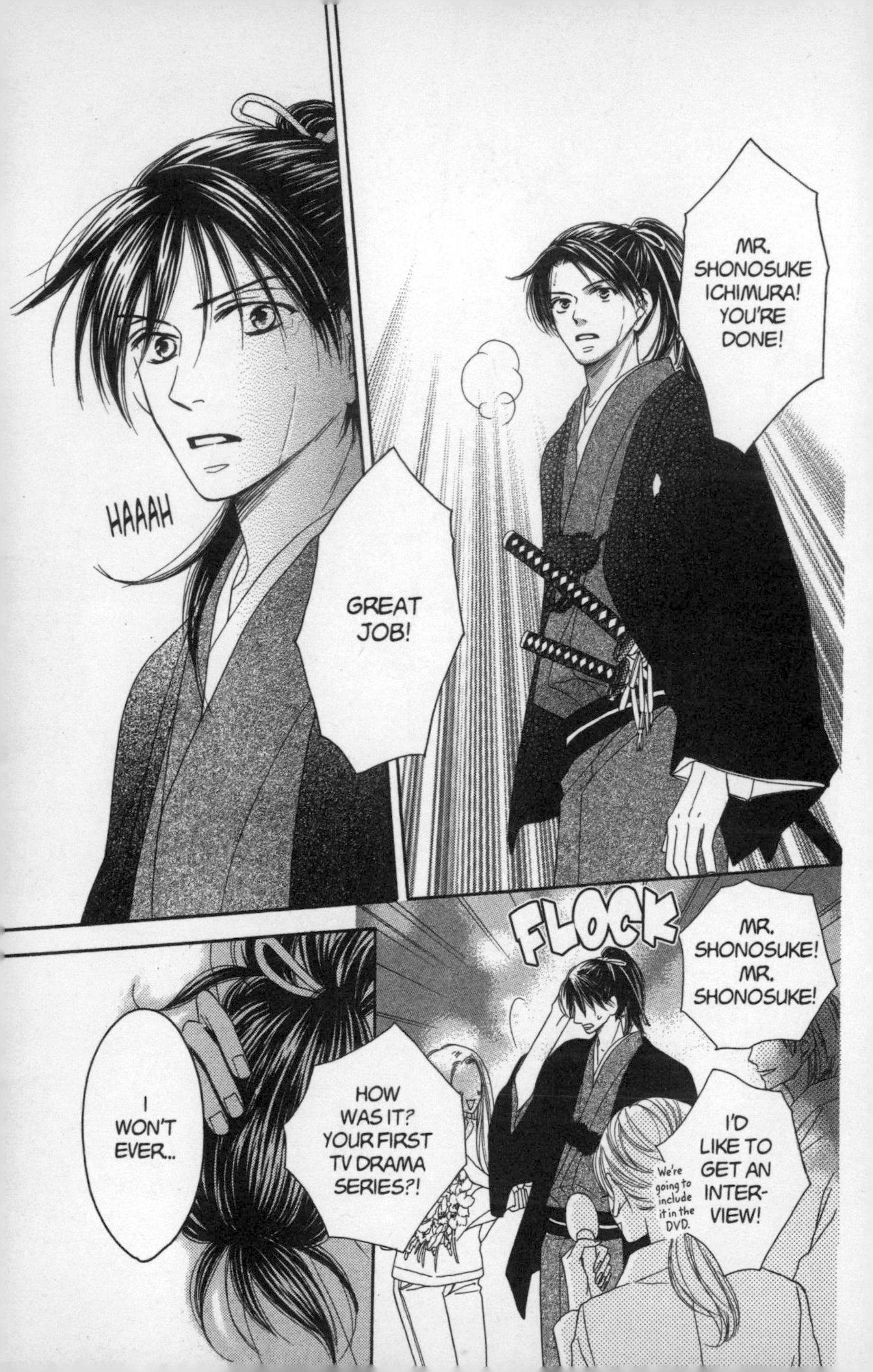
MR. SHONOSUKE ICHIMURA! YOU'RE DONE!
GREAT JOB!
HAAAH
FLOCK
MR. SHONOSUKE! MR. SHONOSUKE!
I'D LIKE TO GET AN INTER-VIEW!
We're going to include it in the DVD.
HOW WAS IT? YOUR FIRST TV DRAMA SERIES?!
I WON'T EVER...

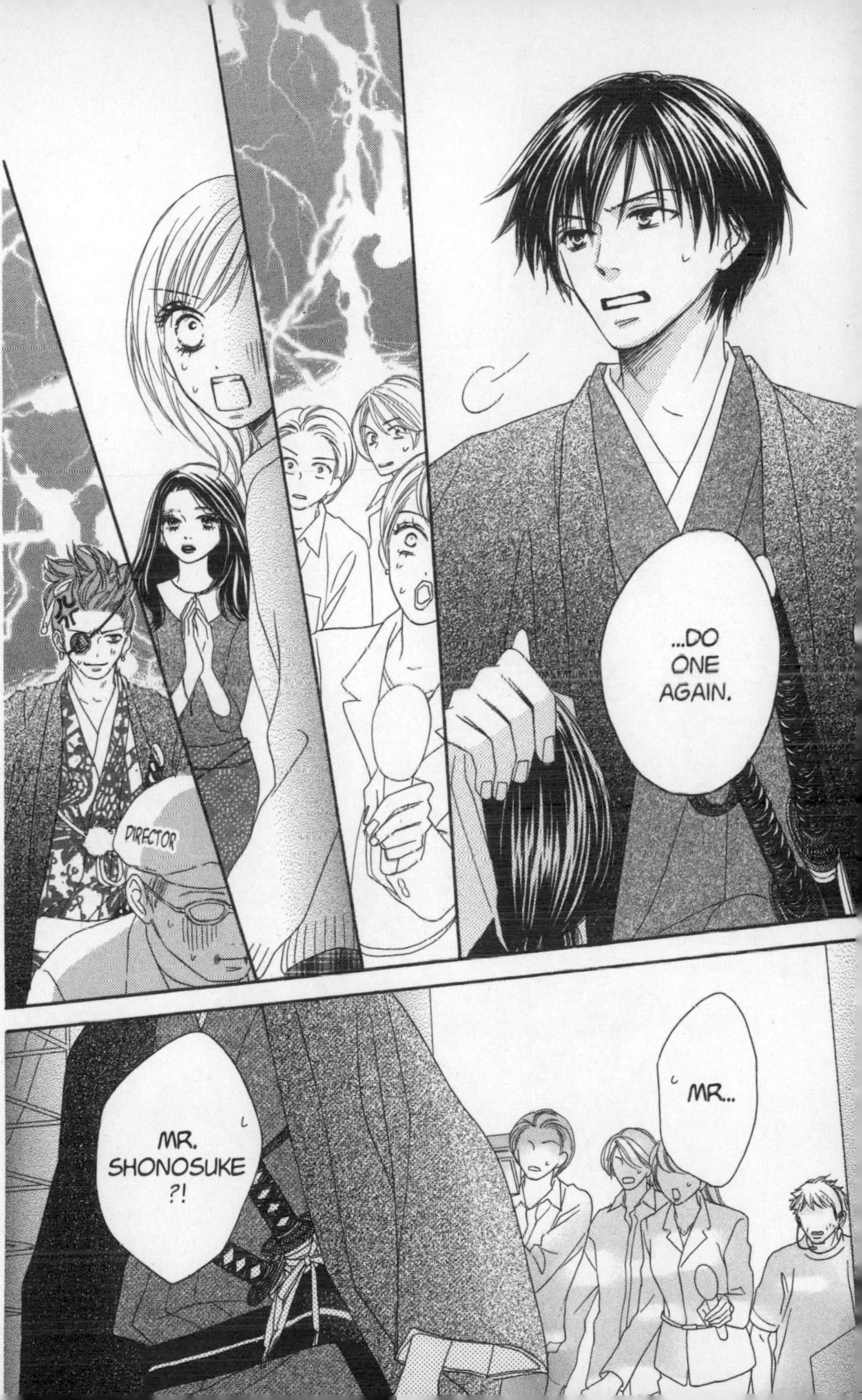
...DO ONE AGAIN.
DIRECTOR
MR...
MR. SHONOSUKE ?!

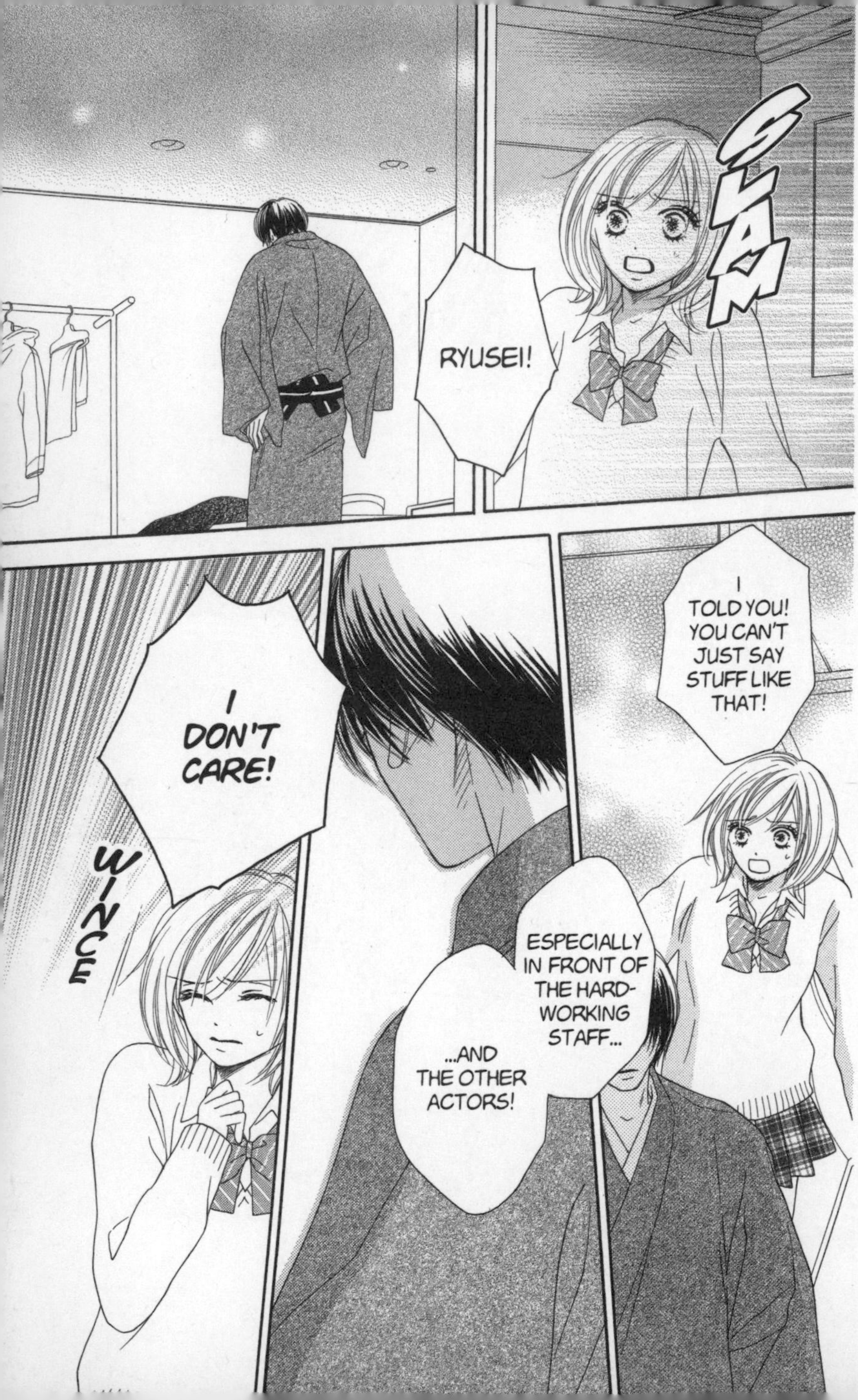
SLAM
RYUSEI!
I TOLD YOU! YOU CAN'T JUST SAY STUFF LIKE THAT!
ESPECIALLY IN FRONT OF THE HARD-WORKING STAFF...
...AND THE OTHER ACTORS!
I DON'T CARE!
WINCE

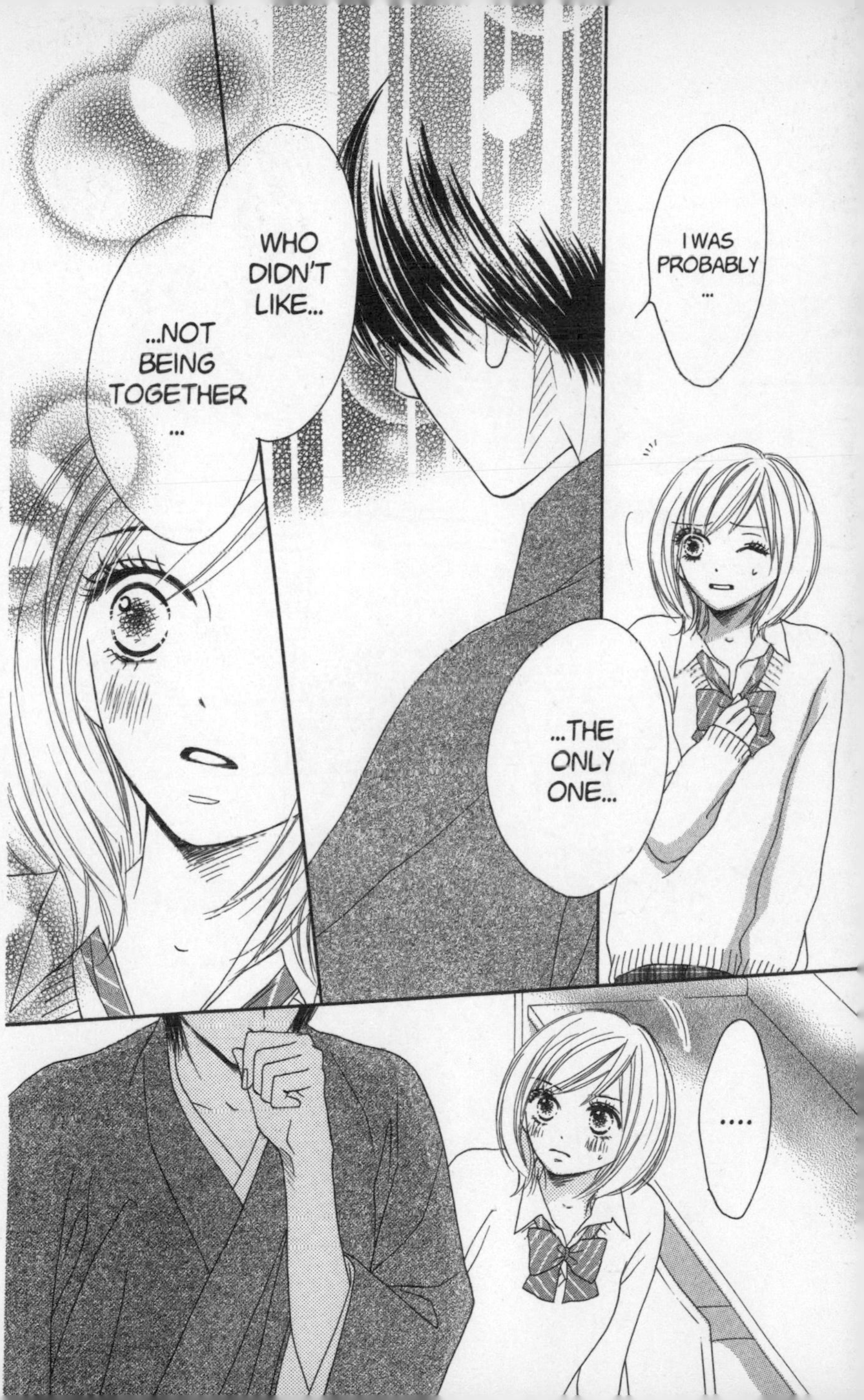
I WAS PROBABLY ...
...THE ONLY ONE...
WHO DIDN'T LIKE...
...NOT BEING TOGETHER ...
....

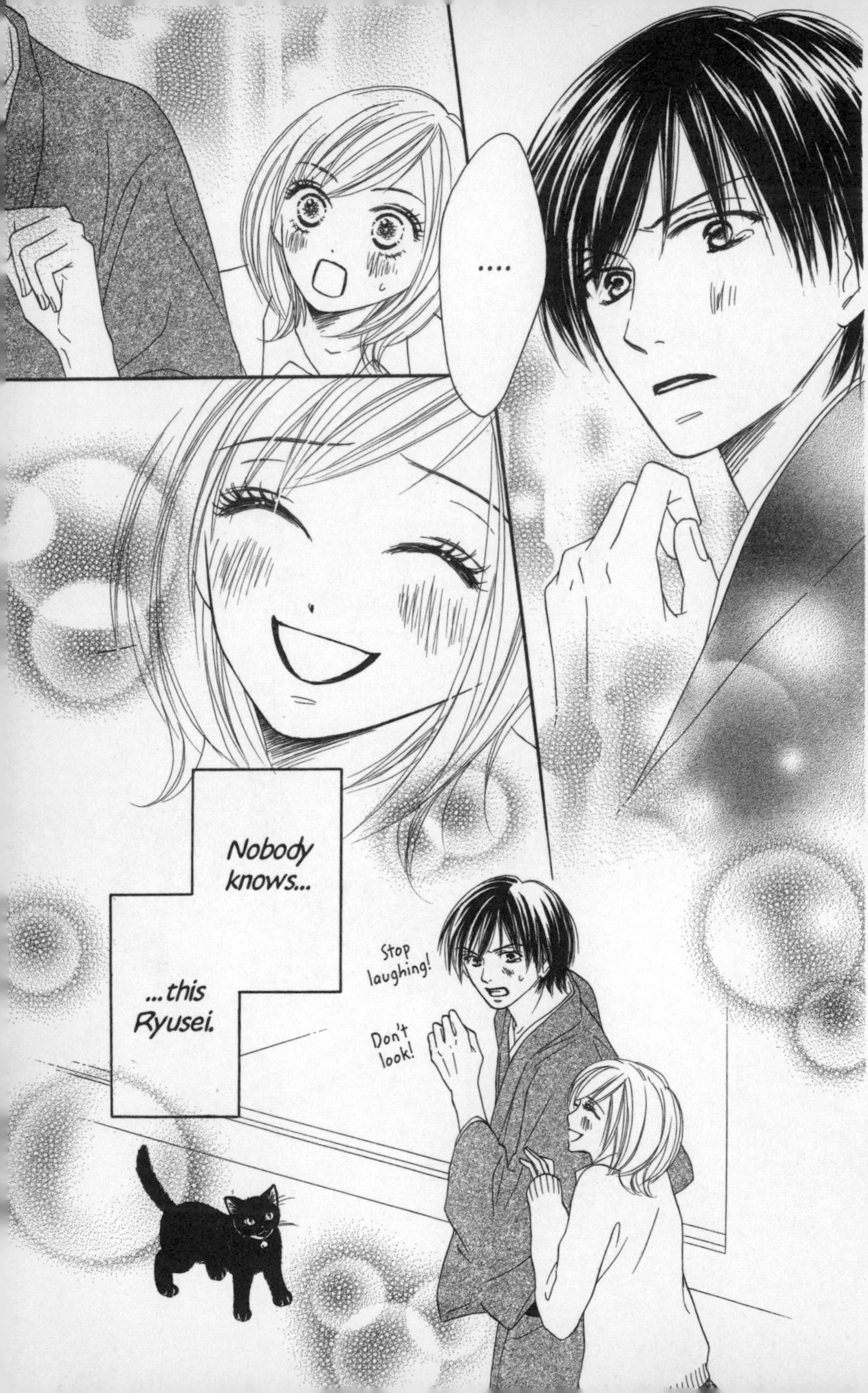
....
Nobody knows...
...this Ryusei.
Stop laughing!
Don't look!

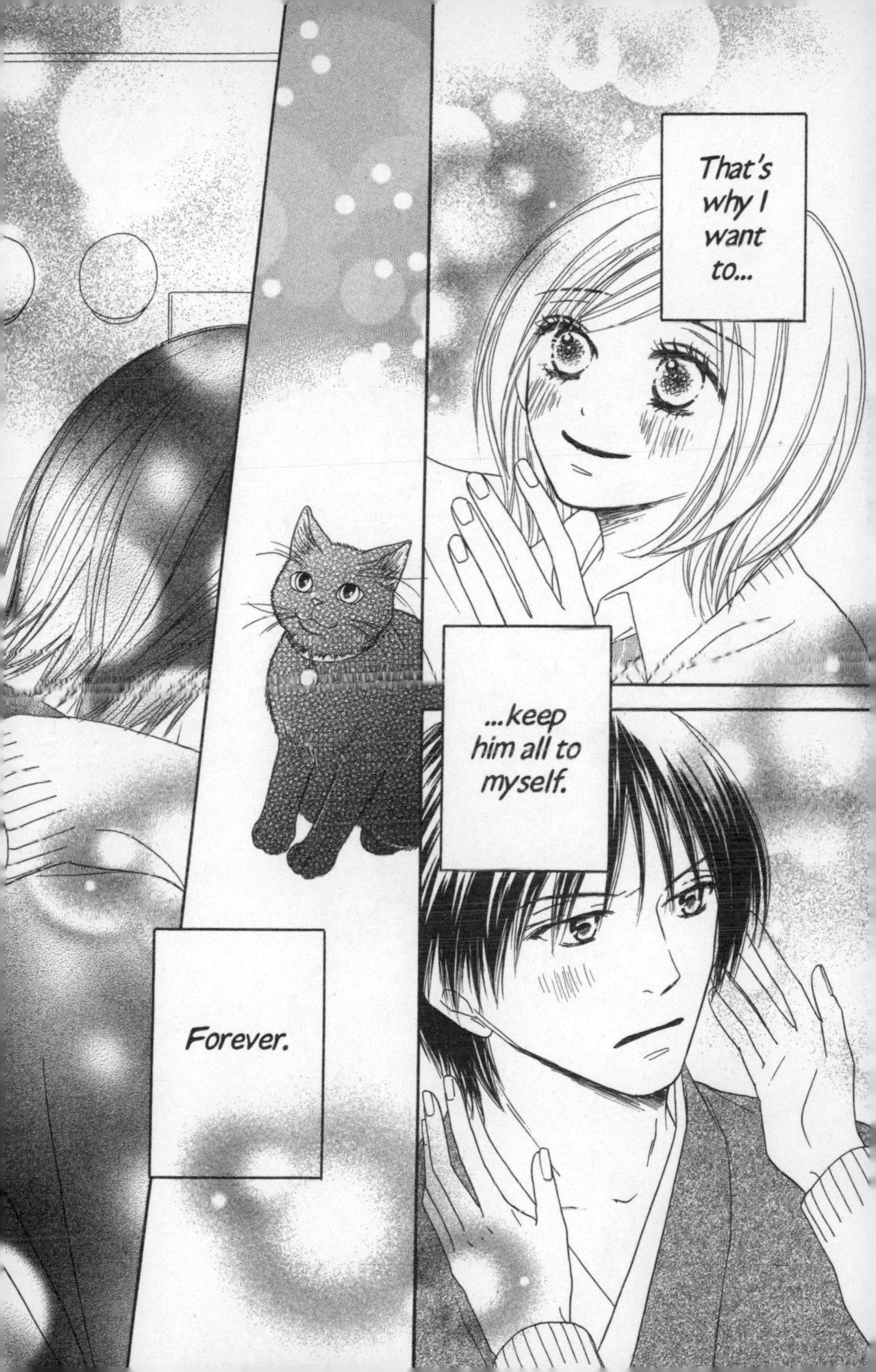
That's why I want to...
...keep him all to myself.
Forever.

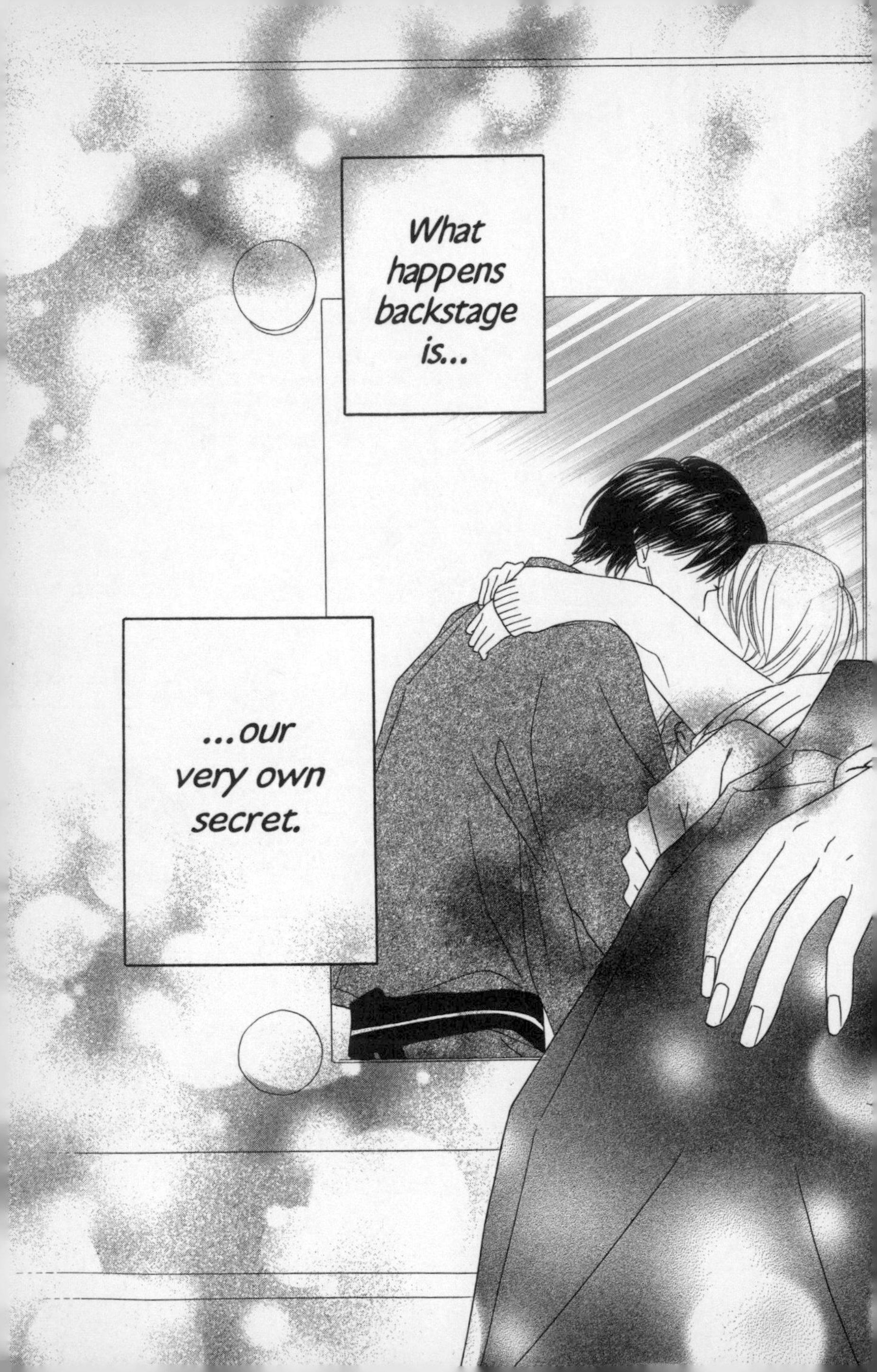
What happens backstage is...
...our very own secret.

Backstage at Backstage Prince: Part 3

IF I MAKE THE TV DRAMA SERIES IN THIS SECOND ACT A MODERN ONE, THERE WON'T BE ANY KIMONOS...BUT EVEN IF I MAKE IT A HISTORICAL DRAMA, MY EDITOR IMPLEMENTS THE "NO SAKAYAKI" RULE!

THEREFORE, THE BELOW SCENARIO IS WHAT I CAME UP WITH AS A LAST RESORT.

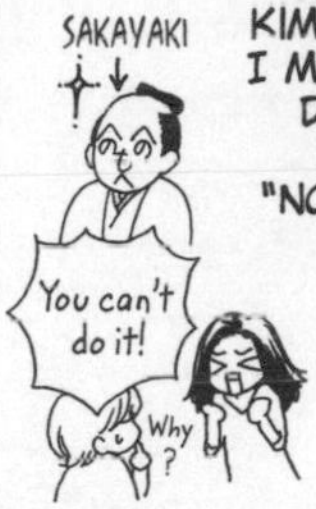
SAKAYAKI
You can't do it!
Why?

YOU DON'T HAVE TO READ IT...

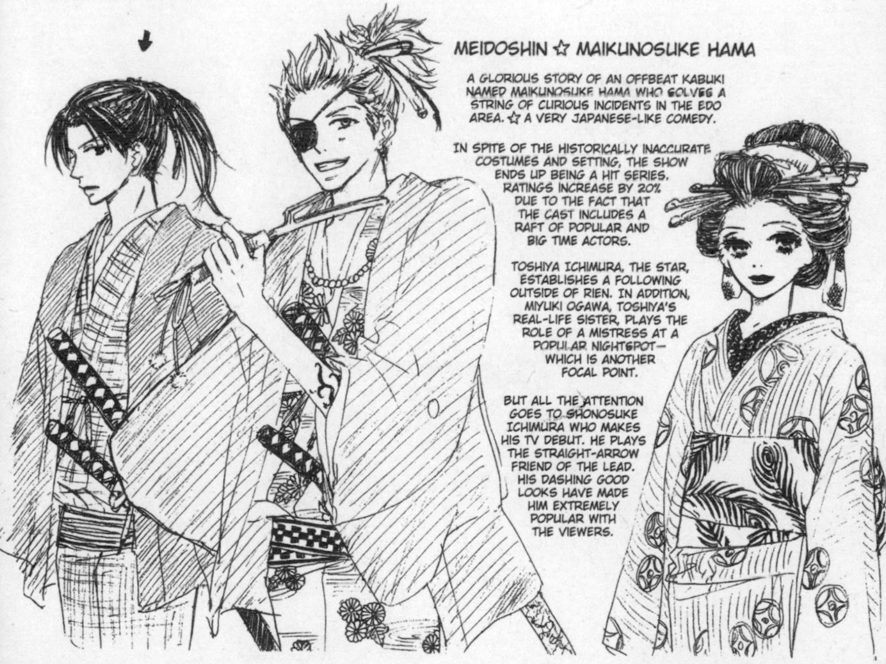

MEIDOSHIN ☆ MAIKUNOSUKE HAMA

A GLORIOUS STORY OF AN OFFBEAT KABUKI NAMED MAIKUNOSUKE HAMA WHO SOLVES A STRING OF CURIOUS INCIDENTS IN THE EDO AREA. ☆ A VERY JAPANESE-LIKE COMEDY.

IN SPITE OF THE HISTORICALLY INACCURATE COSTUMES AND SETTING, THE SHOW ENDS UP BEING A HIT SERIES. RATINGS INCREASE BY 20% DUE TO THE FACT THAT THE CAST INCLUDES A RAFT OF POPULAR AND BIG TIME ACTORS.

TOSHIYA ICHIMURA, THE STAR, ESTABLISHES A FOLLOWING OUTSIDE OF RIEN. IN ADDITION, MIYUKI OGAWA, TOSHIYA'S REAL-LIFE SISTER, PLAYS THE ROLE OF A MISTRESS AT A POPULAR NIGHTSPOT—WHICH IS ANOTHER FOCAL POINT.

BUT ALL THE ATTENTION GOES TO SHONOSUKE ICHIMURA WHO MAKES HIS TV DEBUT. HE PLAYS THE STRAIGHT-ARROW FRIEND OF THE LEAD. HIS DASHING GOOD LOOKS HAVE MADE HIM EXTREMELY POPULAR WITH THE VIEWERS.

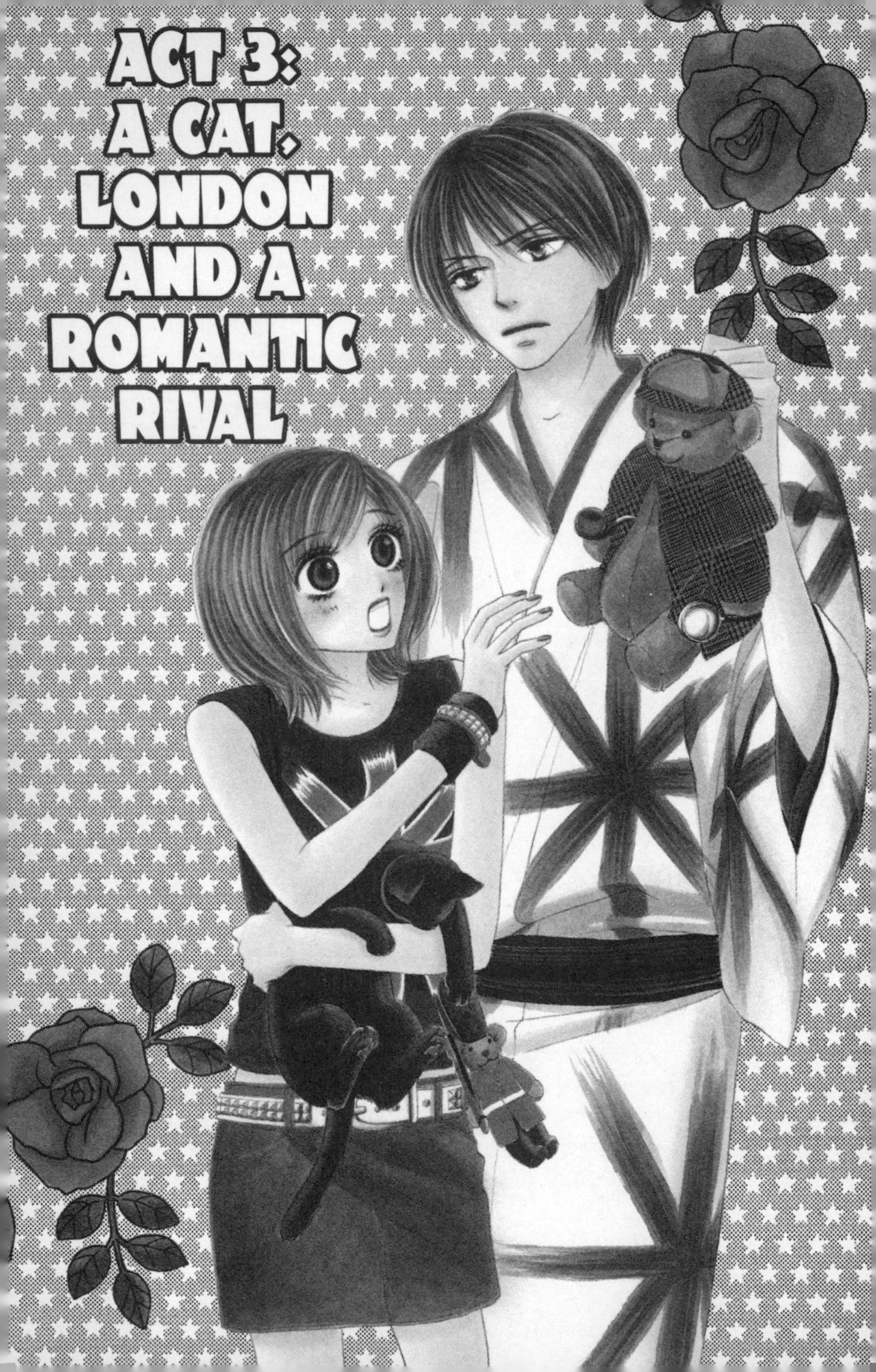
ACT 3:
A CAT,
LONDON
AND A
ROMANTIC
RIVAL

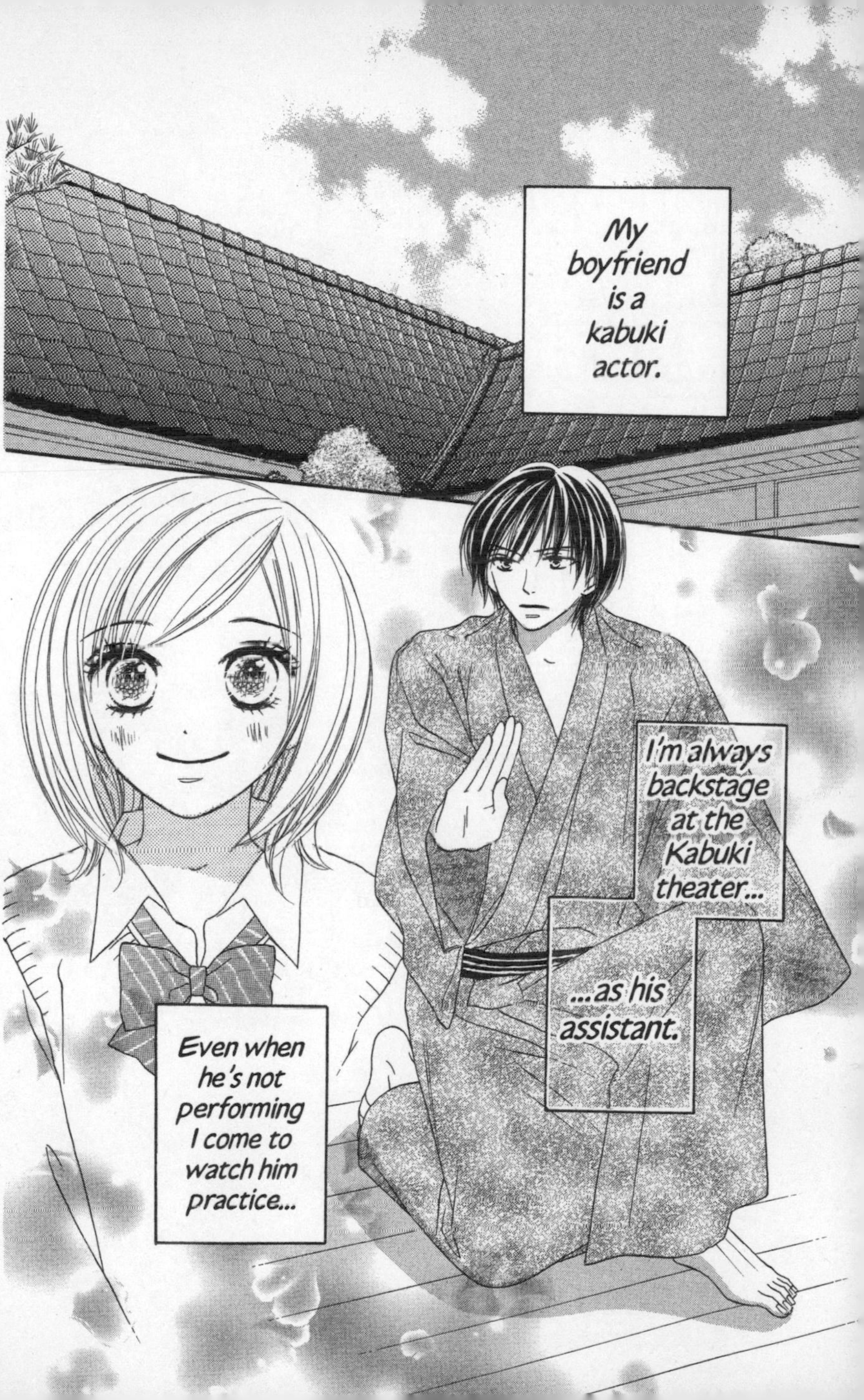
My boyfriend is a kabuki actor.
I'm always backstage at the Kabuki theater...
...as his assistant.
Even when he's not performing I come to watch him practice...

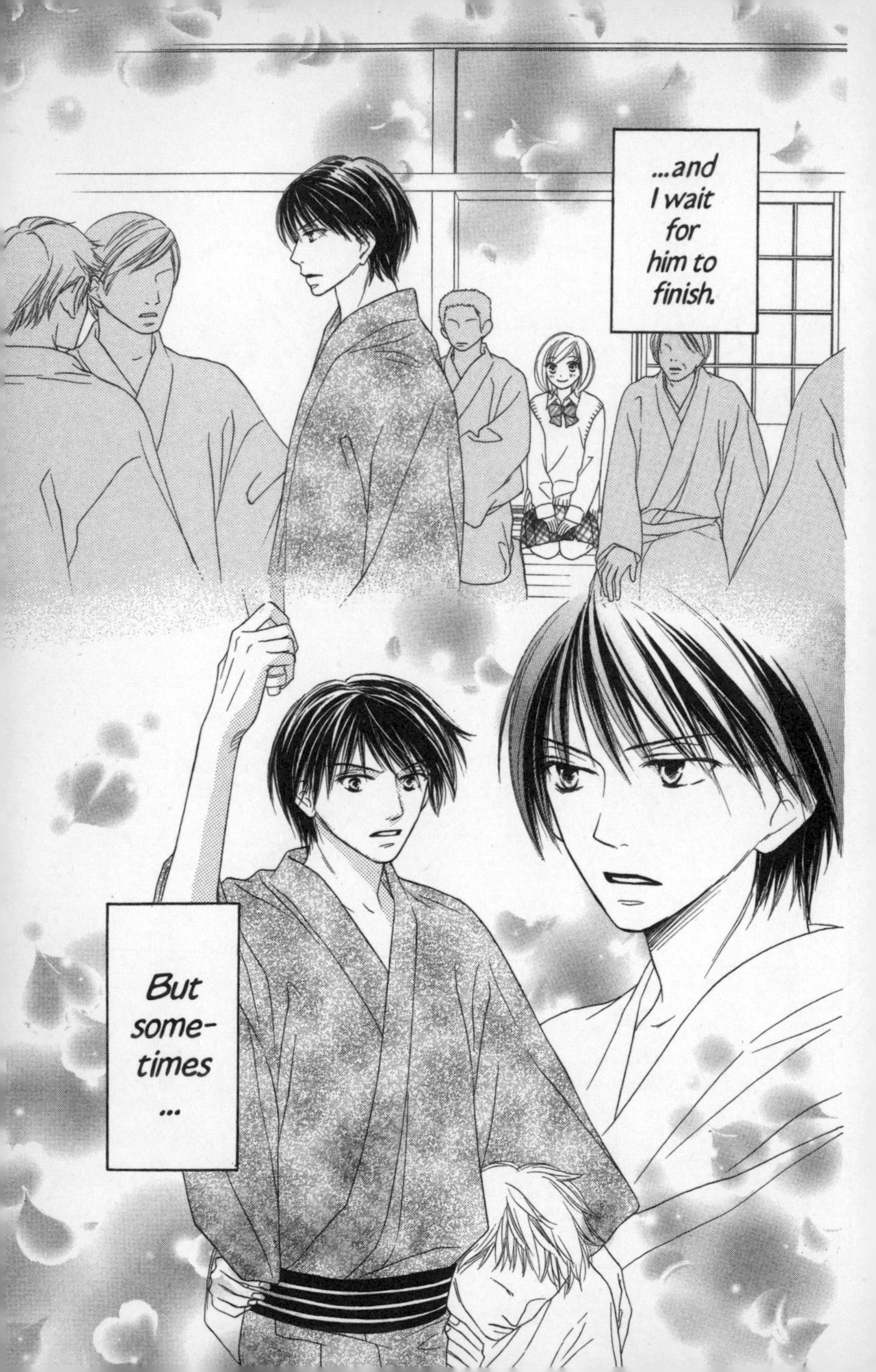
...and I wait for him to finish.
But some-times ...

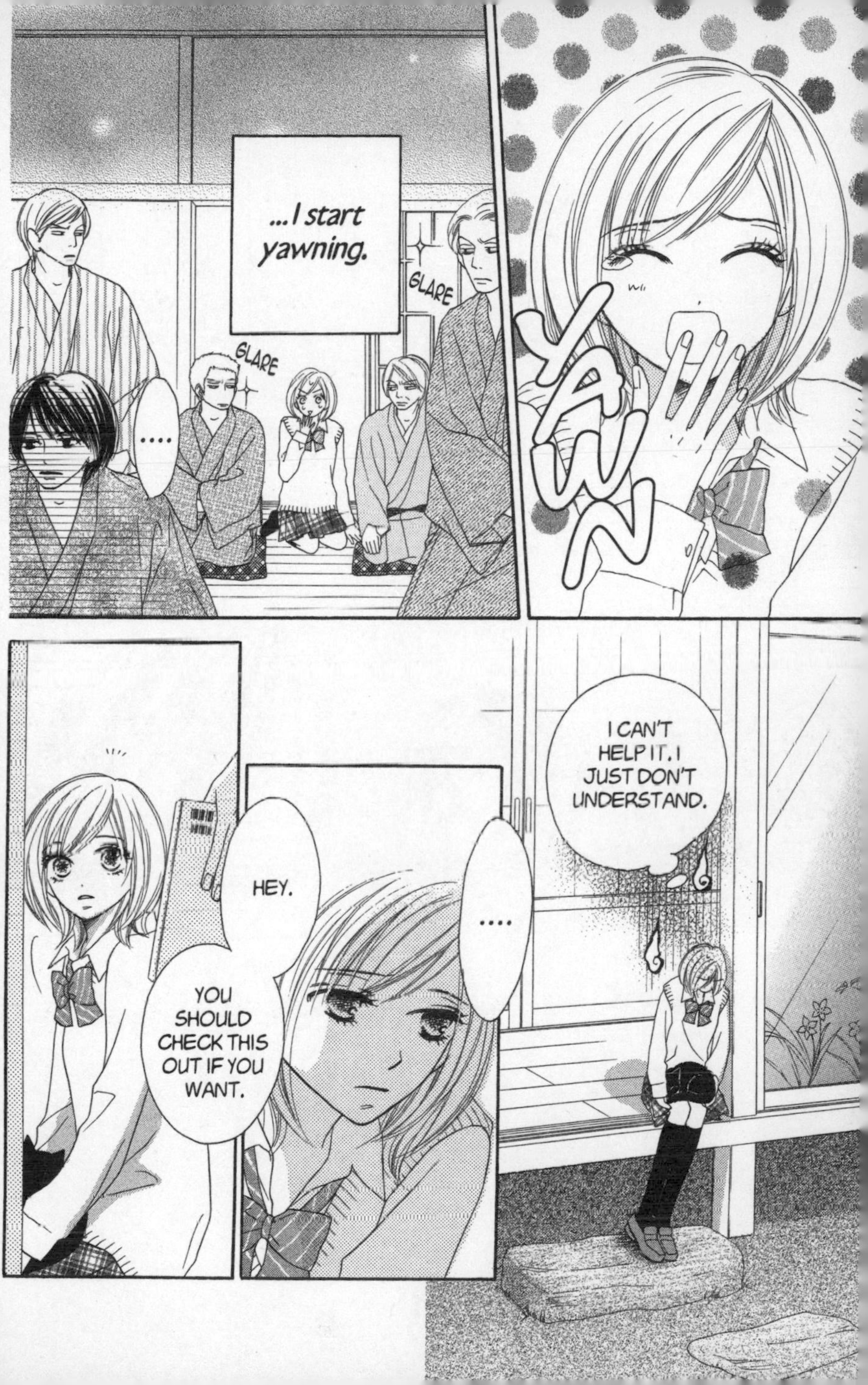
YAWN
...I start yawning.
GLARE
GLARE
....
I CAN'T HELP IT. I JUST DON'T UNDERSTAND.
....
HEY.
YOU SHOULD CHECK THIS OUT IF YOU WANT.

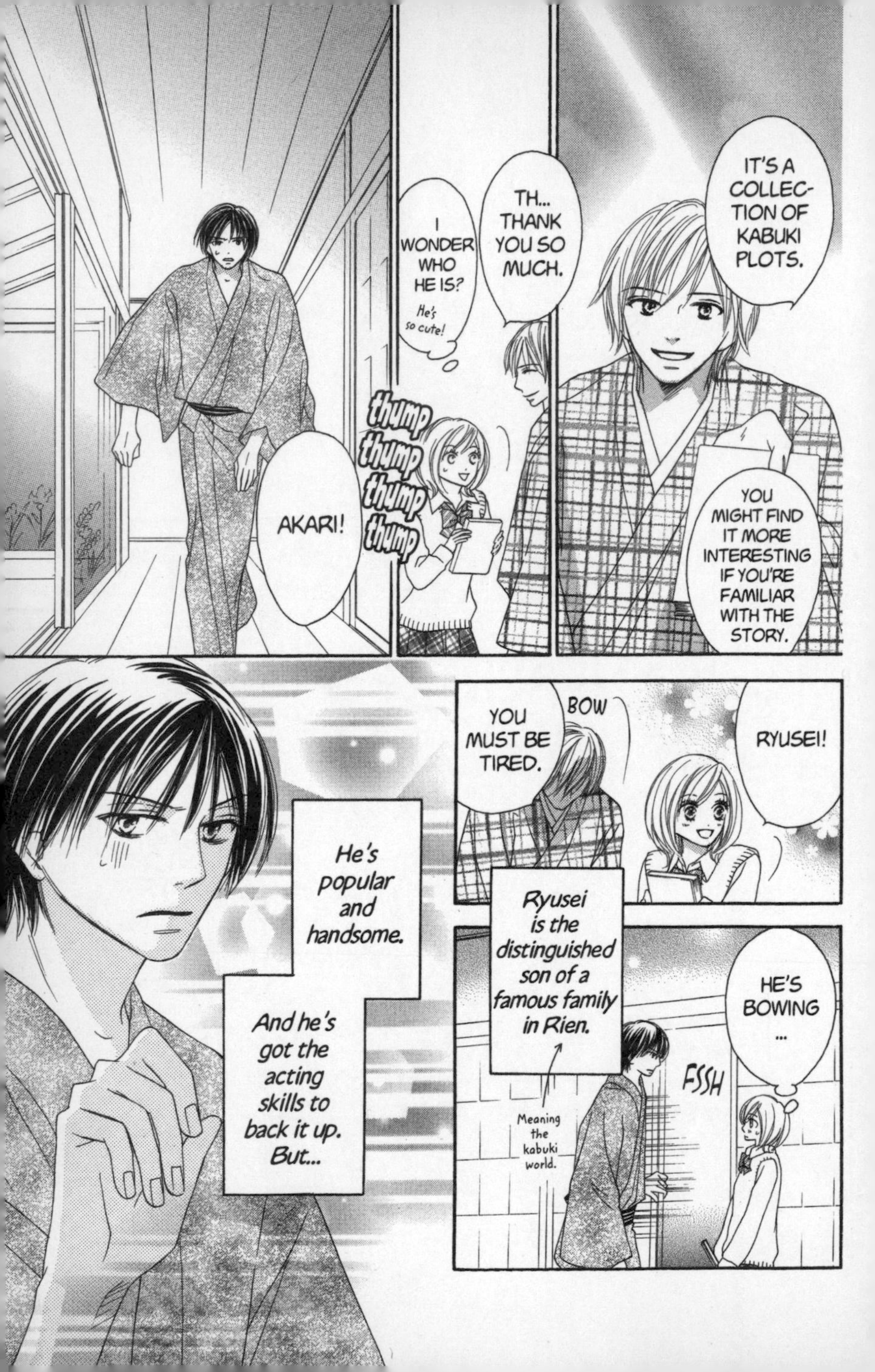
IT'S A COLLECTION OF KABUKI PLOTS.
YOU MIGHT FIND IT MORE INTERESTING IF YOU'RE FAMILIAR WITH THE STORY.
TH... THANK YOU SO MUCH.
I WONDER WHO HE IS?
He's so cute!
thump thump thump thump
AKARI!
RYUSEI!
BOW
YOU MUST BE TIRED.
Ryusei is the distinguished son of a famous family in Rien.
Meaning the kabuki world.
HE'S BOWING ...
FSSH
He's popular and handsome.
And he's got the acting skills to back it up. But...

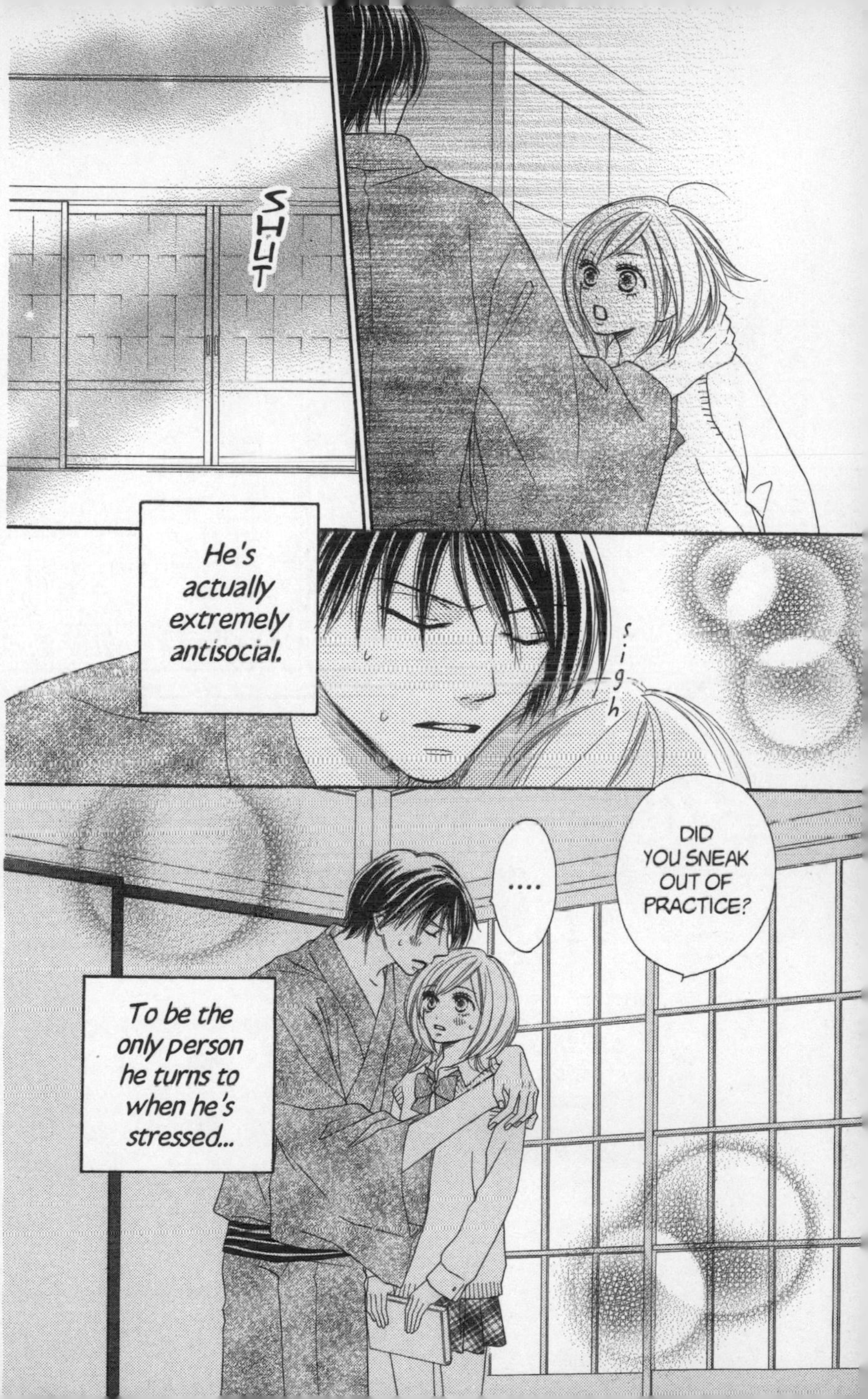
SHUT
sigh
He's actually extremely antisocial.
DID YOU SNEAK OUT OF PRACTICE?
....
To be the only person he turns to when he's stressed...

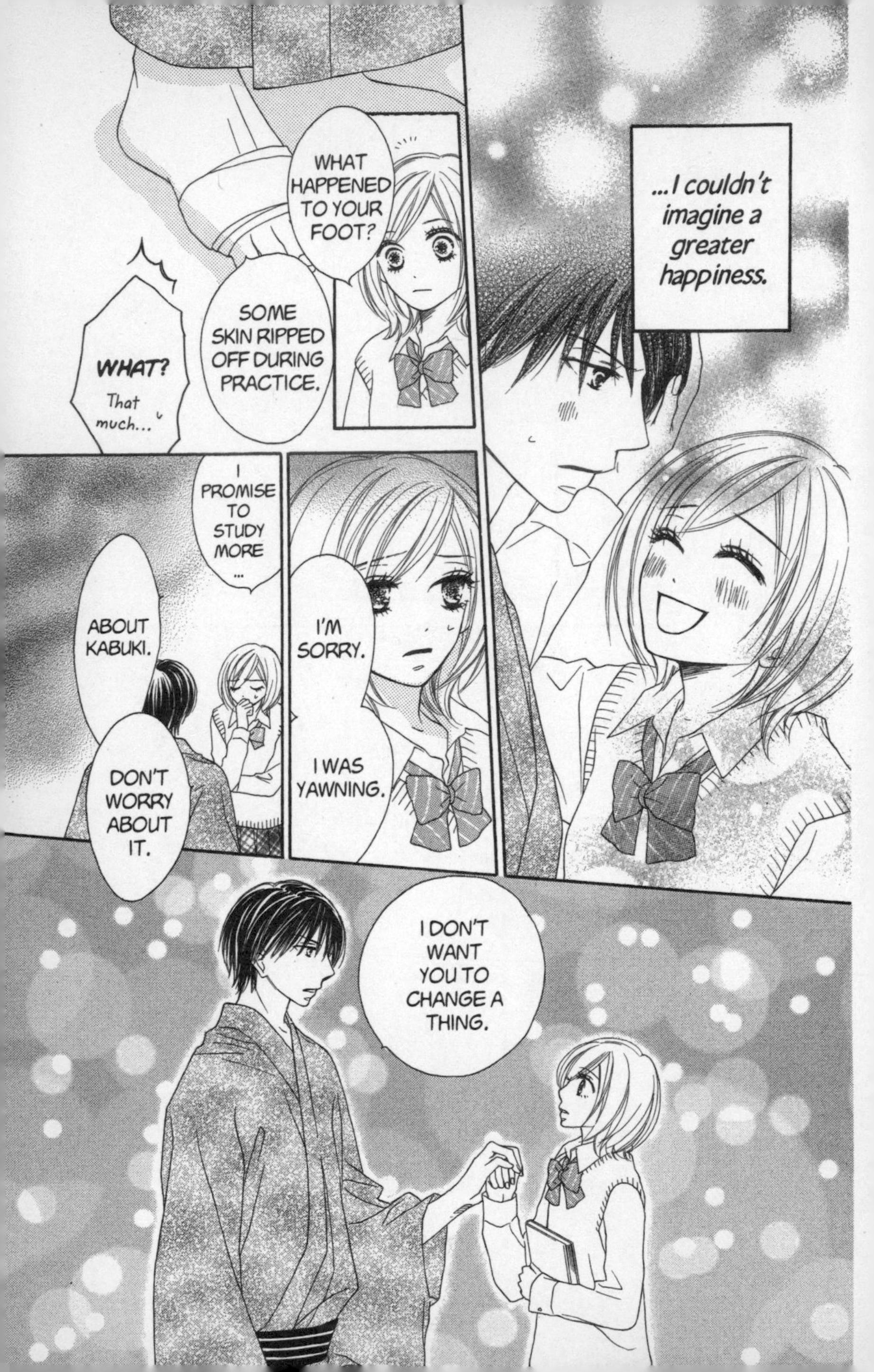
...I couldn't imagine a greater happiness.
WHAT HAPPENED TO YOUR FOOT?
SOME SKIN RIPPED OFF DURING PRACTICE.
WHAT?
That much...
I'M SORRY.
I WAS YAWNING.
I PROMISE TO STUDY MORE...
ABOUT KABUKI.
DON'T WORRY ABOUT IT.
I DON'T WANT YOU TO CHANGE A THING.

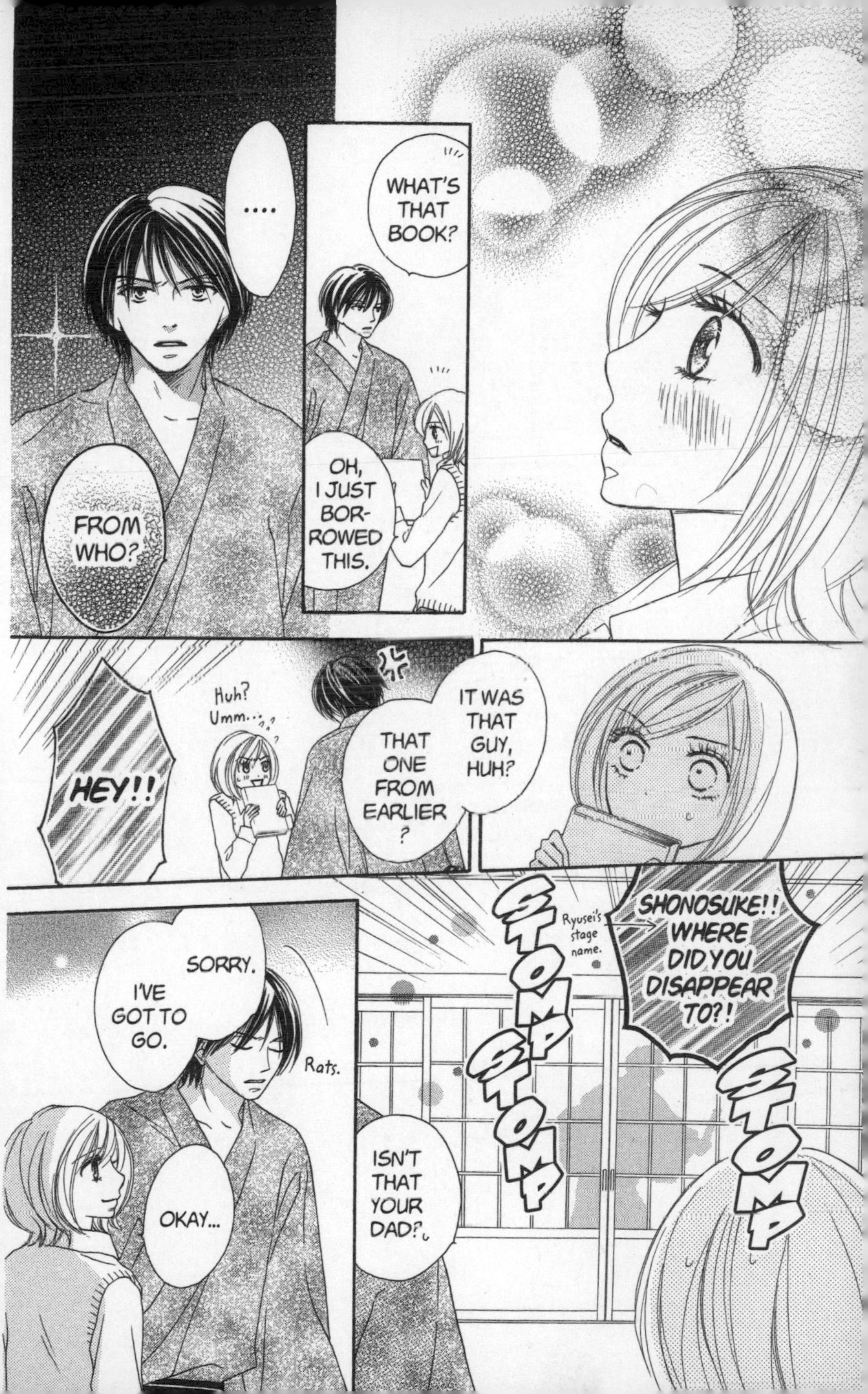
WHAT'S THAT BOOK?
OH, I JUST BOR-ROWED THIS.
....
FROM WHO?
IT WAS THAT GUY, HUH?
THAT ONE FROM EARLIER?
Huh? Umm...
HEY!!
SHONOSUKE!! WHERE DID YOU DISAPPEAR TO?!
Ryusei's stage name.
STOMP STOMP
STOMP
ISN'T THAT YOUR DAD?
SORRY. I'VE GOT TO GO.
Rats.
OKAY...

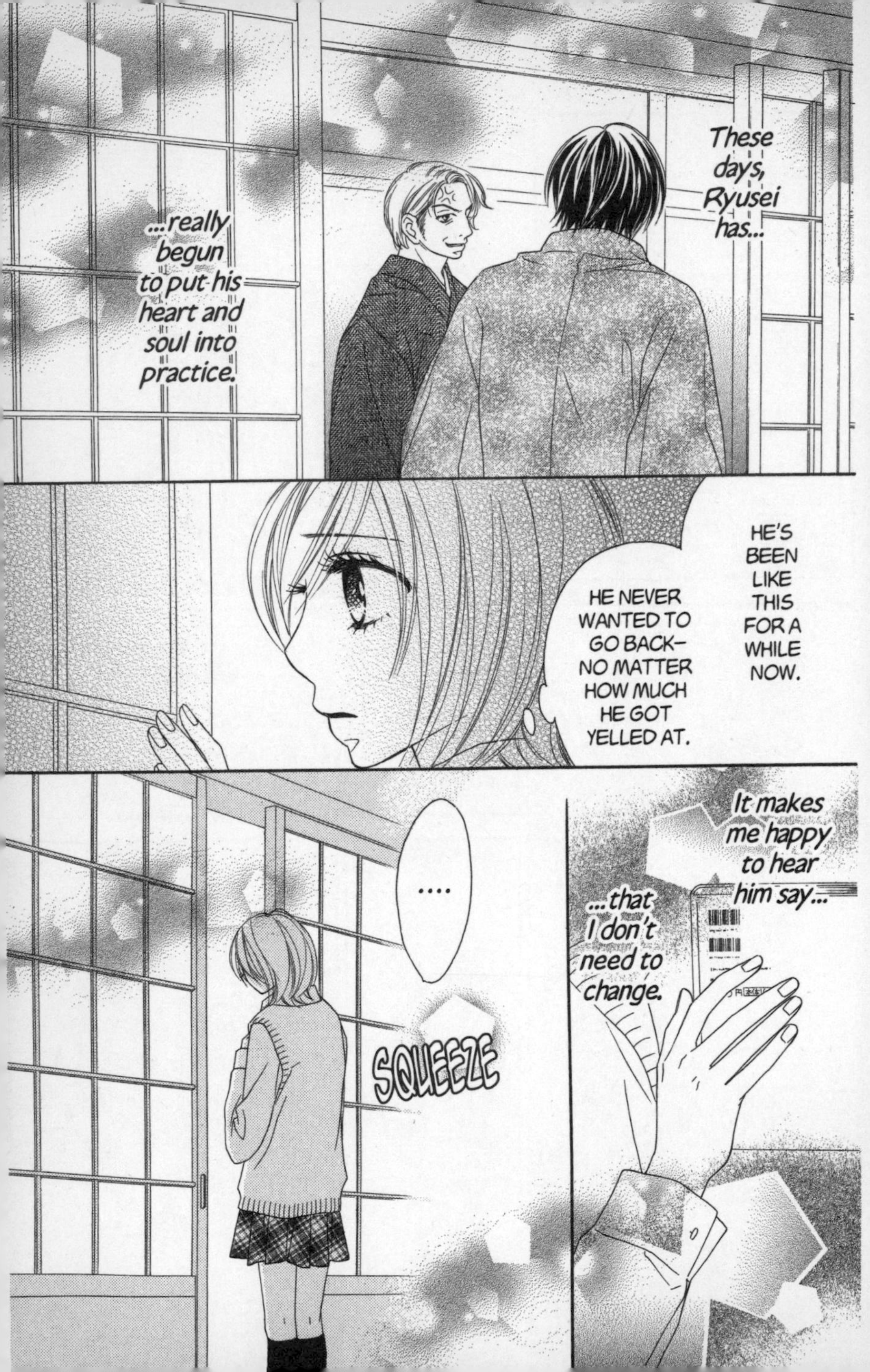
These days, Ryusei has...
...really begun to put his heart and soul into practice.
HE'S BEEN LIKE THIS FOR A WHILE NOW.
HE NEVER WANTED TO GO BACK— NO MATTER HOW MUCH HE GOT YELLED AT.
It makes me happy to hear him say...
...that I don't need to change.
....
SQUEEZE

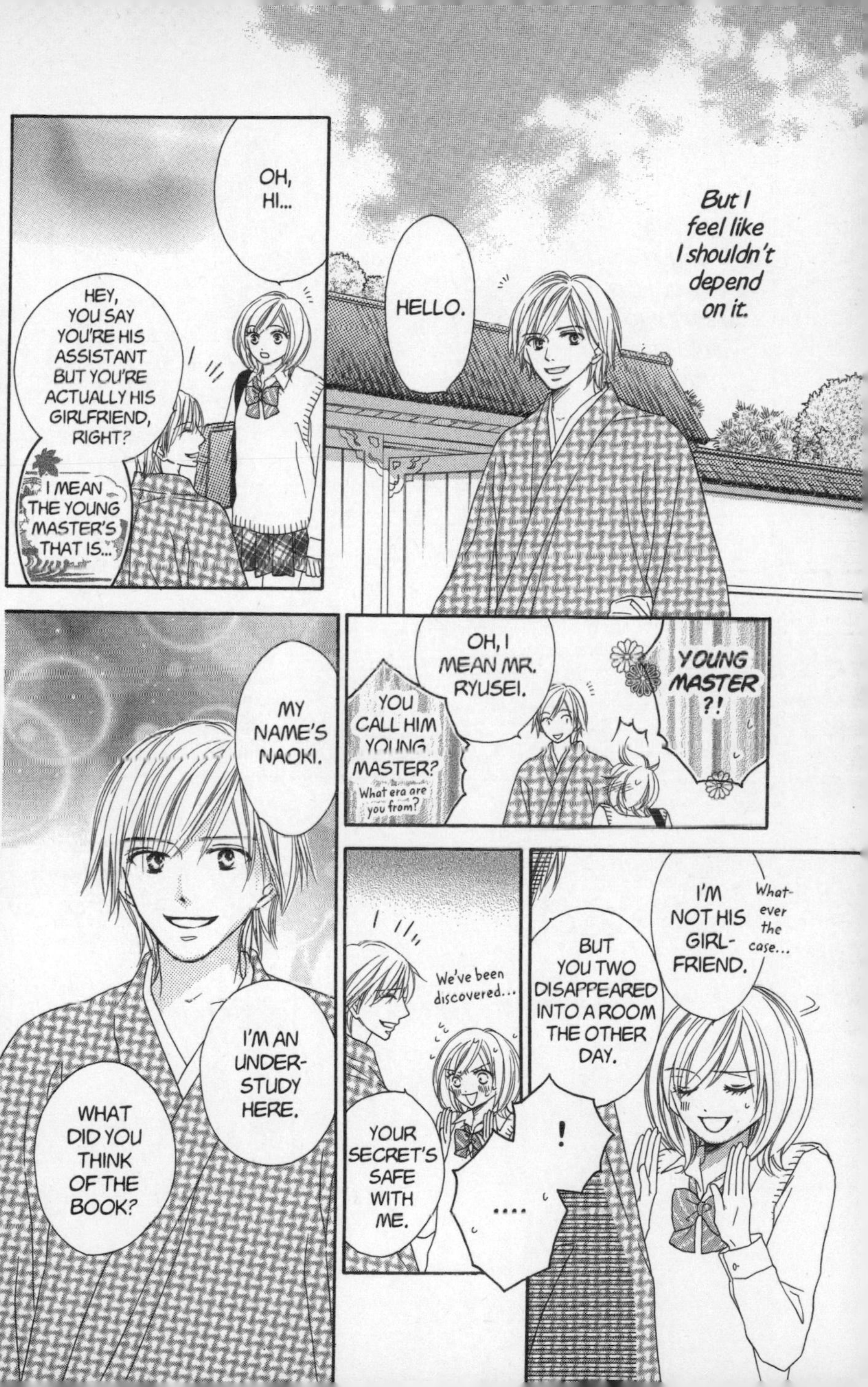
But I feel like I shouldn't depend on it.
HELLO.
OH, HI...
HEY, YOU SAY YOU'RE HIS ASSISTANT BUT YOU'RE ACTUALLY HIS GIRLFRIEND, RIGHT?
I MEAN THE YOUNG MASTER'S THAT IS...
YOUNG MASTER ?!
OH, I MEAN MR. RYUSEI.
YOU CALL HIM YOUNG MASTER?
What era are you from?
I'M NOT HIS GIRL-FRIEND.
What-ever the case...
BUT YOU TWO DISAPPEARED INTO A ROOM THE OTHER DAY.
!
....
We've been discovered...
YOUR SECRET'S SAFE WITH ME.
MY NAME'S NAOKI.
I'M AN UNDER-STUDY HERE.
WHAT DID YOU THINK OF THE BOOK?

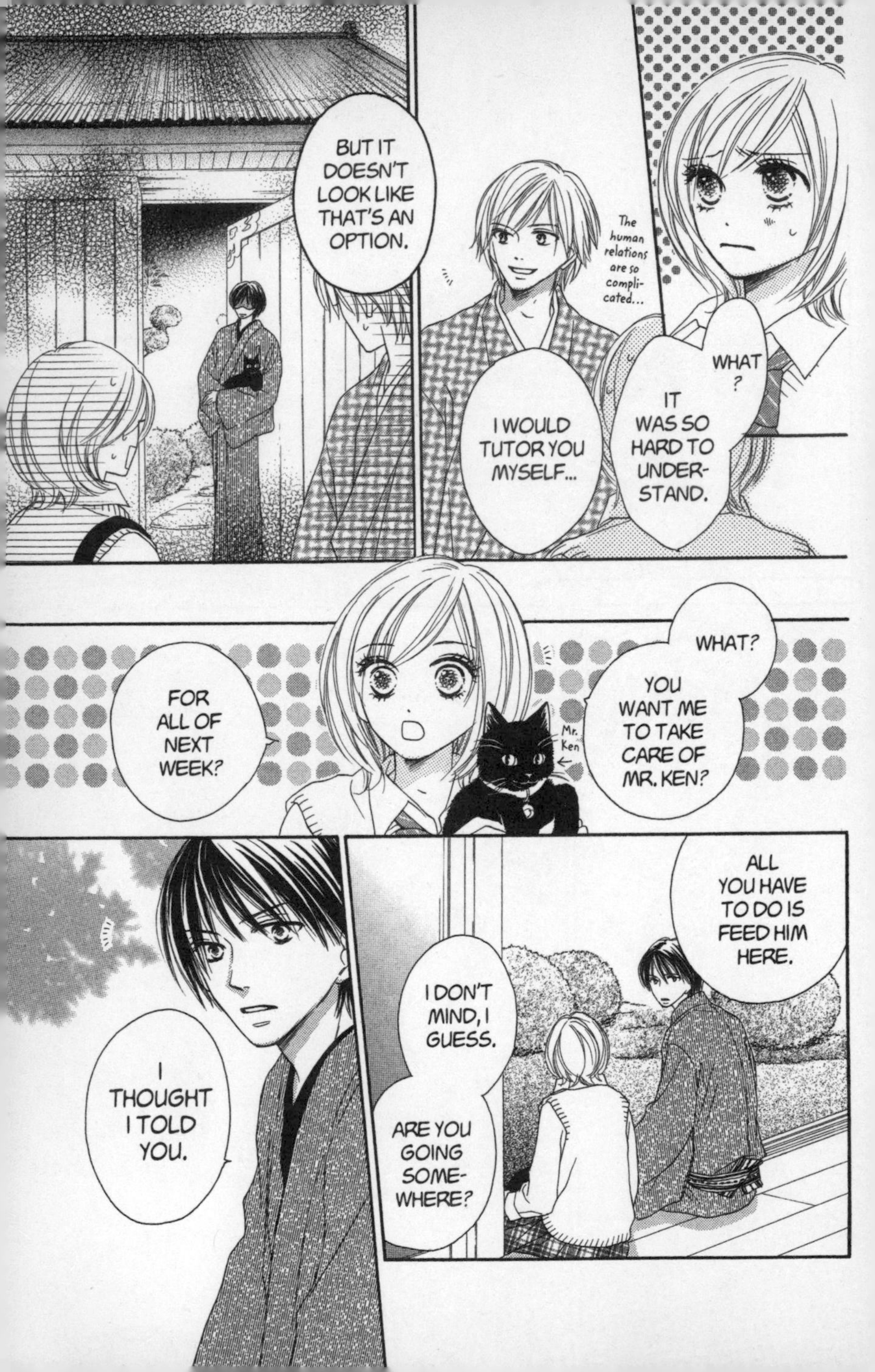
WHAT?
IT WAS SO HARD TO UNDER-STAND.
The human relations are so compli-cated...
I WOULD TUTOR YOU MYSELF...
BUT IT DOESN'T LOOK LIKE THAT'S AN OPTION.
WHAT?
YOU WANT ME TO TAKE CARE OF MR. KEN?
Mr. Ken
FOR ALL OF NEXT WEEK?
ALL YOU HAVE TO DO IS FEED HIM HERE.
I DON'T MIND, I GUESS.
ARE YOU GOING SOME-WHERE?
I THOUGHT I TOLD YOU.

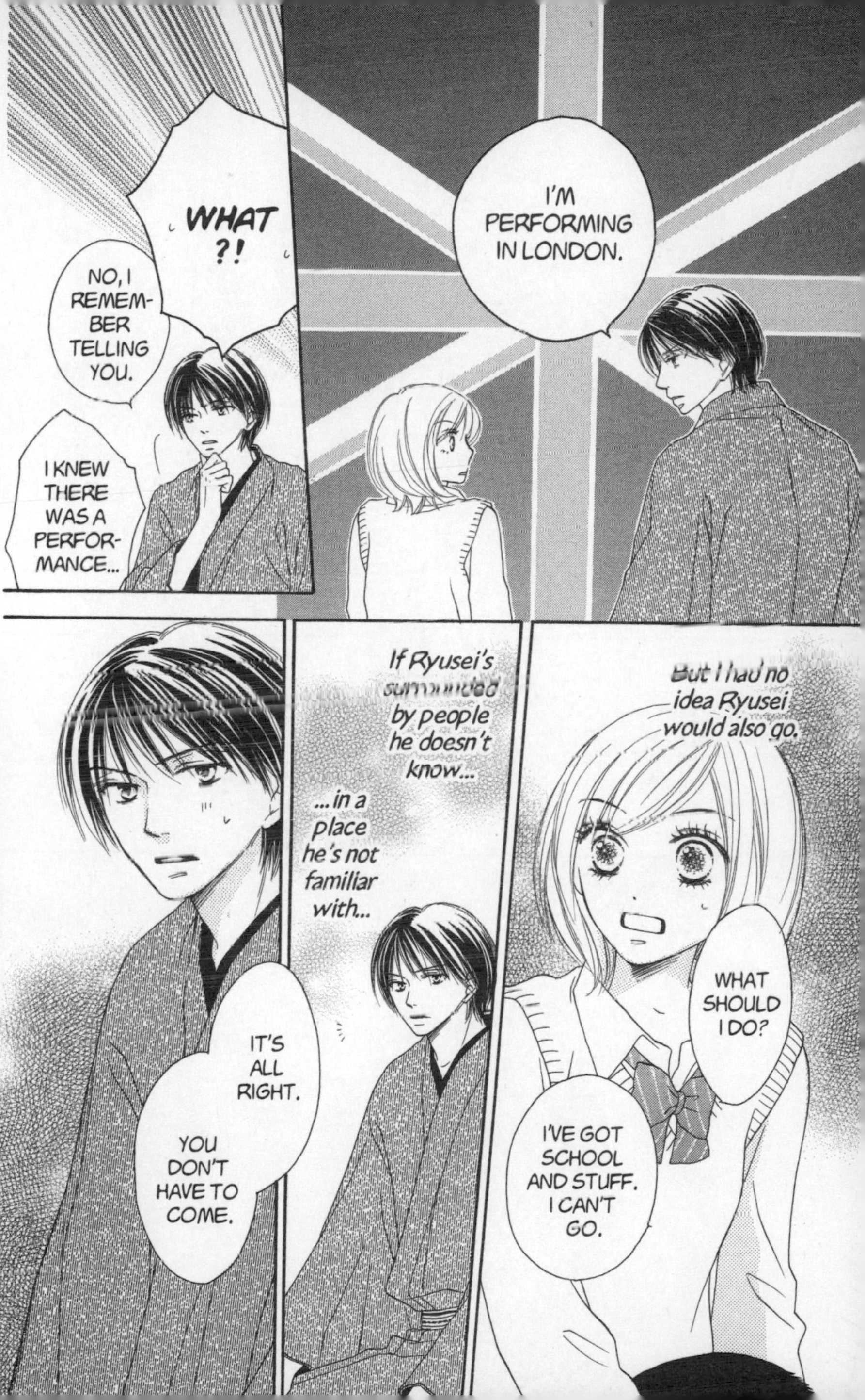
I'M PERFORMING IN LONDON.
WHAT?!
NO, I REMEMBER TELLING YOU.
I KNEW THERE WAS A PERFORMANCE...
But I had no idea Ryusei would also go.
WHAT SHOULD I DO?
I'VE GOT SCHOOL AND STUFF. I CAN'T GO.
If Ryusei's surrounded by people he doesn't know...
...in a place he's not familiar with...
IT'S ALL RIGHT.
YOU DON'T HAVE TO COME.

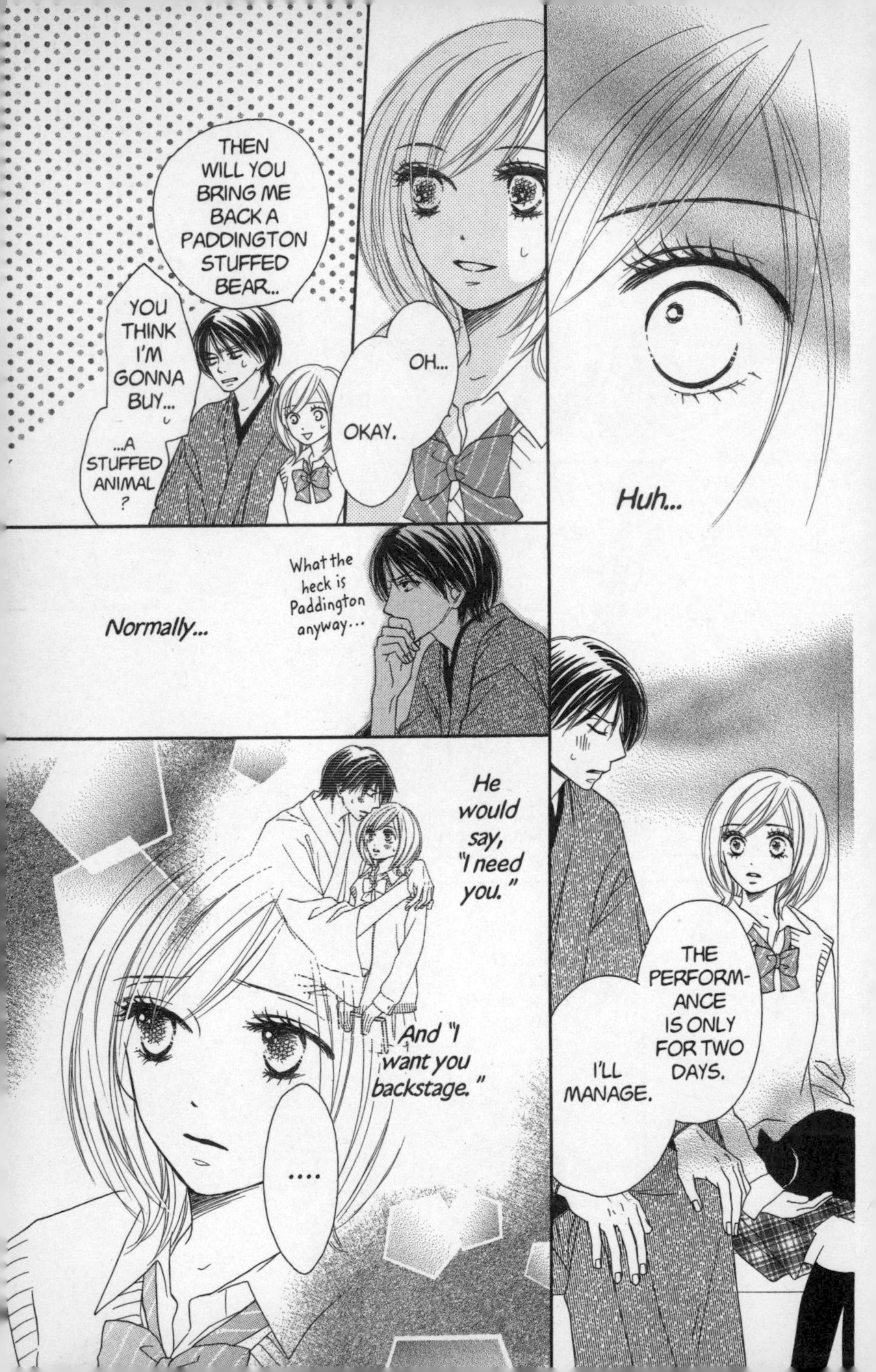
Huh...
OH...
OKAY.
THEN WILL YOU BRING ME BACK A PADDINGTON STUFFED BEAR...
YOU THINK I'M GONNA BUY...
...A STUFFED ANIMAL?
Normally...
What the heck is Paddington anyway...
THE PERFORMANCE IS ONLY FOR TWO DAYS.
I'LL MANAGE.
He would say, "I need you."
And "I want you backstage."
....

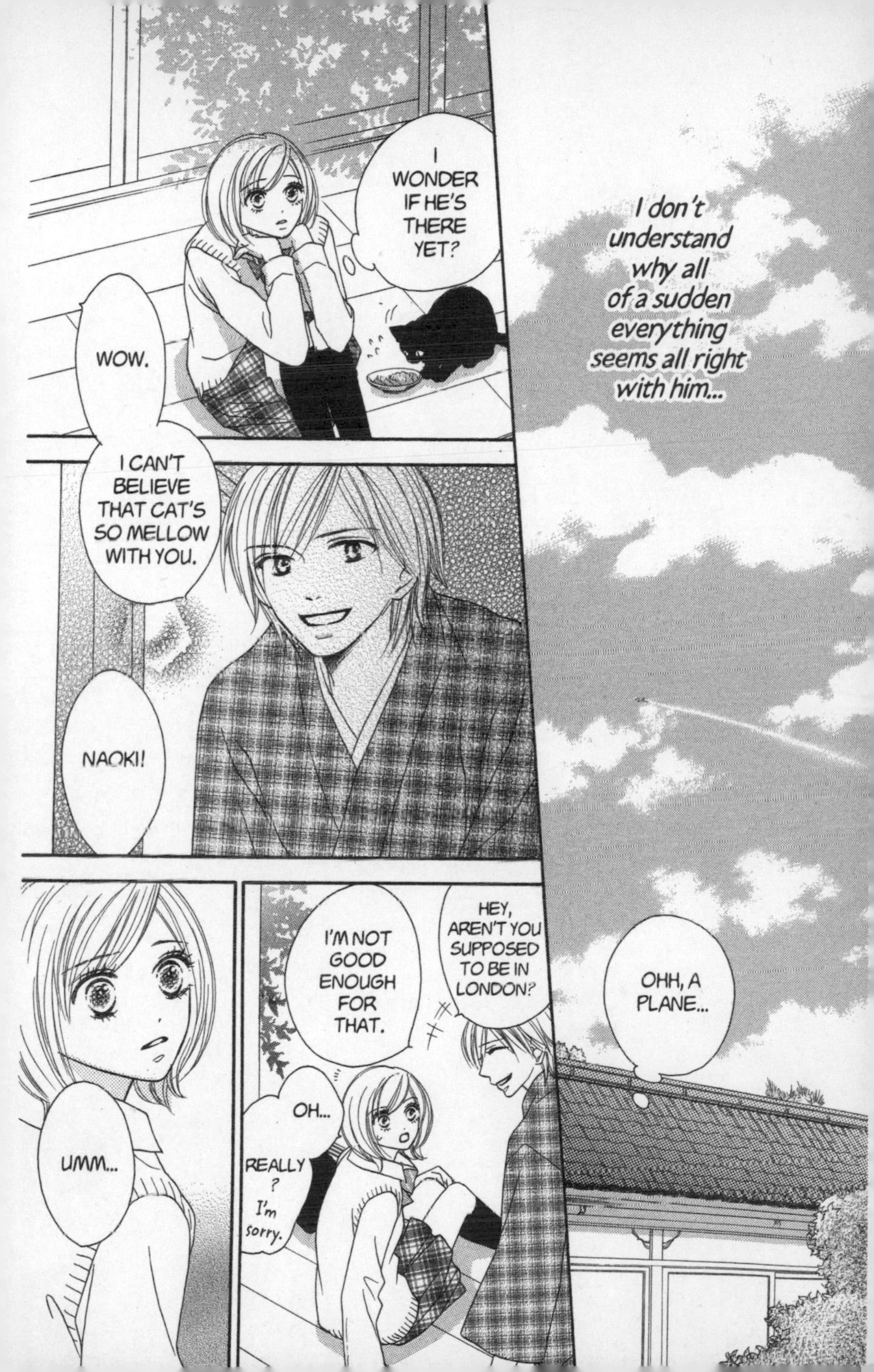
I don't understand why all of a sudden everything seems all right with him...
OHH, A PLANE...
I WONDER IF HE'S THERE YET?
WOW.
I CAN'T BELIEVE THAT CAT'S SO MELLOW WITH YOU.
NAOKI!
HEY, AREN'T YOU SUPPOSED TO BE IN LONDON?
I'M NOT GOOD ENOUGH FOR THAT.
OH...
REALLY?
I'm sorry.
UMM...

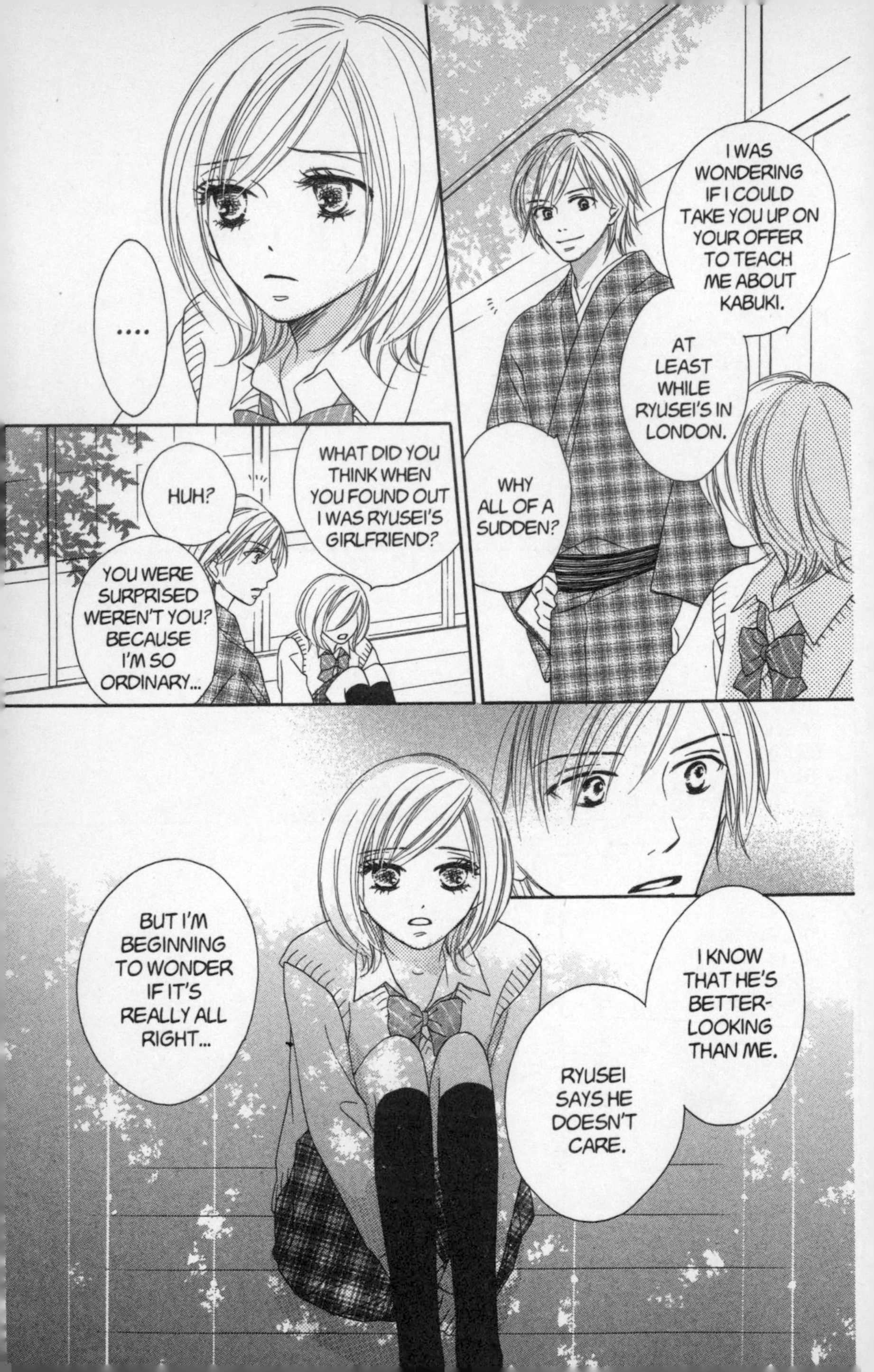
I WAS WONDERING IF I COULD TAKE YOU UP ON YOUR OFFER TO TEACH ME ABOUT KABUKI.
AT LEAST WHILE RYUSEI'S IN LONDON.
WHY ALL OF A SUDDEN?
....
WHAT DID YOU THINK WHEN YOU FOUND OUT I WAS RYUSEI'S GIRLFRIEND?
HUH?
YOU WERE SURPRISED WEREN'T YOU? BECAUSE I'M SO ORDINARY...
I KNOW THAT HE'S BETTER-LOOKING THAN ME.
RYUSEI SAYS HE DOESN'T CARE.
BUT I'M BEGINNING TO WONDER IF IT'S REALLY ALL RIGHT...

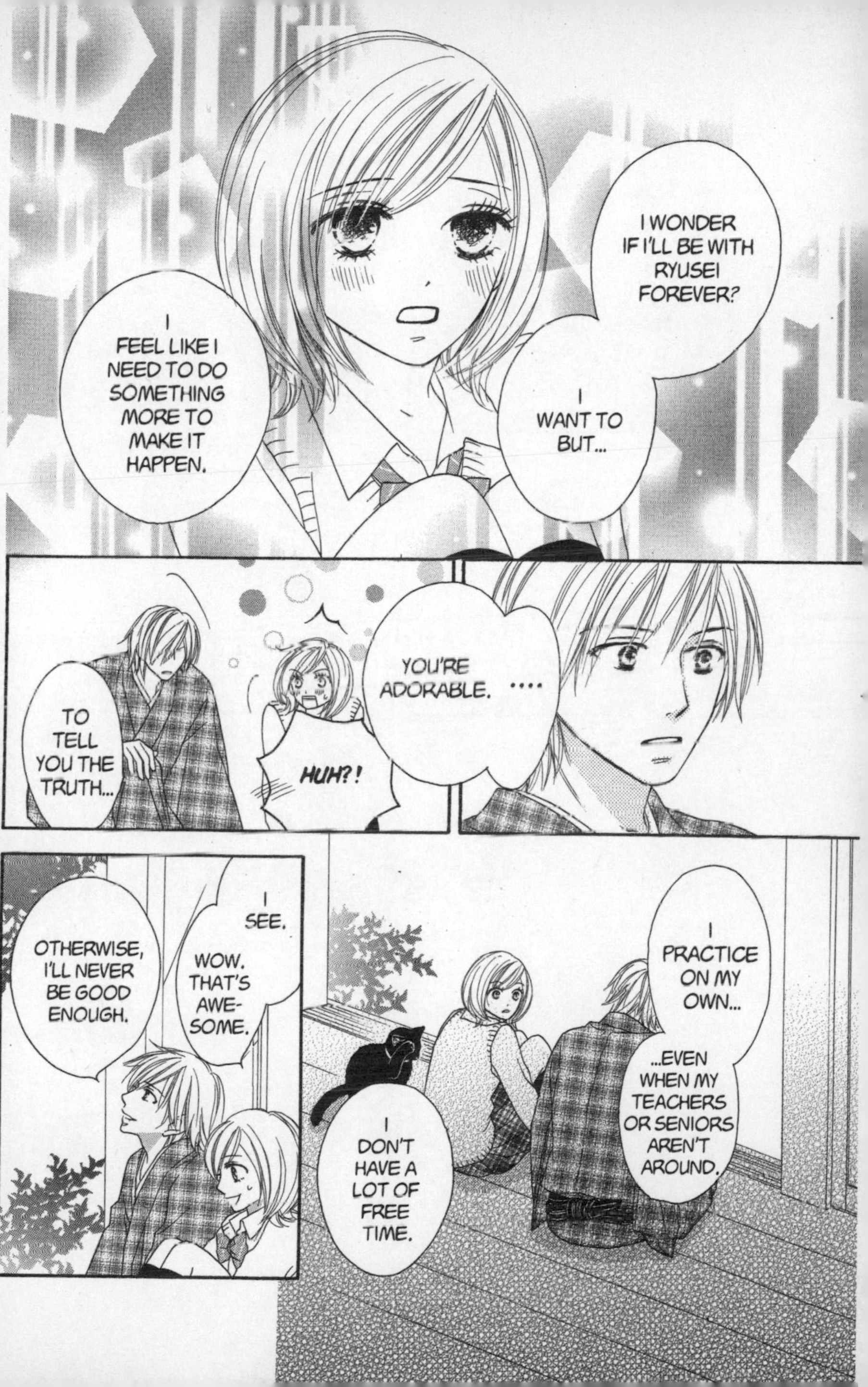
I WONDER IF I'LL BE WITH RYUSEI FOREVER?
I WANT TO BUT...
I FEEL LIKE I NEED TO DO SOMETHING MORE TO MAKE IT HAPPEN.
....
YOU'RE ADORABLE.
HUH?!
TO TELL YOU THE TRUTH...
I PRACTICE ON MY OWN...
...EVEN WHEN MY TEACHERS OR SENIORS AREN'T AROUND.
I DON'T HAVE A LOT OF FREE TIME.
I SEE.
WOW. THAT'S AWE-SOME.
OTHERWISE, I'LL NEVER BE GOOD ENOUGH.

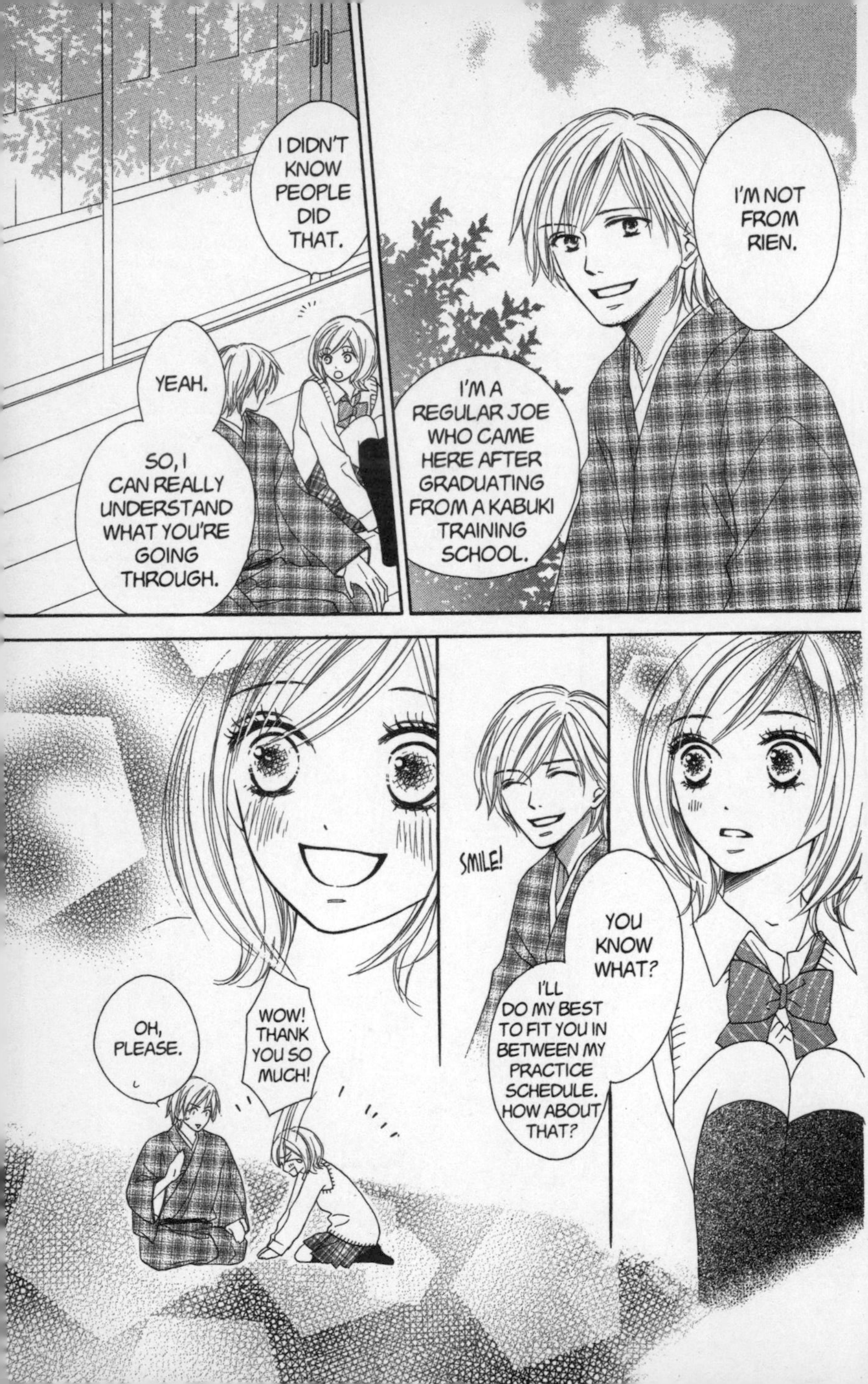
I'M NOT FROM RIEN.
I'M A REGULAR JOE WHO CAME HERE AFTER GRADUATING FROM A KABUKI TRAINING SCHOOL.
I DIDN'T KNOW PEOPLE DID THAT.
YEAH.
SO, I CAN REALLY UNDERSTAND WHAT YOU'RE GOING THROUGH.
SMILE!
YOU KNOW WHAT?
I'LL DO MY BEST TO FIT YOU IN BETWEEN MY PRACTICE SCHEDULE. HOW ABOUT THAT?
WOW! THANK YOU SO MUCH!
OH, PLEASE.

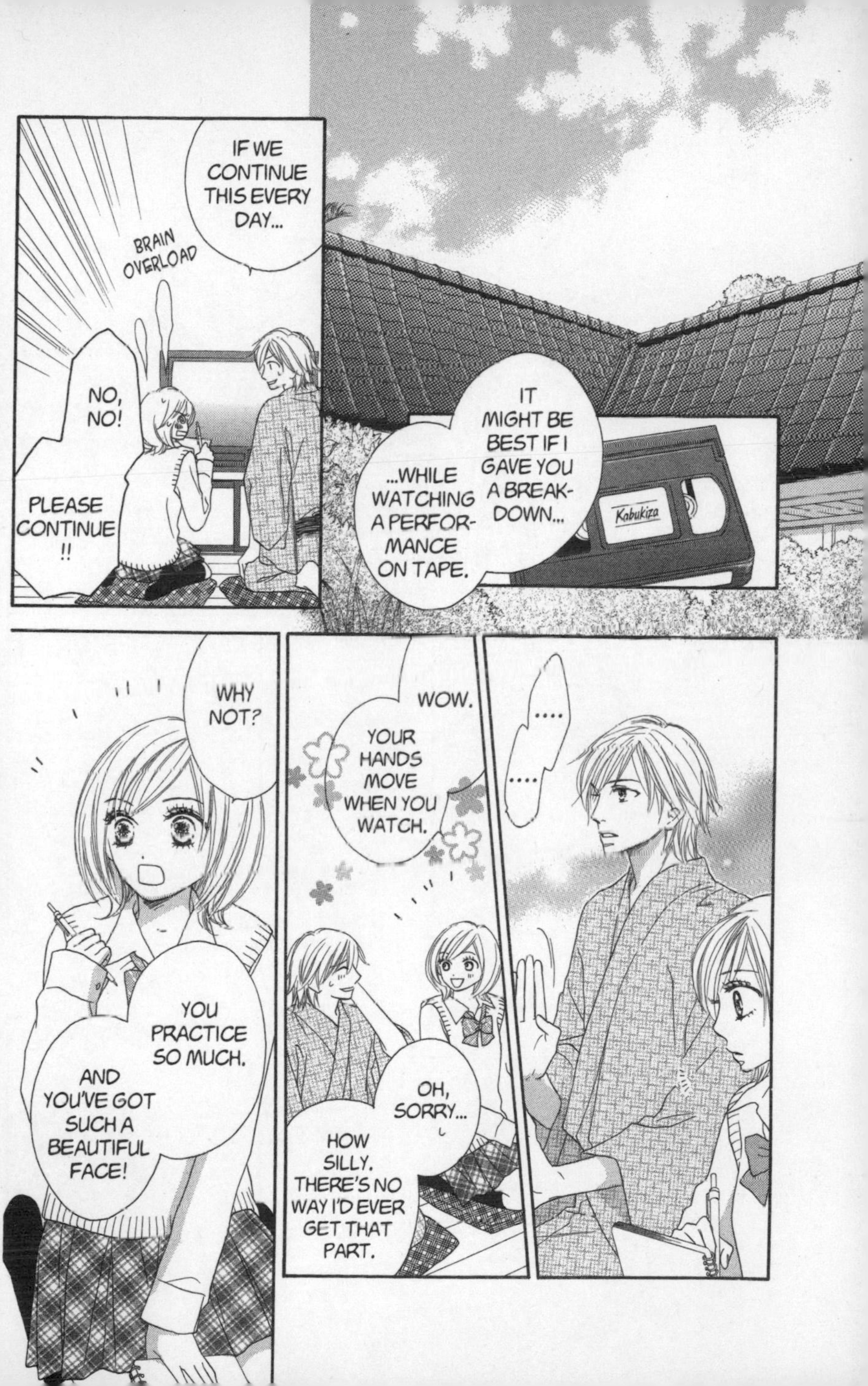
IT MIGHT BE BEST IF I GAVE YOU A BREAK-DOWN...
...WHILE WATCHING A PERFORMANCE ON TAPE.
Kabukiza
IF WE CONTINUE THIS EVERY DAY...
BRAIN OVERLOAD
NO, NO!
PLEASE CONTINUE !!
....
....
WOW.
YOUR HANDS MOVE WHEN YOU WATCH.
OH, SORRY...
HOW SILLY. THERE'S NO WAY I'D EVER GET THAT PART.
WHY NOT?
YOU PRACTICE SO MUCH.
AND YOU'VE GOT SUCH A BEAUTIFUL FACE!

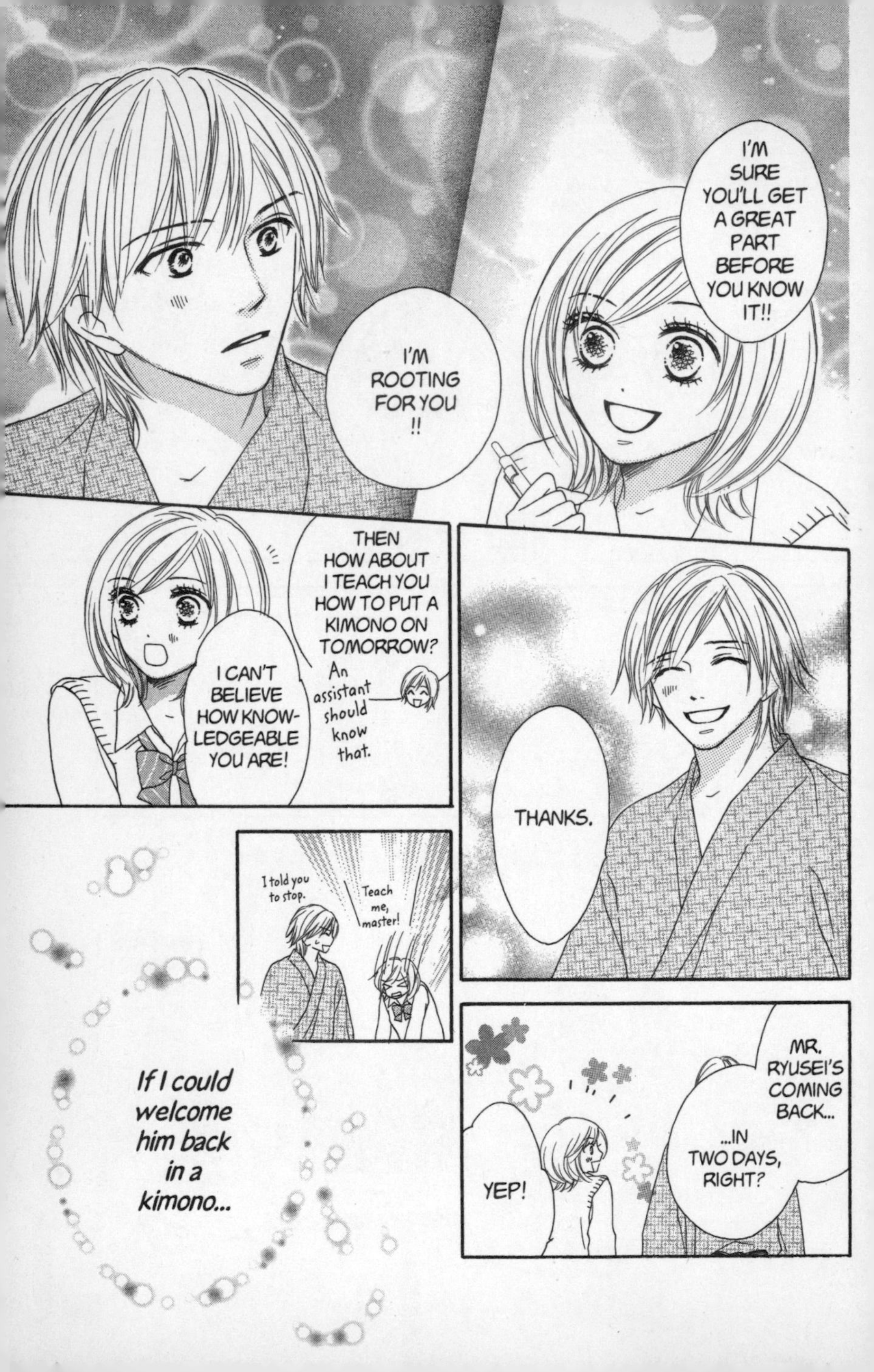
I'M SURE YOU'LL GET A GREAT PART BEFORE YOU KNOW IT!!
I'M ROOTING FOR YOU !!
THANKS.
THEN HOW ABOUT I TEACH YOU HOW TO PUT A KIMONO ON TOMORROW?
An assistant should know that.
I CAN'T BELIEVE HOW KNOW-LEDGEABLE YOU ARE!
Teach me, master!
I told you to stop.
MR. RYUSEI'S COMING BACK...
...IN TWO DAYS, RIGHT?
YEP!
If I could welcome him back in a kimono...

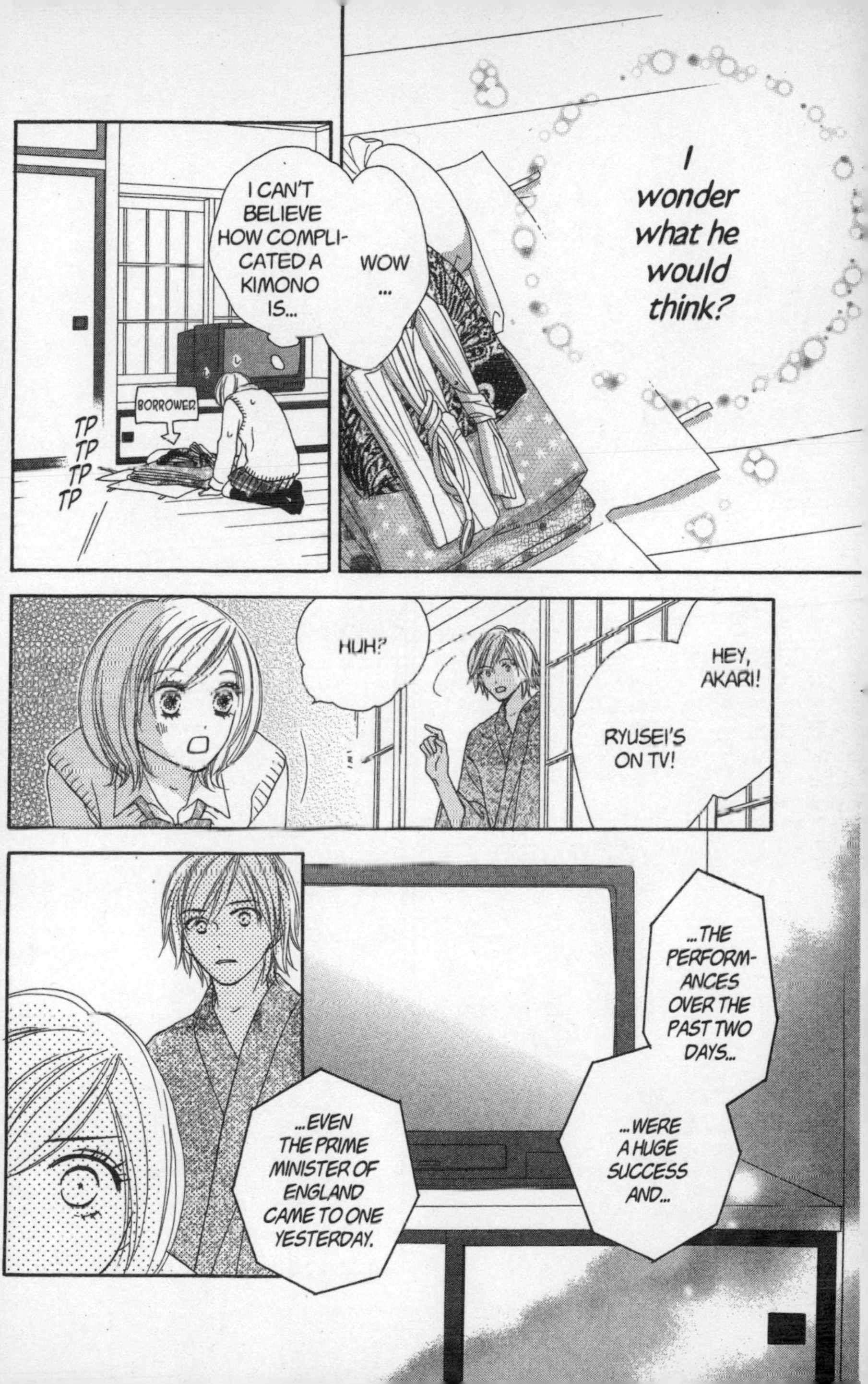
I wonder what he would think?
WOW...
I CAN'T BELIEVE HOW COMPLICATED A KIMONO IS...
BORROWER
TP TP TP TP
HEY, AKARI!
RYUSEI'S ON TV!
HUH?
...THE PERFORMANCES OVER THE PAST TWO DAYS...
...WERE A HUGE SUCCESS AND...
...EVEN THE PRIME MINISTER OF ENGLAND CAME TO ONE YESTERDAY.

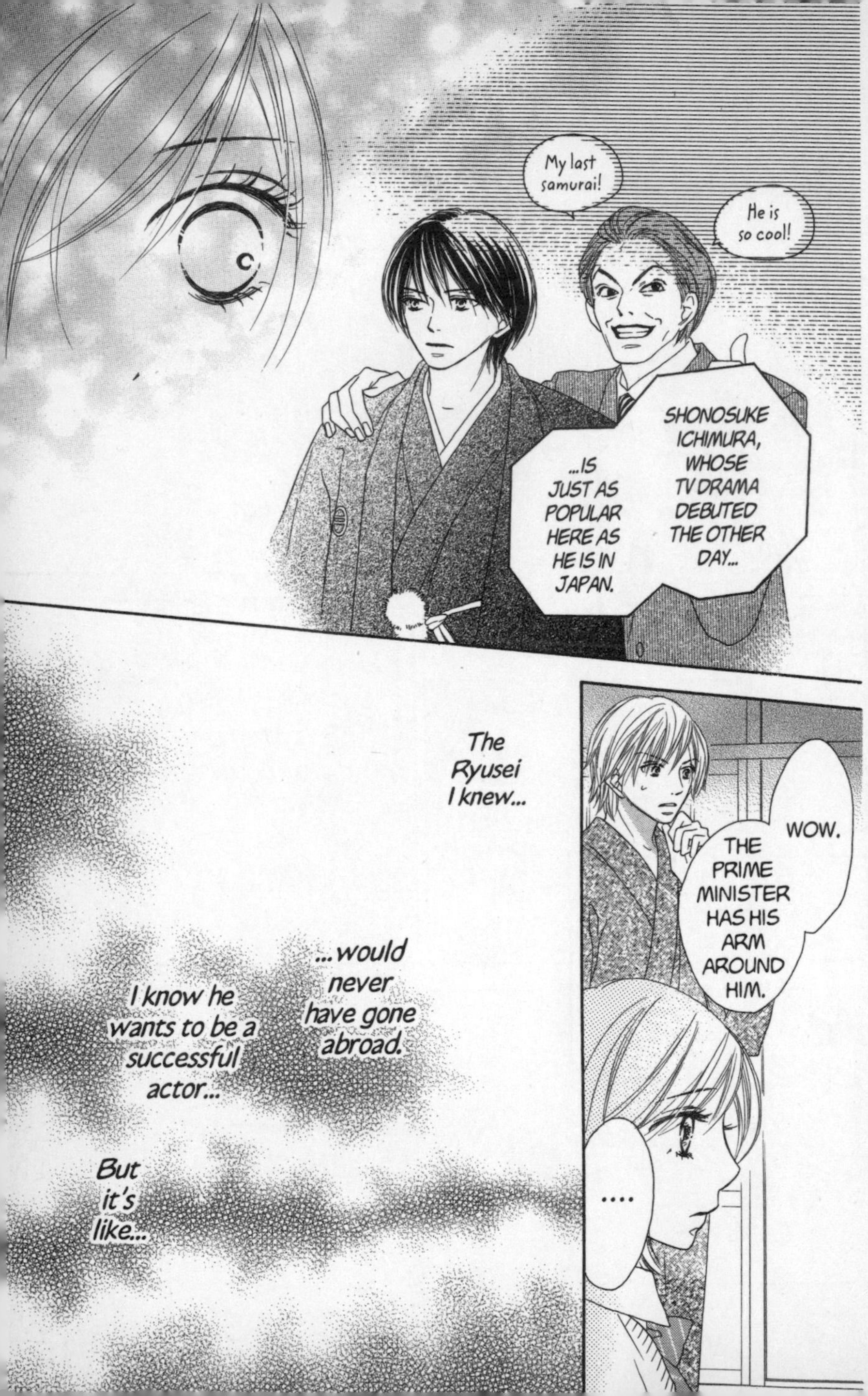
My last samurai!
He is so cool!
SHONOSUKE ICHIMURA, WHOSE TV DRAMA DEBUTED THE OTHER DAY...
...IS JUST AS POPULAR HERE AS HE IS IN JAPAN.
WOW. THE PRIME MINISTER HAS HIS ARM AROUND HIM.
....
The Ryusei I knew...
...would never have gone abroad.
I know he wants to be a successful actor...
But it's like...

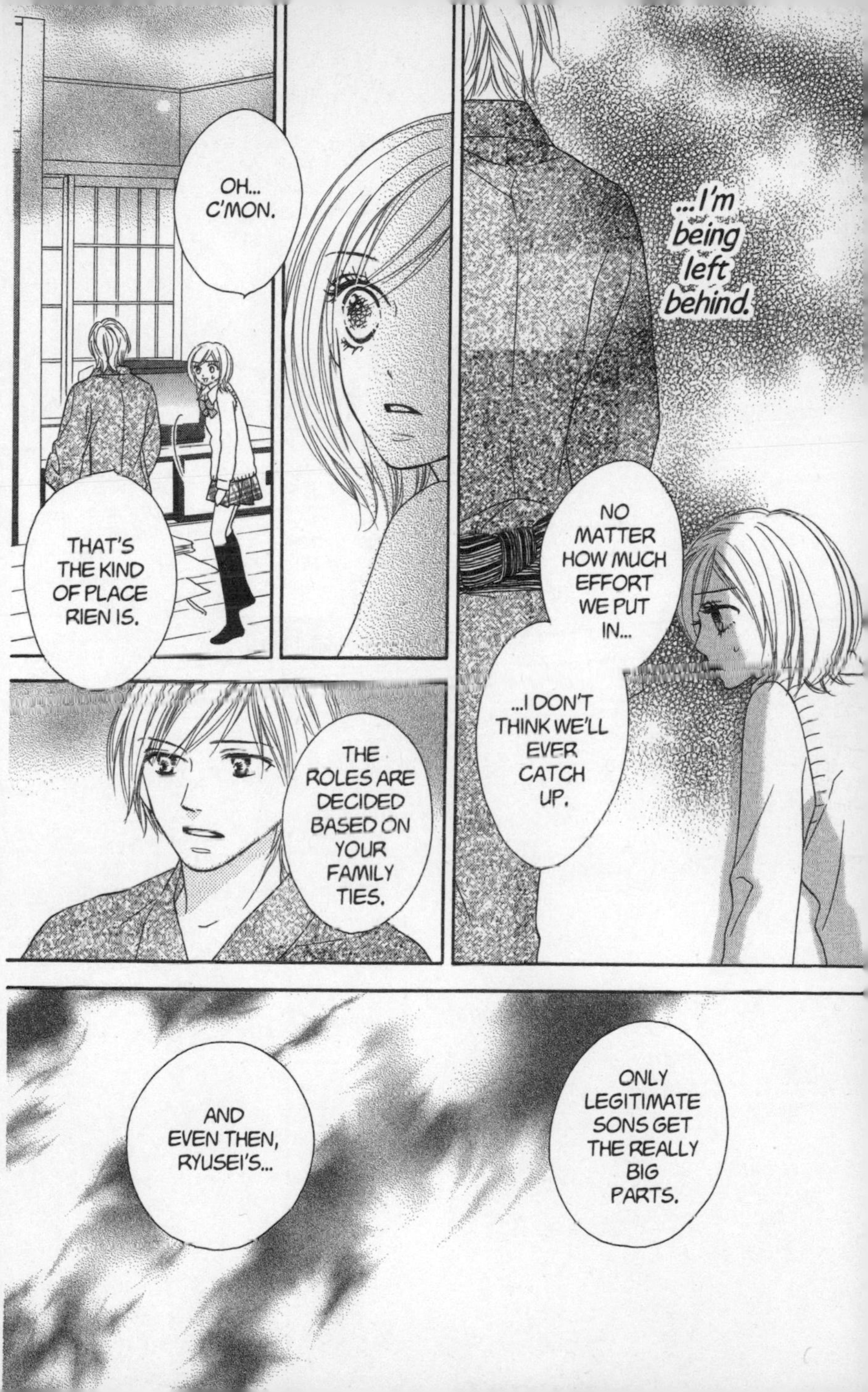
...I'm being left behind.
NO MATTER HOW MUCH EFFORT WE PUT IN...
...I DON'T THINK WE'LL EVER CATCH UP.
OH... C'MON.
THAT'S THE KIND OF PLACE RIEN IS.
THE ROLES ARE DECIDED BASED ON YOUR FAMILY TIES.
ONLY LEGITIMATE SONS GET THE REALLY BIG PARTS.
AND EVEN THEN, RYUSEI'S...

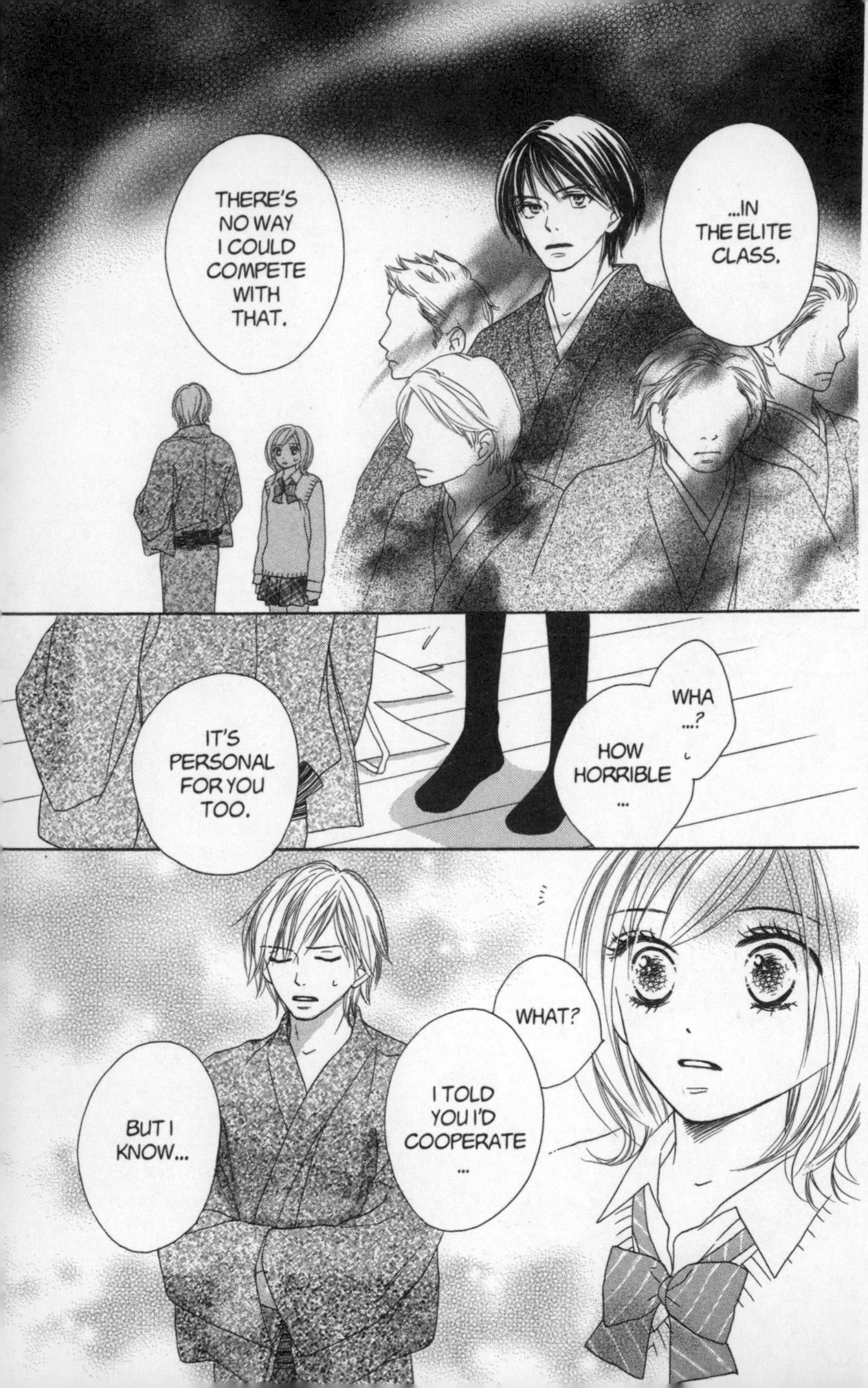
...IN THE ELITE CLASS.
THERE'S NO WAY I COULD COMPETE WITH THAT.
WHA ...?
HOW HORRIBLE ...
IT'S PERSONAL FOR YOU TOO.
WHAT?
I TOLD YOU I'D COOPERATE ...
BUT I KNOW...

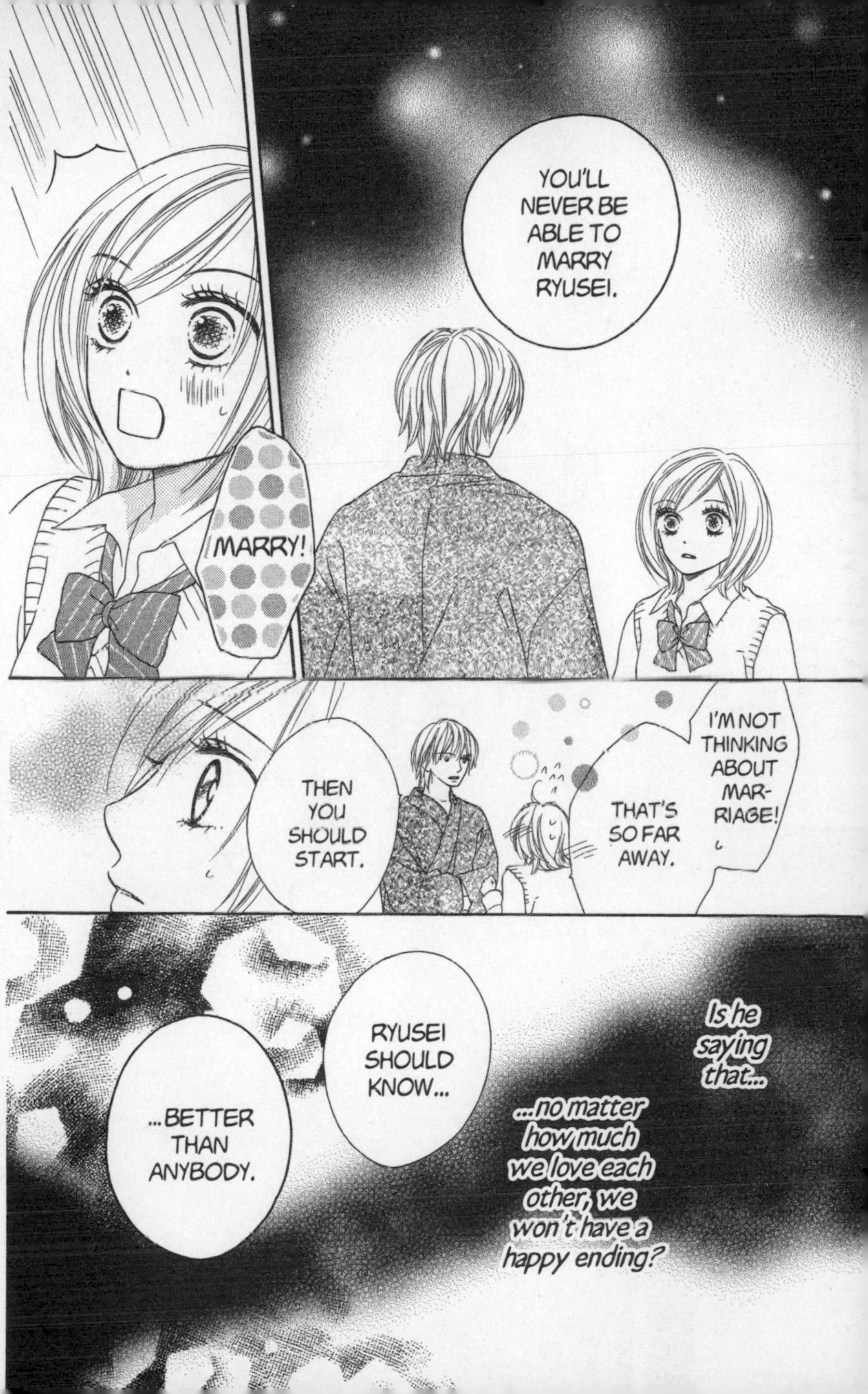
YOU'LL NEVER BE ABLE TO MARRY RYUSEI.
MARRY!
I'M NOT THINKING ABOUT MAR-RIAGE!
THAT'S SO FAR AWAY.
THEN YOU SHOULD START.
Is he saying that...
...no matter how much we love each other, we won't have a happy ending?
RYUSEI SHOULD KNOW...
...BETTER THAN ANYBODY.

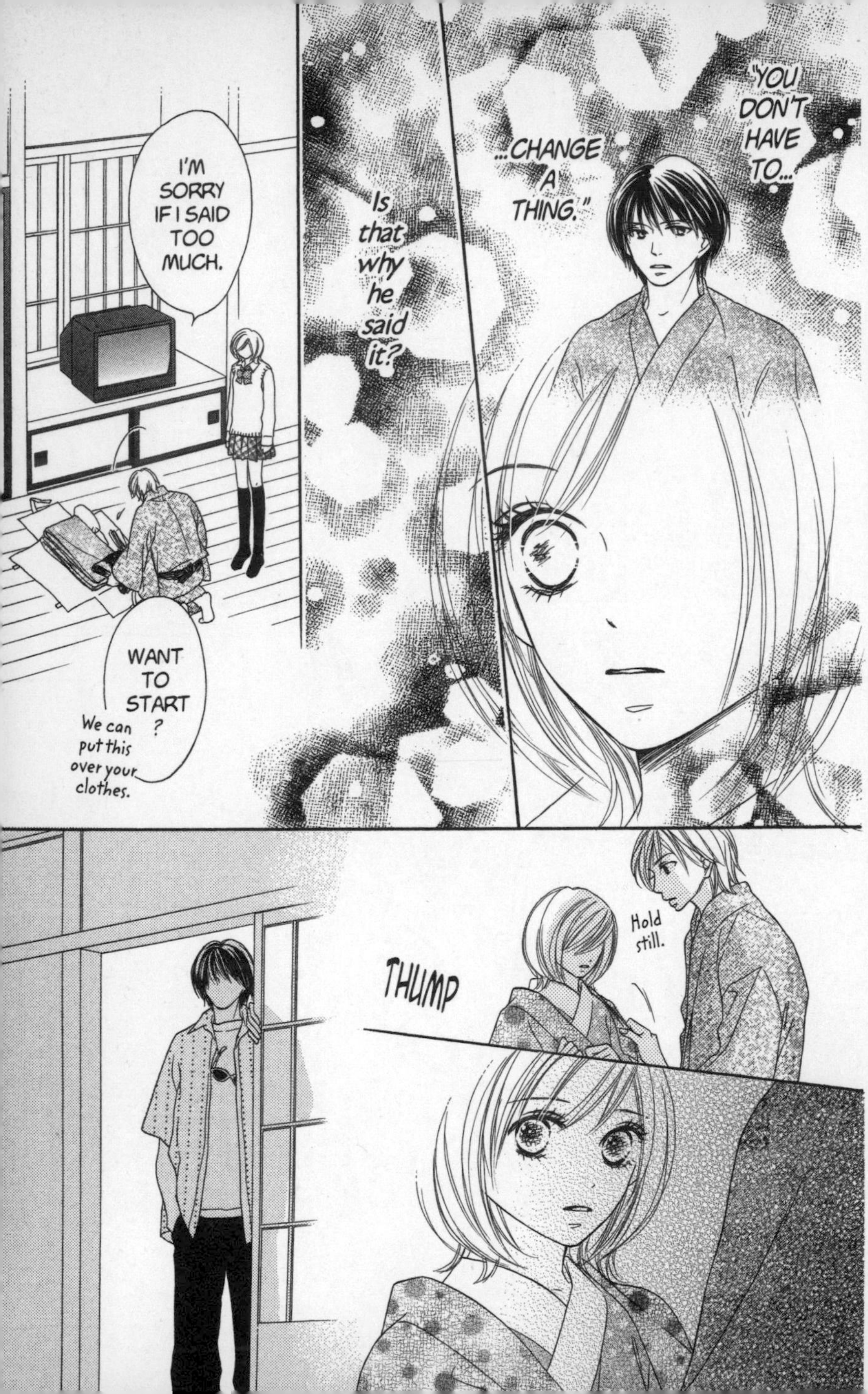
"YOU DON'T HAVE TO...
...CHANGE A THING."
Is that why he said it?
I'M SORRY IF I SAID TOO MUCH.
WANT TO START?
We can put this over your clothes.
Hold still.
THUMP

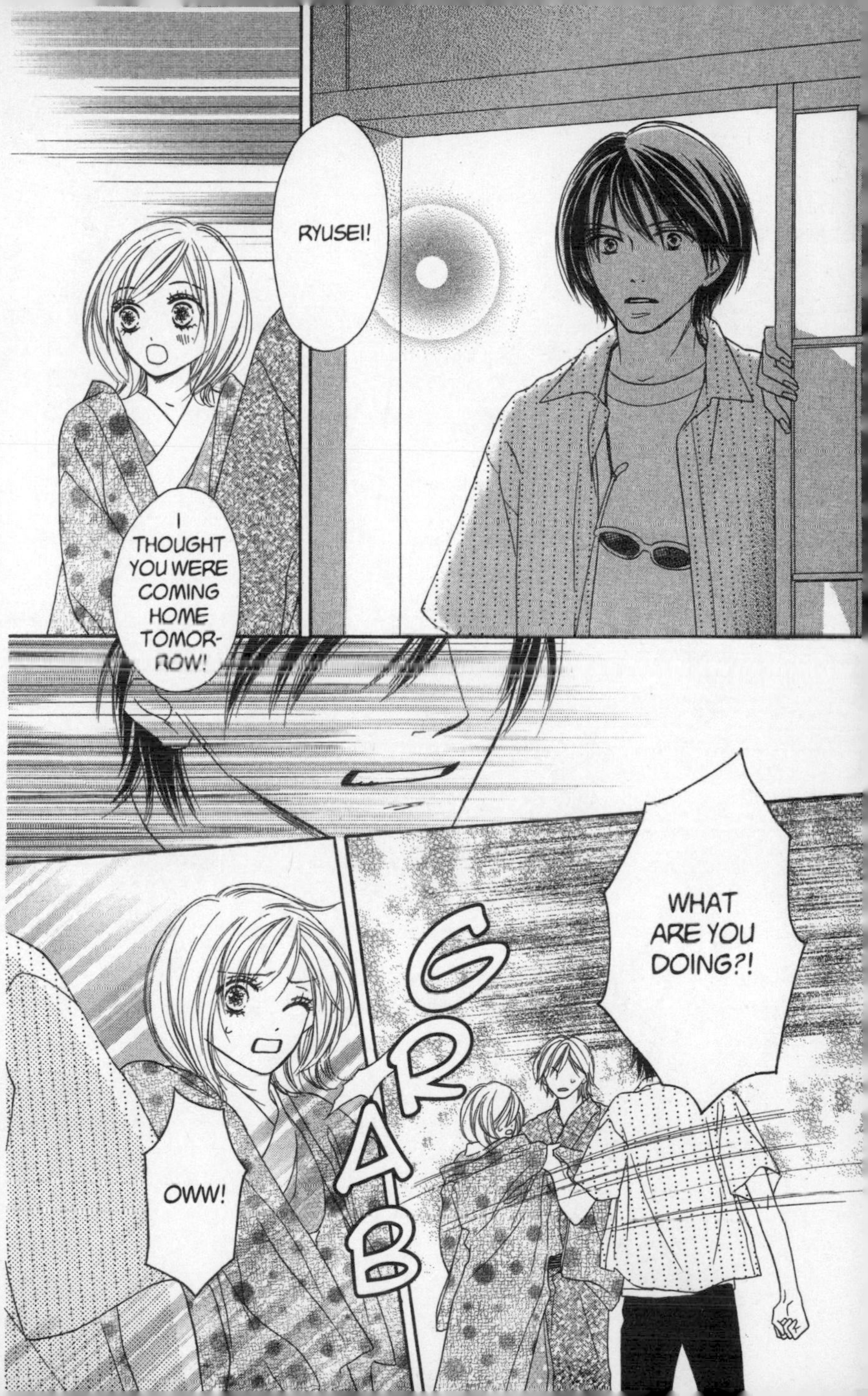
RYUSEI!
I THOUGHT YOU WERE COMING HOME TOMOR-ROW!
WHAT ARE YOU DOING?!
GRAB
OWW!

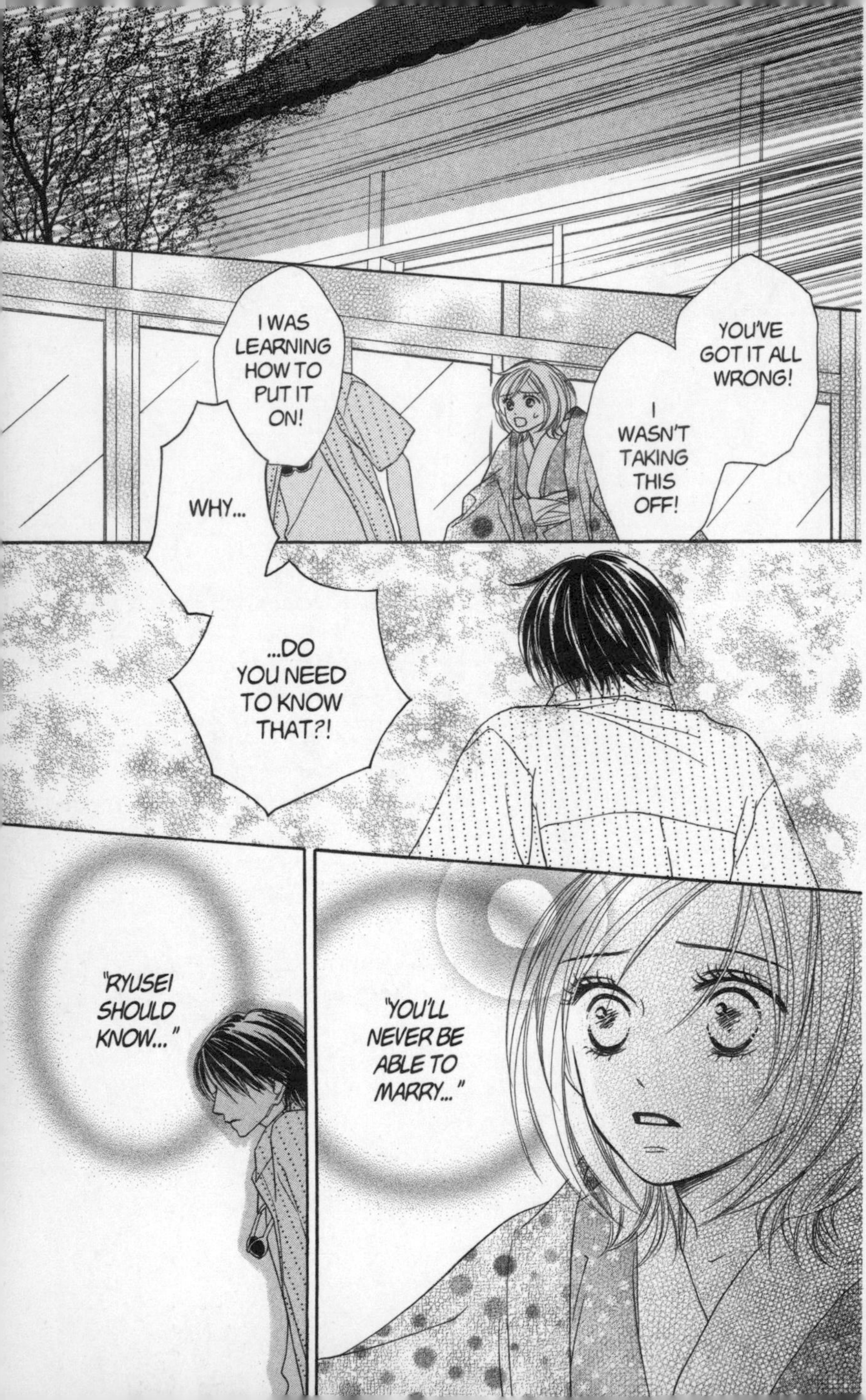
YOU'VE GOT IT ALL WRONG!
I WASN'T TAKING THIS OFF!
I WAS LEARNING HOW TO PUT IT ON!
WHY...
...DO YOU NEED TO KNOW THAT?!
"YOU'LL NEVER BE ABLE TO MARRY..."
"RYUSEI SHOULD KNOW..."

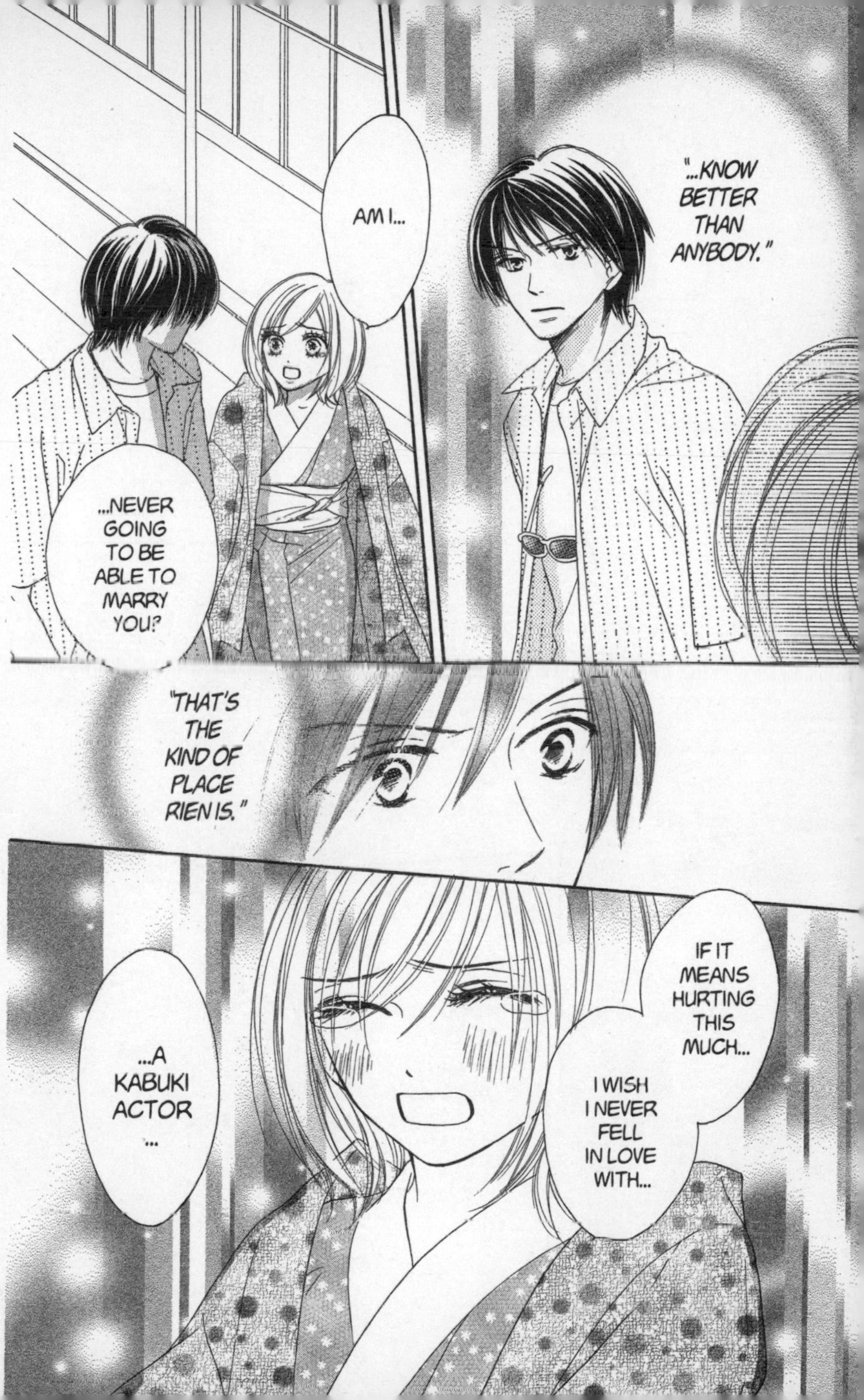
"...KNOW BETTER THAN ANYBODY."
AM I...
...NEVER GOING TO BE ABLE TO MARRY YOU?
"THAT'S THE KIND OF PLACE RIEN IS."
IF IT MEANS HURTING THIS MUCH...
I WISH I NEVER FELL IN LOVE WITH...
...A KABUKI ACTOR ...

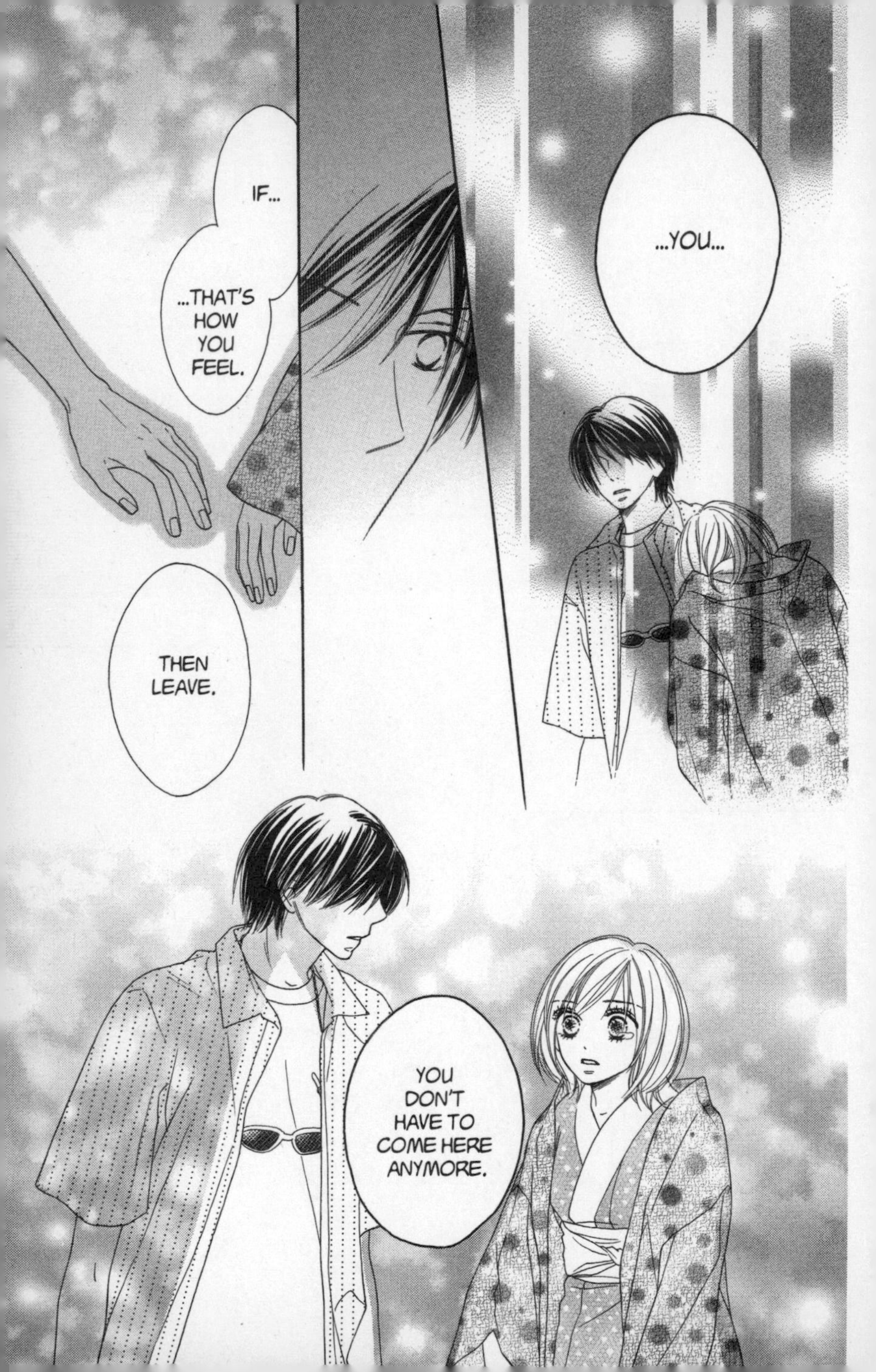
...YOU...
IF...
...THAT'S HOW YOU FEEL.
THEN LEAVE.
YOU DON'T HAVE TO COME HERE ANYMORE.

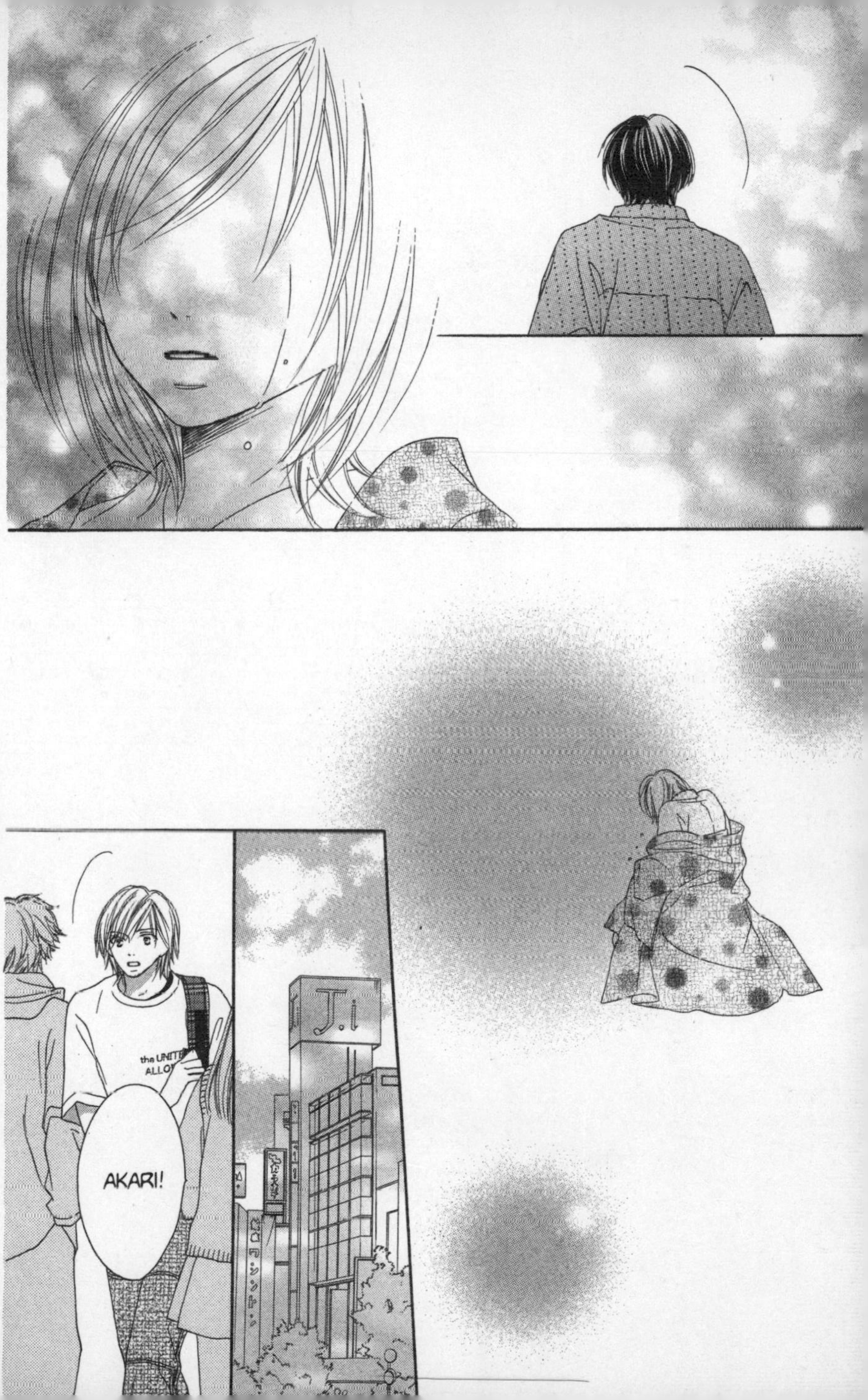
AKARI!

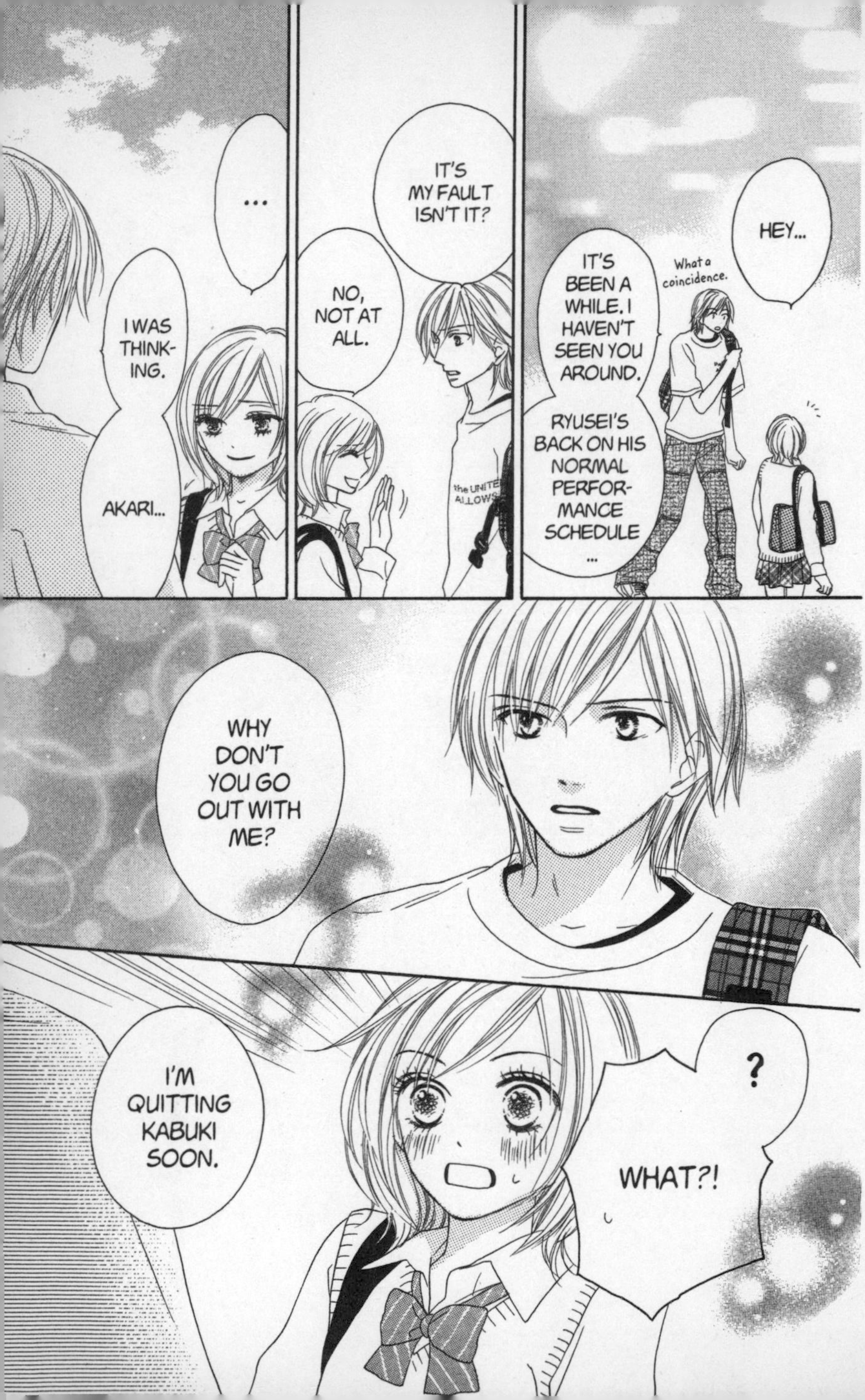
HEY...
What a coincidence.
IT'S BEEN A WHILE. I HAVEN'T SEEN YOU AROUND.
RYUSEI'S BACK ON HIS NORMAL PERFORMANCE SCHEDULE ...
IT'S MY FAULT ISN'T IT?
NO, NOT AT ALL.
...
I WAS THINKING.
AKARI...
WHY DON'T YOU GO OUT WITH ME?
I'M QUITTING KABUKI SOON.
?
WHAT?!

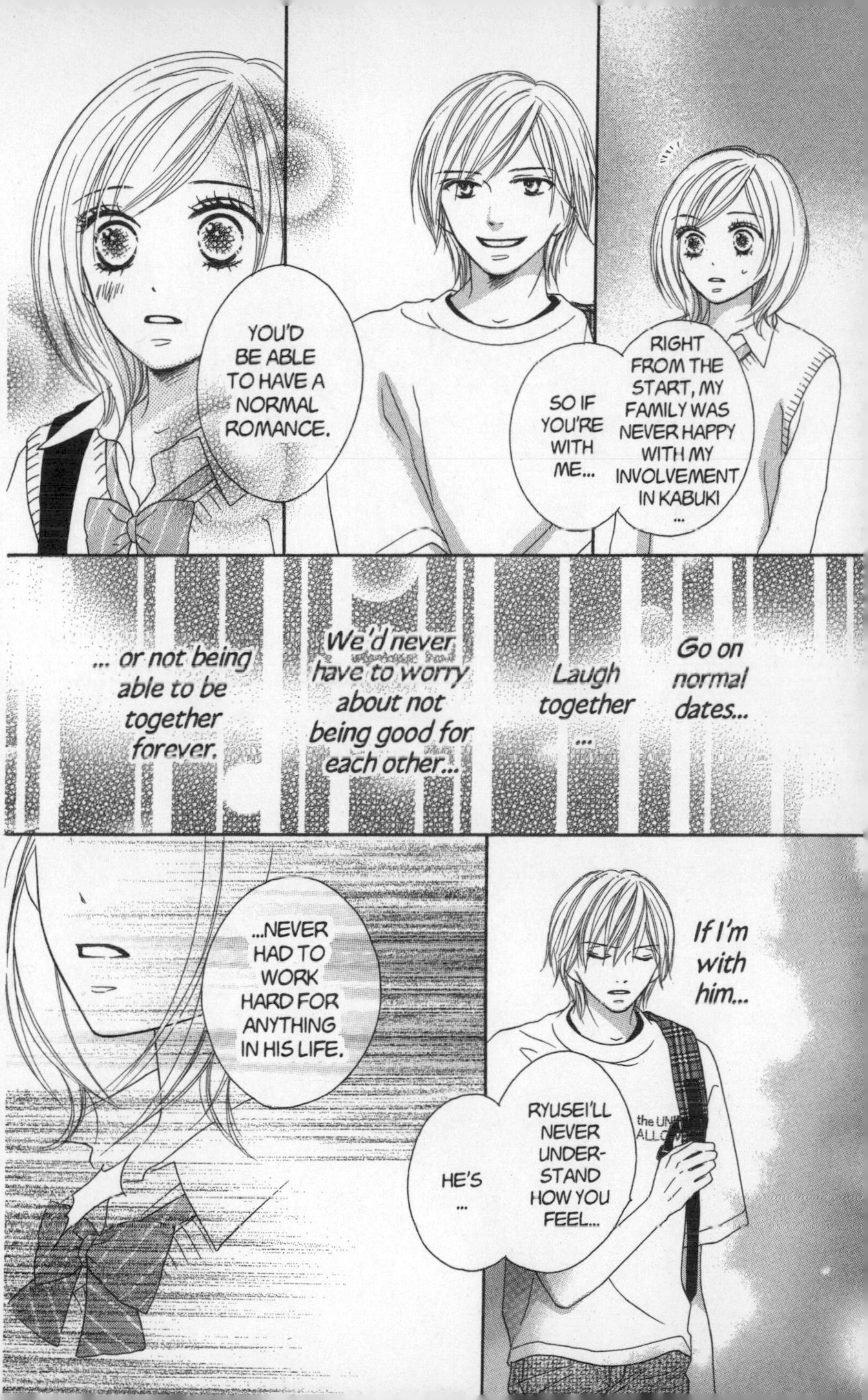
RIGHT FROM THE START, MY FAMILY WAS NEVER HAPPY WITH MY INVOLVEMENT IN KABUKI ...
SO IF YOU'RE WITH ME...
YOU'D BE ABLE TO HAVE A NORMAL ROMANCE.
Go on normal dates...
Laugh together ...
We'd never have to worry about not being good for each other...
... or not being able to be together forever.
If I'm with him...
RYUSEI'LL NEVER UNDER-STAND HOW YOU FEEL...
HE'S ...
...NEVER HAD TO WORK HARD FOR ANYTHING IN HIS LIFE.

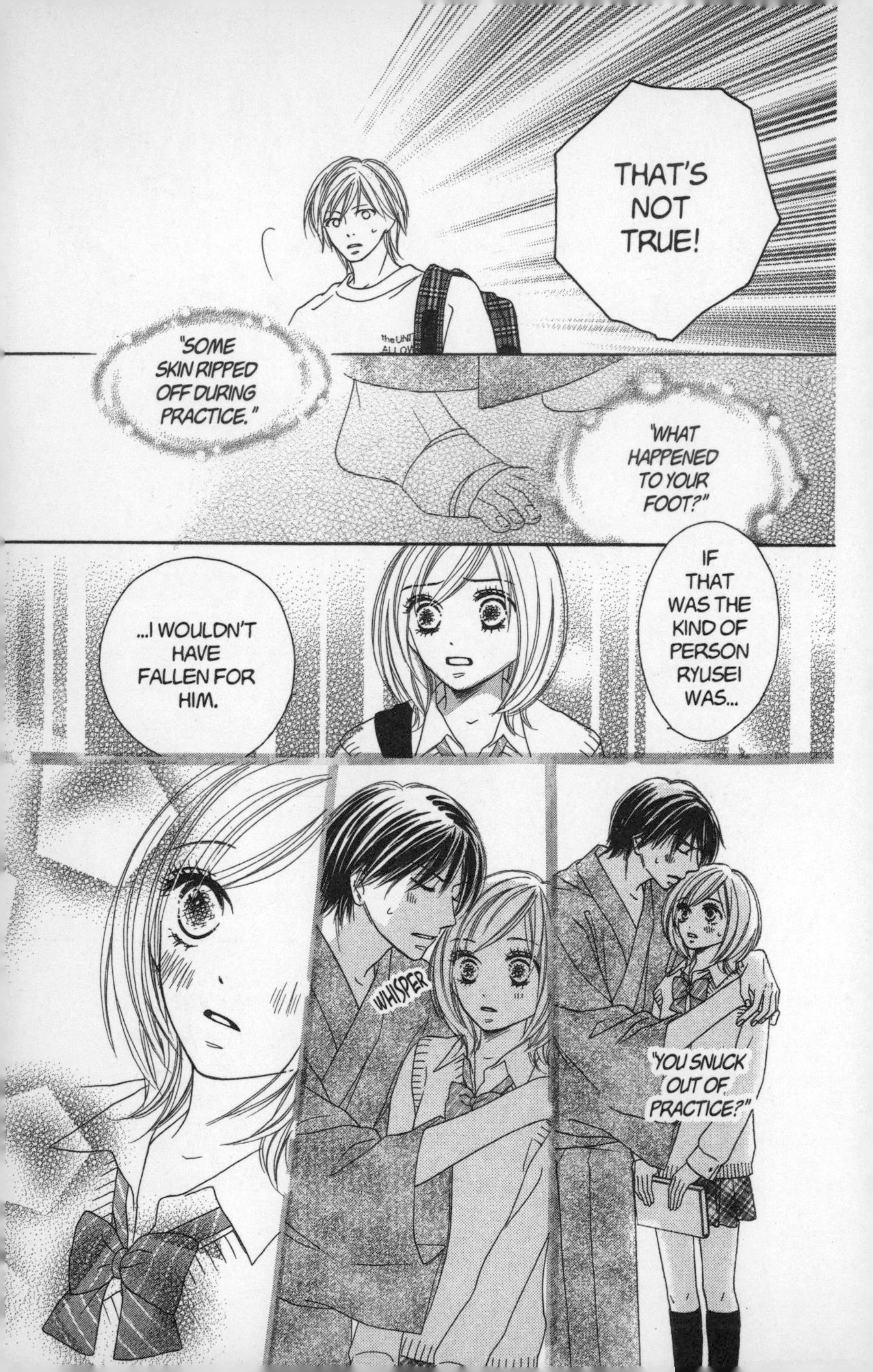
THAT'S NOT TRUE!
"WHAT HAPPENED TO YOUR FOOT?"
"SOME SKIN RIPPED OFF DURING PRACTICE."
IF THAT WAS THE KIND OF PERSON RYUSEI WAS...
...I WOULDN'T HAVE FALLEN FOR HIM.
"YOU SNUCK OUT OF PRACTICE?"
WHISPER

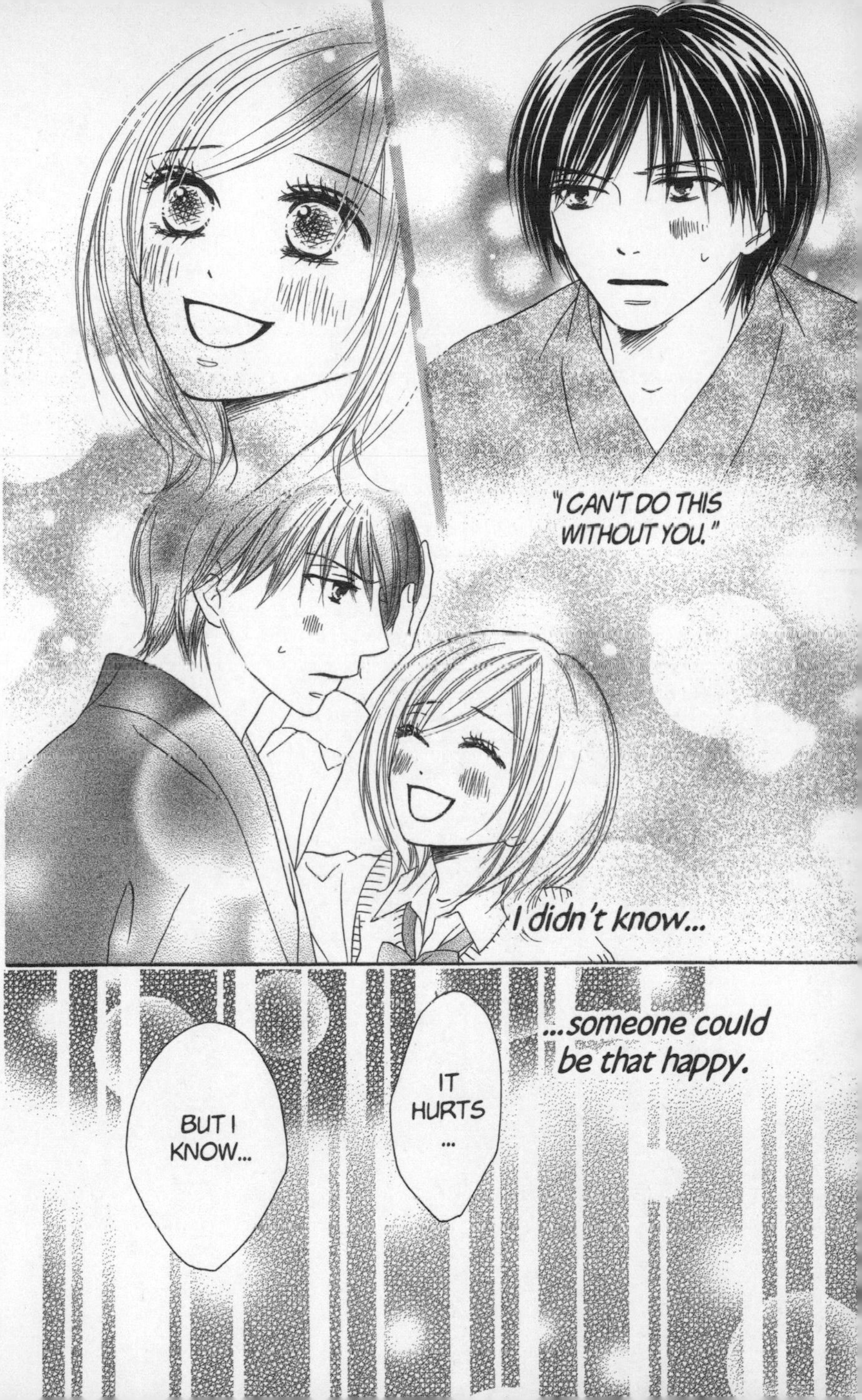
"I CAN'T DO THIS WITHOUT YOU."
I didn't know...
...someone could be that happy.
IT HURTS ...
BUT I KNOW...

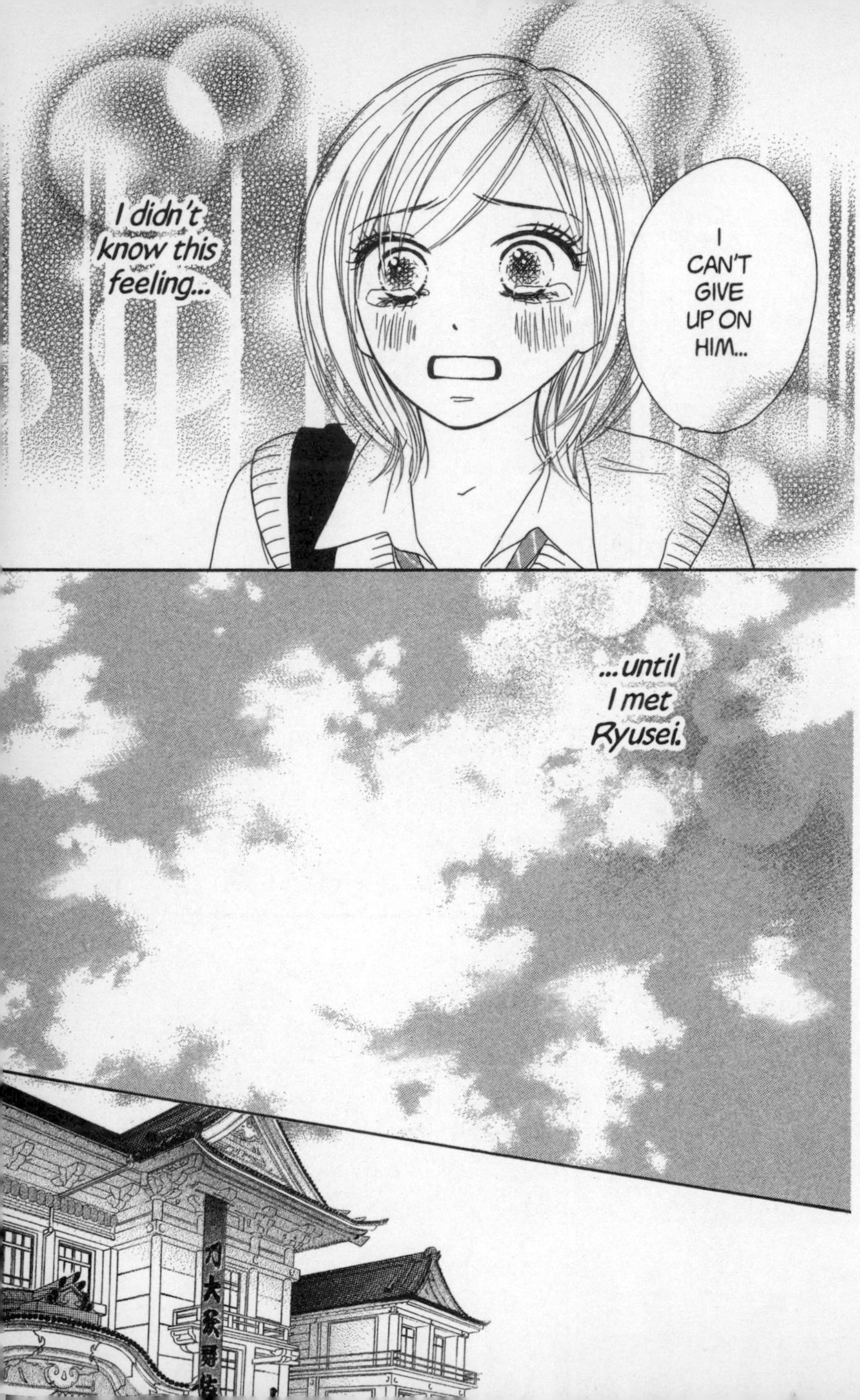
I CAN'T GIVE UP ON HIM...
I didn't know this feeling...
...until I met Ryusei.

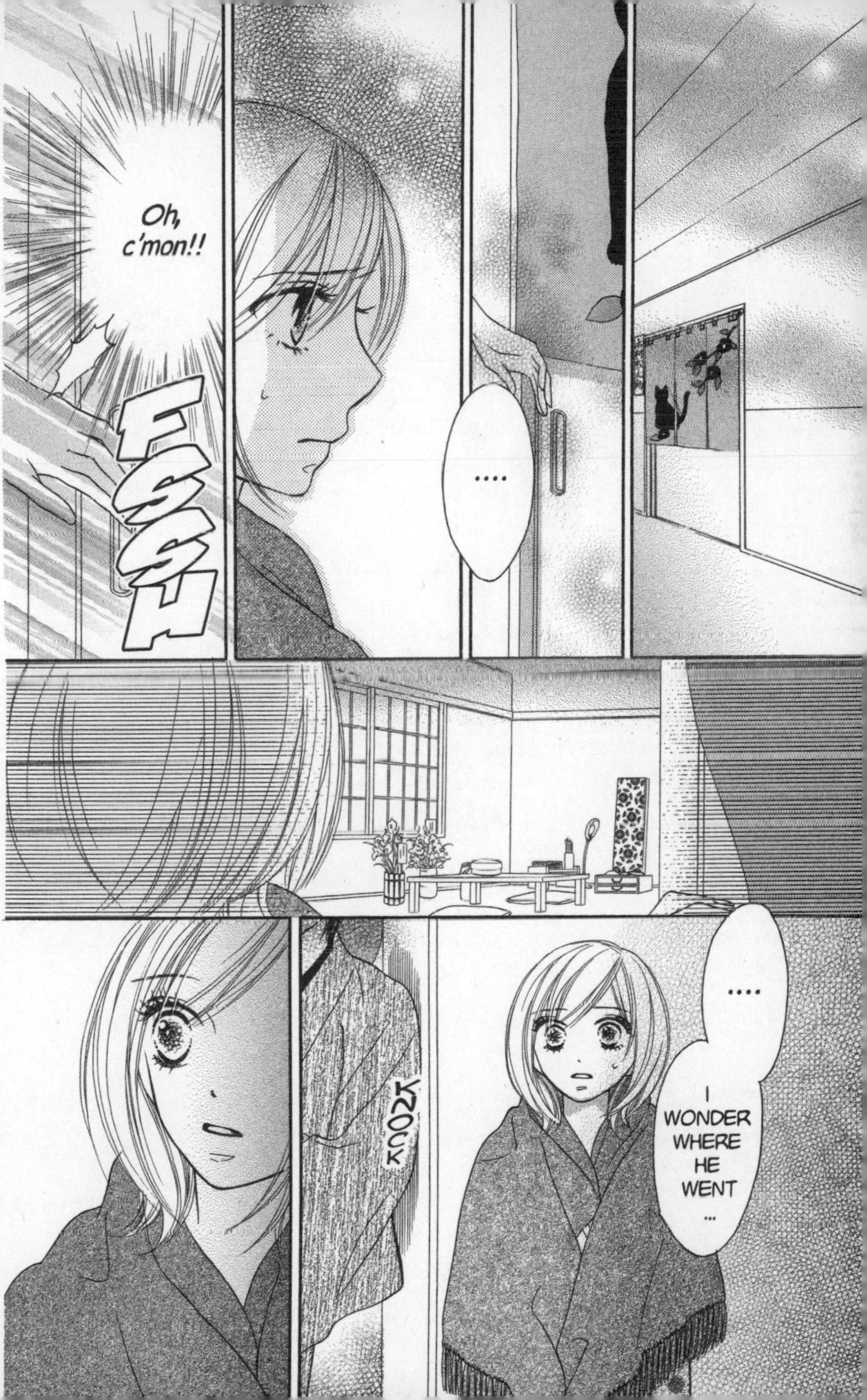
....
Oh, c'mon!!
FSSH
....
I WONDER WHERE HE WENT ...
KNOCK

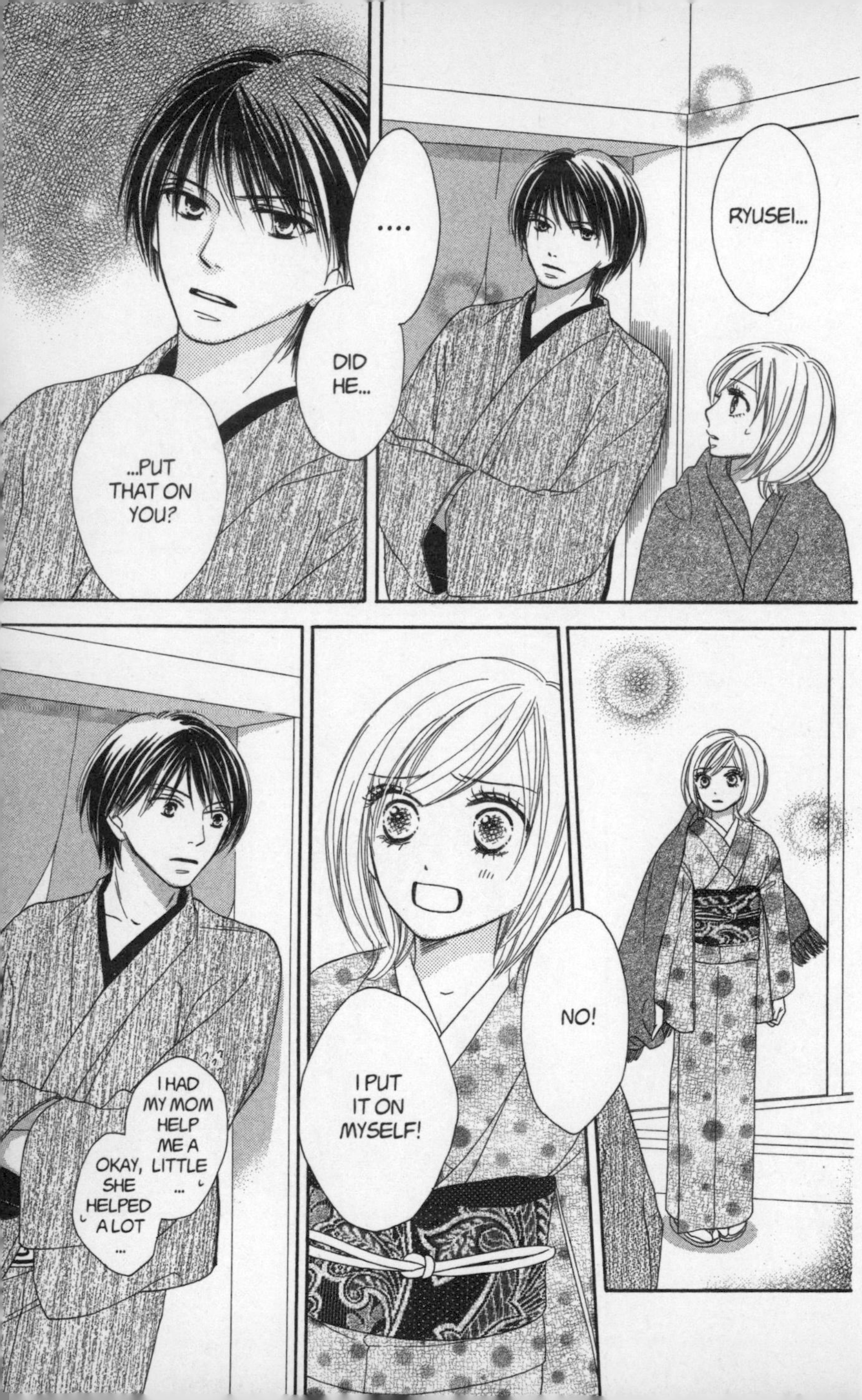
RYUSEI...
....
DID HE...
...PUT THAT ON YOU?
NO!
I PUT IT ON MYSELF!
I HAD MY MOM HELP ME A LITTLE...
OKAY, SHE HELPED A LOT...

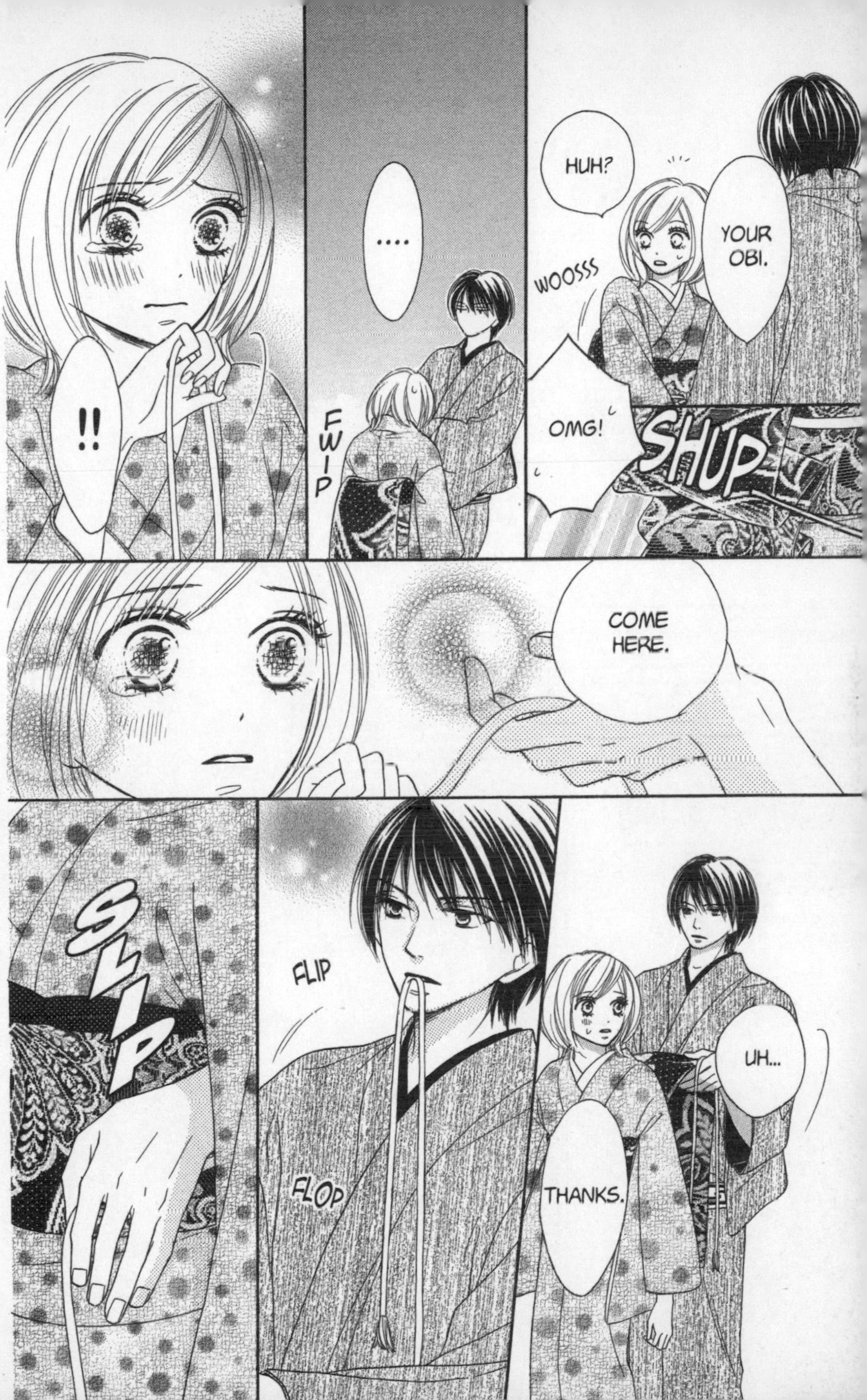
YOUR OBI.
HUH?
WOOSSS
OMG!
SHUP
....
FWIP
!!
COME HERE.
UH...
THANKS.
FLIP
FLOP
SLIP

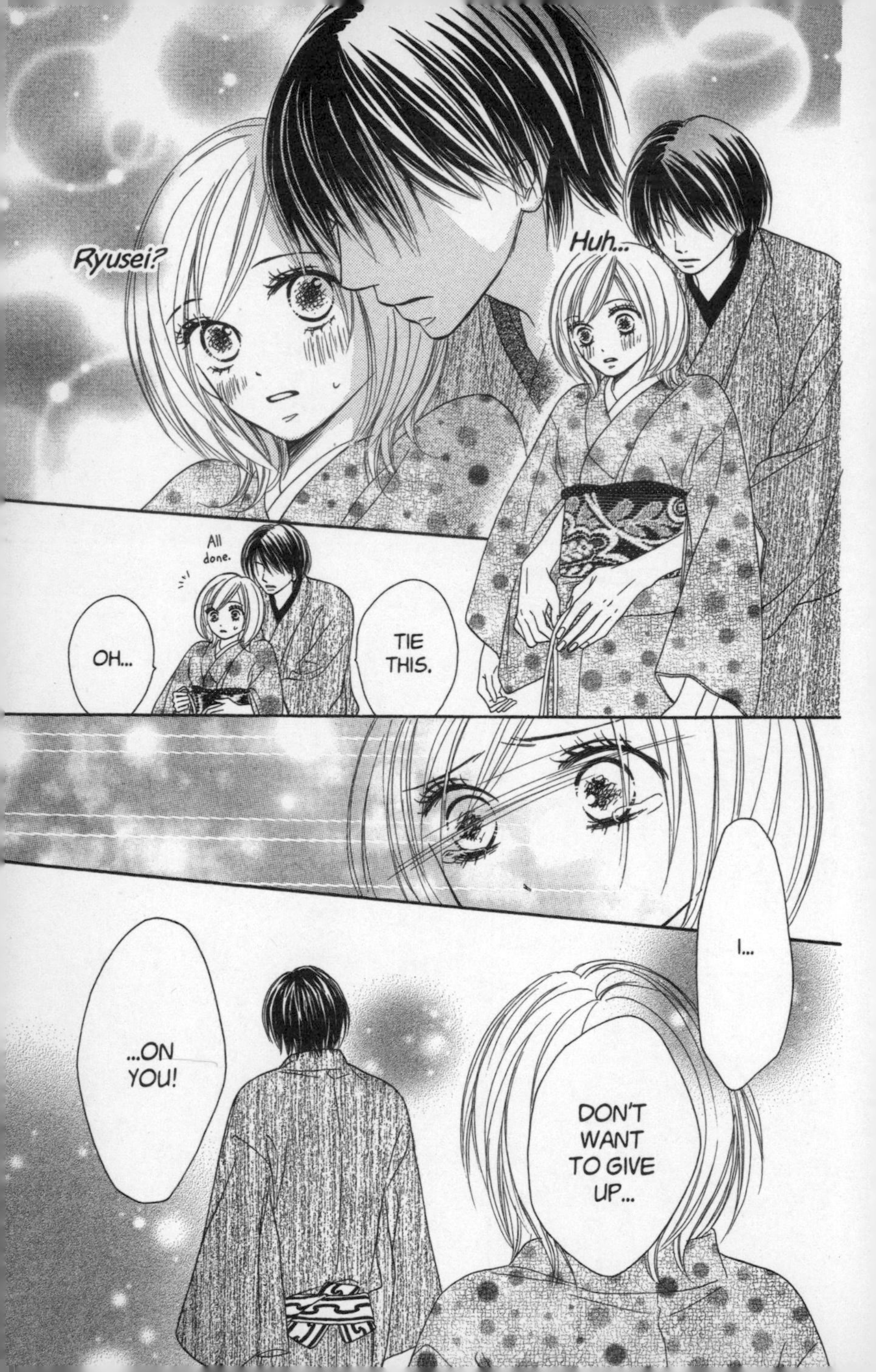
Huh...
Ryusei?
TIE THIS.
All done.
OH...
I...
DON'T WANT TO GIVE UP...
...ON YOU!

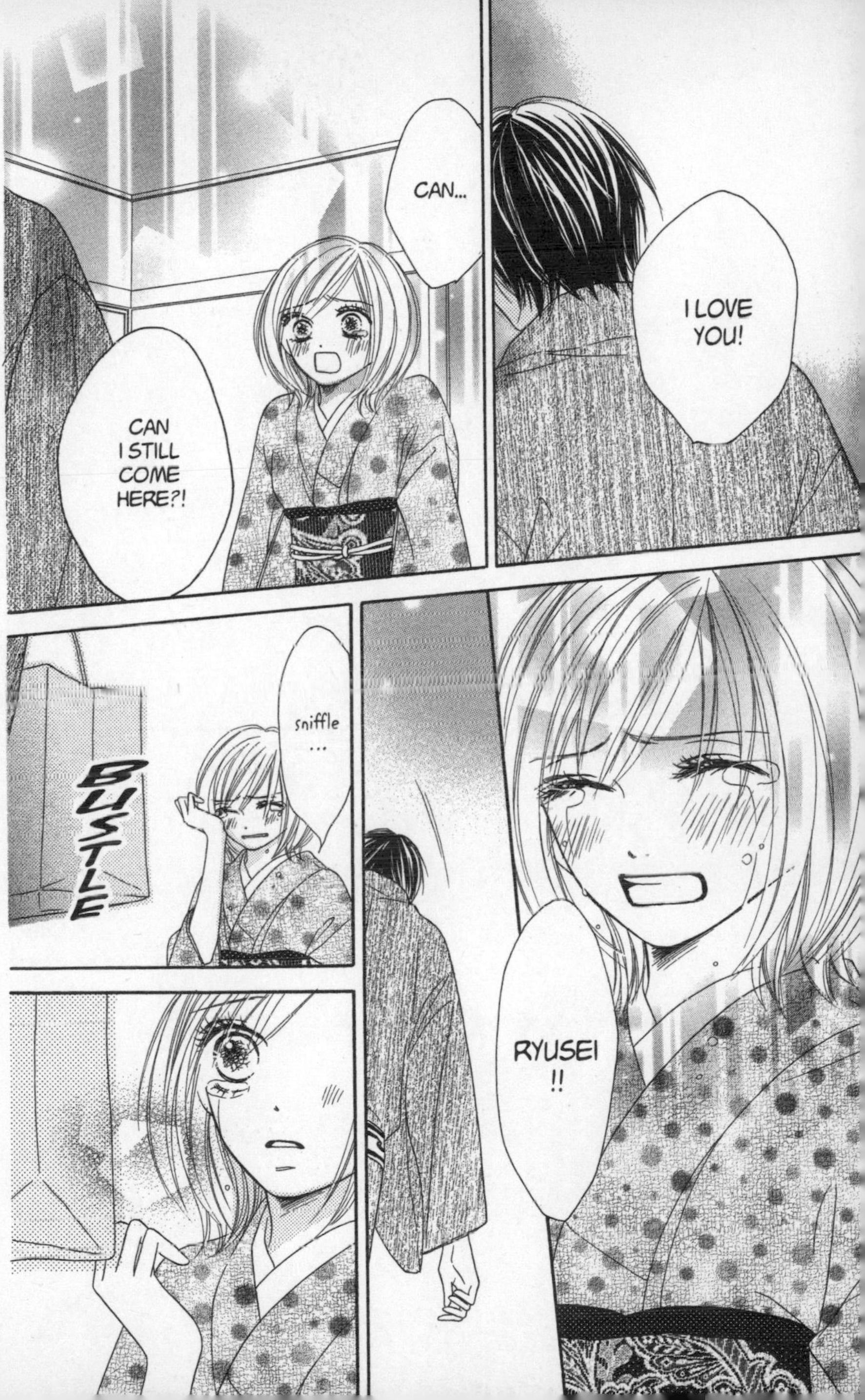
I LOVE YOU!
CAN...
CAN I STILL COME HERE?!
RYUSEI !!
sniffle ...
BUSTLE

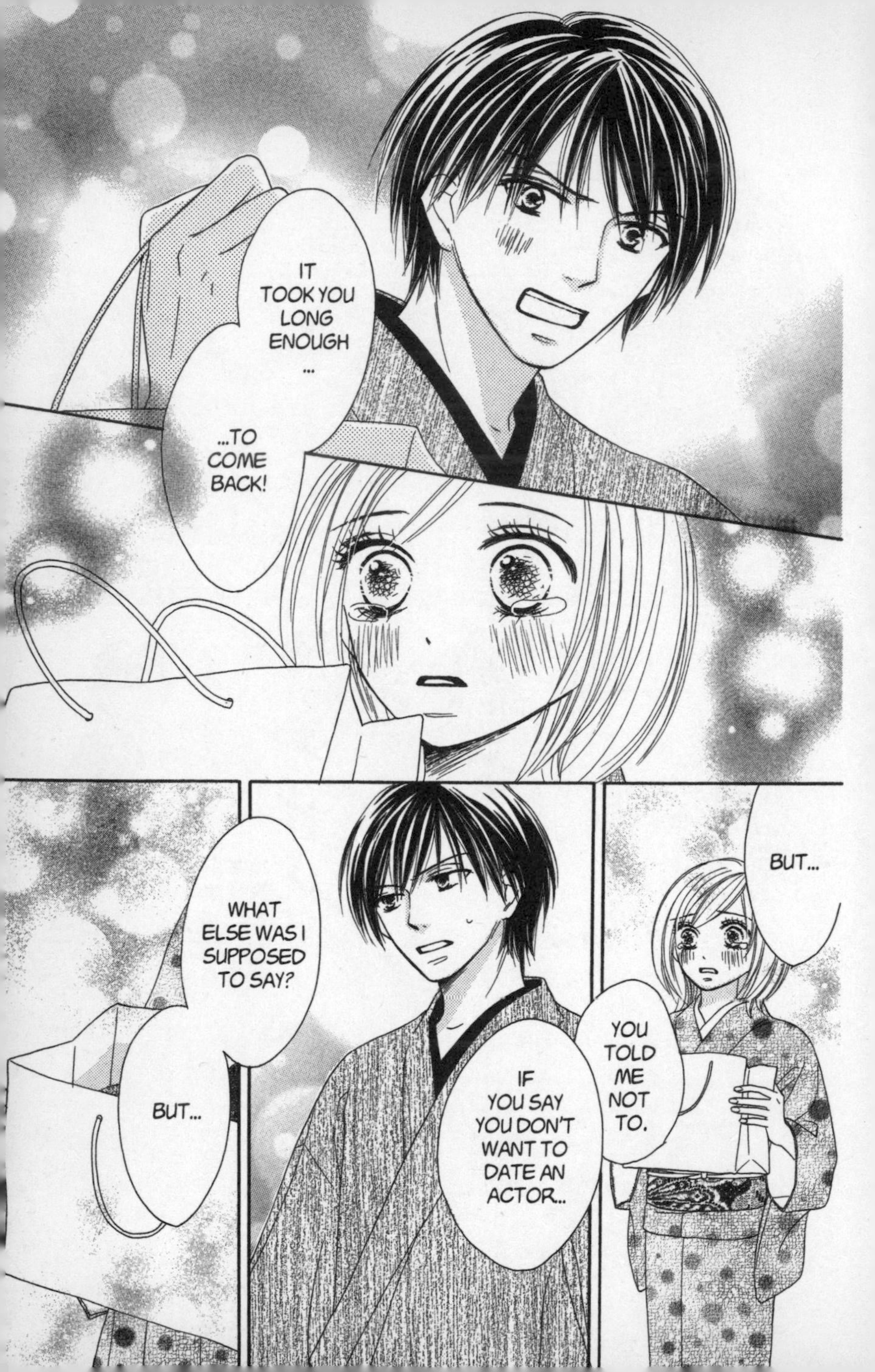
IT TOOK YOU LONG ENOUGH ...
...TO COME BACK!
BUT...
YOU TOLD ME NOT TO.
IF YOU SAY YOU DON'T WANT TO DATE AN ACTOR...
WHAT ELSE WAS I SUPPOSED TO SAY?
BUT...

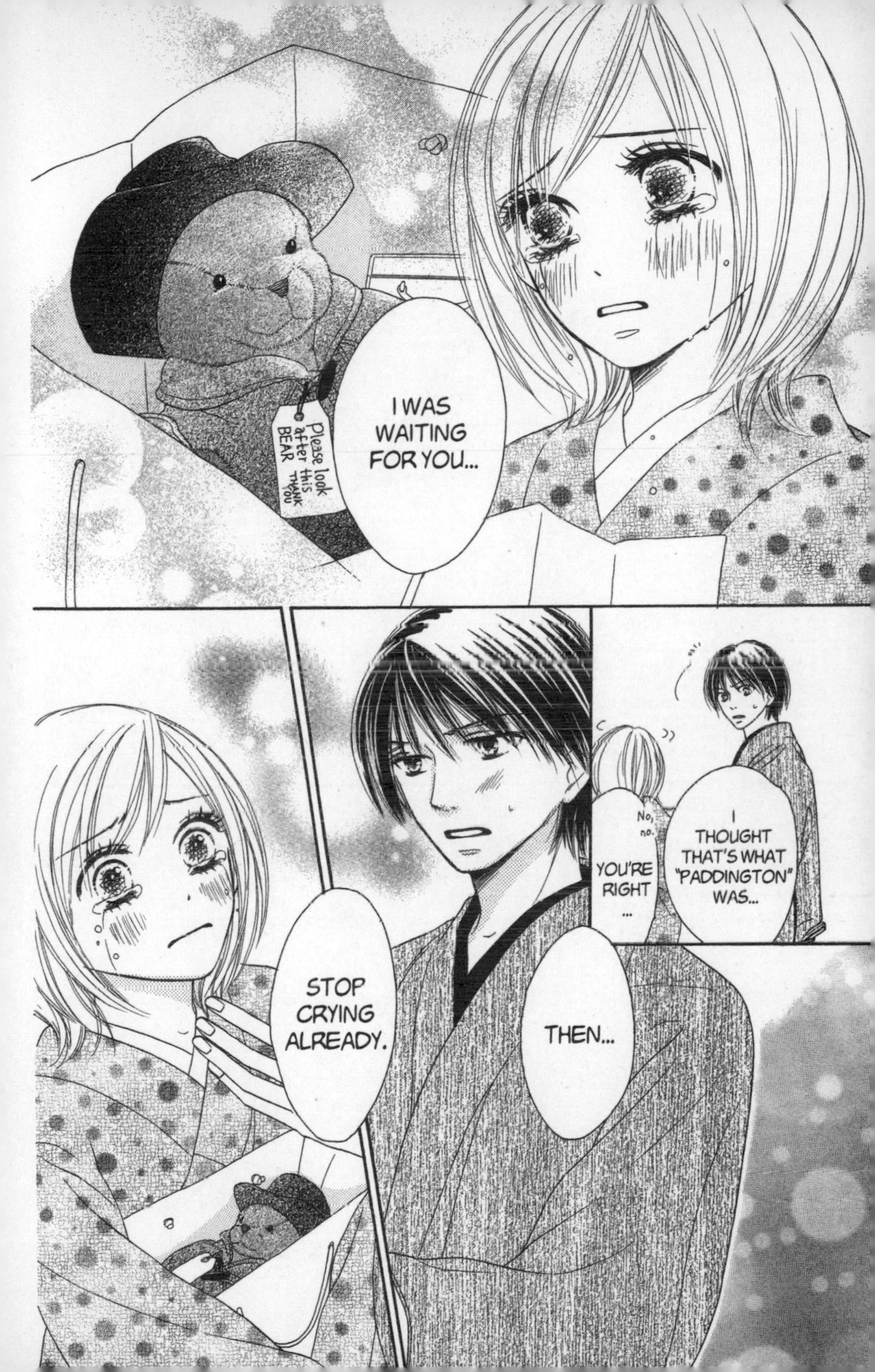
I WAS WAITING FOR YOU...
Please look after this BEAR THANK YOU
I THOUGHT THAT'S WHAT "PADDINGTON" WAS...
No, no.
YOU'RE RIGHT ...
THEN...
STOP CRYING ALREADY.

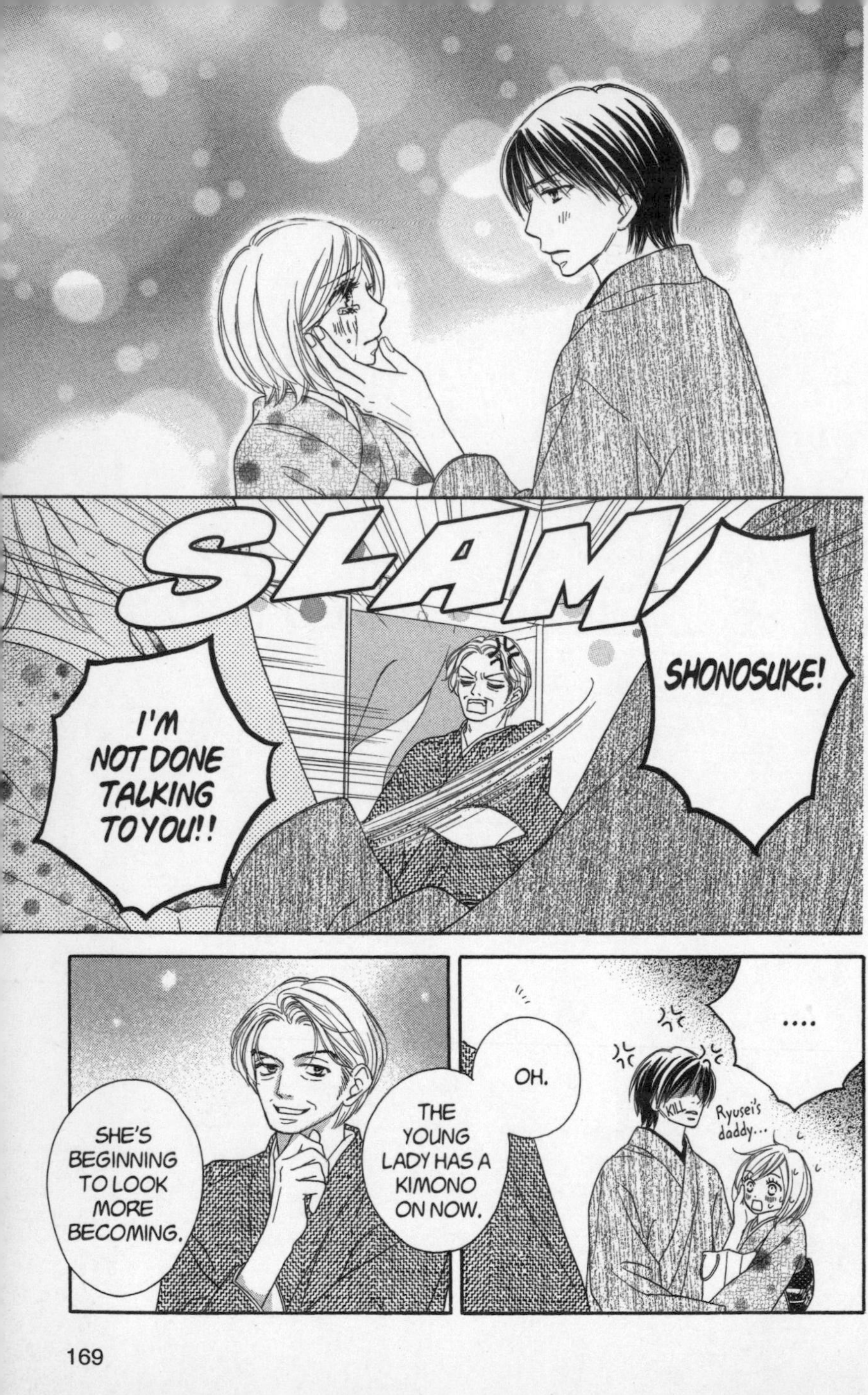
SLAM
SHONOSUKE!
I'M NOT DONE TALKING TO YOU!!
....
OH.
KILL
Ryusei's daddy...
THE YOUNG LADY HAS A KIMONO ON NOW.
SHE'S BEGINNING TO LOOK MORE BECOMING.

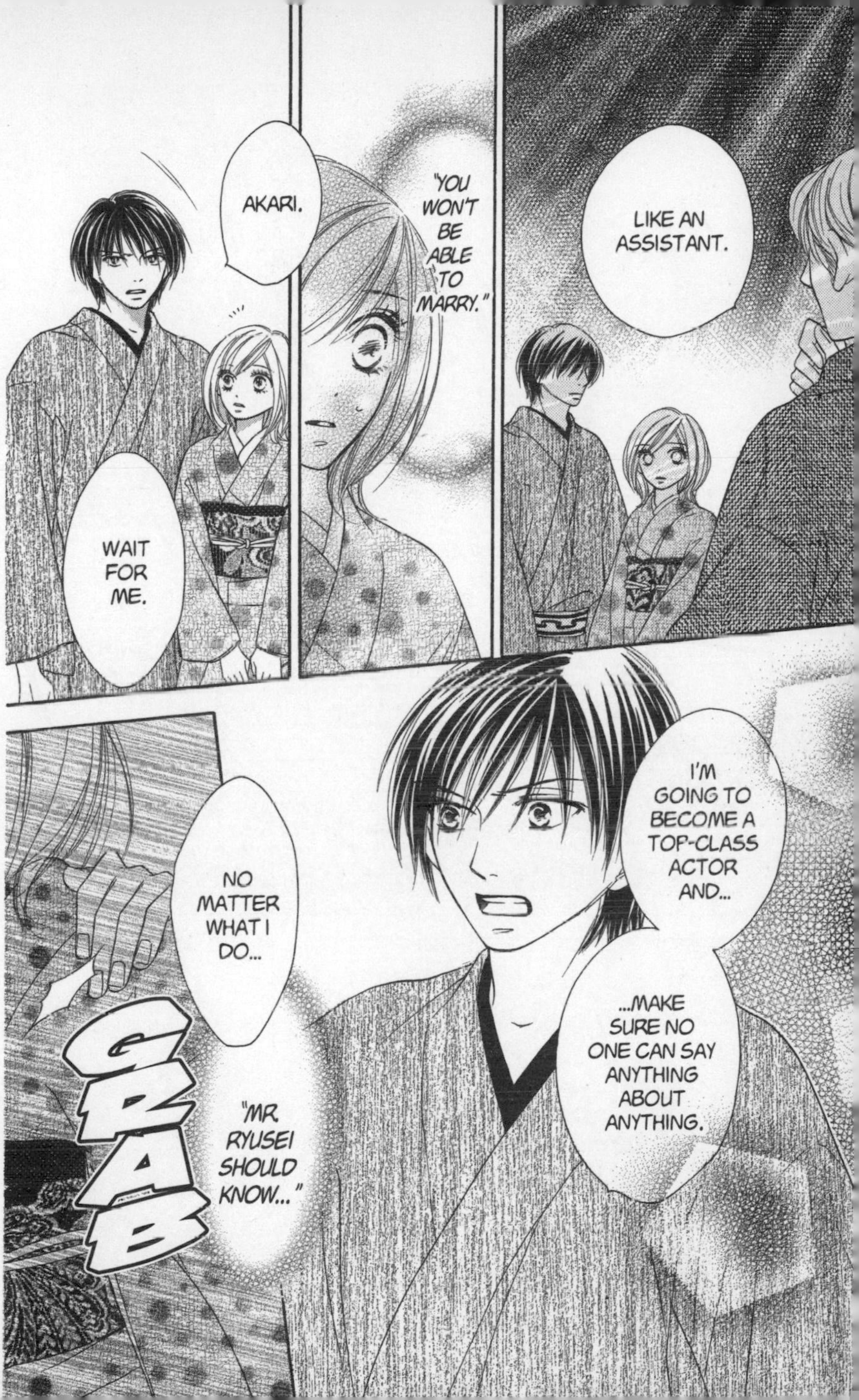
LIKE AN ASSISTANT.
"YOU WON'T BE ABLE TO MARRY."
AKARI.
WAIT FOR ME.
I'M GOING TO BECOME A TOP-CLASS ACTOR AND...
...MAKE SURE NO ONE CAN SAY ANYTHING ABOUT ANYTHING.
NO MATTER WHAT I DO...
"MR. RYUSEI SHOULD KNOW..."
GRAB

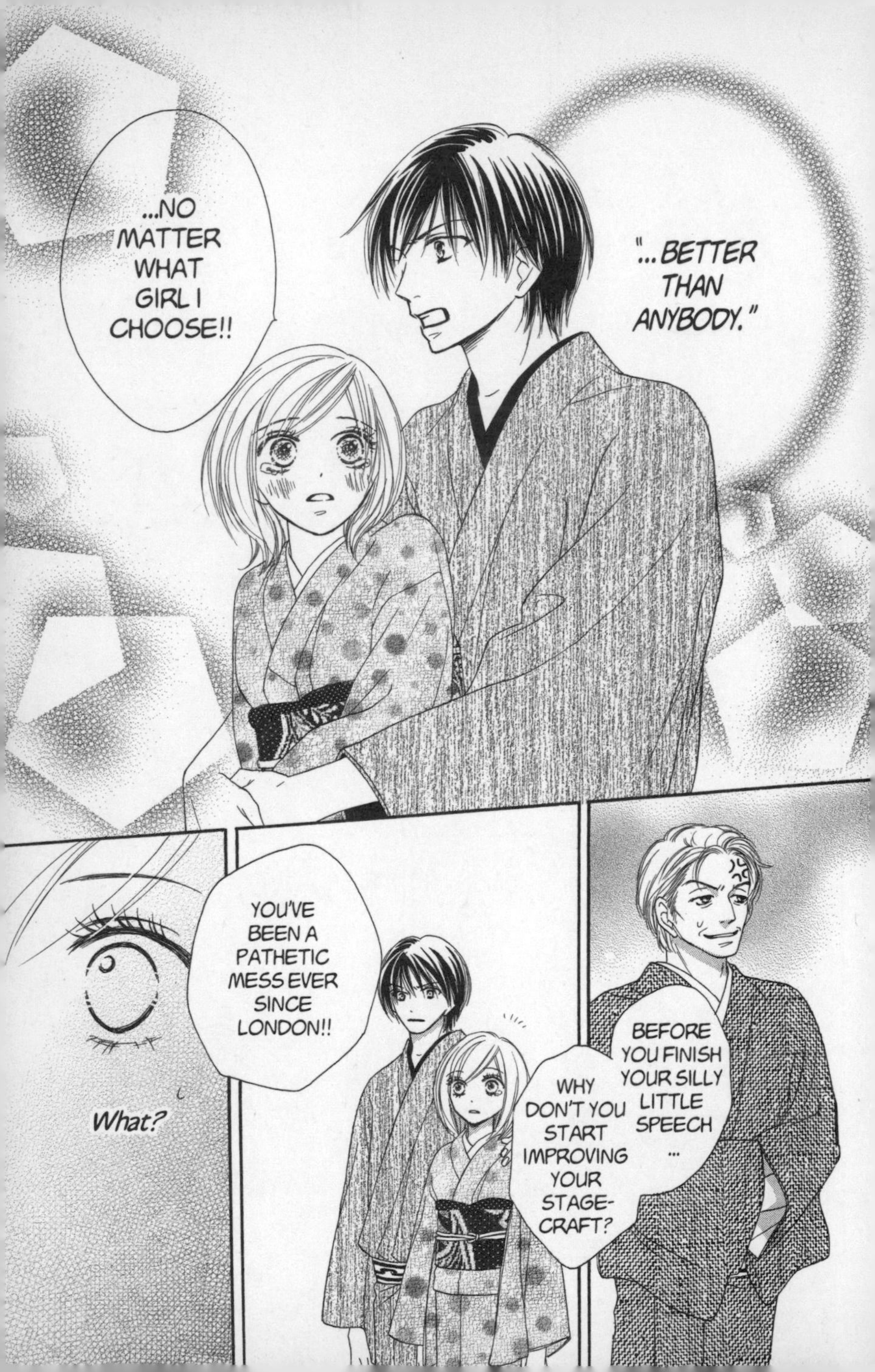
"...BETTER THAN ANYBODY."
...NO MATTER WHAT GIRL I CHOOSE!!
BEFORE YOU FINISH YOUR SILLY LITTLE SPEECH...
WHY DON'T YOU START IMPROVING YOUR STAGE-CRAFT?
YOU'VE BEEN A PATHETIC MESS EVER SINCE LONDON!!
What?

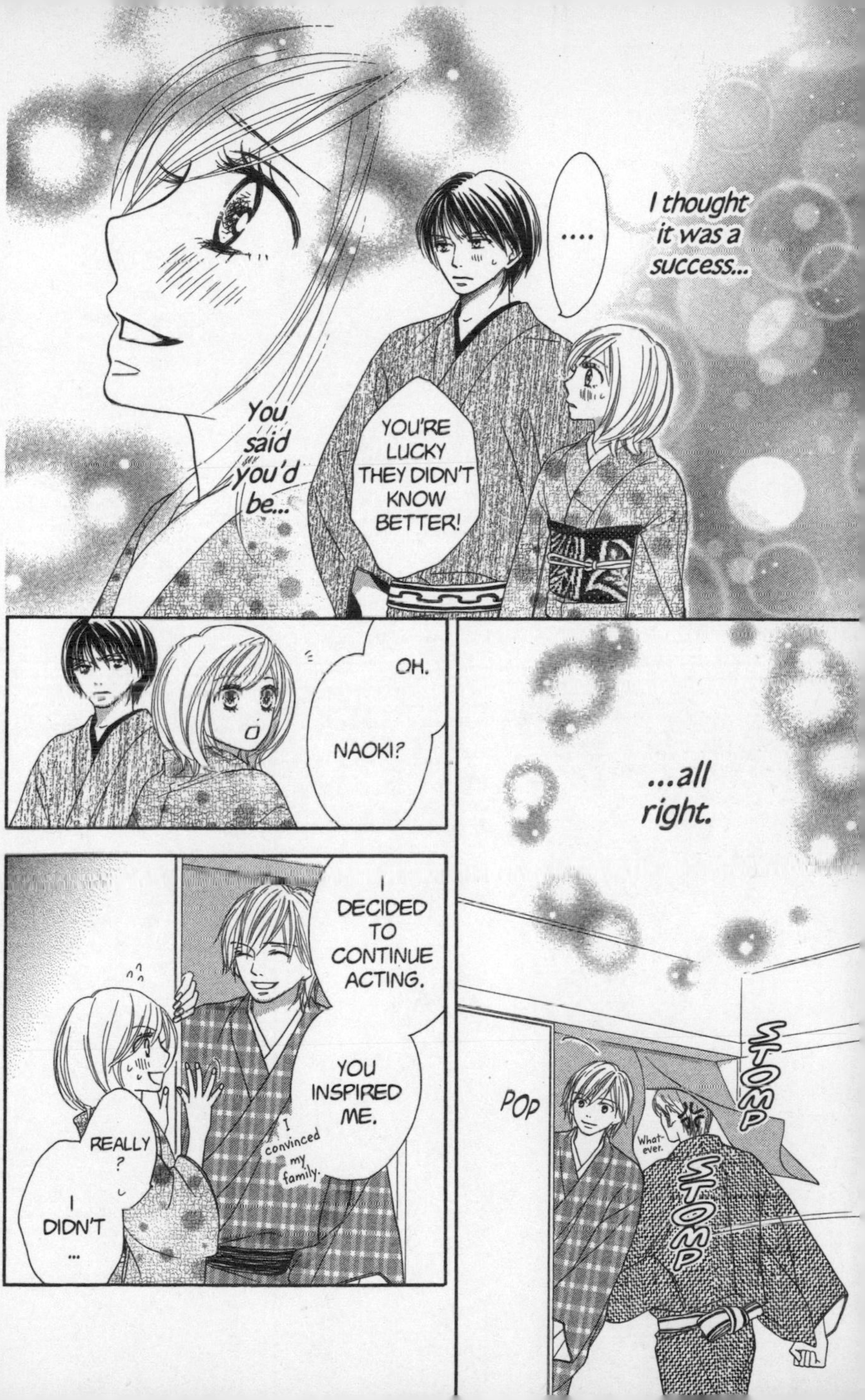
I thought it was a success...
....
YOU'RE LUCKY THEY DIDN'T KNOW BETTER!
You said you'd be...
...all right.
STOMP
POP
What-ever.
STOMP
OH.
NAOKI?
I DECIDED TO CONTINUE ACTING.
YOU INSPIRED ME.
I convinced my family.
REALLY?
I DIDN'T ...

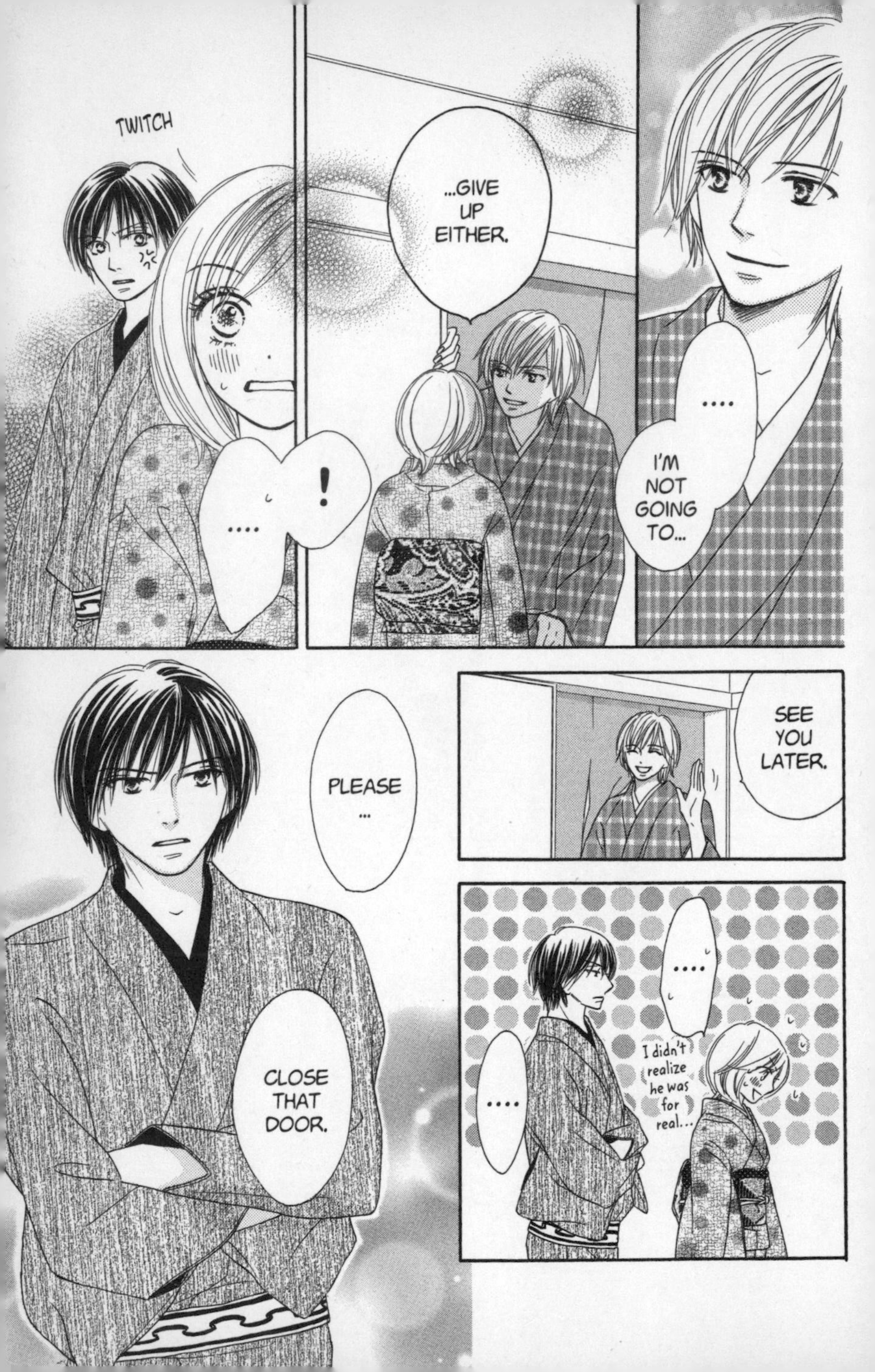
....
I'M NOT GOING TO...
...GIVE UP EITHER.
TWITCH
!
....
SEE YOU LATER.
....
I didn't realize he was for real...
....
PLEASE ...
CLOSE THAT DOOR.

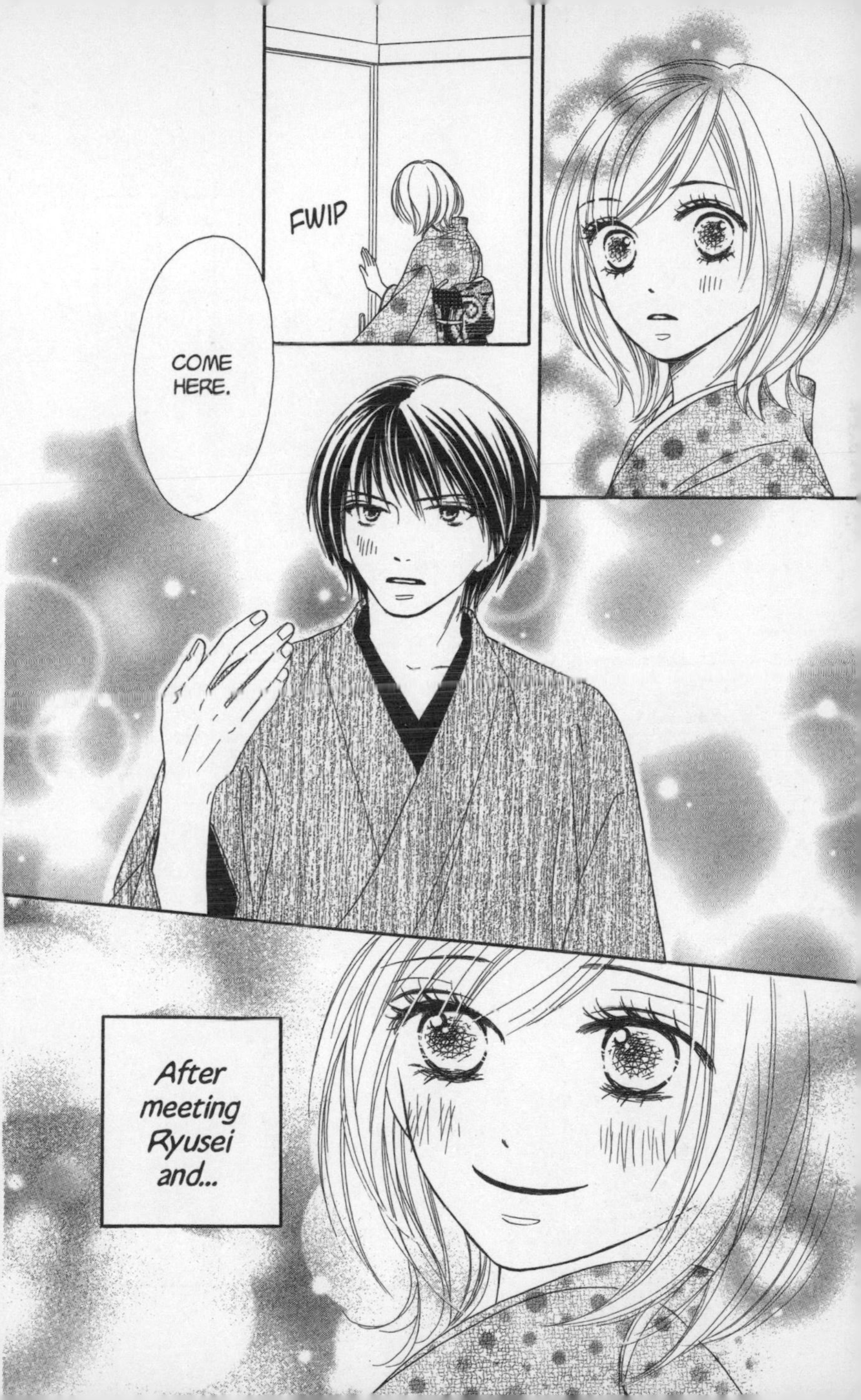
FWIP
COME HERE.
After meeting Ryusei and...

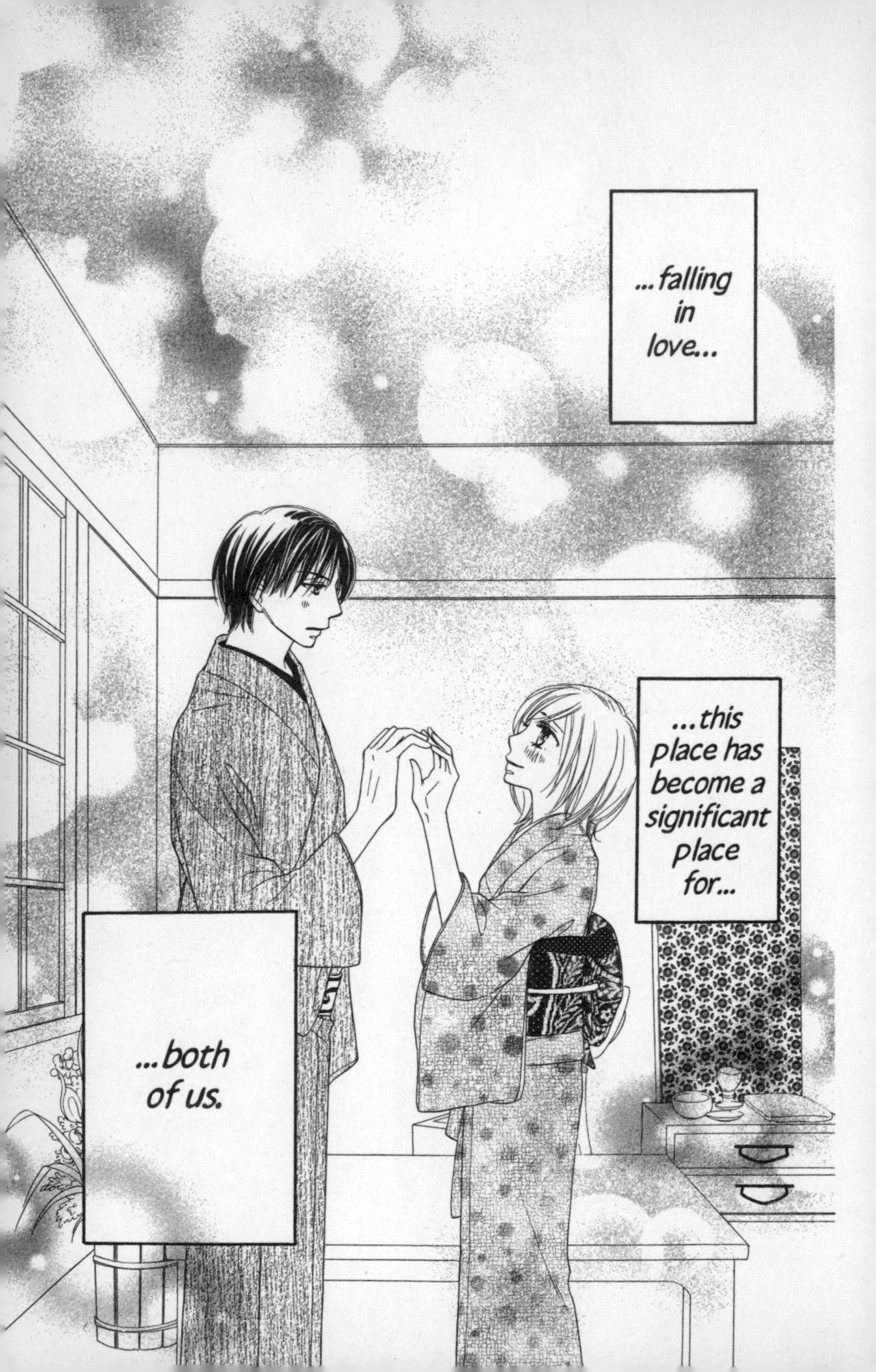
...falling in love...
...this place has become a significant place for...
...both of us.

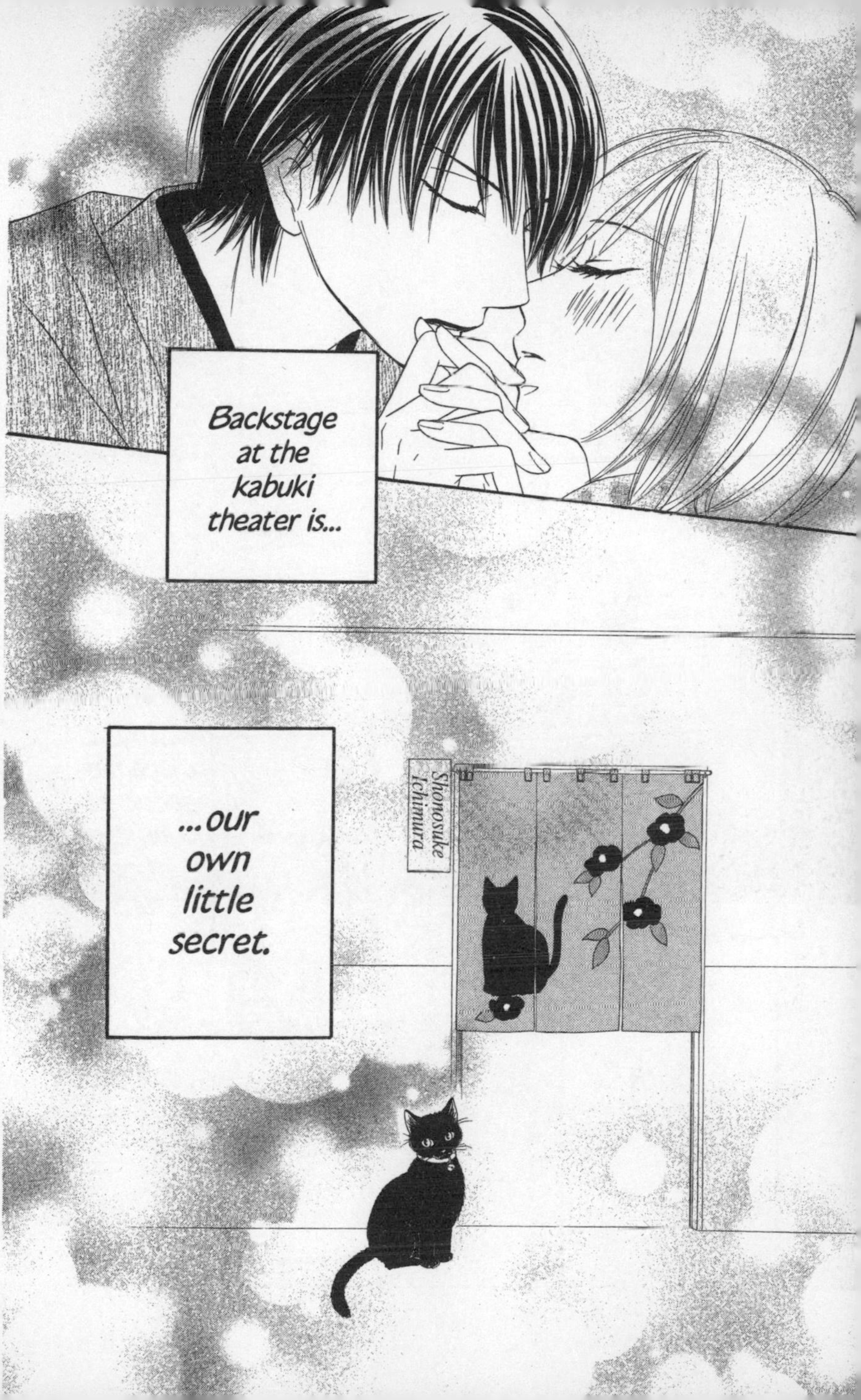
Backstage at the kabuki theater is...
...our own little secret.
Shonosuke Ichimura

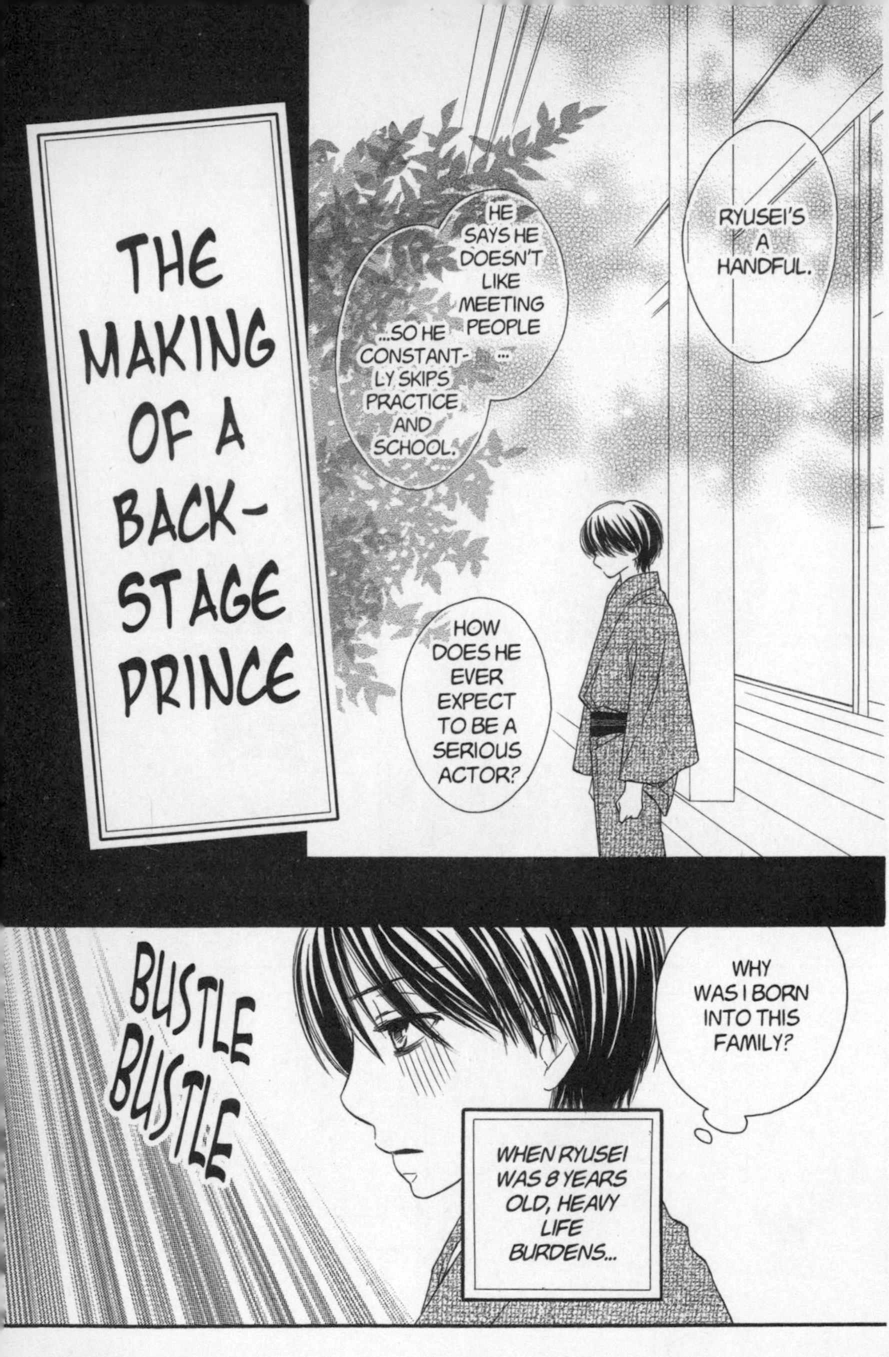
RYUSEI'S A HANDFUL.
HE SAYS HE DOESN'T LIKE MEETING PEOPLE...
...SO HE CONSTANT-LY SKIPS PRACTICE AND SCHOOL.
HOW DOES HE EVER EXPECT TO BE A SERIOUS ACTOR?
THE MAKING OF A BACK-STAGE PRINCE
WHY WAS I BORN INTO THIS FAMILY?
BUSTLE BUSTLE
WHEN RYUSEI WAS 8 YEARS OLD, HEAVY LIFE BURDENS...

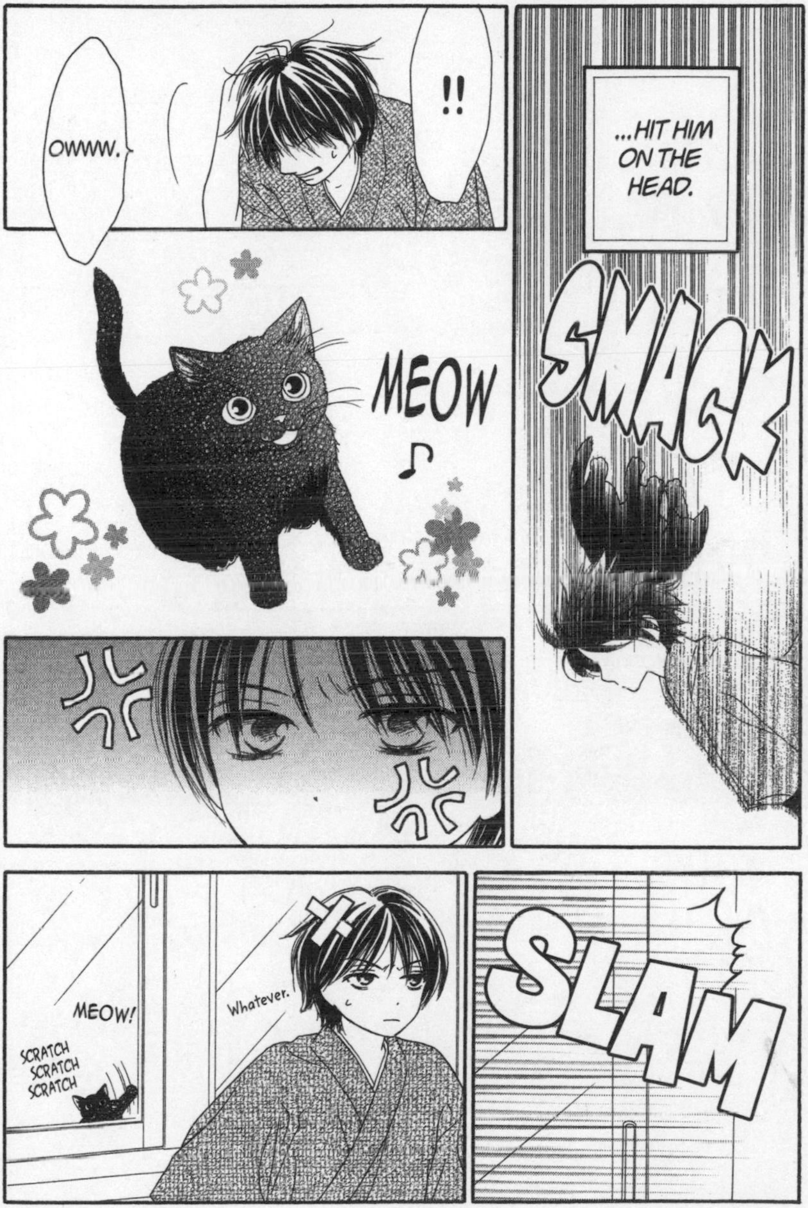
...HIT HIM ON THE HEAD.
SMACK
!!
OWWW.
MEOW ♪
SLAM
Whatever.
MEOW!
SCRATCH SCRATCH SCRATCH

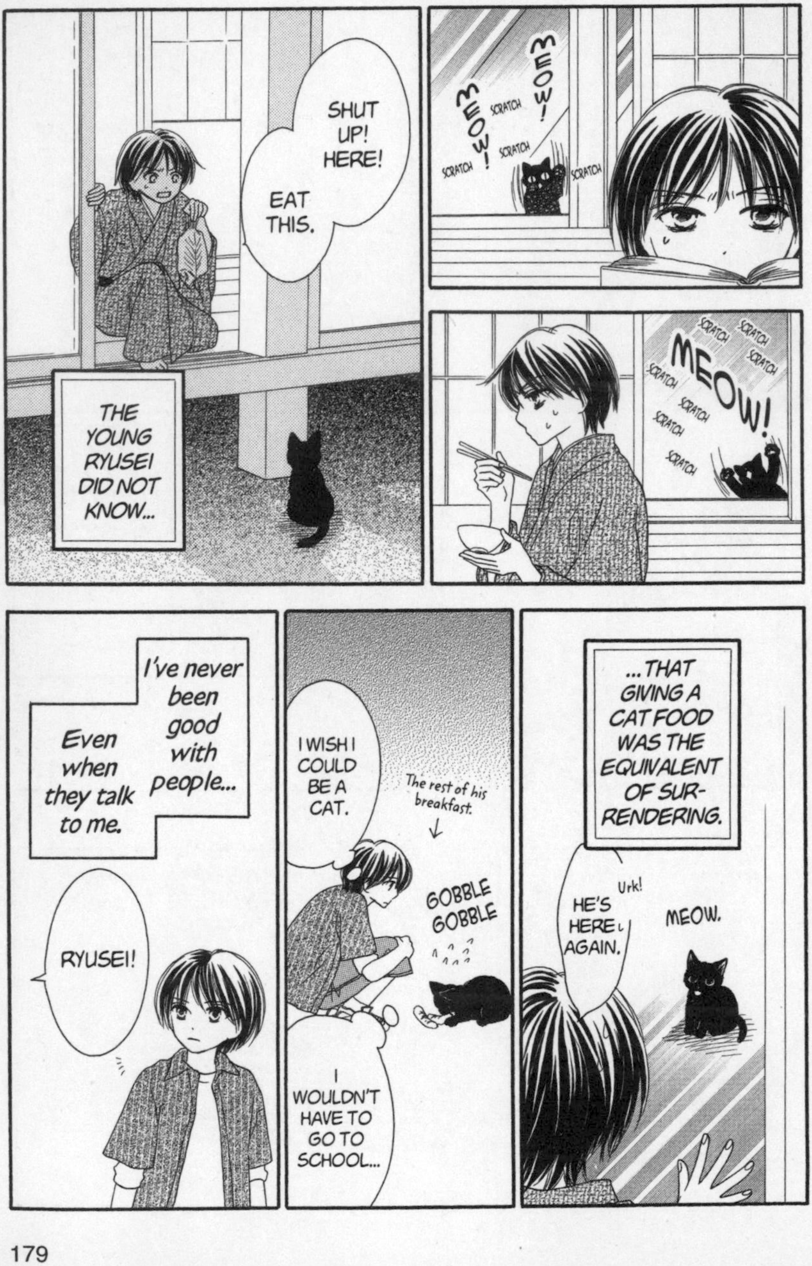
MEOW!
SCRATCH
MEOW!
SCRATCH
SCRATCH
SCRATCH
SCRATCH
SCRATCH
MEOW!
SCRATCH
SCRATCH
SCRATCH
SCRATCH
SCRATCH
SHUT UP! HERE!
EAT THIS.
THE YOUNG RYUSEI DID NOT KNOW...
...THAT GIVING A CAT FOOD WAS THE EQUIVALENT OF SUR-RENDERING.
HE'S HERE AGAIN.
Urk!
MEOW.
I WISH I COULD BE A CAT.
The rest of his breakfast.
GOBBLE GOBBLE
I WOULDN'T HAVE TO GO TO SCHOOL...
I've never been good with people...
Even when they talk to me.
RYUSEI!

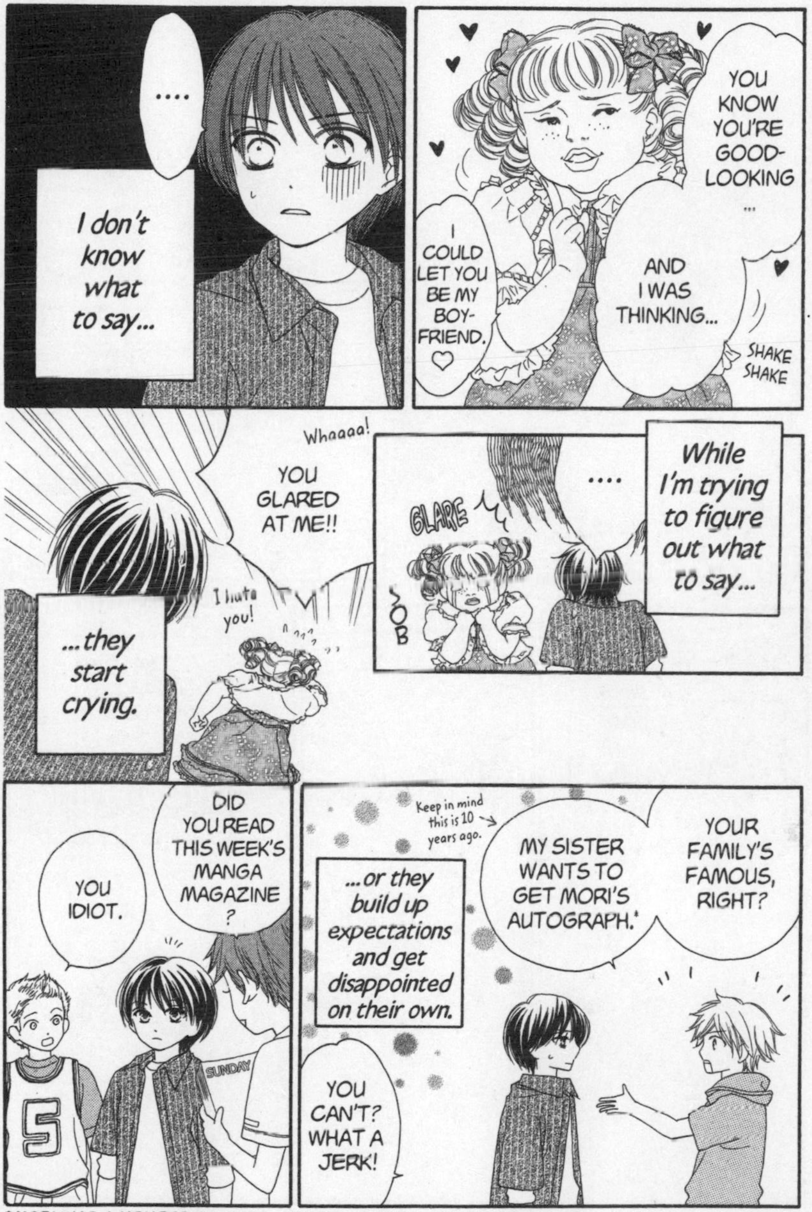
YOU KNOW YOU'RE GOOD-LOOKING ...
AND I WAS THINKING...
I COULD LET YOU BE MY BOY-FRIEND.
SHAKE SHAKE
....
I don't know what to say...
While I'm trying to figure out what to say...
....
GLARE
SOB
Whaaaa!
YOU GLARED AT ME!!
I hate you!
...they start crying.
YOUR FAMILY'S FAMOUS, RIGHT?
MY SISTER WANTS TO GET MORI'S AUTOGRAPH.*
Keep in mind this is 10 years ago.
...or they build up expectations and get disappointed on their own.
YOU CAN'T? WHAT A JERK!
DID YOU READ THIS WEEK'S MANGA MAGAZINE?
YOU IDIOT.
SUNDAY

*MORI WAS A MEMBER OF SMAP, A POPULAR JAPANESE BOY BAND. -ED

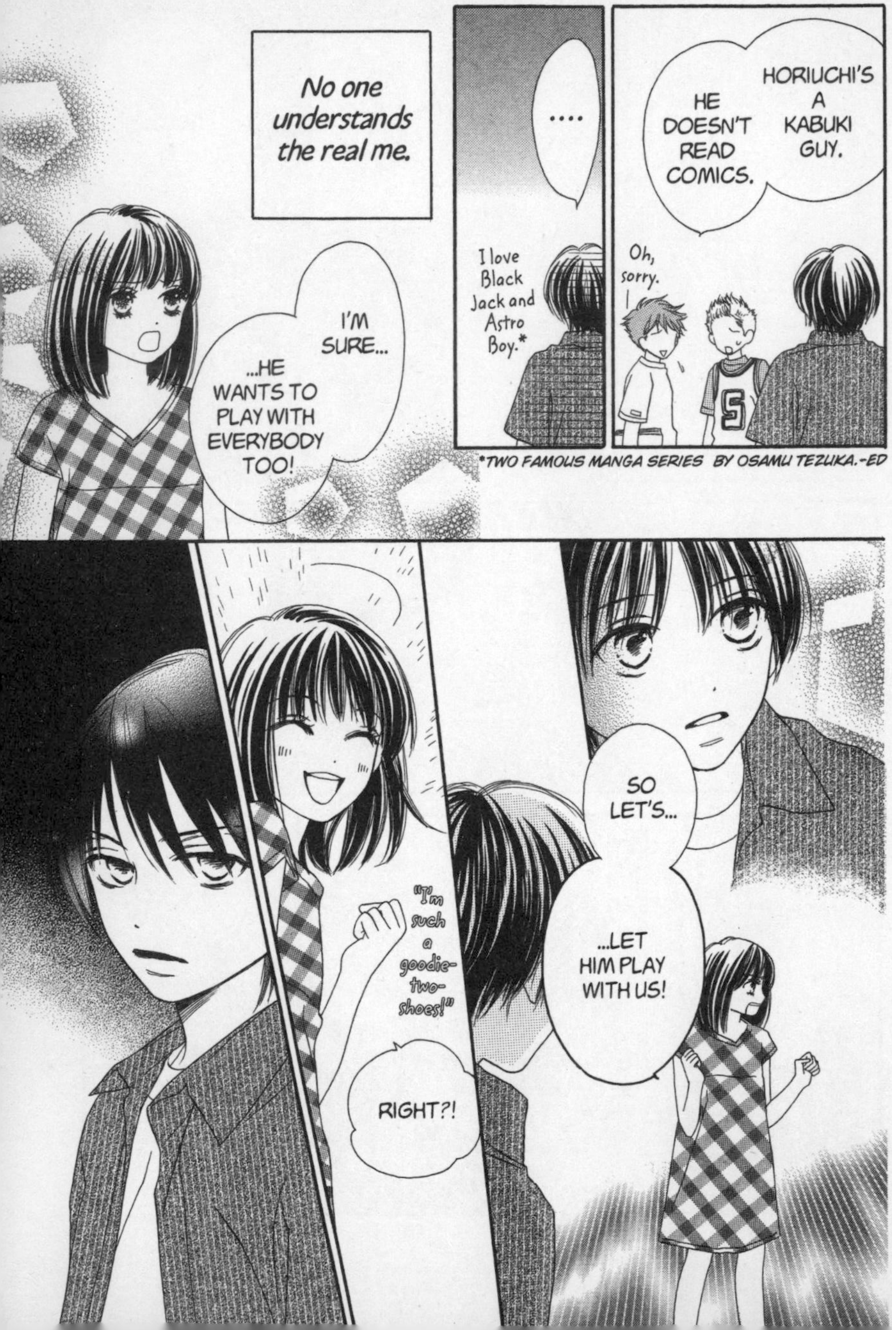
HORIUCHI'S A KABUKI GUY.
HE DOESN'T READ COMICS.
Oh, sorry.
....
I love Black Jack and Astro Boy.*
No one understands the real me.
I'M SURE...
...HE WANTS TO PLAY WITH EVERYBODY TOO!
*TWO FAMOUS MANGA SERIES BY OSAMU TEZUKA.-ED
SO LET'S...
...LET HIM PLAY WITH US!
RIGHT?!
"I'm such a goodie-two-shoes!"

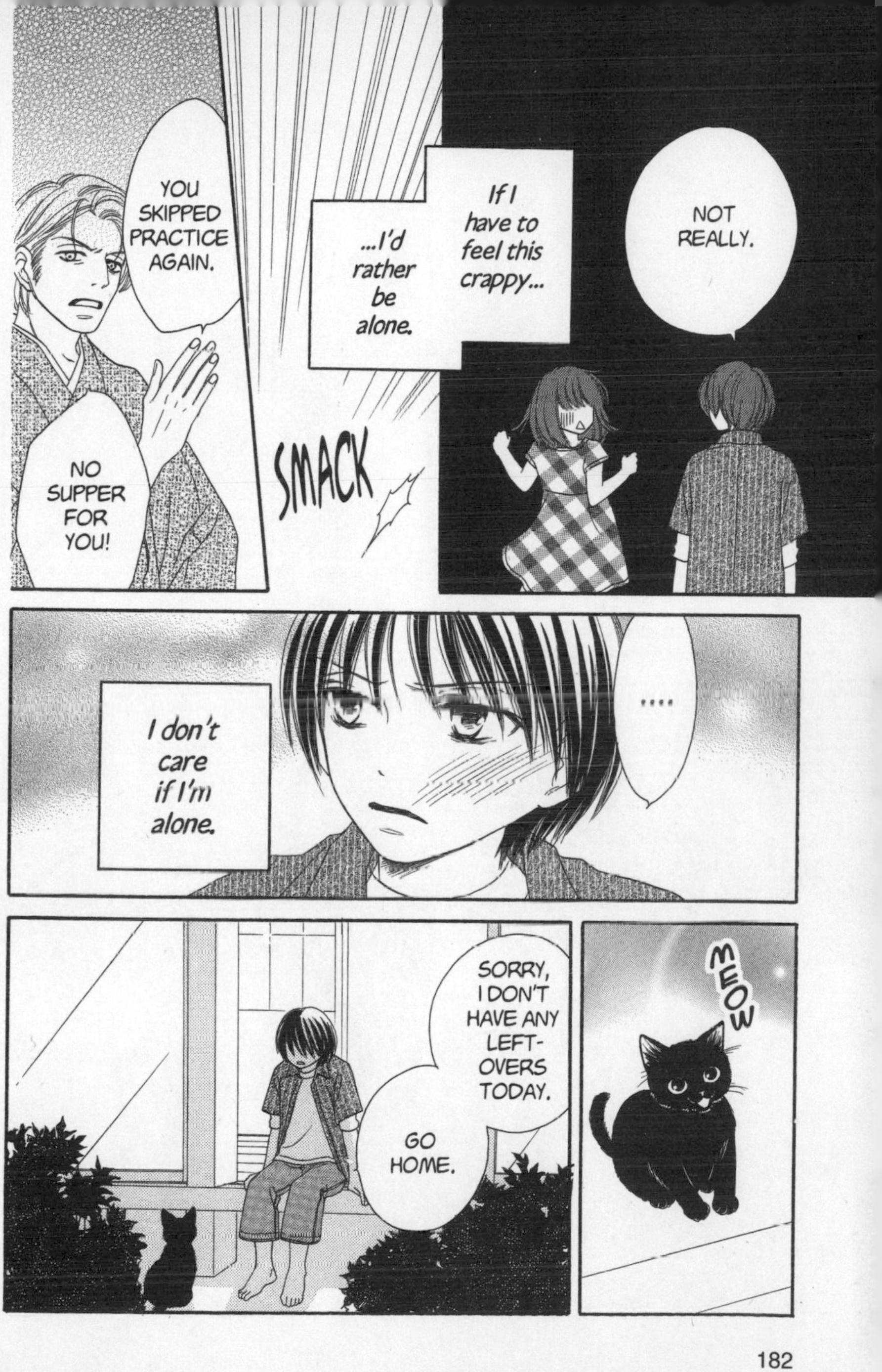
NOT REALLY.
If I have to feel this crappy...
...I'd rather be alone.
SMACK
YOU SKIPPED PRACTICE AGAIN.
NO SUPPER FOR YOU!
....
I don't care if I'm alone.
MEOW
SORRY, I DON'T HAVE ANY LEFT-OVERS TODAY.
GO HOME.

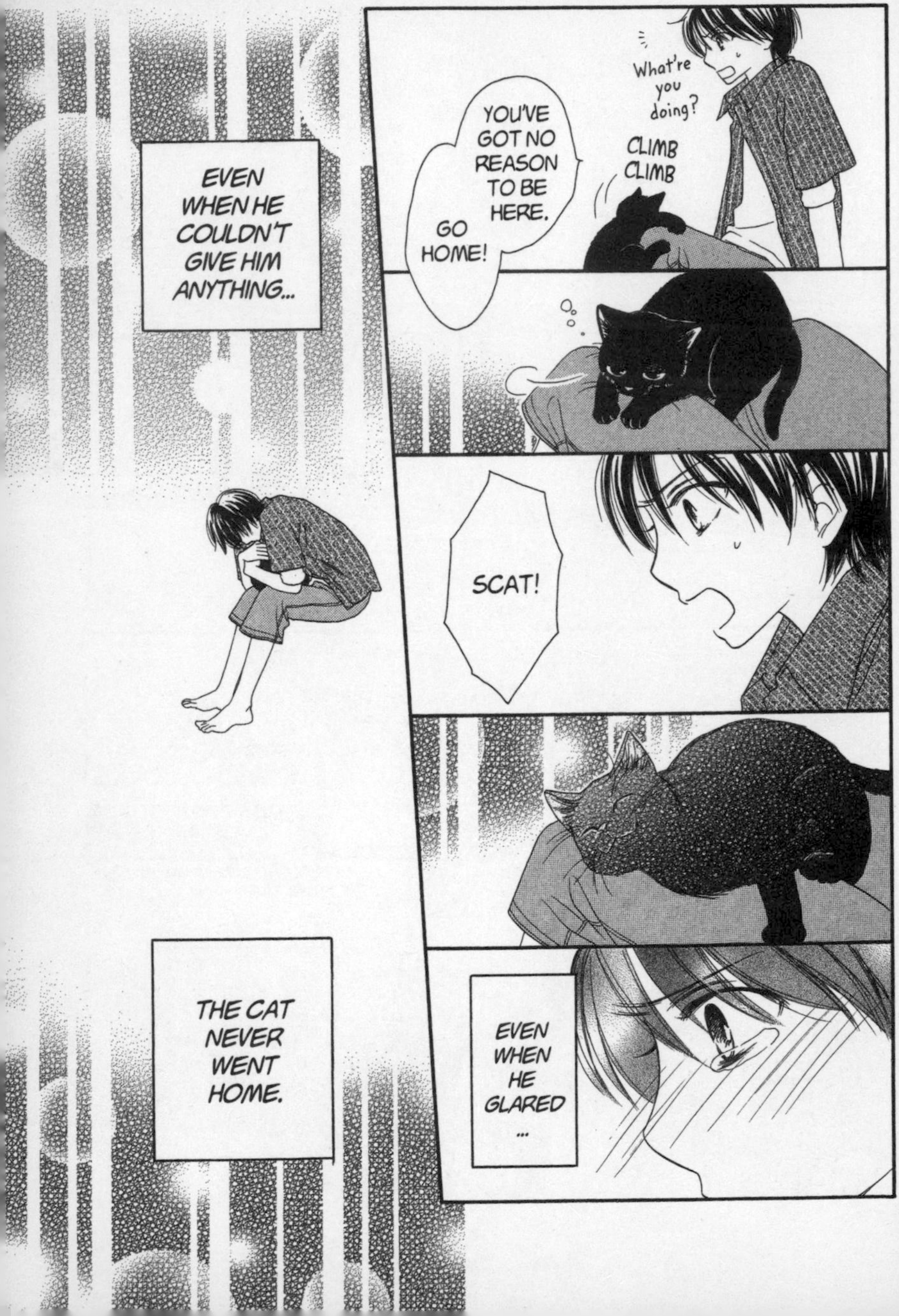
What're you doing?
YOU'VE GOT NO REASON TO BE HERE.
GO HOME!
CLIMB CLIMB
SCAT!
EVEN WHEN HE GLARED...
EVEN WHEN HE COULDN'T GIVE HIM ANYTHING...
THE CAT NEVER WENT HOME.

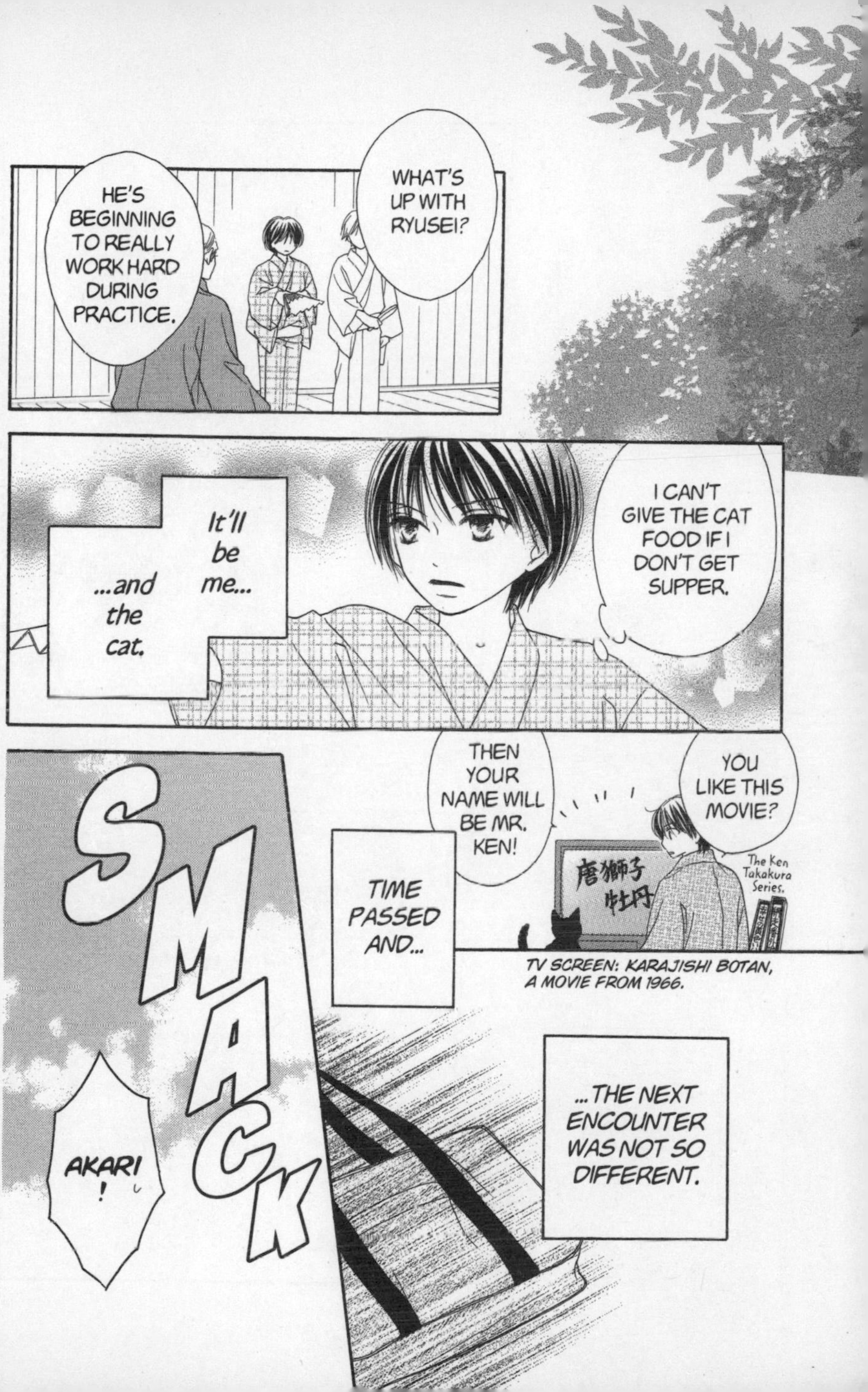
WHAT'S UP WITH RYUSEI?
HE'S BEGINNING TO REALLY WORK HARD DURING PRACTICE.
I CAN'T GIVE THE CAT FOOD IF I DON'T GET SUPPER.
It'll be me...
...and the cat.
YOU LIKE THIS MOVIE?
THEN YOUR NAME WILL BE MR. KEN!
唐獅子牡丹
The Ken Takakura Series.
TV SCREEN: KARAJISHI BOTAN, A MOVIE FROM 1966.
TIME PASSED AND...
...THE NEXT ENCOUNTER WAS NOT SO DIFFERENT.
SMACK
AKARI!

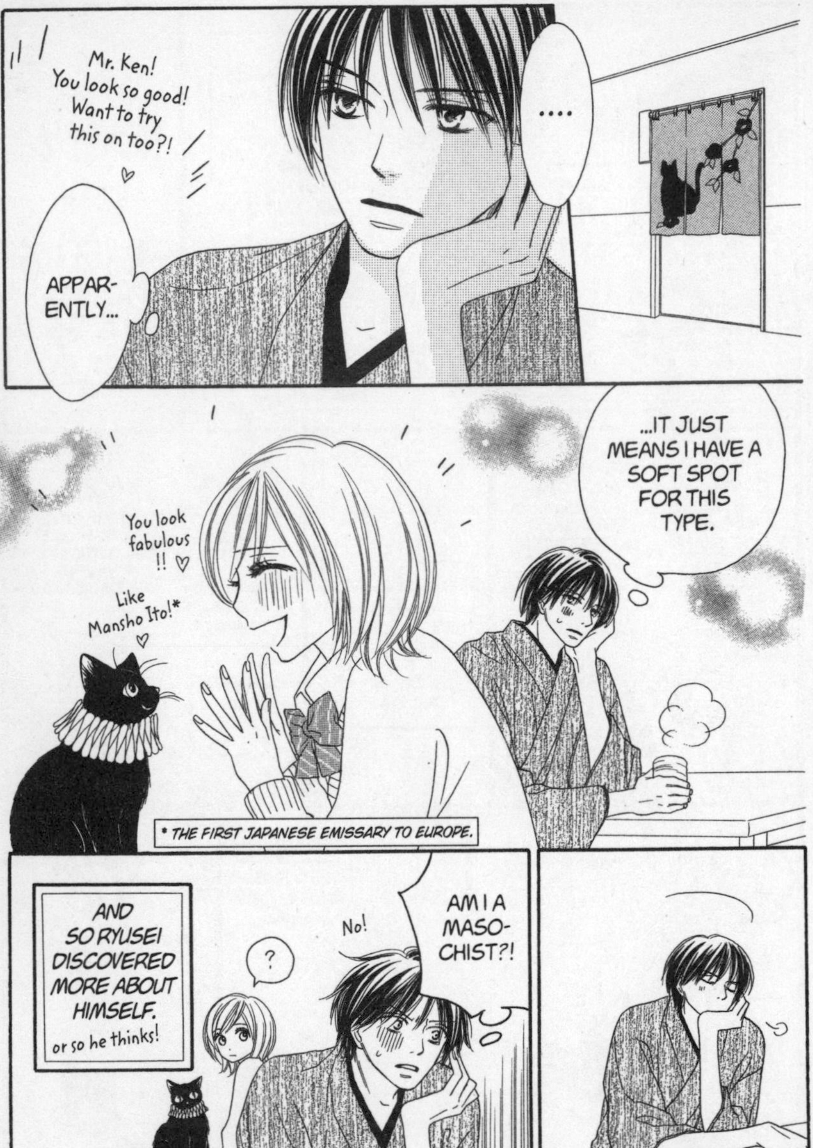
....
Mr. Ken! You look so good! Want to try this on too?!
APPARENTLY...
...IT JUST MEANS I HAVE A SOFT SPOT FOR THIS TYPE.
You look fabulous!!
Like Mansho Ito!*
* THE FIRST JAPANESE EMISSARY TO EUROPE.
AM I A MASOCHIST?!
No!
?
AND SO RYUSEI DISCOVERED MORE ABOUT HIMSELF.
or so he thinks!

THE END

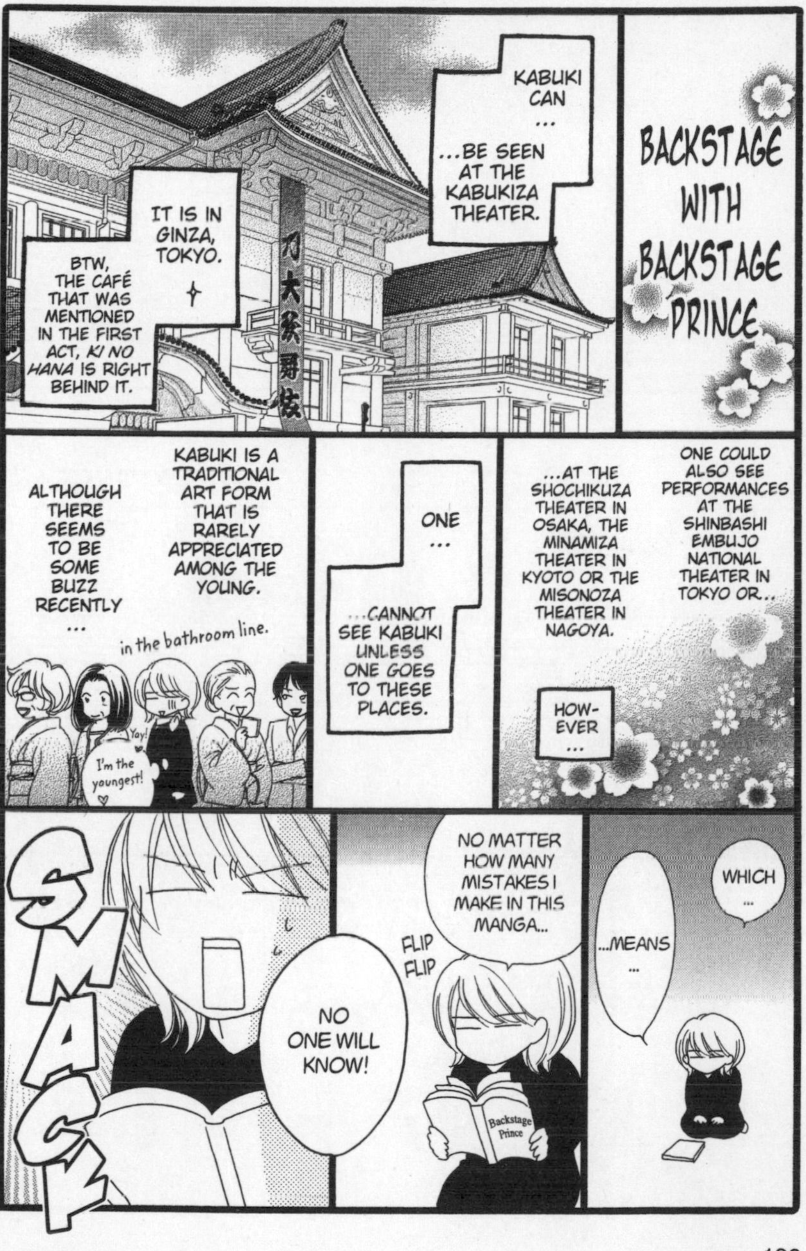
BACKSTAGE WITH BACKSTAGE PRINCE
KABUKI CAN ...
...BE SEEN AT THE KABUKIZA THEATER.
IT IS IN GINZA, TOKYO.
BTW, THE CAFÉ THAT WAS MENTIONED IN THE FIRST ACT, *KI NO HANA* IS RIGHT BEHIND IT.
ONE COULD ALSO SEE PERFORMANCES AT THE SHINBASHI EMBUJO NATIONAL THEATER IN TOKYO OR...
...AT THE SHOCHIKUZA THEATER IN OSAKA, THE MINAMIZA THEATER IN KYOTO OR THE MISONOZA THEATER IN NAGOYA.
HOW-EVER ...
ONE ...
...CANNOT SEE KABUKI UNLESS ONE GOES TO THESE PLACES.
KABUKI IS A TRADITIONAL ART FORM THAT IS RARELY APPRECIATED AMONG THE YOUNG.
ALTHOUGH THERE SEEMS TO BE SOME BUZZ RECENTLY ...
in the bathroom line.
Yay!
I'm the youngest!
WHICH ...
...MEANS ...
NO MATTER HOW MANY MISTAKES I MAKE IN THIS MANGA...
FLIP FLIP
Backstage Prince
NO ONE WILL KNOW!
SMACK

"I have John Lennon's autograph."

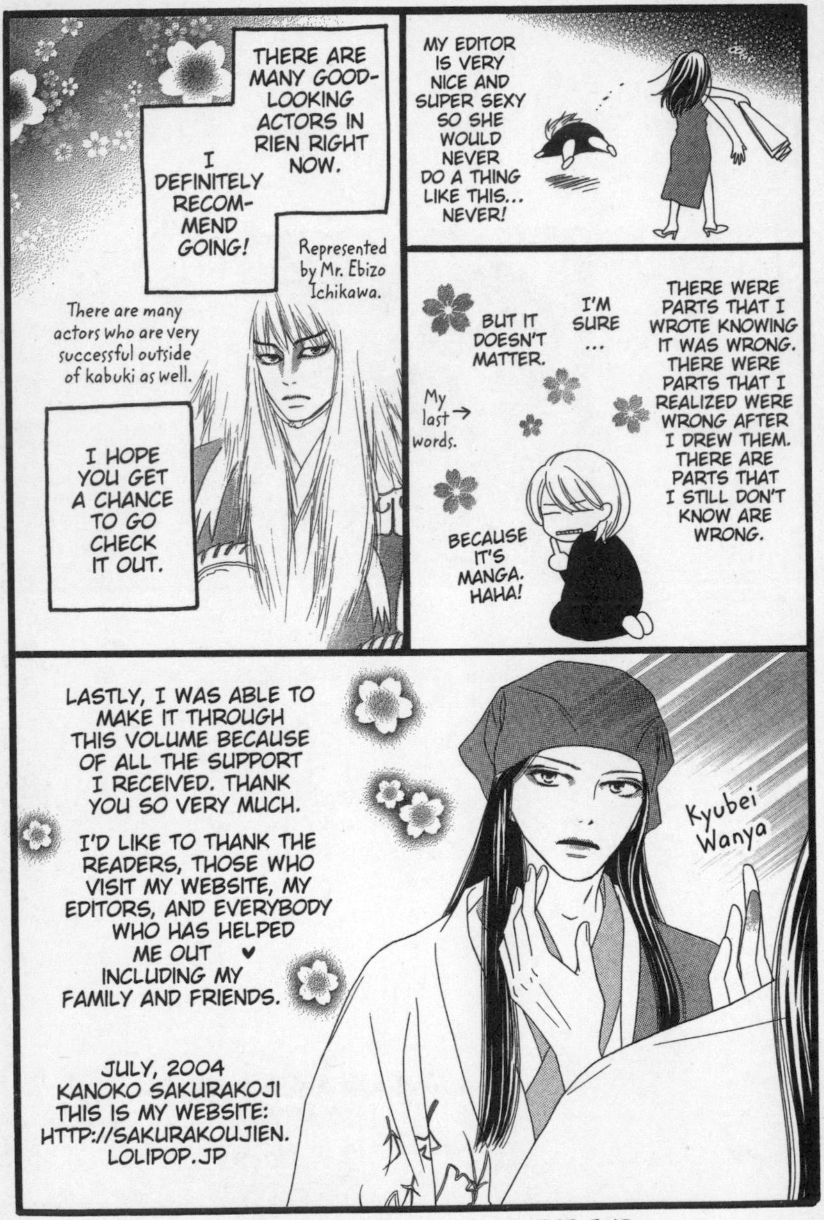

MY EDITOR IS VERY NICE AND SUPER SEXY SO SHE WOULD NEVER DO A THING LIKE THIS... NEVER!
THERE WERE PARTS THAT I WROTE KNOWING IT WAS WRONG. THERE WERE PARTS THAT I REALIZED WERE WRONG AFTER I DREW THEM. THERE ARE PARTS THAT I STILL DON'T KNOW ARE WRONG.
I'M SURE ...
BUT IT DOESN'T MATTER.
My last words. →
BECAUSE IT'S MANGA. HAHA!
THERE ARE MANY GOOD-LOOKING ACTORS IN RIEN RIGHT NOW.
I DEFINITELY RECOMMEND GOING!
Represented by Mr. Ebizo Ichikawa.
There are many actors who are very successful outside of kabuki as well.
I HOPE YOU GET A CHANCE TO GO CHECK IT OUT.
Kyubei Wanya
LASTLY, I WAS ABLE TO MAKE IT THROUGH THIS VOLUME BECAUSE OF ALL THE SUPPORT I RECEIVED. THANK YOU SO VERY MUCH.
I'D LIKE TO THANK THE READERS, THOSE WHO VISIT MY WEBSITE, MY EDITORS, AND EVERYBODY WHO HAS HELPED ME OUT ♥ INCLUDING MY FAMILY AND FRIENDS.
JULY, 2004
KANOKO SAKURAKOJI
THIS IS MY WEBSITE: HTTP://SAKURAKOUJIEN.LOLIPOP.JP

BACKSTAGE PRINCE VOL. 1: THE END

Kanoko Sakurakoji's debut title, *Raibu ga Hanetara* (When the Live Jumps) was serialized in *Deluxe Betsucomi* in 2000 and won the 45th New Manga Artist Award of Shogakukan in the same year. Sakurakoji's stories often include cats—in her serialized title *Suzu-chan no Neko* (Suzu's Cat), most of the main characters are feline! *Backstage Prince* was originally serialized in Japan's *Betsucomi* anthology in 2004.

BACKSTAGE PRINCE

Vol. 1

The Shojo Beat Manga Edition

This manga volume contains material that was originally published in English in *Shojo Beat* magazine, October-December 2006 issues.

STORY & ART BY
KANOKO SAKURAKOJI

Translation & Adaptation/Mai Ihara
Touch-up Art & Lettering/Rina Mapa
Additional Touch-up/Kam Li
Design/Izumi Hirayama
Editor/Pancha Diaz

Managing Editor/Megan Bates
Editorial Director/Elizabeth Kawasaki
VP & Editor in Chief/ Yumi Hoashi
Sr. Director of Acquisitions/Rika Inouye
Sr. VP of Marketing/Liza Coppola
Exec. VP of Sales & Marketing/John Easum
Publisher/Hyoe Narita

Printed in Canada

Published by VIZ Media, LLC
P.O. Box 77064
San Francisco, CA 94107

Shojo Beat Manga Edition
10 9 8 7 6 5 4 3 2 1
First printing, March 2007

store.viz.com

PARENTAL ADVISORY
BACKSTAGE PRINCE is rated T for Teen and is recommended for ages 13 and up. This volume contains suggestive situations.

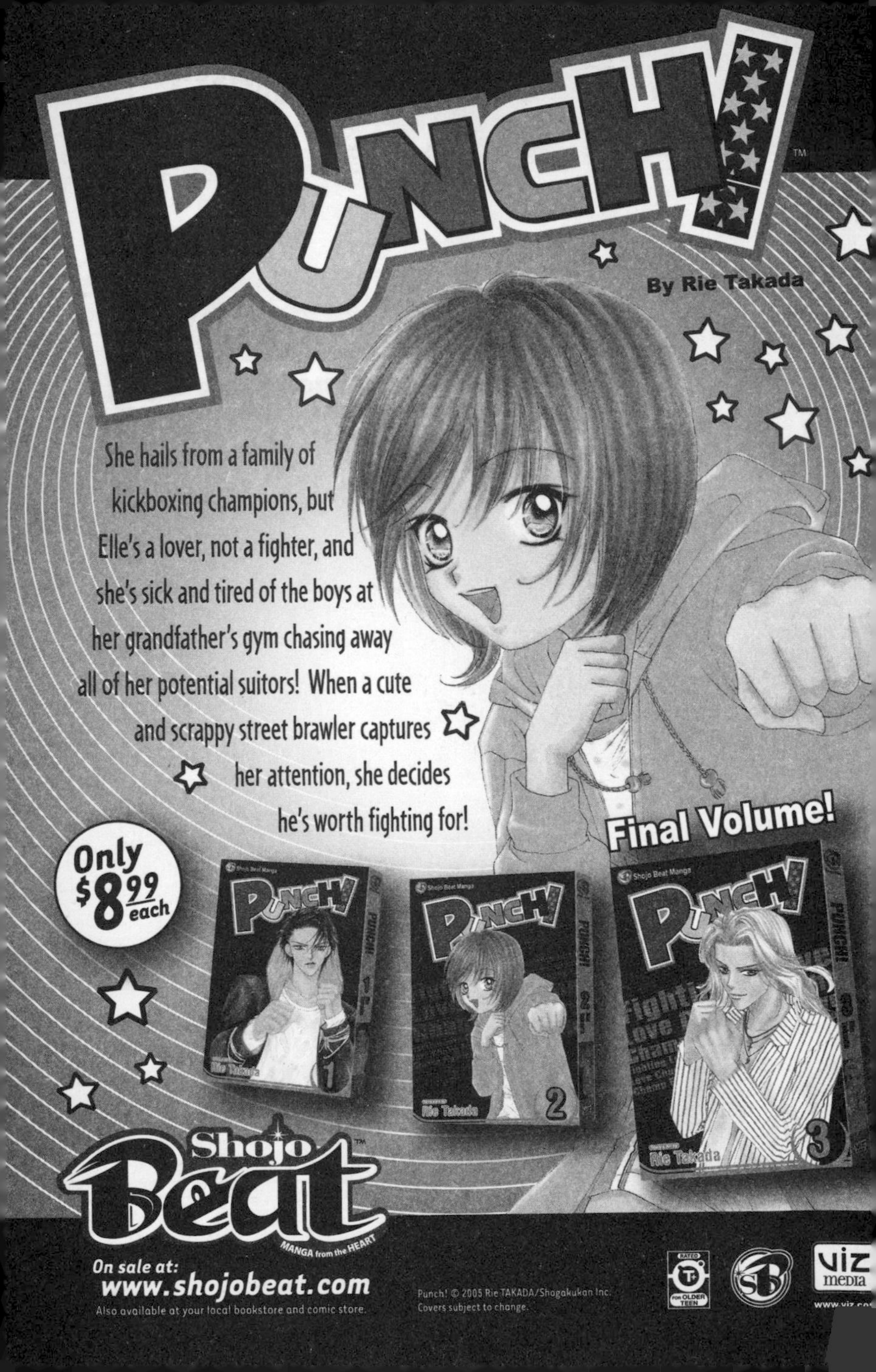
PUNCH!™
By Rie Takada
She hails from a family of kickboxing champions, but Elle's a lover, not a fighter, and she's sick and tired of the boys at her grandfather's gym chasing away all of her potential suitors! When a cute and scrappy street brawler captures her attention, she decides he's worth fighting for!
Only $8.99 each
Final Volume!
Shojo Beat Manga
PUNCH!
Rie Takada
1
2
3
Shojo Beat™
MANGA from the HEART
On sale at:
www.shojobeat.com
Also available at your local bookstore and comic store.
Punch! © 2005 Rie TAKADA/Shogakukan Inc.
Covers subject to change.
RATED T+ FOR OLDER TEEN
SB
VIZ media

Tell us what ... about Shojo ...

Help us make our product offerings better!

VIZ media

Shojo Beat

THE REAL DRAMA BEGINS IN...

MANGA from the HEART

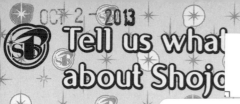